Outer Hebrides
The Western Isles of Scotland, from Lewis to Barra

the Bradt Travel Guide

Mark Rowe

edition
2

www.bradtguides.com

Bradt Travel Guides Ltd, UK
The Globe Pequot Press Inc, USA

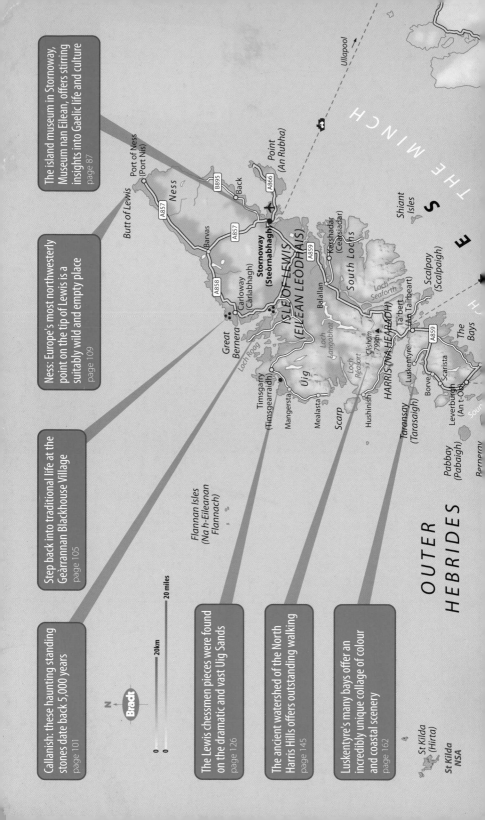

The island museum in Stornoway, Museum nan Eilean, offers stirring insights into Gaelic life and culture
page 87

Ness: Europe's most northwesterly point on the tip of Lewis is a suitably wild and empty place
page 109

Step back into traditional life at the Gèarrannan Blackhouse Village
page 105

Callanish: these haunting standing stones date back 5,000 years
page 101

The Lewis chessmen pieces were found on the dramatic and vast Uig Sands
page 126

The ancient watershed of the North Harris Hills offers outstanding walking
page 145

Luskentyre's many bays offer an incredibly unique collage of colour and coastal scenery
page 162

THE MINCH

Ullapool

Butt of Lewis

Port of Ness (Port Nis)

Ness

Back
B895

Point (An Rubha)
A866

Barvas
A857
A857

Stornoway (Steòrnabhagh)

A858

Carloway (Càrlabhagh)

Keshadar (Ceasaidar)
A859

South Lochs

Shiant Isles

Scalpay (Scalpaigh)

Great Bernera

Balallan

Loch Seaforth

Loch Roag

Loch Langabhat

Tarbert (An Tairbeart)

A859

Timsgarry (Timsgearraidh)

Loch Resort

Gisham 799m

HARRIS (NA HEARADH)

The Bays

Mangersta

Uig

Mealasta

Luskentyre

Scarp

Hushinish

Borve
Scarista

Taransay (Tarasaigh)

Leverburgh (An t-Ob)

Flannan Isles (Na h-Eileanan Flannach)

Pabbay (Pabaigh)

Berneray

OUTER HEBRIDES

ISLE OF LEWIS (EILEAN LEÒDHAIS)

N

20km

20 miles

Bract

St Kilda (Hirta)

St Kilda NSA

Loch Eynort: woodland walks await above the shores of this picturesque South Uist loch
page 253

Glorious wild flowers, lochs and beaches make North Uist a delight for wildlife lovers and walkers
page 198

Tràigh Mhòr: enjoy the world's only scheduled beach landing strip from the less bumpy comfort of the dunes
page 272

Arguably the most beautiful beach in the Outer Hebrides can be found near its southernmost tip on Vatersay
page 286

KEY
Main town
Other town
Airstrip, airport
Tarred road
Other important road
Railway
Parks/reserves

Outer Hebrides

Don't miss...

Island produce

From fresh fish to soup from the croft, community cafés to fine dining, the Outer Hebrides serve up superb cuisine for all budgets

(PB) page 53

Luskentyre

The mesmerising sands, dunes and currents of Luskentyre's many bays on Harris seem to change their patterns and colour with every tide

(KL/VS) page 162

Callanish

Haunting and truly ancient, the stones of Callanish on Lewis remain an enigma to explore in a solitude that is impossible at Stonehenge

(KL/VS) page 101

Barra

The Outer Hebrides in miniature, the island of Barra has it all: wonderful beaches, good food, a picturesque port and marooned Kisimul Castle offshore

(PT/VS) page 267

Wildlife

Otters, red deer, golden and sea eagles, and other charismatic animals are so commonly spotted that the islands can feel like walking into an episode of the BBC's *Springwatch*

(LC) page 10

Outer Hebrides in colour

above left   The harbour at Ness is located near the wild, northernmost tip of Lewis (LC) page 109

above right   The old whaling station of Bunavoneadar on the lonely road to Hushinish in North Harris is
testament to the failed dreams of the island's former owner, Lord Leverhulme (LC) page 143

below left   The classic way to arrive on the islands is by CalMac ferry from the mainland (D/D) page 41

below right   The sea stacks and sheer cliffs of remote Mangersta in Uig, southwest Lewis, make for elemental
coastal views (LC) page 129

top   Vatersay Bay is among the most beautiful beaches of the Outer Hebrides (S/S) page 286

above   Such signs are no gimmick: the many causeways that connect the islands offer good prospects of spotting otters (MR) page 193

below left   At low tide, enchanting rivulets run across the vast sands of Luskentyre on the west coast of Harris (LC) page 162

below right   The North Harris Hills – viewed here from Northton, South Harris – form a spectacular backdrop to the many bays of Luskentyre (LC) page 145

bottom   The dramatic sweeping landscapes of Hirta and Dùn on St Kilda resemble those of a South Pacific idyll (c/S) page 180

above   The hillsides of Hirta on St Kilda are dotted with storehouses known as cleits, where islanders kept eggs and bird meat right up to the 20th century (SS) page 189

left   Flodda, southwest Lewis, is one of more than 100 islands and skerries that make up the Outer Hebrides (LC) page 230

below   A trip around the island of Boreray offers a breathtaking finale to any visit to St Kilda (SS) page 190

AUTHOR

Mark Rowe is a qualified journalist with more than 25 years' experience of writing for national newspapers and magazines and, nowadays, increasingly online. Born in the wilds of Hertfordshire, his love of travel was stirred by a visit to the former USSR at the age of 12, later living in Minsk as part of his degree in Russian and English, and by a six-month solo backpacking trip around China in 1991, which led to his first published piece

– a tale of how to slurp noodles in China, published in *The Independent*. Having completed a postgraduate course in journalism at City University in London, he cut his teeth on the *Grimsby Evening Telegraph*, covering stories of haddock smuggling and dancing-pet competitions in Cleethorpes. He worked as staff writer for *The Independent* and *Independent on Sunday* for five years and continues to contribute to their travel pages on a freelance basis. He specialises in environmental issues, wildlife and the Great Outdoors and is the author of Bradt's *Orkney*, which was published in 2019. For 15 years, Mark wrote a regular 'Walk of the Month' column for *The Independent*. He is author of the 'Behind the Headlines' column for *BBC Countryfile* magazine and contributes to its sister title *BBC Wildlife*. He writes regularly for *Geographical*, the magazine of the Royal Geographical Society, and *Nat Geo Traveller* from the National Geographic stable. He lives in Bristol with his wife and three children. You can follow him on Twitter (🐦 @wanderingrowe) or visit his website (**w** markrowe.eu).

USE OF GAELIC AND ENGLISH PLACES NAMES

The vast majority of place names in the Outer Hebrides have both a Gaelic and an Anglicised name. Generally, this guide gives both names for the most popular places (eg: Steòrnabhagh/Stornoway; Calanais/Callanish; Losgaintir/Luskentyre); and also for smaller locations where the two are different (An t-Ob/Leverburgh; Baile nan Cailleach/Nunton). For other places, where the two forms are very similar (Fleoideabhagh/ Flodabay), the Anglicised spelling is used for reasons of space or to avoid maps appearing cluttered. With a handful of exceptions for commonly climbed peaks (eg: An Cliseam/Clisham), hills and their summits are given their Gaelic name only.

For more on the wonderful ways in which Gaelic place names identify the landscape in which they are found, see the box on page 5.

PUBLISHER'S FOREWORD *Adrian Phillips, Managing Director*

Bradt is known for covering far-flung destinations, but we also have more guides to British regions than almost anyone else. The Outer Hebrides brings the far-flung and the British together. Mark Rowe is a hugely respected travel writer and a regular visitor to the Outer Hebrides, so there could be no better author to lead you around the islands' wildlife, food and ancient heritage. The archipelago has so often been relegated to a few pages within guidebooks encompassing all the Scottish highlands and islands. Here Mark gives it the attention it really deserves.

Second edition published April 2020
First published 2017
Bradt Travel Guides Ltd
31a High Street, Chesham, Buckinghamshire, HP5 1BW, England
www.bradtguides.com
Print edition published in the USA by The Globe Pequot Press Inc,
PO Box 480, Guilford, Connecticut 06437-0480

Text copyright © 2020 Mark Rowe. Translation by Margaret Fay Shaw and John Lorne Campbell on page 235 reproduced with kind permission of the National Trust for Scotland – Canna House. Diagram on page 17 reproduced and adapted with kind permission of Scottish Natural Heritage – Canna House.
Maps copyright © 2020 Bradt Travel Guides Ltd; includes map data © OpenStreetMap contributors. Contains Ordnance Survey data © Crown copyright and database right 2015.
Photographs copyright © 2020 Individual photographers (see below)
Project Manager: Susannah Lord
Cover research: Pepi Bluck, Perfect Picture

ISBN: 978 1 78477 596 4

British Library Cataloguing in Publication Data
A catalogue record for this book is available from the British Library

Photographs AWL Images: Tom Mackie (TM/AWL); Borrisdale Tweed, Isle of Harris (BTIH); Paul Brown (www.lewislonghouse.com) (PB); Laurie Campbell (www.lauriecampbell.com) (LC); Dreamstime.com: Donaldford (D/D), Luca Quadrio (LQ/D), Silviaanestikova (S/D); Mhairi Law (ML); Dena Macleod (DM); Steve Morgan (SM); Mark Rowe (MR); Shutterstock.com: corlaffra (c/S), Joe Gough (JG/S), Spumador (S/S); SuperStock (SS); James Smith (JS); Mairi Thomson (MT); VisitScotland: Kenny Lam (KL/VS), Paul Tomkins (PT/VS); Chris Whitelaw (www.flickr.com/photos/whitez73) (CW)

Front cover Mangersta Sea Stacks, Isle of Lewis (TM/AWL)
Back cover Puffin (LC); Machair at Howmore, South Uist (MT)
Title page Callanish standing stones (SM); Highland cow (SS); Hushinish, North Harris (LC)

Maps David McCutcheon FBCart.S

Typeset by Ian Spick, Bradt Travel Guides Ltd; and Geethik Technologies, India
Production managed by Jellyfish Print Solutions; printed in India
Digital conversion by www.dataworks.co.in

Acknowledgements

A huge thank you must go to Rob McKinnon, Christina Morrison and Mairi Thompson of Outer Hebrides Tourism, who have been generous with their knowledge and ideas and incredibly supportive of this project, and who go about their work with great skill, passion and imagination.

My sincere thanks also go, in no particular order, to the following individuals, organisations and companies who have often given up their time and insights and given support to make this book possible: John Groom, Bill Lawson, Andy and Jan Biddles, Kevin Murphy, Steve Duffield, Chris Ryan, Carol Graham and Rob English, Elaine Fothergill and Richard Inger, Seamus Morrison, David Maclennan, Lewis Mackenzie, Christina Miller, Mary Schmoller, Liam Alastair Crouse, Eilidh MacMillan, Kathryn Goodenough, John Merritt, Peter Clarke, Kathryn and Angus Johnson, Heather Beaton, Andrew Ross, Catriona Macleod, Steve Morgan, Harris Bari, Magaidh Smith, Alan and Isobel Graham, Ian Riches and Lyn Turner at the National Trust for Scotland, Tim Malseed and Loganair, Caledonian MacBrayne, Car Hire Hebrides, Cross Country trains, Bristol Airport, and ScotRail and the Caledonian Sleeper.

I also give my heartfelt thanks to Rachel Fielding at Bradt for supporting my proposal for this book so enthusiastically; my editors at Bradt, Claire Strange and Susannah Lord, and cartographer David McCutcheon for painstakingly plotting Gaelic hill names deep into the night; and, finally, the late Helen Trickett for friendship and laughter from Minsk to the Minch.

DEDICATION

To Lucy, Hannah, Thomas and Oscar: Horgabost, every time.

FOLLOW US

Tag us in your posts and share your adventures using this guide with us – we'd love to hear from you.

 BradtGuides
 @BradtGuides & @wanderingrowe
 @bradtguides
 bradtguides
 bradtguides

Contents

I first became aware of the Outer Hebrides in the 1990s when, finding myself in Yugoslavia near the end of an Interrail trip, I used my remaining days to travel the furthest distance possible – so I headed for Inverness. I took a bus from there to Skye, where I watched a ferry bouncing out to sea over choppy waters. In my ignorance, I had no idea there *was* anything further west.

And in all honesty, most guidebooks to Scotland can leave you with the same impression: I've rarely seen a guidebook dedicated solely to these islands. Invariably, the few national and international publishers that do cover the islands shoehorn them into tomes of the 'highlands and islands' genre, yielding space to Mull, Skye and even Orkney and Shetland. That means much of the wonder of these islands is skimmed over. Benbecula and Barra are often lucky to get a paragraph, let alone a page or two. Here, they get their own chapters, which I hope you feel they deserve.

A good deal of my professional work and interest focuses on the natural environment and both human and social geography, which run through these islands like the rivers and burns through the North Harris Hills. I felt there were wonderful travel experiences to share. Researching and updating this, the second edition of *Outer Hebrides*, has been as much a labour of love as was the first and now draws on more than ten years of visiting these islands.

People move on, people move in. The most striking change I have noticed while researching this second edition to *Outer Hebrides* is the increase in younger people relocating to the islands. Some are incomers; others are returning home, sometimes with young families. All of them bring fresh ideas, from how to manage their ancestral croft, to offering outdoor pursuits, providing a stylish twist to traditional tweed designs or sprinkling that pub menu with a bit of flair. Other, small, changes are also making a visit to these islands easier and include better waymarking for walkers and the incredible support network of pit stops that has grown up around the Hebridean Way route for cyclists and walkers.

The concept of slow travel has caught on in recent years, yet the Outer Hebrides was such a destination long before the term was even coined. For that reason, I should add my gratitude to Bradt Travel Guides for recognising that the islands sit comfortably within their remit of promoting sustainable travel and, indeed, the road less travelled.

At Bradt Travel Guides we're aware that guidebooks start to go out of date on the day they're published – and that you, our readers, are out there in the field doing research of your own. You'll find out before us when a fine new family-run hotel opens or a favourite restaurant changes hands and goes downhill. So why not write and tell us about your experiences? Contact us on ☏ 01753 893444 or e info@bradtguides.com. We will forward emails to the author, who may post updates on the Bradt website at w bradtupdates. com/outerhebrides. Alternatively, you can add a review of the book to w bradtguides.com or Amazon.

Introduction

The inhabited isles of the Outer Hebrides run from the Butt of Lewis in the north to Vatersay in the south, tapering at both ends to an unbroken ocean. Along the way, they encompass places with evocative names strung out in a gentle arc: Lewis, Stornoway, Harris, Uig, Berneray, the Uists, Benbecula, Eriskay and Barra. Collectively, they make up a breathtakingly gorgeous spine of cliffs, dunes, hills, beaches, peat, moorland, lochs and volcanic rocks.

Like many before and after, I fell first for the picture-postcard beaches of the Outer Hebrides, the endless miles of shell-sand that deliver Robinson Crusoe moments where your footprints are often the sole dents in the fine substrate. You could easily compile a case for the top ten beaches in the UK all being located in the Western Isles.

The wildlife is astonishing too. You will see big animals for sure on any visit, from red deer to eagles and seals. Getting around takes time but is, as the cliché goes, part of the journey. And some trips, such as the ferry across the Sound of Harris between South Harris and Berneray, have few equals in the UK, or, in the case of the beach landing on Barra, are unique.

All the islands have a distinctive appeal and differ remarkably from one another in character. Lewis is smothered with moorland and home to the truly ancient Callanish stones, while its western and eastern coasts provide the first introduction to those magnificent beaches.

Conjoined with Lewis, Harris is more rugged, with ancient and undentable rocks giving way to magnificent sands running down its western flank. The Uists have a different flavour: more windswept, less populated and with an extraordinary undulating flatness to their western coasts that contrasts with the jagged sea lochs to the east.

Benbecula squeezes in between the Uists, a shimmering collection of lochs and islets that somehow coalesces into an island. Barra, tucked away at the bottom, is a small parcel of everything the Outer Hebrides have to offer, its village of Castlebay, the most serene of all ports, overlooking the clanking medieval gem of Kisimul Castle, which stands ankle deep in the bay.

Offshore lie intriguing smaller islands: the Shiants and the Monachs whose landscape and wildlife repay the excursion. The greatest island jewel of them all, St Kilda, lies 40 miles to the west, deep in the Atlantic Ocean: a place of haunting beauty and spine-tingling history, it represents a once-in-a-lifetime journey for many visitors.

But the Outer Hebrides are about more than their natural wonders. You quickly come to appreciate the warmth and hospitality of the islanders. Your accommodation hosts, the skipper of a boat trip, will often be among the memories you take home. The revival of Gaelic, which here has long preceded the rise in nationalism on mainland Scotland, is striking; and music retains its distinctive rhythms and cadences. The ancient heritage is palpable, from Iron Age brochs to Celtic chapels. Many blackhouses, a form of traditional shelter where families and animals lived under the same roof, are still standing, gateways to an immediate past that were occupied until the 1970s.

Food, too, is a revelation. Pioneers here have for years drawn on the natural resources of fish, lamb and beef. Now word is getting out. There's a food trail that embraces community cafés run by volunteers and chefs who take their food extremely seriously. The quality is remarkably high, and you really have not tasted salmon until you have eaten it here.

A bewitching sense of remoteness accompanies you around this ancient landscape of islands on the edge of the UK, something that is reinforced when the weather bares its teeth, as it often does. Turn on the radio and the news from Edinburgh seems as distant and irrelevant as do reports from London, as though it comes from another country. In many respects it does. A different outlook on life still prevails here: people working the land, drawing to a significant degree on their natural resources, which not only sustain them but determine to a large degree how they live the way they do. The traditions of crofting, fishing, weaving are uncontrived and meaningful strongholds of that culture. For those in search of a place where travel is slow in all senses of that word, these islands are for you.

And, should you travel all the way from north to south, there are few more evocative journey's ends than Bàgh a Deas, the bay at the bottom of the island of Vatersay. This graceful bay, grazed by cattle and walked by very few people indeed, marks the conclusion of a dreamy island chain. *Fàilte!*

HOW TO USE THIS GUIDE

AUTHOR'S FAVOURITES Finding genuinely characterful accommodation or that unmissable off-the-beaten-track café can be difficult, so the author has chosen a few of his favourite places throughout the country to point you in the right direction. These 'author's favourites' are marked with a ✻.

PRICE CODES Throughout this guide we have used price codes to indicate the cost of those places to stay and eat listed in the guide. For a key to these price codes, see page 52 for accommodation and page 54 for eating out; see also the inside front cover.

ENTRANCE FEES AND FARES Prices are set out as adult/child; where applicable a family ticket price is added on.

MAPS
Keys and symbols Maps include alphabetical keys covering the locations of those places to stay, eat or drink that are featured in the book. Note that regional maps may not show all hotels and restaurants in the area: other establishments may be located in towns shown on the map.

Grids and grid references Several maps use gridlines to allow easy location of sites. Map grid references are listed in square brackets after the name of the place or site of interest in the text, with page number followed by grid number, eg: [70 C3].

Part One

GENERAL INFORMATION

THE OUTER HEBRIDES AT A GLANCE

Location 43 miles off the northwest Scottish mainland 57.76°N 7.02°W
Size 135 miles north–south by 35 miles east–west
Area 1,190 square miles
Islands 119 officially named, 14 inhabited
Heights Sea level to 799m (2,621ft)
Climate January 6°C; summer 14°C
Population 26,830 (2018)
Density 22.65 people per square mile
Capital Stornoway
Status Unitary authority answering to both the Scottish Parliament and Westminster, part of both Scotland and the United Kingdom
Language English, Gàidhlig (Scottish Gaelic)
Religion Church of Scotland, Free Church of Scotland, Roman Catholic
Currency Pound sterling £
Exchange rate US$1= £0.76, €1= £0.84 (February 2020)
International telephone code +44
Time GMT (winter), GMT+1 (summer)
Electrical voltage 230V
Weights and measures Road signs in miles; elsewhere both metric and imperial widely used
Public holidays Same as mainland Scotland: 1 January; 2 January; Good Friday; early May bank holiday (first Monday of month); spring bank holiday (last Monday of month); summer bank holiday (first Monday of August); St Andrew's Day (30 November); Christmas Day; Boxing Day

1

Background Information

GEOGRAPHY

The Outer Hebrides comprise 119 islands (14 inhabited) to the west of the stretch of waters that separates them from the Inner Hebrides and from islands such as Skye and Mull. They spread out, in a roughly northeast–southwest orientation, over some 135 miles. To the islands' west lies the North Atlantic, and there is no land in that direction until the rocky pinprick of Rockall, 230 miles west and, beyond that, Newfoundland along Canada's northeastern coast.

The islands of Lewis and Harris are a single landmass, by far the biggest Hebridean island at 217,898ha; in comparison with a disparate cast of places, they are six times the size of the Isle of Wight, the same size as Comoros and slightly smaller than Luxembourg and the third largest in the British Isles overall (after the

WHAT'S IN A NAME?

The islands described in this guidebook are known as the Outer Hebrides, but you will often see them referred to as the Western Isles or by the Gaelic name for the Western Isles, Na h-Eileanan Siar, though you will also see it written as Na h-Eileanan an Iar. In reality, people locally will rarely refer to them as the Western Isles. Na h-Eileanan an Iar is the name of the constituency for the UK Parliament, while Comhairle nan Eilean Siar has been the official name of the local authority since 1999.

'The Western Isles is a strange term,' says Ian Fordham, former owner of Broad Bay House in the village of Back on Lewis. 'It's quite vague – the Western Isles of where? People might think Mull, Skye are Western Isles too. The Outer Hebrides is a defined area: you can draw a neat ring around the islands.'

In Gaelic, the Outer Hebrides are also called Innse Gall, 'islands of the strangers', a name that originates in the 9th century, when it was applied to the incoming Viking raiders and settlers. Just occasionally, you may hear them referred to as An t-Eilean Fada, 'The Long Island'.

The name Hebrides, meanwhile, is generally believed to be a garbled modern English form of the classical Latin 'Hebudes', with the earliest references being made by Pliny the Elder and Ptolemy. This in turn is thought to have originated from 'Epidii', a Pictish tribal name whose root may come from *epos*, or horse. Others argue that 'Hebudes' is a corruption of the Old Norse 'Havbredey' or Isles on the Edge of the Sea. A handful of romantic types cling to the pseudo-Gaelic 'Ey-Brides', 'the Isles of St Bridget', the pre-Christian fire goddess Brigid or Bride. This last interpretation is given virulent short shrift by academia.

mainland and Ireland). The other main inhabited islands are North Uist, which covers 30,305ha, South Uist (32,026ha), Benbecula (8,203ha), Barra (5,875ha), Great Bernera (2,122ha), Berneray (1,010ha), Vatersay (960ha), Eriskay (703ha) and Scalpay (653ha). The waters between these islands and the Inner Hebrides/mainland are known as The Minch in the north, off the coast of Lewis and Harris; the Little Minch off the shores of North Uist; and the Sea of the Hebrides off South Uist and Barra.

Stornoway, with a population of just over 8,000, is the only settlement that fits the description of a town. The remaining population is scattered among more than 280 townships, tiny communities that often straggle for a mile or more and are characterised by standalone croft houses. Everywhere, scattered remains of fractured, broken croft houses, stone cross-beams and gables front thin air, a mournful reminder of just how hard physically, geologically and politically it is to make a living in these lands.

Lewis is by far the most populated island, with 19,658 registered at the 2011 census, nearly three-quarters of the total population of the Outer Hebrides. Harris is the next largest island area with 1,916 people, followed by South Uist (1,897), North Uist (1,619), Benbecula (1,330) and Barra and Vatersay (1,264).

The landscapes of the islands are extraordinarily varied. Lewis is dominated by peat-covered uplands that sweep remorselessly south across an almost tundra-like wilderness towards the rocky hills of North Harris. Further south lie the sweeping sandy beaches of the Uists, punctuated by lochs, while the island of Barra squeezes into its modest size elements of all its neighbours.

GEOLOGY *With thanks to Scottish Natural Heritage and the British Geological Survey*
Dramatic forces of nature have shaped the Outer Hebrides over billions of years. Over that time the land that was to become these islands moved from close to the South Pole through every climate zone on the planet, creating a landscape that is stark and dramatic, haunting and sometimes drably beautiful. Within a few short miles you can encounter some of the oldest rocks on the planet, bleak flatlands of peat bog and gorgeous grassy sea meadows, known as the *machair* (pronounced *much-ur*, with a Scottish *ch* as in loch), that back on to wild Atlantic beaches.

Freshwater lochs characterise the machair, and while the islands account for barely 1.3% of the UK landmass, these inland lochs account for 15% of the UK's fresh water. Meanwhile, vast sea lochs take giant chunks out of the seemingly impermeable hard rock of the east coast, creating a coastline as indented as the Norwegian fjords.

Volcanic forces Lewis is predominantly formed of metamorphic Lewisian gneiss. Some 2.8 billion years old, this rock is among the world's oldest and is named after the island. Gneisses are metamorphic rocks, ie: rocks that have been altered under extraordinary temperature or pressure. Most of the gneisses that make up the Outer Hebrides started off as igneous rocks, formed by the cooling and crystallisation of magma nearly 3 billion years ago. The majority of these were types of granite, but some were more iron- and magnesium-rich rocks with less silica, called gabbros. Associated with this igneous geology were small amounts of sedimentary rocks such as limestone and mudstone. The rocks were subsequently scoured by ice and scarred by rivers. Along the way, they have been squashed, folded, melted and bent to give the fantastically contorted shapes you see today along the west coast of Lewis, particularly around Ness and Dalbeg.

According to Dr Kathryn Goodenough and Jon Merritt, authors of *Outer Hebrides Landscape Fashioned by Geology*, the Lewisian gneiss has helped to create the

Gaelic has more than 80 words for hill, mountain or elevated ground. A good deal of place names and landmarks yield their meaning only in Gaelic. Benbecula's Gaelic name is Beinn na Faoghla which means 'Mountain of the Fords'. Near Scarista on Harris is Tober Ruadh, or the red well, where iron minerals were extracted from a rivulet. (Scottish writer Martin Martin observed early in the 18th century how 'the natives found [these minerals] efficacious against cholicks, stitches and gravels'.) Some species of wildlife, too, have names that tell a tale in Gaelic. For example, the oystercatcher is known as Gille Bhrighde, or servant of Bride, or Bridget: the story goes that when St Bridget arrived on the Outer Hebrides in the 5th century, she did so with an oystercatcher perched tamely on each wrist.

COMMON PLACE NAMES *With thanks to Dr Simon Taylor, the Ordnance Survey and Bill Lawson*
These common place names are Gaelic in origin, unless otherwise stated.

abhainn river
acarsaid anchorage, harbour
allt burn, stream
-aigh/ay/ey (Norse) island
àird height, promontory
àth ford
bàgh bay
baile village/township
barpa chambered cairn
beag little
bealach pass/glen
beinn hill, mountain
-bost farm (Norse)
bùth hut/cottage
cairn pile of stones, hill
caladh harbour/port
càrnan small cairn
ceann headland
clach stone
clachan village
cladach shore/beach
cleit rock/cliff
cnoc hill
corie corrie/hillside hollow
creag/craig rock, cliff
crò sheep pen
-dal/dail (Norse) valley
deas south
dubh black
dùn fort
ear east
eilean island
frith deer forest/heath/moor

geàrraidh land around a township/enclosure
geodhar/geo chasm/ravine
glas grey
gleann narrow valley/glen
iar west
lochan small loch
lùb/lùib meander/bend
machair low-lying fertile ground
meall round hill
mòine peat/moor
mol shingly beach
mòr big
-nis (Norse) headland
rathad road/way
rois promontory/isthmus
rubha headland
sgeir skerry
sgùrr rocky peak/steep hill
shader (Norse) farm, dwelling or township
sròn nose/point
sta (Norse) homestead
tairbeart isthmus
taobh side
tom small hill
tòb bay
tràigh beach
tuath north
-val (Norse) hill
vat (Norse) loch
vig (Norse) bay

In a land of unrelenting winds and plateaus of moorland, the reforestation of the Outer Hebrides seems formidably ambitious. Today, much of the Western Isles are dominated by a bleak, drably beautiful 'peat-scape' that draws away to the horizon, pitted with lochans, ancient gneiss rocks and clumps of heather. Trees, to put it bluntly, are as rare as hen's teeth. Those trees you do see have been grown mainly over the past 150 years (there are some exceptions, such as the millennia-old copse of aspen found on the shores of Loch Trolamaraig near Rhenigidale).

This triumph of peat, though, turns out to be a relatively recent development. Around 5,000 years ago, the climate of the Outer Hebrides was warmer, and studies suggest tree cover was almost complete. This sylvan landscape was recognised by the communities who erected the haunting Calanais stone circle on the west coast of Lewis. Slowly, however, the climate began to change, becoming cooler and wetter. Combined with grazing and clearing, peat began to take over.

The Hebridean Ark (w horshader.com/hebridean-ark-tree-project) project seeks to return parts of the islands to their erstwhile state. Supported by the Woodland Trust and the Forestry Commission, Ark involves taking cuttings and seeds from surviving trees and propagating 100,000 saplings to plant across Lewis and Harris.

'There's a place for moorland,' says David Murdo MacKay, who is building up a bank of seeds at Horshader on the west coast of Lewis. 'But nature can bounce back really strongly and reverse the damage we've done to it. If we plant trees, we reverse the process of soil erosion. Give birds some shelter and they will come and roost. We [the Outer Hebrides] are a metaphorical ark out in the sea.'

peat-scapes that prevail over much of the islands: gneiss is not porous, so rainwater quickly accumulates and bogs develop. Over hundreds of years, the waterlogged acid-soil-loving plant matter slowly breaks down to form a dense, dark layer of peat. The gneiss also appears on Harris, although the more common geology here, along with southern Lewis, comprises igneous and metamorphic rocks around 2.2 billion years old. By contrast, the Shiant Isles and St Kilda are geologically youthful, formed as the Atlantic began to widen about 55 million years ago.

The hills of the southernmost part of Harris, and Beinn Mhòr and Hecla on South Uist, are formed from large masses of igneous rocks which are slightly younger. Most of these consist of gabbro, but the peak of Roineabhal above Leverburgh – bare, stony and the most southerly of the Harris summits – is made up of a rare white-coloured igneous rock known as anorthosite, which consists almost entirely of the mineral feldspar. At times on the south and east coasts of Harris, you feel you are looking at a lunar landscape. Indeed, in some respects you are: anorthosite may be rare in Britain but is common on the Moon, where it has created its own lunar highlands.

Around 1.7 billion years ago, Lewisian gneiss underwent a second period of burial, heating and metamorphism. All rocks, including the dykes and younger igneous rocks, were changed fundamentally, creating new minerals such as the red crystals of garnet that can be seen in some igneous rocks. Meanwhile, more magma intruded into the gneisses of South Harris and western Lewis, to form veins and sheets of hard, pink granite. This granite is less easily eroded than the surrounding gneiss and forms well-developed sea stacks on the western side of the Uig Hills on Lewis.

The final event in the ancient history of the Outer Hebrides, more than 500 million years ago, was the development of a structure called the Outer Hebrides

Aspen, holly, juniper, birch and rowan may be native, but that is not always enough. 'The environment is very extreme here,' says David. 'Trees from the mainland don't do as well. They don't have the genetic make-up of the Hebrides trees. They get contorted by the wind; the local ones grow straight up. The trees here have evolved to deal with the salt spray and gale force winds.'

David has identified original Hebridean species of aspen and willow, though they can require some effort to obtain. 'They grow on cliff edges, crags, inaccessible places. These are very resilient trees in places that can't be reached by deer.' Sometimes, he says with a chuckle, 'they seem to grow from pure rock, from seeds dropped by birds.' Aspen is particularly tenacious, with truly ancient specimens somehow ploughing upwards through the subsoil. 'Some aspen can be linked back to the Bronze Age,' says David. 'It's a treasure house for genetic material, so it can easily disappear. The seeds are so important.'

The RSPB has been supporting these efforts and also encourages native tree growth further south, along the shores of Loch Eynort and Loch Hamascleit on South Uist. 'It's perfect, absolute heaven,' purrs Heather Beaton, the Uists' warden for the RSPB. 'The small woodland areas are full of native ash, aspen and hazel, it has a really fabulous understorey. To go here is simply to step into the past.' Bird species include willow warbler, cuckoo, goldfinch, goldcrest, wren, chiffchaff, blackbird and woodcock. Sparrowhawks enjoy rich pickings, while dippers are now also present on the burn. Heather recognises the long timescales involved in turning the tide against peat. 'I'm talking 200 years here,' she says. 'I'm never going to see it through but perhaps my children's children will.'

Fault, a major fracture in the Earth's crust, along which rocks moved against each other. Deep beneath the Earth's surface, the fault has continued to move episodically through geological time; the Lewisian gneisses have ground against each other along this fracture and created large amounts of friction that melted the rocks. The tiny amounts of melt created in this way were squeezed into cracks in the gneiss, where they rapidly cooled and solidified to form a network of black, glassy veins. This welded the rocks together, making them more resistant to erosion. Today, a line of low hills, comprising erosion-resistant melted gneisses, follows the fault, from Heaval on Barra northwards through South Uist to Eaval on North Uist and reappearing in North Harris and Lewis.

Around 500 million years ago, the crust of Scotland was lifted up to expose the Lewisian gneisses at the surface. During the Permian and Triassic periods, around 200 million to 300 million years ago, Scotland lay in the centre of a large continental mass with a hot, dry climate. The waters of the Minch were a broad valley or basin, into which rivers flowed from the surrounding high ground. At the start of the Jurassic period, some 200 million years ago, the Minch basin was flooded by a shallow sea. Sediments laid down in this sea were slowly compressed to form mudstones, sandstones and limestones.

Around 60 million years ago, large-scale tectonic movements led to the crust of Scotland being stretched and thinned. Deep in the Earth, rocks melted to form magma, which rose up through fractures in the thinned crust. This magma cooled and crystallised to form thick, gently sloping sheets of igneous rock, known as sills; some of these sills formed the cliffs of the modern-day Shiant Isles. The cliffs of the Shiants are characterised by dramatic columnar structures, which formed as the

1

magma cooled and crystallised into hexagonal columns, a process similar to that which created the Giant's Causeway in Northern Ireland.

Volcanic activity around the Outer Hebrides and St Kilda continued until almost 50 million years ago, with lavas pouring on to the seabed. When volcanic activity ceased, the exposed rocks on land were weathered and continuously eroded under warm and humid conditions for the next 45 million years.

Ice ages The ice ages then began to play their role in shaping the Outer Hebrides, and the islands have been glaciated at least three times, the most recent episode creating much of the rugged and desolate beauty we see today. The last of these major glaciations reached its peak about 22,000 years ago, when an ice cap was centred over the remote mountains of southern Lewis and Harris. Across the Uists, the ice flowed eastwards towards the mainland, while another vast expanse of ice flowed westwards for about 40 miles, reaching but not engulfing St Kilda.

The glacial legacy is one of angular, frost-shattered blocks of rock, pinnacles and tors along with smooth, ice-scoured slopes lower down the mountainsides.

The ice flowed over watersheds, scoured away loose and weathered rocks, and further deepened, widened and straightened the existing fjord-like valleys. Ice-scoured basins were filled with water or peat, surrounded by ice-moulded crags. This type of landscape – known as *cnoc-and-lochan*, where *cnoc* means 'round hill' – is best seen on South Harris, but also occurs along the eastern coasts of the Uists and Benbecula.

In northern Lewis, the ice laid down smooth, thick, gently undulating sheets of rubbly glacial material called till, over which the characteristic peatlands were formed. In the corries and glaciated valleys of the Harris hills, boulder-strewn ridges were formed when sediment was deposited at the ice front as moraines.

Impact of the Gulf Stream A sudden switch 11,500 years ago from a severe, dry Arctic climate to a relatively warm, wet one dominated by the Gulf Stream brought about the most recent profound changes in the landscape. By then, the sea was less than 45m (150ft) below its present level and the coastline well to the west of its current position. Global sea levels then rose rapidly as the great continental ice sheets of the last Ice Age melted. By 4000BC, the sea level was only 18m (60ft) lower than today.

PEAT CUTTING

Everywhere in the Outer Hebrides you will notice deep incisions in the moors and frequently catch sight of people labouring to cut peat. Before the availability of relatively low-cost coal, oil and electricity, peat was the most important source of domestic heat available. For crofting families, the annual peat cutting was a time-consuming task that could involve the whole family and often the neighbours. Up to 50–60 cart loads of dried peat were needed to keep a croft house in fuel for a year. The job of cutting, drying and transporting the peats home – traditionally carried out between March and 21 June – would have equated to about one month's full-time work for a single man. The way peats are cut by hand has changed little for generations: the main tool, a *treisger*, slices and then levers the chocolatey slabs of wet peat out of the ground. Once the peat has significantly dried and become firm, it is lifted into stooks, or spread layers; when fully dry, the hardened peats are heaped up with the outer layer stacked like roof tiles to repel the rain.

As sea levels rose, stones and boulders derived from glacial deposits on the sea-floor were – and still are – continuously ground and polished by beach processes, rolled shorewards over many thousands of years to form the storm beach shingle that backs many of the shorelines today. The dazzling, creamy-white beaches are also partly derived from glacial deposits, but most of the sand consists of tiny shell fragments and an assortment of broken spines and other remains of marine animals and algae.

Tree cover on the islands, in geological terms, has come and gone in the blink of an eye. A pioneer community of herbaceous plants began to colonise the thin, stony soils some 11,500 years ago, followed by heather, juniper and grass. Birch scrubland was replaced by mixed birch, hazel and oak woodland. These forests reached their greatest extent around 6000BC. As the climate became cooler and wetter, extensive areas of blanket peat began to form, a presence reinforced by Mesolithic man's gradual removal of trees for grazing and small-scale cultivation.

The islands were probably largely devoid of trees by the end of the Bronze Age, some 3,000 years ago.

Today, the peat moors are home to vast areas of heather. Three species are involved: bell heather and cross-leaved heath flower in June and the more common ling flowers in August. Thanks to the combination of wind, acidic soil and grazing, trees remain few and far between, and it's a tenacious sapling that thrives anywhere other than in a secluded glen or on the leeward side of houses. The exception is the wind-pummelled, dwarf-like juniper, which often appears plaintively prostrated before the elements.

The vast forces that shaped the Outer Hebrides continue today. The islands are separated from the mainland by the Minch, which lies along a tectonic fault and acts as a hinge. As the Scottish mainland rises, pushing against this hinge, the Outer Hebrides are being slowly forced downwards in a process known as isostatic readjustment. Lewis and Harris are sinking into the sea – so much so that it is thought that they may be 5m (15ft) lower than they were 5,000 years ago.

CLIMATE

The Outer Hebrides are regularly exposed to the extremes of wind and rain but – relatively speaking – enjoy a mild climate, with frosts rare. Many places where you stay will helpfully print out the weather forecast for you to peruse over breakfast: it's not uncommon for such forecasts to predict winds to be 'minimum 2mph, maximum 58mph'. Not only can you experience all four seasons in one day here; stand on a headland in sunshine watching hail across the sea, and it can feel as though you can experience them all at once.

In Stornoway, winter temperatures average 7°C by day with lows of 1.8°C at night; springtime temperatures climb to 9.9°C in the afternoon with overnight lows of 3.8°C. Summer's average high temperatures are 15.2°C, though they can reach the mid 20s°C any time between April and September, with lows of 9.3°C. Come autumn, temperatures typically drop to 11.5°C during the day and lows of 6°C.

Rainfall averages 1,173mm, and Harris and Lewis – with the exception of Ness – have had significantly higher rainfall over the past 30 years than the southern islands; they are also wetter than most places on the mainland, with the exception of the western Highlands, the Lake District and Snowdonia.

On average, there are 1,234 hours of sunshine a year: Stornoway sees just 50 minutes sunlight a day in December. On Midsummer's Day the islands enjoy 18¼ hours of daylight, the sun rising at 04.20 and setting at 22.35, though the nautical twilight continues all night, so it doesn't ever really get pitch black.

CLIMATE CHANGE IMPACTS The impact of climate change on the islands is expected to be disproportional to their minimal contribution to greenhouse gas emissions. Scenarios for the Outer Hebrides were graphically pointed out in a paper produced for Scottish Natural Heritage (SNH) that in turn drew on a Regional Climate Model from the Met Office Hadley Centre. This envisaged a combination of rising sea levels, increased winter rain, and more frequent and severe winter storms. By the 2080s, rainfall from December to February could increase by 8%, with a likely increase in storm surges, reflected in higher wave height.

The report identified the flat, low-lying machair lands of the Uists as particularly vulnerable, not only from sea waters overtopping coastal dune ridges, but also from inland flooding and limited natural drainage, which may increase the duration and extent of seasonal standing waters within the machair lands. The paper found that 'any future change in water levels would impose significant environmental shifts' but reported that there was already 'a perception within the Western Isles that seasonal winter water on the machair now covers a greater area and takes longer to disperse than previously'. The research also estimated that sea levels would rise between 8.9cm and 68.6cm by the 2080s.

In the summer of 2019, SNH went further and reported that South Uist, Benbecula and North Uist – with their soft coastline, low-lying plains and lochs – may be the first Scottish communities to suffer from the effects of climate change and rising sea levels. SNH said that storm surges and further sea-level rises could undermine the natural coastal defences offered by the underwater 'forests' of kelp. The machair at Cille Pheadair on South Uist was said to be in particular danger of inundation by the sea if the dunes were to breach during a storm.

Sea-level rises could also reduce the effectiveness of the canal system, known as the *ligidhean* (page 237), which drains water from South Uist, as there would be less time at low tide to expel surface water. The forecast increase in the prevalence of storms has also raised concerns about the need for greater marine and coastal protection. During a Force 10 storm in August 2016, an oil rig being towed along the west coast broke loose and was washed up on to Dalmore beach north of Carloway on Lewis. On this occasion, fears of a major oil spill proved unfounded, but it nevertheless prompted calls for a review of whether such vessels should follow navigation routes further out into the Atlantic.

The report raises the possibility that: 'if local people believe that climate change will make any stage of their arable operation so difficult that it is no longer worth the considerable effort involved, then there will be wide-ranging impacts on machair and its associated habitats: not only might arable cropping cease, but cattle-rearing might also cease without the availability of locally grown fodder.' However, the report also found that measures such as sluice gates may well protect freshwater lochs from saltwater intrusions on high tides.

Climate change already appears to be having an impact on seabirds in the North Atlantic. The warming seas mean fewer zooplankton on which sand eels – in turn an important staple for kittiwakes and puffins – depend. So far, the impact appears greater off the west coast of the islands, and the seas of the Minches are as yet unaffected, according to bodies such as Marine Scotland, the marine and fisheries directorate of the Scottish government.

NATURAL HISTORY

For many people, the extraordinary wildlife of the Outer Hebrides is a highlight of a visit. The islands boast three National Nature Reserves: St Kilda, Rona and Sula Sgeir, and the Monach Isles; along with 53 Sites of Special Scientific Interest (**w** gateway. snh.gov.uk/sitelink). The islands also boast three National Scenic Areas (a Scottish designation given to areas of great scenic beauty that affords them protection in planning law): South Lewis, Harris and North Uist NSA; St Kilda NSA; and the South Uist Machair NSA. Perhaps the most striking thing about the fauna and flora of these islands is just how visible it is: you can almost feel short-changed should you fail to see an otter, a white-tailed eagle or a red deer stag. All the hours you may have spent trying and failing to see charismatic mammals and uncommon birds elsewhere in the UK are likely to be brushed away by the ease with which they are found here: it can feel as if you have walked into an episode of *BBC Springwatch*. 'For me it's the sheer diversity of wildlife that makes it magical,' says David Maclennan of Scottish Natural Heritage (SNH). 'There's such a contrast between the different islands: they all have such distinctive characters. There are areas of the Outer Hebrides that are truly unique.'

MAMMALS Arguably, the most iconic species is the **red deer**, an animal you may spot from your car while walking the hills, or from the vantage point of a cosy bar or café. I once drove on South Uist in thick mist which suddenly parted to reveal a stag stood on raised ground just metres from the road. Native to the islands, red deer number around 5,000–6,000 and reside on all the inhabited islands apart from Barra, and most are descended from the original herds. The deer are 'managed' – a euphemism for culled – by sporting estates and also under licence if they cause problems for agricultural produce on crofts.

The Outer Hebrides have the densest population of **otters** in the UK, and the fetching 'otters crossing' roadside warning signs are not just there for holiday snaps. Another native animal, otters are an important part of the ecosystem, adapted to catch fish in both rivers and fresh- and seawater lochs. Despite their ability to fish in saltwater, these are European otters, not sea otters (which inhabit the Pacific Ocean). You are most likely to see them in the early morning or late evening. You may also see mountain hare on Lewis, particularly on the moors abutting the northeast coast between Tolsta and Ness (they can also be found on North

---

DEADLY SPECIES: THE HEDGEHOG

Another invasive species is a more unlikely villain: the **hedgehog**, introduced to control garden slugs or arriving as stowaways in bales of hay from the mainland. Given the current concern on the mainland about their decline, it can seem odd that they are considered a pest in the Outer Hebrides. The evidence has appeared to be overwhelming, however, as fixed cameras have caught hedgehogs taking eggs and young chicks from the nests of many waders, including golden plover, redshank, lapwing and ringed plover. The biggest impact has been on dunlin, of which the machair of the Uists once boasted the world's largest breeding population. It should be emphasised, though, that hedgehogs may not be the only ones in the frame: climate change and changes in farming practices may also be affecting the breeding success of birds.

For now, the hedgehog remains rampant, though environmental groups have applied for European funding to establish an eradication programme. The image of hundreds of Mrs Tiggy-Winkles being culled, however, has prompted a re-think on the PR implications; SNH has accordingly gravitated to relocation of the animals to the mainland.

Harris but there have been no sightings further south for several years; despite the introduction of mountain hares on North Uist a century ago, the population is deemed to have fizzled out long ago). From October until early April they sport striking white winter coats.

Invasive species have caused many environmental headaches. The main culprit has been the **American mink**, whose presence is attributed to the failure of a handful of mink fur-farms in the 1950s. By the 1990s, mink had colonised both Lewis and Harris, thriving in a perfect combination of sea lochs, rivers and a year-round food supply from prey unaccustomed to such a predator. Mink particularly targeted nesting black-headed gulls and Arctic terns, destroying whole nests rather than taking a single egg or chick and caching up to 50 birds in a single night. In defence of the animal, this is their normal behaviour, which works well in their native Canadian tundra habitat, where the eternal rhythms of the predator–prey balance keep matters in check. In the more limited confines of the Outer Hebrides, the effect was devastating, and there could only be one winner. Domestic chickens and ducks were targeted too, forcing several smallholders to cut their losses and quit.

Matters came to a head in the 1990s, when mink made landfall on the Uists. This was a tipping point, graphically demonstrating how quickly the animals could spread and raising concerns for the corncrake, a bird that had made North Uist something of a stronghold. A major eradication programme was launched by Scottish Natural Heritage and others, and today the battle is nearly won. The mink population has been all but exterminated, but efforts continue to catch the remaining individuals. The news is not uniformly good – the absence of mink has been a boon for rabbits that are now rampant on the machair and await the correction of their own numbers by some other means.

Another problem relates to greylag geese. While skeins of these birds provide superb photo opportunities for visitors, crofters view them as nothing more than pests. The goose was once classed as a migratory species but numbers have expanded and many are now resident year-round, taking advantage of the milder winters that are coming with climate change. Crofters say that large flocks trample, soil and ruin grassland.

Until 2018 restricted culls were carried out locally, during which a team of experienced, volunteer shooters operated under licence to cull the greylag geese on the Uist machair, Lewis and Harris; some of those killed were turned into burgers and sausages for sale at local shops. The culling scheme has now ended, but the Western Isles Crofters Committee warns that without any mitigation 'it is inevitable that the goose population will rise to the further detriment of croft land, our communities and our already fragile local economy'.

Among domestic mammals roaming the islands, you will often see **Highland cattle**, distinguished by their shaggy coats and curved horns. Some claims are made that the animal originated in the Outer Hebrides, or was first introduced to Britain there by Vikings. The most common sheep is the **Highland blackface**, a breed well adapted to the weather and climate. Here and there, you will see enormous, seemingly overweight castrated male sheep known as **wedders**. Other specialist breeds are reared by crofters seeking a premium price for a special product. All breeds form an important part of the ecosystem, grazing tough grasslands and enabling rare flowers to flourish, particularly on the machair. The importance of grazing can be seen on the more northerly moorlands and interior of Lewis, where sheep rearing has declined over the past couple of decades to the detriment of the landscape. As crofters have given up sheep grazing – mainly as it has become uneconomic – or as people move out of the area, the heather becomes rank.

This has knock-on effects for birds such as redshank and golden plover, which struggle to raise chicks in what quickly becomes unsuitable habitat.

BIRDS More than 320 species of bird have been recorded in the Outer Hebrides, and at least 100 species breed here. One reason for this diversity is the near-complete absence of mammalian predators: foxes, stoats and weasels remain at bay on the mainland while black rats were confined to the Shiant Isles, where an eradication campaign in 2015/16 led to the isles being declared rat free in 2018. Another is the superb habitat: marine waters rich in fish for seabirds and insect-rich machair for landbirds, which in turn feed eight species of birds of prey. Field voles and other small mammals such as mice and brown rats also provide short-eared owls and other predators – including even the occasional barn owl – with a plentiful supply of food. There are regular flurries of excitement among the UK's birding community when unexpected birds such as the black-billed cuckoo (a North American species that graced the islands in May 2016), the Baltimore oriole (which turned up on Barra in October 2018) and the brown shrike (also appearing on Barra in November 2019), are blown off course and make landfall. A regularly updated list of unusual feathered flutterings can be found at w https://western-isles-wildlife.co.uk/templates/latest_sightings_outer_hebrides_birds.html.

The greatest success story of recent years is that of the **white-tailed eagle** (or 'sea-eagle'). The return of the UK's largest raptor to the Outer Hebrides represents a heart-warming coda to a sad story. When the eagle was persecuted to national extinction a hundred years ago, the Outer Hebrides was its last sanctuary. The reintroduction of the species has been natural: Norwegian birds that were translocated to Mull and Skye have simply extended their population and range, thriving on the fish of the sea lochs and the large seabird populations. There are about 29 breeding pairs of white-tailed eagle across the islands – 19 on Lewis and Harris – and they are breeding with increasing success, from southeast Lewis down to South Uist. You may often be close enough to identify them without binoculars, as they drill through the air above a loch.

EXTREME INSECTS – HOW CITIZEN SCIENCE CAN HELP

Until 2012, no-one was quite sure just how many animal species could be found in the Outer Hebrides, and in what numbers. Beyond the most charismatic mammals, it was unclear just how wildlife-rich the islands were. Specialists might come and study hoverflies or butterflies in great detail but would then head home leaving a wider audience none the wiser. To address the issue, the Outer Hebrides Biological Recording (OHBR; w ohbr.org.uk) project was set up to enumerate and quantify the extent of biodiversity. The OHBR comprises a group of amateur but informed naturalists and has a public engagement remit: its findings are not jealously guarded but instead are freely accessible on the website. 'Some findings have been extraordinary,' says William Neill, a wildlife artist (see box, page 258), who also leads the South Uist branch of the OHBR. 'This is a fairly rigorous environment for butterflies and the like, but it is also a clean environment. There are almost no insecticides and pesticides, they are only used by some gardeners who haven't got the message yet. The crofters are not prone to using pesticides.' Unexpected sightings include a number of solitary bees and a high number of moth species. The OHBR always welcomes visitor reports of sightings, best done via their website.

The **golden eagle** is even more numerous, with up to 90 breeding pairs across the islands. They generally inhabit mountainous areas, such as Harris and the eastern side of South Uist. While they can be seen year-round, February and March are good times to see males and females pair-bond, soaring in unison and locking talons. In some places, the golden eagle has been gradually displaced by the larger white-tailed eagle. Generally, conservationists view this as nature reasserting itself: the golden eagle flourished when its larger relative was eradicated, and the latter is now reclaiming its strongholds. At this stage, the phenomenon is thought to pose little overall threat to the golden eagle population.

Hen harrier (see box, page 226) is another bird that thrives on the islands, free from the persecution it suffers in parts of the mainland. A helpful **Birds of Prey Trail** (w visitouterhebrides.co.uk, search 'birds of prey trail') lists 11 locations and two ferry journeys where you have a decent chance of spotting both eagles, hen harrier, short-eared owl and merlin.

Just as dramatic as the birds of prey can be the spectacle of voracious **Arctic skuas** on the hunt and the **great skua** (or bonxie), described pithily by the RSPB as 'an aggressive pirate of the seas', which harasses birds such as puffin and even (the large) gannet to steal a free meal by forcing them to drop their own catch.

One of the most endearing birds is the **puffin**, which you can expect to see during late spring and early summer, particularly around the Shiant Isles and at St Kilda. You can often spot them in the waters of the Minch, along with **guillemot**, **shag** and **razorbill**; more rarely, in autumn and late winter you may spot little auks. **Gannets** – gloriously described by Adam Nicolson in *Sea Room* (page 297) as 'a fuselage with stiletto wings' – can be seen plunging dramatically into the offshore waters and sea lochs the length and breadth of the islands. All the gannets you see will have flown in search of food from their colonies on either St Kilda (see box, page 185) or Sula Sgeir (see box, page 111).

There are an estimated 80–90 pairs of **short-eared owl** on the Uists and Benbecula. **Snowy owls** very occasionally drop in and will typically be spotted at the foot of wooden fence posts, where they are bombarded by defensive terns and gulls. More **gyrfalcons** seem to divert to the islands from the Arctic than anywhere else in the UK, while **snow bunting** is a common winter visitor from the same area. Another species more commonly associated with the high north is the **eider**, with its green nape and distinctive 'Frankie Howerd' cooing call. Along the shoreline, look out for **turnstone** and large flocks of **sanderling**. East-coast lochs are good places to see **red-throated** and **great northern divers**.

Cuckoos arrive every spring and, away from Stornoway, you will rarely be out of earshot of one. The Outer Hebrides are perhaps the easiest place in the UK to see them, since they perch on telephone wires where you might expect to see swallows. The doughtiest migrant is the **Arctic tern**, distinguished by its red beak, which easily travels 10,000 miles each year to live in perpetual summer. **Swift**, **swallow** and **house martin** also return from Africa to breed as far north as the Butt of Lewis.

Waders abound, thriving on the boggy moorland interior of Lewis, Harris and the Uists: the needle-billed (and very rare) **red-necked phalarope**, **curlew**, **redshank**, **greenshank** and **golden plover**, the last of these a bird that will often lift your heart after a weary uphill slog over open ground. It's not uncommon during bad weather to see such birds taking cover in bus shelters. Other birds that fill the sky include **oystercatcher** and **lapwing**, a bird with a hint of iridescent green and a foppish quiff that performs a striking spiral dive to deter nest predators.

The Outer Hebrides are a stronghold for the embattled **corncrake**, whose range and numbers crashed during the 20th century, for the most part as a result of early harvesting that destroyed nests before chicks had the chance to fledge. They can be seen – but their rasping call more commonly heard – around the west-coast machair. **Mute and whooper swans** exploit the islands' many resources, while many **greylag geese** now stay year-round rather than flying to Iceland to breed. Thousands of Greenland **barnacle geese** overwinter.

Extreme **butterflies** are something of a feature of the Outer Hebrides, with hardy species doing surprisingly well in a rigorous climate. The low use of insecticides and other pest-control measures is thought to be a major factor in their well-being. The most common sighting is likely to be **green-veined white**, widespread across the archipelago, while **common blue** has a Hebridean version that is thought to be the largest of this species. Others include **red admiral** in late summer and autumn, **small tortoiseshell** on any sunny day and, on Lewis and Uig, **meadow brown**.

On the southern islands, you have a good chance of spotting the speckled **dark green fritillary** where violets grow. South Uist, Eriskay and Barra provide good habitat for **grayling**. The **peacock** is a summer immigrant to the Uists, where you may also see the migrant **small white**. Other flutterers to look out for include **monarch** (from North America, typically after westerly winds in autumn), **clouded yellow**, **painted lady** and **ringlet**. Not all the butterflies are universally welcome: **large white** caterpillars happily munch through cabbages wherever they are grown. As for moths, the star species is the stunning day-flying **belted beauty**, whose chocolate tones and white streaks can often be seen on the machair of South Uist.

Bee species include the rare 'true' bee, the **moss carder bee** and the **great yellow bumblebee**; the latter was once common across the British Isles but is now confined to northern Scotland.

MARINE LIFE The fish-rich waters of the Minches and the Atlantic attract whales, porpoises, dolphins and **basking shark**. The eastern waters are good for **harbour porpoise**, **bottlenose** and **white-beaked dolphins**; **Risso's dolphin** can be seen off the northeast of Lewis. Other sightings around the islands may include **minke whale** and **orca** along with **humpback**, **fin**, **sperm** and other species of whales. The Hebridean Whale and Dolphin Trust (w whaledolphintrust.co.uk) is a good source of detailed further information. Species are fully protected, so matters have moved on since Martin Martin recorded in the early 18th century that whales were chased into the sea lochs of west Lewis to be slaughtered and 'sea-pork', as he put it, was a central component of the local diet. **Harbour (or common) seals** are frequently encountered, and **grey seals** are usually found on the western Atlantic coasts. They gather in their thousands on the Monach Islands.

Strandings of whales occur occasionally: pilot whales, with their propensity to act and swim in unison, seem particularly vulnerable. The Scottish Marine Animal Stranding Scheme (SMASS; w strandings.org) provides useful background and a range of contact numbers. For live animals, contact the British Divers Marine Life Rescue (✆ 01825 765546) or the Scottish SPCA Animal Helpline (✆ 03000 999 999). For dead animals, inform SMASS (✆ 01463 243030; m 07979 245893; e strandings@ sruc.ac.uk).

The elemental battering the coasts of the Outer Hebrides receive has created thousands of **rockpools**. The exposed shorelines of Hushinish and the vast bays of Luskentyre and Uig Sands will keep children occupied for hours. (My own children refer to the shores around Borve on Harris as 'Planet Clanger' on account of the almost lunar landscape revealed at low tide.) The southern islands also offer rich pickings. Places to linger include Borgh on Berneray, the northwest coast of

Up to 23 species of whale, porpoise and dolphin – more than a quarter of the world's 89 known cetacean species – either reside or pass through the waters off the west coast of Scotland, and many of these are frequently spotted from the coastline of the Outer Hebrides.

Such sightings are, of course, down to good fortune and timing, but to help nudge the odds in your favour, the Hebridean Whale and Dolphin Trust (HWDT) has created a Hebridean Whale Trail (w whaletrail.org). The trail marks 30 points across the Hebrides – including ten in the Outer Hebrides – where you have a sporting chance of seeing whales or dolphins. The aim is that each location will feature an interpretation board telling you what to look out for.

The Outer Hebrides locations are: Tiumpan Head on the east coast of Lewis; the Butt of Lewis; Gallan Head on Lewis's Àird peninsula; Hushinish on North Harris; Scalpay to the east of Harris; Balranald and Lochmaddy on North Uist; Rubha Àird a'Mhuile on the west coast of South Uist; Tràigh Mhòr on Barra; and St Kilda.

'Tiumpan Head, on the east coast of Lewis, is good for sightings of humpback and sperm whales, while off Barra you may spot "the Barra boys", a resident pod of bottlenose dolphins,' says Karl Stevens of the HWDT.

A Whale Track app can be downloaded from the HWDT website which will enable you to identify and register what you see, as well as find out what has been spotted recently. There are also plans for the app to feature a real-time alert for sightings.

'In the Outer Hebrides you feel on the edge of Europe, even of the world,' says Karl. 'The trail is not necessarily just about the cetaceans. The places in themselves – dramatic headlands, lighthouses, huge beaches – are wonderful places to visit even if you don't see cetaceans there.

'The next bit of land across the ocean is America. You just have these amazing seascapes so far from the mainland and who knows what is out there. It's a mysterious place of dramatic sea cliffs at the top of Lewis and the waterlands of the Uists. There just feels to be more of a link to the sea in the Outer Hebrides than anywhere else I've been in the world.'

North Uist, Balivanich on the west coast of Benbecula, the southwest coast of South Uist, and the beaches of Eriskay and Barra.

The causeways that link the Uists to Benbecula are always good for rockpools, but be mindful here of the rapidly rising tides. Signature animals to look for include the **shore** (or **green**) **crab** and the **velvet swimming crab** with its distinctive red eyes: handle this one with care as it's quite temperamental and will defend itself. Try to pick out the **shanny**, a small fish with chameleon-like qualities, green where found with seaweed and grey where among more exposed rocks. A more exotic-looking challenge is the **butterfish**, which has a distinctive row of spots on its back and gets its name from its slippery texture and habit of wriggling down crevices if threatened. The **beadlet anemone**'s red colour makes it an easy spot just below the surface of rockpools. On the southern islands, look out at tourist information centres for an excellent leaflet, *The Tidal Shores of the Uists and Barra*.

MACHAIR The defining landscape features of the Outer Hebrides' west coast are the long strips of sea meadows and coastal grasslands known as the machair.

As smooth and polished as a snooker table for much of the year, they transform into an astonishing riot of wild flowers in summer, providing an extreme and dazzling contrast with the bare, rugged rocks inland. Abundant on almost all the islands, they are a rare habitat in Europe.

They were formed 3,000–4,000 years ago, when sand derived from abraded sea shells was driven ashore on to the glacial soils. 'The machair of the Uists in particular is unique. There is really nowhere else like it anywhere but parts of Ireland. The flowers in summer are amazing and it teems with waders,' says David Maclennan of Scottish Natural Heritage.

Machair sand is largely composed of tiny shell fragments, which provide an ideal, well-drained, lime-rich soil to sustain rich grassland. Extreme winds blow beach sand inland to form belts of dunes that slowly become stabilised by marram grass. As the latter takes hold and stabilises the sand, flowers soon follow. A square metre of machair can contain up to 45 species of wild flowers: summer brings millions of emergent bright red and white clover, buttercup, yellow iris, harebell, vetches, gentians, eyebright, daisies, thyme and orchids such as frog and northern marsh orchid. Some botanists believe that North Uist even has its very own orchid, Hebridean marsh orchid, found nowhere else in the world.

Brackish lagoons, freshwater lochans and bogs associated with the machair provide a wealth of different habitats for plants, birds and other animals. Finer-grained sand blows farther inland where it settles to create broad, flat, turf-covered plains. In severe gales, bare or loosely vegetated areas of sand lying above the water table can be blown away in hours to form deep, elliptical hollows that may take years to repair naturally. The machair supports around a third of all the breeding dunlin and ringed plover in Britain as well as lapwing and oystercatcher.

The machair soil is much better for agriculture than acid peat and is important for grazing cattle. It is also used by crofters for bedding animals within byres. Sand is traditionally taken from the beaches, dunes and machair for a range of building purposes and for spreading on inland farmland. There have been some problems

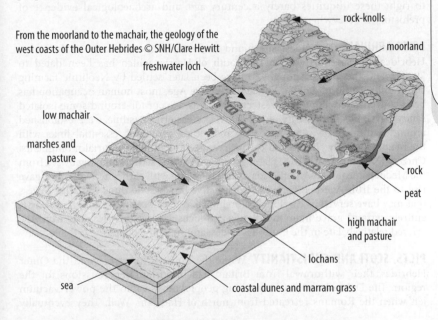

From the moorland to the machair, the geology of the west coasts of the Outer Hebrides © SNH/Clare Hewitt

rock-knolls

moorland

freshwater loch

low machair

marshes and pasture

rock

peat

high machair and pasture

lochans

sea

coastal dunes and marram grass

in recent years with uncontrolled commercial extraction from dunes and machair. This can leave the machair vulnerable to erosion by wind, while the blowing sand can make life unpleasant for local communities.

Flowers are not confined to the machair, however. Nutrient-poor lochs encourage the presence of tough specialist flowers that have carved out their own ecological niche, such as the often semi-submerged **bogbean**, which can suddenly flower over large areas, throwing a translucent blend of white and pink across a peaty landscape. These peatlands and bogs are dominated by **purple moorgrass** and **deergrass** along with **milkwort**, **cotton-grass**, **sundew** and **butterwort**, while the lochans support **bulbous rush** and **water lilies**.

Coastal interest includes **sea sandwort** and **sea ivory**, while rocks are often colonised by the pale grey **crab-eye lichen**. Curracag (**w** curracag.org.uk), a small local natural history society, is a good source for recent animal and plant sightings of oddities and rarities.

HISTORY

History can feel very tangible in the Outer Hebrides. Ruined and abandoned houses are a legacy both of the clearances (page 20) and economic upheaval, striking monuments pay homage to the land riots whereby islanders sought to right these iniquities barely a century ago, and archaeological evidence of prehistory is everywhere.

FIRST ARRIVALS The oldest site found so far for hunter-dwellers in the Outer Hebrides is near Northton in the south of Harris, which has been dated to 7000BC and the area is thought to have been later settled by Neolithic farming communities around 4000BC. Since the Bronze Age, most human occupation has been concentrated along the western seaboards. Except for around some isolated sandy bays, any settlements along the rocky eastern coastline were established around natural deep-water harbours and jetties, providing essential links with the mainland. Early chambered cairns have been identified as burial monuments. Current DNA research shows a later group of Neolithic settlers arriving by sea from the Mediterranean and Atlantic coasts and mingling with earlier arrivals. They gave rise to the Iron Age people, whose distinctive broch-style duns (circular towers that may have served as dwellings, storehouses or fortifications, though no-one is entirely certain) grace many headlands and lochs around the isles. The Iron Age arrived relatively late in the Outer Hebrides, around 400–300BC.

PICTS, SCOTI AND CHRISTIANITY While the Romans never reached the Outer Hebrides, their withdrawal from Britain had important repercussions for the region. The Dalriada, an Irish-speaking people, moved into the power vacuum left when the Romans retreated from north of Hadrian's Wall. They eventually became known as the Scoti or Scots, and their expansion pushed the indigenous Picts to extend their own influence into the Hebrides. Excavations have uncovered fortifications and weapons from 1000BC to AD500 and linked to an expanding Pictish population. From AD500, the Irish 'Scoti' peoples moved up the west coast of the isles. The coming of Christianity during the 6th and 7th centuries is demonstrated by many religious sites around the islands. St Columba certainly travelled as far as Skye, but little is recorded about whether he made it to the Outer Hebrides, so it remains unclear if Christianity was introduced to the islands from Iona or another missionary source. However, place names suggest that Christianity was present by around AD700 or even earlier: Pabbay derives its name from the Norse *papar-oy* meaning 'island of the priest', which suggests the presence of early monastic sites. The Gaelic name *cille* (church) also occurs in several places.

THE NORSEMEN COMETH Vikings moved in from AD700 to AD900. The north of Lewis was thoroughly settled by Norsemen, but farther south they were more of a ruling caste, though raiding, settling and conquering remained their modus operandi. Their main legacy in the islands has been place names and perhaps a love of the sea. By the end of the 11th century, the Outer Hebrides had become part of the Norse kingdom of Man and the Isles, and dependent on the king of Norway. In the mid 12th century, however, a revolt led by Somerled (half-Norse, half-Celt) against the kingdom led to greater links with Ireland and Gaelic culture.

CLAIMED BY SCOTLAND The Outer Hebrides were part of Norway until the mid 13th century when, after Scotland was victorious at the Battle of Largs in 1263, they were ceded to the Scottish Crown under King Alexander III by the Treaty of Perth in 1266. The islanders became known as the Gall-Gaidheil, or foreign Gaels. Although nominally under the Scottish Crown, effective control remained elusive until as late as 1598, when Stornoway was designated a burgh town (a status that reflected its burgeoning size and gave it a degree of trading autonomy). In between times, warfare and strife predominated. By the end of the 13th century, the Outer Hebrides were effectively under the control of the Clan Ruairi (or Mhic Ruairidh), and in 1346 they passed to John of Islay, as a result of his political marriage to Amie MhicRuairidh, heiress to her clan's lands. Most of the Hebrides were now brought together under a single Lordship, with John of Islay the first of the Lords of the Isles. While the Lordship was officially controlled by the Scottish Crown, in reality the local power base was located in the Hebrides, and the resulting independence allowed Gaelic culture to flourish: the period is often referred to as the 'Golden Age' of the islands. Kinship ties and rights to land were maintained through the clan system, and power held firmly by a few major families. The clan Donald, descendants of Somerled, emerged to control the islands as Lords of the Isles.

The Lordship collapsed in the late 15th century, and the power passed to the clan chiefs: Macneil on Barra, Clanranald on South Uist, Clan Uisdein on North Uist and Macleod on Harris and Lewis, each building their own castles and churches throughout the islands. The Lordship of the Isles was officially forfeited in 1493, but the clans dug in to maintain their political power. During the reign of James VI (James I of England and Ireland), the Statutes of Iona and other legislation outlawed the Gaelic learned orders and attempted to eradicate the Gaelic language.

The first comprehensive account of everyday life in the Outer Hebrides was published in 1703 in Martin Martin's *Description of the Western Islands of Scotland*.

Martin depicted a world in which islanders lived in blackhouses, farming and fishing in the same manner as they did up to, and after, the introduction of crofting. Settlement patterns remain largely unchanged throughout the medieval period, and the landscape was characterised by small hamlets of up to five houses, known as *bailes*, surrounded by cultivated land characterised by *feannagan* (azybeds, ie: raised furrows of land).

THE JACOBITE UPRISINGS When James VII (James II of England and Ireland) was deposed during the Glorious Revolution of 1688, he fled to France, planning to recover Scotland with the help of the French king. Events were to unfold that would have huge implications for all the Western Isles. James died in 1701, but the torch was picked up by his son, James Edward Stewart, known as the Old Pretender, whose followers became known as Jacobites. The first Jacobite uprising to challenge the union with England took place in 1715; a second in 1745 was led by James Edward Stewart's son, Charles Edward Stewart, better known as Bonnie Prince Charlie. The prince first set foot on Scottish soil on Eriskay, his aim to regain the throne on behalf of his father. Highland chiefs were dismayed that the prince had brought no French troops, few arms and very little money. Some refused outright to support him, and in any case not all the clans backed the Catholic prince: some favoured the Protestant Hanoverian king, George II. After some success, Bonnie Prince Charlie was defeated at Culloden on 16 April 1746 and fled once more to the Outer Hebrides with a £30,000 bounty (worth £4.6 million today) on his head. Famously, under a code of hospitality and honour, not even his enemies would betray him to the Crown, and he slipped away to Skye dressed as a maid with Flora MacDonald (page 225). The consequences of the venture, though, were to prove disastrous to the Highland clans and their Gaelic culture.

THE CLEARANCES In the immediate aftermath of Culloden, the Duke of Cumberland (the youngest son of George II) led the British army on a 'pacification' process of the Highlands, killing both surviving army forces and non-combatants thought to be sympathetic, as well as burning settlements and seizing livestock. At the same time, the clan system that had dominated the Outer Hebrides and the rest of the Highlands was eviscerated; swords were surrendered to the triumphant Crown, and the wearing of tartan and kilts was banned. While this contributed to the major waves of depopulation that followed, many other factors were at play.

According to Bill Lawson of the Seallam! Visitor Centre (page 167) on Harris, those other factors included: the changes in attitudes to land holdings that had begun in the later medieval period became more widespread, and the idea of the land belonging to the people – protected by a chief – was eroded. In its place came the notion that land was a commodity that could be bent to the will of private hands.

Another important factor was the move on Highland estates away from arable and mixed farming, which supported a large tenant population – subsistence-based and centred mainly on cattle raising – to more profitable sheep farming, which required the removal of those tenants. Emigration had begun around 1725, well before Culloden, but increased in the 1770s, after a series of years of poor harvests. The process intensified as crofters used their capital to pay their fare across the Atlantic, from Lewis to mainland Nova Scotia, from North Uist and Harris to Cape Breton, and from South Uist to Cape Breton and Prince Edward Island. Emigration continued up to, and beyond, the potato blight and famine of 1846. Every island in the Outer Hebrides was significantly affected, with families either forcibly evicted at the point of a gun or left with no choice but to leave. Island owners such as

Colonel John Gordon of Cluny gained fearsome notoriety for the brutality and lack of compassion with which he evicted inhabitants. Islanders were forcibly moved or chose the option of exchanging the fertile west coasts of the islands for the barren, rocky eastern shores, where there was little productive land but a wealth of seaweed.

The island landowners encouraged settlement on the sea lochs of these east coasts, and a booming marine-based industry grew up, greatly to the economic advantage of the landowners, but also providing a source of small capital for the crofters. The ash of kelp – seaweed – proved to be a source of minerals and fertiliser, in great demand during the French wars of the late 1700s and early 1800s.

ECONOMIC COLLAPSE If anything, the clearances and depopulation of the Outer Hebrides sped up in the early 19th century. After the Battle of Waterloo in 1815 and the end of the French wars, the market for kelp collapsed in the face of foreign competition, and the whole economy of the islands slumped. The suddenness of events left the islands devastated and bequeathed landlords a huge redundant population. Crofters no longer had an income with which to pay rent, and the landlords had lost their main source of revenue. Most landlords went bankrupt and almost all the remaining clan chiefs lost their estates to creditors. In the 1840s, the potato blight struck the islands, and famine on the Irish scale was only averted by well-organised charitable bodies from the Scottish mainland.

Matters got even worse when Lewis and Harris were bought by the merchant James Matheson in 1844. Townships were increasingly consolidated in groups of up to 15–30 houses, which were allocated land that was invariably the same size or smaller than that previously enjoyed by a single settlement. Ever-more centralised crofting and consequent migration towards the east coast and even emigration to Canada, the Carolinas and Australia ensued. This allowed Matheson and his 'factors' – estate managers, but effectively enforcers – to create larger farms and push rents ever higher. The most notorious factor was Donald Munro, nicknamed 'the Shah', who rigidly imposed regulations that prevented crofters from offering land to relatives or friends who had been evicted, and he ousted anyone who flouted the rules.

Tenants were each given a croft of 8 acres (3.2ha), an area insufficient to farm profitably, and they soon struggled to pay rent and feed their families. Tenants may have held the right to grow crops and graze cattle, but in return they gave the chief – the factor and, ultimately, the landowner – either military service or a share of their crop. The tacksman, who held the lease to the land, would collect this rent on behalf of the chief. The poorer farms were shared by joint tenants; those who had no land squatted on the outskirts of townships.

The new owners felt no responsibility to their tenants and were quite willing to dispossess them in favour of sheep farmers offering higher rents. Ever greater numbers of tenants left the islands, and many more were forced to leave as the best lands were cleared for sheep. Emigration continued, even though few could afford the fares, and many only left for Australia with the assistance of bodies such as the Highlands and Islands Emigration Society.

LAND REFORM In the first half of the 19th century, townships were generally governed by 'runrig' systems, a kind of shared-field agreement whereby every household took turns on a different plot of land to ensure that no single person had an enduringly better plot. By 1850, however, these arrangements were being replaced by the new crofting townships. Several steps of varying enthusiasm and success were taken by the British government to resolve the iniquities of the clearances and clarify land rights. Part of the impetus came from a series of riots over land rights. These protests were characterised by deliberate seizures of land and livestock or hunting of deer rather than mass violence. Riots of particular significance took place on Great Bernera in 1874, in the Pairc area of southeast Lewis in 1887 and in Aiginis on Point in 1888. The Great Bernera riot was the first successful legal challenge to 19th-century ownership of land that had emerged from the clearances.

Meanwhile, the Napier Commission, created by the government to appease land-reformers and crofters, had begun gathering evidence across the highlands and islands as part of a public inquiry into how issues could be resolved. The Commission concluded that landowners and crofters should work out their differences without recourse to law, which left all sides unhappy. It did, however, have the effect of politicising and organising crofters, enabling them to push for land reform in a more co-ordinated way. In 1886, the Crofters Holdings (Scotland) Act was passed, guaranteeing security of tenure to crofters and the right to compensation if they relinquished a holding. In the following years, many rents were reduced by nearly half and almost two-thirds of outstanding rent arrears were cancelled. Discontent and pressure continued, with important protests on Vatersay in 1906 and 1907. The following year, the Congested Districts (Scotland) Act provided money to create holdings. After World War I, the Land Settlement (Scotland) Act created powers and a fund to break up farms into smallholdings and to provide homes and income for returning soldiers.

THE OUTER HEBRIDES TODAY – AND TOMORROW It's fair to say that not everything is rosy in the Outer Hebridean garden. The islands face challenges common to other island communities around the world: emigration, holding on to the younger generation and encouraging inward migration. Incomes are lower than on the mainland, and the prevailing culture of self-sufficiency is not always enough to compensate for this. The islands are classified as an 'economically fragile area' and costs of imported commodities such as fuel and meat are high. Islanders don't have time to wallow nostalgically in the past, not least because historically there has not been much to be nostalgic about. Mains tap water arrived only in the 1960s; before that time many islanders washed their laundry in the nearest loch.

Yet the islanders have seen off, or assimilated, Norse invaders, and the English and Scottish crowns, as well as enduring and surviving the Highland Clearances.

In 2003, the Scottish government introduced the Land Reform Act, giving crofters and communities the right to buy their own land, with the weighty responsibility that brings in terms of managing the land responsibly and at a profit. Several communities on the islands have done so, moving to reverse the historical processes of enclosure and privatisation through community land purchase. Well over half of the islands' area is now registered in community trusts, and more than two-thirds of the population lives on community-owned estates, which include the North Harris Trust (see box, page 140), the Stornoway Trust and Stòras Uibhist on the southern isles.

Island demographics Depopulation of the islands did not stop with the end of the clearances. While the total population has actually increased slightly in recent years, the prevailing trend has been one of migration, whether within the islands to Stornoway and Lewis or to the mainland and further afield. In the past 60 years, 13 islands have become uninhabited, eight of them since the 1970s: these include Taransay, Scarp, Pabbay and Sunamal.

The pattern of long-term decline is clear: the population of the Outer Hebrides has dropped by 5,000 (almost 14%) since 1961. Islands such as Eriskay, Harris, Scalpay and Berneray have seen a particularly marked decline in population over the last 50 years. The population of Harris plummeted by 48% between 1951 and

2011, from 3,121 to 1,625. South Uist's population declined by 15% between 1981 and 2001, while Barra and Vatersay's dropped by 11% over the same period. Lewis may still be the most populated island, but the population dropped from 23,344 to 19,406 between 1961 and 2011, a decline of 17%.

Since 2001, some islands have reversed this trend: Barra and Vatersay have experienced the highest population increase at 8%. Lewis and Benbecula have each experienced a 6% increase. Overall, between 2001 and 2011 there was a 4.5% increase in the island chains' population. Generally, though, this uptick is viewed in official circles as a blip. While demographic analysis predicts an even higher population by 2022, by this time, according to conclusions drawn from the 2011 census, there will be fewer school-age children, working-age adults and women of child-bearing age. The long-term decline in the number of women of child-bearing age from around 4,500 in 2004 to around 3,500 in 2019 – around 23% – was identified by the islands' council (now known only by its Gaelic name, Comhairle nan Eilean Siar) as an area of key concern. Despite a higher than average fertility rate (the second highest in Scotland), annual births are projected to decline by 50% in the next 20 years.

Several small schools have closed or amalgamated in recent years. Resentment is still palpable in small communities at the events of 2010 when 11 small schools were axed at a single council meeting: Cross primary, Sandwickhill primary, Scalpay primary, Daliburgh secondary, Stoneybridge, Balallan, Bragar and Carloway primaries, Lionel secondary, Shawbost secondary and Seilebost primary. The smallest remaining schools are now Uig with 11 pupils and Berneray with 12. In September 2017, school rolls showed there were 3,360 pupils in full-time education (1,906 in primary schools and 1,454 in secondary schools). This compares with 2,100 primary school children and 2,100 secondary school children in 2004.

Young people from the islands do well at school (the Outer Hebrides ranks 12th among all local authorities in Scotland), but then often leave to study at university and college. Consequently, the area has an increasingly ageing population profile, with the highest proportion of elderly people in Scotland. If current trends persist, the population is set to continue to decline and age at what the council calls 'a worrying rate'.

That said, it is possible to read too much into official data, which are now several years out of date. In slight contradiction to these data, the local authority has built seven new schools (though to some extent, since these have larger catchment areas, they represent a consolidation of schools that have been closed). Furthermore, while secondary school numbers have declined in the long term (down by 15% since 2010/11), primary school rolls have been quite steady since the last census in March 2011. At that time (the school year 2010/11), there were 1,870 primary pupils in the Outer Hebrides. In 2018/19 there were 1,875. This implies that the coming years will see an increase in secondary school numbers.

The evidence on the ground may also suggest a different picture as a small but statistically significant number of innovative young people are returning, or moving to, the islands. Whether this is driven by improved internet and related services, a desire for a lifestyle away from the rat race or the re-emergence of an importance of identity and sense of place, is as yet undefined. The driver may perhaps be a combination of all these factors. The 2021 census may confound or confirm this perception. A good website to peruse is CoDeL (w codel.scot), which was set up on North Uist in 2018 with the aim of identifying trends that can fall between the cracks of aggregated big data. Data on the website, which are focused on North Uist, paint a more upbeat picture of population trends. Headline figures state that the age profile for agricultural committees on North Uist and South Uist is now a generation younger than a decade ago; and the number of children attending playgroups has doubled in just a few years to 20 on North Uist and a dozen on Benbecula.

Contrary to the anti-immigration mood that was so conspicuous during the UK's EU referendum in 2016, migration of one kind or another will have to be part of any solution to the demographic challenges the Outer Hebrides face. The number of incomers is increasing every year; in some communities, as few as 50% of residents were born on the islands. Incomers can bring new ideas, but people escaping city life can sometimes unwittingly impose their own values; meanwhile, there is a risk that some local people end up feeling financially and socially ostracised. So far, evidence of this is scant; the majority of incomers seek a lifestyle change and are keen to assimilate.

ARCHAEOLOGY

At the latest count – December 2019 – the Outer Hebrides were home to precisely 13,348 identified archaeological sites and monuments, which represents an extraordinary increase of 500 over the past four years. The number rises steadily as the weather exposes fragments of Iron Age pottery or medieval houses. This is particularly the case on the western seaboard, which is characterised by machair (page 16). The documented sites include 232 individual entries from the Mesolithic period (10000–4001BC), 358 Neolithic entries (4000–2351BC) and 400 Bronze Age entries (2350–751BC).

According to the archaeology department of Comhairle nan Eilean Siar, the geography of the western side of the islands is key to the survival of the archaeology. The machair represents the interaction of man with domestic cattle. Before that, there were Mesolithic farmers, but the sand just covered up what they did. But if the sand erodes, then history can simply appear before your eyes. It's not uncommon for a village on the island that nobody remembers to be revealed after a storm blows in.

Rising water levels have been a common feature of the islands up to the present day. While this meant constant readjustment for early communities, it makes for ideal conditions for archaeologists to gain information from the past as all interesting features – from woodland remains in tidal peats to stone structures and midden deposits (pottery, bone and shell) from the eroding coastline – have been preserved, offering insights into early domestic life. What keeps the islands special in archaeological terms is that farming techniques have never reached industrial levels. The light footprint and low impact of farming practices through the ages has left much of what went before undisturbed. Rabbits play their part too, by offering occasional and tantalising glimpses of what lies below the surface. The entrances to their burrows can show the evidence of pottery fragments or worked quartz. Furthermore, not everything that looks old actually is: ceramic croganware was made until the 1920s and shares many characteristics with shard material of the Bronze and Iron Ages and medieval pottery.

The earliest known sites in the Outer Hebrides date to the Mesolithic (Middle Stone Age), at Northton on South Harris, and Cnip headland on the Bhaltos peninsula on Lewis. The visible remains from later times can be seen from ruins such as Grimsay wheelhouse on North Uist, Kisimul Castle off Barra, Borve Castle on Benbecula and St Columba's Church at Aiginish on Lewis. The islands are awash with archaeological treasures and include the unique site of the Callanish Stones complex. Many of these remain in implausibly remote locations awaiting closer inspection, most notable of which are the *shielings*. Made from turf and stone (and many of corbelled construction), these structures were summer dwellings where farmers – usually women – would take cattle for summer grazing. Some structures may date back into pre-history, while others remained in use during the 20th century.

Until the last century, the main routes of communication for the Outer Hebrides were by sea, something clearly indicated by the shared material culture (everyday items, pottery, tools) and decorative styles from the Neolithic onwards that are found along the coasts and which have origins overseas. These material remains show the importance of the maritime trade routes from Ireland, Orkney, Shetland and Scandinavia. Another indicator that remains today is the strong Scandinavian influence seen in many place names, such as Habost ('high farm') or **Chàrlabhaigh (Carloway)**, which originates from Karlavàgr, or Karli's Bay.

Should you come across any artefacts, be mindful of Scotland's Treasure Trove legislation (w treasuretrovescotland.co.uk), which states that any find belongs to the government of Scotland. This can be done easily by reporting any finds directly to Treasure Trove or by contacting the Museum nan Eilean (✆ 01851 822746; e museum@cne-siar.gov.uk). Any skeletal remains suspected of being human should be reported to Police Scotland. For those keen to drill deeper into these islands, several excellent books are listed on page 295. Three fine online resources are: w megalithic.co.uk, run by passionate amateur Andy Burnham; w www.canmore.org, the website of Canmore and operated by Historic Environment Scotland; and w pastmap.org.uk, which allows you to search over a wide area for everything from ancient monuments to listed buildings – type in 'Callanish', for example, and the map will show you all the Callanish-related sites on Lewis.

GOVERNMENT AND POLITICS

To the outsider, the Outer Hebrides appears a neat and tidy entity, governed by a single council, Comhairle nan Eilean Siar, the only Scottish council to have a Gaelic-only name; it was renamed from Western Isles Council in 1997.

Thirty-one councillors are elected from nine wards across the islands under the Single Transferable Vote, whereby voters use numbers instead of a cross and rank candidates in order of preference. A quota and formulae system then decides who is elected, based on the preferences as indicated by the voters.

At the time of writing, to say that women and the BAME community are under-represented in civic life is something of an understatement: all 31 councillors are white men.

Before Comhairle nan Eilean Siar was established, the straggling Outer Hebridean islands answered to three local authorities and their accordingly vested interests. While not short of critics, the unitary authority has by general consensus introduced a greater degree of co-ordination, oversight and cohesive funding to development with regard to transport and infrastructure – the causeways being among the most obvious examples. More than £30 million has been spent on major projects over the past decade or two; these include a bridge to Scalpay, causeways to Berneray and Eriskay, ferry terminals at Stornoway and Leverburgh, and car ferries on the routes between Harris and the Uists and from the mainland to Barra and Stornoway. Above all, the single local government appears to have given cohesion to an internal market created by the north–south spinal route from Lewis through to the bottom of South Uist.

The islands return one MP to the UK Parliament for the seat of Na h-Eileanan an Iar. The seat represents the smallest electorate (21,780) in the UK and has been held since

2005 by the Scottish National Party (SNP). The islands also elect a single member to the Scottish Parliament. Traditionally, this seat has been a two-way marginal between the SNP and Labour, with the former holding the seat since the 2011 election. In the 2014 referendum on Scottish independence, the Outer Hebrides voted against the motion by 53% to 47%, on a turnout of 86%. In the 2019 general election, the islands returned the SNP candidate to the UK parliament with an increased majority of 2,400, a swing of 5% from Labour to the SNP. (In this last election, a ferry breakdown meant that a number of Barra voters could not return to the island to vote.)

ECONOMY

I once got chatting in a shop with a man from Harris. What did he do for a living, I asked. On the one hand, he did a bit of fishing, came the reply. On the other, he grazed some cattle. On the other, he continued, he did a bit of decorating. When I pointed out we'd now reached three hands, he simply nodded. You'll get a similar reply from many people in the Outer Hebrides: you often need several income streams to keep your head above water, partly because one income alone is rarely sufficient, but also to cover yourself should market forces or the weather – often one and the same – intervene.

In *Sea Room*, Adam Nicolson's captivating account of an outsider who inherited the Shiant Isles, the author captures the prevailing mentality to resources. He contrasts it with that of the mainland, which he describes as 'the world beyond here [the Outer Hebrides], the world of cheap options, of short cuts, the world of "most boats" where the rigour of this man and his workshop was not applied.' Nicolson was talking about a boat-maker, but it reflects a wider point about utilising resources at hand, where you can't just pop down the local out-of-town DIY store should you run out of materials.

Self-employment and part-time work are higher in the Outer Hebrides than in Scotland overall. For other parameters, the Outer Hebrides follows the Scottish trend, with more men than women in full-time work or self-employed, and more females than males in part-time work. Average pay is £461 a week, compared with the Scottish average of £518. The unemployment rate was 5.2% in 2014, compared with the Scottish average of 6.25%. Some 71% of the Outer Hebrides population aged 16–74 was economically active. The Outer Hebrides has a higher percentage of retired people than in Scotland overall and has a higher percentage of retired women, more women looking after family and more men who are long-term sick or disabled. The Outer Hebrides have Scotland's highest percentage (17%) of people aged 65 or over living alone. Life expectancy is 77.2 years for men (slightly higher than the Scottish average) and 80.4 years for women (slightly lower).

The Outer Hebrides has more people working in construction, transport and storage, education, and human health and social work activities than the Scottish average.

PRINCIPAL ECONOMIC ACTIVITIES The economy has four major sectors: crofting, tourism, tweed and fishing. **Crofting** is in simple terms the management and cropping of small areas of land, and the crofting rights enshrined in the 1886 Crofters Holding Act – security of tenure and fair rents – still determine the shape of crofting today. This is the predominant land use in the Outer Hebrides: about 77% of land is held in crofting tenure, with some 6,000 crofts distributed among

280 townships. Of these, 94% provide fewer than two days' work a week for their occupiers and typically average 2.8ha in size. The quality of land and sizes of crofts and grazings vary considerably but, generally, the smallest crofts are to be found on the poorest land, and most of the large full-time crofts are on the Uists.

Modern-day crofts tend to have more conventional rectangular cultivation plots and are large enough to include stone enclosures for stock management and storage of winter fodder. Raising lambs is the most important crofting activity in the Western Isles; lambs are fattened for slaughter elsewhere in the UK or in Europe. The rearing of calves as hardy breeding stock is also carried out, mainly on the Uists and Barra.

One characteristic of crofting has remained unchanged: the traditional method of farming. Crofting involves a low-input system, with little added in the form of chemicals. Traditional use of seaweed and dung fertiliser is still widespread, particularly on the Uists, Barra and Taransay.

As a form of land use, crofting has been extremely successful in maintaining rural populations in areas where they would otherwise certainly have disappeared. However, it faces many problems, of which the most pressing is an ageing population of crofters.

Tourism was worth £65 million to the local economy in 2017 and is projected to rise to £74 million in 2020 as visitor numbers grow from 219,000 in 2013 to a projected 260,000 in 2020. The limited Sunday services – from buses (non-existent) to cafés (rarely open) – in the northern part of the isles are often seen as a constraint to tourism by visitors, but strong voices within the tourism sector argue this is a unique selling point that should be marketed to appeal to visitors interested in local culture. It sounds counter-intuitive: only by car or by bicycle can you travel meaningful distances on a Sunday – if you have neither, you are marooned – but the argument is that this forces you to explore a particular locality that day and gives you an insight into how locals plan their week, from buying petrol ahead of Sunday to enjoying landscapes that are even emptier than usual.

Harris Tweed employs more than 250 craftsmen and women on the islands, with many specialist weavers creating their own niches and designs. The unique cloth of Harris Tweed can be produced only in the Outer Hebrides by weavers working in their own homes; however, once woven the cloth is then transferred to one of three local mills, where the finishing touches are made to the cloth. Finished

PRICE PREMIUMS

For many years, islanders have complained that they pay a price premium for goods and services to remote and rural areas. Petrol and domestic fuel prices are high as the Outer Hebrides rely almost entirely on imported energy and are located at the extremities of a centralised electricity-generation and -distribution model. Other concerns focus on delivery charges and impacts on shopping, education, employment and other key services, particularly in relation to service distribution and the need for many people to travel long distances for work or for health care. Several companies flatly refuse to deliver goods and parcels. The Office of Fair Trading has visited the islands to collect evidence amid claims that the price premium can be as high as 20%. In the past decade, the introduction of the Road Equivalent Tariff has made travelling to and from the islands by ferry cheaper, but the tariff does not apply to freight, which means your guesthouse or hotel must pay a higher cost for everything from fuel and potatoes to window frames and toilet seats.

Harris Tweed items and rolls of cloth are exported to more than 50 countries. The industry is emerging from a period of decline and has re-established itself as a luxury global product.

Many weavers are crofters but are usually only part-time farmers. Weaving, however, combines well with the seasonal demands of crofting, harvesting, planting, peat-cutting, shearing and milking.

Aquaculture and **sea fisheries** are increasingly important to the islands. Shellfish accounts for around 90% of total landings, while deep-sea and white fish account for the remainder. A significant proportion of shellfish is exported.

Despite the economic pressures facing fishing, the total numbers employed in the catching sector remain fairly stable. As well as the 680 people directly employed in fish catching, a further 300 are employed in ancillary activities, including 200 in processing and around 100 in vessel maintenance and repair. The fish-farming industry provides around 550 jobs. Due mainly to lower market prices, many smaller companies have been forced out of salmon farming, and three companies now account for more than 80% of production. In theory, remote working has the potential to attract more skilled professionals seeking lifestyle changes, though this would first require the ubiquitous introduction of super-fast broadband.

The *Outer Hebrides Migration Study*, published in 2006, continues to inform much of the thinking of the council and other agencies. This found that the lack of job opportunities was behind the long-term population decline; in particular the lack of skilled jobs with progression opportunities, and the limited range of training and education opportunities. The study recommended that the solution involved 'a stable and growing economy based around a skilled workforce' that drew upon the islands' wealth of natural resources, such as food production, energy and crafts, plus a greater emphasis on opportunities for graduates and skilled workers.

GREEN ENERGY With their direct exposure to the aggressive North Atlantic climate regime, the Outer Hebrides have some of the richest wind, wave and tidal resources in Europe. Marine Scotland identifies the seas west of Lewis as one of the country's leading wave-resource areas; and the Scottish government sees similar potential for a large area north of Lewis. Already, the turbines that have been erected produce energy well above the UK turbine average of 25% of the time and, together with Orkney and Shetland, the Outer Hebrides have the potential to provide 5% of the UK's entire electricity needs by 2030.

Comhairle nan Eilean Siar (see box, page 3) has a vision that, by the end of 2020, the Outer Hebrides will be generating 1 gigawatt of onshore wind and at least the same of marine energy (half each from wave and offshore wind). Other projects explore the feasibility of community-generated hydrogen fuelling local road transport.

Some projects are also proving contentious. A proposal for a 36-turbine wind farm a few miles outside Stornoway on Lewis, financed by EDF, has been opposed by crofters who have plans for their own community wind schemes and are also alarmed by the proposed turbine heights of 187m. The council has also come under pressure from other crofting groups who feel local ownership should be at the heart of the islands' renewable energy projects.

The main obstacle, however, is the limited connection and capacity both to transport energy to the mainland and to distribute it within the islands. In the short term, the island grids are effectively 'full', making it difficult to connect to any major generation or even link up private households and community projects. Key to the success of green energy on the islands, some argue, is the construction of a sub-sea interconnector cable that would transport surplus electricity from Lewis to Inverness, a proposal that has stalled over just who will underwrite the £780 million cost. Many supporters of green energy say that the current charges to access the transmission network for green energy projects are also prohibitive.

PEOPLE

The portrait of the Outer Hebrides painted by early visitors was of a land steeped in remnant medievalism, islanders bound by superstition and an area where even cows had second sight. The observation of Martin Martin in his early 18th-century *A Description of the Western Islands of Scotland* is typical: a chapter heading is entitled 'Their Admirable and Expeditious Way of Curing Most Diseases by Simples of Their Own Product. A Particular Account of the Second Sight, Or Faculty of Foreseeing Things to Come, by Way of Vision, So Common Among Them'. Even cows, Martin was told, could presage their master's death by yielding blood rather than milk from their udders.

Things have moved on somewhat since then. Culturally, the Outer Hebrides are typical of many islands in that they retain a distinct cultural identity, based around family and crofts, music and oral literature. The islands have a higher percentage of those identifying themselves as White Scottish (86.9%) and White Other British (10.5%) than mainland Scotland. Those identifying themselves as Asian, Asian Scottish or Asian British were far fewer than mainland Scotland, at 0.5%. Other ethnic groups were 0.4%. In the Outer Hebrides, single-person households are the largest household type at 37.2%, slightly above the Scottish average (34.7%).

Whereas some other Scottish islands have slowly shed some of their warmth, inhabitants' hospitality jaded by the sheer number of visitors, you will be struck by the lack of 'side' among Outer Hebrides islanders: they tend to be straight, sometimes to the point of directness, with you and each other. Artist Anthony Barber, of Ness, put it well when we met to discuss his paintings (see box, page 110):

Background Information PEOPLE

GENEALOGY

The Hebridean diaspora has spread far and wide, and recent years have seen a significant increase in people seeking to trace their roots. Tony Robson, one of the organisers of the Lewis 2014 Homecoming Tattoo says that event attracted many descendants of those who left the island in desperate circumstances. 'There are a lot of people in the US, Canada and Australia whose families originate in the Outer Hebrides,' says Tony. 'There are a tremendous amount of links to the 1800s, when people were either poor, or were shoved out by landlords and the Highland Clearances. People don't tend to forget; those events are still felt today.' The islands have 19 genealogical centres – archives and places of research usually housed in museums or community centres – of which 11 are now connected to the Hebridean Connections website (w hebrideanconnections.com), which should be the first port of call for anyone wanting to root around their family history. The website enables descendants to search by name, village and even occupation. All the centres are helpful, though some are more adept at using 21st-century technology than others. Other useful sites include w hebridespeople.com and w tasglann.org.uk, an archive collection database with information on Gaelic-language collections and details of heritage groups and collections.

'People here make you feel very welcome. They are very straight and trusting. I've often wondered why that is and I think it is because the population here has so many relatives who have gone abroad. They want to think that their relatives are being treated well wherever they go and so they want to do the same here.'

The *Outer Hebrides Migration Study* (page 28) offered intriguing insights into the outlook of islanders and concluded that the strong sense of community that attracts many people to the Outer Hebrides could also be viewed as suffocating and excluding by some, particularly 'by individuals who consider themselves to be different'.

LANGUAGE

Gaelic was sown into us like grains
of oats, turnip-seed, split potatoes
ploughs folded below earth each spring
Language by Donald S Murray

The islands are the only places in the UK where you will hear Scottish Gaelic spoken freely. In some places, such as Barvas on the west side of Lewis, Harris, Barra and North and South Uist, more than 60% of residents speak it. The language spoken in the Outer Hebrides is more accurately known as Gàidhlig, but for consistency and to avoid confusion, this book refers to the language as it is most widely known: 'Gaelic'. Overall, the number of people who speak Gaelic is around 53%, down from 61% in 2001; it is spoken by just 43% of people in Stornoway.

Scottish Gaelic is closely related to Manx and Irish Gaelic, as well as to Welsh, Cornish and Breton. The Gaelic language was introduced in Scotland around the 4th century by settlers from Ireland. Scottish Gaelic developed around the 12th century and became spoken by most of Scotland, replacing Cumbric, Pictish and Old English. The language began to decline in mainland Scotland during the 15th century and a north–south divide in Gaelic usage began to form. The language suffered further decline when many of Scotland's languages and traditions were banned after the Battle of Culloden in 1746.

Developments over the past couple of decades suggest the centuries-old downward trend may be levelling off. Thanks in part to the 2005 Gaelic Language Act, just over half of all children in the Outer Hebrides now go to Gaelic-medium schools, where they speak and learn Gaelic exclusively in their early years.

'Our first language is Gaelic; it is engraved in our traditions,' says Bill Lawson of the Seallam! Visitor Centre on Harris. 'For many years it wasn't cool to speak vernacular Gaelic. The whole system tried to tell you that Gaelic was a dying language. There is no point in resurrecting languages that are already dead, but Gaelic is alive.'

Alasdair Macleod, an island councillor involved in the promotion of Gaelic, adds that 'Gaelic has a rich heritage of song and poetry, of looking at the environment and the world in a different way. Gaelic permeates every strand of the community from crofting to the church – it's our heritage. The weather, the landscape, the moors, the names of hills resound with Gaelic. If Gaelic died out, we would lose a part of our soul. Why does Gaelic matter to me?' he continues. 'It's my first language, the first language in the community I live in. It's part of my being, my heritage and it's difficult to imagine life without it. We are not backward-looking; this is forward-looking.'

In 2020, the island council announced that children starting school would be taught in Gaelic, unless their parents opted out, with English introduced in the fourth year.

RELIGION

To generalise, Lewis, Harris and North Uist are Protestant, while the more southerly islands are Catholic. The northern islands are a stronghold of **Presbyterianism**, whereby control of religious affairs is in the hands of ministers and a group of church elders rather than those of the bishop. The influence of both John Calvin and John Knox is apparent in the practices and outlook of the Presbyterian Church, and the Free Church of Scotland – known colloquially as the Wee Frees – is arguably stronger in the Outer Hebrides than on the mainland. The Wee Frees are seen as adhering to a particularly rigorous interpretation of Presbyterianism, with a fiercely Calvinistic reading and literal interpretation of the Bible. All this explains why the Sabbath is so strictly observed in the northern islands (hence there is no public transport and no supermarkets and very few cafés open that day).

The southern islands of South Uist and Barra, meanwhile, are considered the last remnant of native pre-Reformation Scottish Catholicism, and Barra has been described as 'the island the Reformation did not reach'.

Almost no records exist of Christianity in the Outer Hebrides before the 11th century, though it is known that Irish monks and the abbey of Iona established both presence and influence before this time. A monastery was established by the 6th century on Benbecula and the 12th-century Cille-bharra church on Barra is believed to have been built on an earlier chapel. Viking rule was accompanied by paganism until Norse leaders converted to Christianity in the 11th century. Following the Treaty of Perth in 1266, when the isles were ceded to the Scottish Crown, the Church remained part of the Diocese of the Isles, also known as the Diocese of Sodor. Until the Scottish Reformation of 1557, Lewis and Harris were Catholic islands remaining part of the archbishopric of Trondheim and later St Andrews. Afterwards, the bishops of the isles were Protestants, and whether an island chose to accept the new religion or continue with Catholicism depended on the local chief. During the 16th century, Irish missionaries were active in the islands, and some converted back to Catholicism.

The 1843 Disruption saw the widespread schism in the Church of Scotland and the formation of the Free Church of Scotland by breakaway believers in a dispute over the relationship between Church and State. One of the key points of division centred on land ownership: the Free Church opposed the right of a landowner to nominate a parish minister.

Upheavals sporadically enter the national consciousness. In 2014, a group of 250 worshippers left Stornoway High Church to join the Free Church after the church's general assembly voted for a proposal that would allow gay men and women to become ministers. The group of 250 included the entire kirk session, while only around 100 remained in the Church of Scotland.

The 2011 census found that, of all Scottish regions, the Outer Hebrides had the lowest proportion of people stating that they had no religion (18.1%, less than half the Scottish average of 36.7%). Berneray had the highest proportion of people stating their religious denomination as Church of Scotland (60%), while Eriskay took top billing for Roman Catholicism (82%). Scalpay had the highest percentage of 'other Christian' – for the most part, this means the Free Church of Scotland – at 58%. While religion is an integral part of life on the islands, there is no evidence or modern-day history of tension or sectarian divisions between these very different interpretations of Christianity.

For visitors, attending a church service can provide an insight into island culture, and visitors are welcome to attend any services. 'Out of phase' or 'precenting' Gaelic psalm singing is a feature of services in most island Presbyterian churches. Two series of the BBC documentary *An Island Parish* were filmed on Barra and South Uist in 2011 and 2012, following the work of Father John Paul. The islands also boast a small Muslim community, which dates back to the 1950s. In 2018 the first mosque was completed on the islands, housed in an unassuming, renovated building in Stornoway.

CULTURE

The elemental landscapes and light of the islands have long attracted artists, and you will find contemporary sculptors, painters, ceramicists and others working from their studio homes the length and breadth of the islands.

Music in the form of *duan* – songs or poems – is another powerful expression of local culture and follows a long tradition that ranges from church music known as 'precenting', *waulking* songs (waulking was the laborious process of shrinking and tightening woollen tweed) sung while weavers worked their raw tweed materials, to *baird baile*, community poets from the Gaelic oral song tradition.

A number of organisations are powerful drivers of island and Gaelic culture, including Ceòlas on South Uist (see box, page 241) and The Islands Book Trust (w islandsbooktrust.org), which was formed in 2002 with the aims of furthering understanding of the history of Scottish islands in their wider Celtic and Nordic context, and of generating economic, social and cultural benefits for communities.

MUSIC The Benbecula campus of the University of the Highlands and Islands, in particular, has developed an international reputation for the teaching of traditional music and for providing many opportunities for performance and skills development related to the music professions. The fiddler and orchestra player Anne-Wendy Stevenson is a lecturer at the college, while the island also gave rise to the trio of musicians of Lurach: Naomi Harvey, Rachel Harris and Lucy MacRae, whose combination of vocals, whistles, flute and fiddle have proved popular in the UK and across Europe.

Other contemporary interpretations of traditional music plus accordions, pipes, whistles, and guitars abound. Perhaps the best-known exponents are The Vatersay Boys, who have established a large following on the mainland. The hugely popular Stornoway band Peat and Diesel plays a mixture of folk and rock and, as 'Peatlemania' gathers momentum, they have sold out at venues across Scotland.

Gillebride MacMillan from Milton on South Uist, meanwhile, starred as Gwyllyn the Bard in the dramatisation of the *Outlander* series of time-travel novels by Diana Gabaldon. MacMillan's musical work includes *Air Fòrladh/On Leave*, a collection of songs with family connections and others from Uist tradition.

Others include Sinneag MacIntyre, a South Uist Gaelic primary school teacher and singer, and Kathleen McInnes, another native of South Uist, who has produced two solo albums and appeared on the soundtrack to the 2010 Ridley Scott film *Robin Hood*. Julie Fowlis from North Uist was nominated for the Folk Singer of the Year award at the 2015 BBC Radio 2 Folk Awards and describes herself as 'a quiet torchbearer for her native tradition'. She sang the theme song to *Brave*, Disney Pixar's Oscar-, Golden Globe- and BAFTA-winning animated film.

Much of this culture finds its expression in *cèilidhs* and gatherings in community halls; it reaches a larger stage and audience in the form of *mods* (Gaelic singing festivals), where you see the bigger stars as well as a great deal of amateur and emerging talent.

ARCHITECTURE The prevailing traditional architecture of the islands is unlikely to win any prizes for aesthetic beauty: houses from the early 20th century onwards were battened down against the winds and increasingly rendered with pebble-dash; others are even more basic with corrugated-iron roofing. There are few of the whitewashed houses that adorn towns such as Portree on Skye or Plockton on the west coast of the mainland. Although they can be eyesores on such a stirring landscape, rather like electricity pylons you may find that you stop noticing them after a while; moreover, their appearance can belie interiors of charm and décor.

A number of historical buildings, particularly manses – a clergy house inhabited by a minister, usually of Presbyterian disposition – have survived. In 1823, Thomas Telford was hired for a government-funded programme of church building across the Hebrides. To keep costs down, Telford designed all the churches on the same simple T-shaped plan, each with a manse attached. Elsewhere, thatched buildings with traditional pitch-and-eave details survive and are subject to conservation plans. The most characteristic – and evocative – properties are the traditional drystone-walled blackhouses, built in the North Atlantic longhouse tradition, with sleeping quarters for humans, a central hearth, a sloped area for livestock and a thatched roof. The best examples of these are to be found at Na Geàrrannan (page 105) and Arnol (page 107), both on the west coast of Lewis. Owing mainly to the vagaries of landownership, few houses pre-date the 1880s and the blackhouses gave way to newer white houses with rendered stone walls.

More recently, a sleeker, more aesthetic 'Hebrinavian' design has emerged: clean Scandinavian lines, lots of wood, and more sympathetically blended into the landscape. Such properties are generally low-lying, with windows reaching from ground to ceiling. Others are more substantial, use local material and seek to blend into the landscape (see box, page 165).

Stornoway has a conservation area in recognition of its special character which includes an extensive collection of cast-iron decoration featuring railings and finials. The area extends to the north and east of the town centre and features distinctive circular chimney cans and cast-iron roof lights.

The thought that goes into some of this architecture can take you by surprise, too. On Barra, the Cuithir Houses provide social housing in properties designed with curved ends similar to Viking longhouses which help reduce heat loss from wind chill.

The extraordinary mix of architecture on the islands can be enjoyed by following the Architectural Trail. An illustrated leaflet with photographs by John Maher (page 171) is available to download at w visitouterhebrides.co.uk/see-and-do/culture-and-heritage/architectural-trail, as well as at the tourist information centre in Stornoway and the Welcome Points across the islands. The trail includes a range of architecture from recent landmark buildings such as Talla na Mara at Nisabost to weather-smashed storehouses such as the Girnal at Rodel (page 172).

THE OUTER HEBRIDES IN FILM AND LITERATURE Read *The Lewis Trilogy* by Peter May and you may decide to stay at home, as a disproportionate number of horrors are visited upon these lightly populated and extremely safe islands. The trilogy – *The Blackhouse*, *The Lewis Man* and *The Chessmen* – centres on the work and life of Detective Inspector Fin Macleod. A trail based on the books (w petermaytrail.com) takes you around many of the sights and can be a good vehicle for getting under the skin of the more elemental side of these islands.

Destinations in the guide include the Bridge to Nowhere on Lewis, which was the scene of a scooter race to determine who would name a Celtic rock band in

The Chessmen; the cemetery at Sacrista, which features in *The Lewis Man* (where a body is found in a peat bog); and a shieling on Barvas Moor on Lewis, where Fin's parents were killed in a car crash, in *The Blackhouse*.

On a lighter note, the award-winning children's television series *Katie Morag*, based on stories by Mairi Hedderwick, was filmed on location in Uig and Ness on Lewis. A more comprehensive anthology of fiction- and non-fiction-related titles can be found on page 295.

Whisky Galore, Compton Mackenzie's unforgettable account of a ship containing thousands of bottles of whisky wrecked in a storm, and the subsequent film *Whisky Galore!*, were set on Eriskay and Barra (see box, page 266). The bizarre attempts to launch mail over the water to the island of Scarp off Harris has been the subject of two films, both called *The Rocket Post* (see box, page 144). An insightful BBC documentary, *The Isle of Rust* by Jonathan Meades, can be downloaded online (type the author and title into a search engine to bring up various versions) and offers a corrective antidote to the understandable temptation of visitors to over-romanticise these islands. The title is one of the monikers for Lewis and Harris and refers both to the corroding machinery that occasionally pockmarks the landscape and the more ubiquitous russet-blue tones of deergrass and heather.

2

Practical Information

WHEN TO VISIT

The islands on the edge of the British Isles offer great extremes – not only of interest throughout the year but also of weather. Late April to the end of June is probably the best time to visit. The days quickly become much longer – although you are some way south of the midnight sun, it never gets completely dark in mid-June – and wildlife, on a mission to breed and rear young, is at its richest. April can often be a fine month for weather. A ridge of high pressure driven by anticyclones is a recognised, if not consistent, phenomenon across the islands at the end of May and the start of June.

July and August herald the striking spectacle of carpets of wild flowers along the grasslands, known as the machair, along the west coast. Summer also brings many outdoor events, such as Gaelic singing festivals, agricultural shows and local versions of Highland games. It can be hard to get accommodation at short notice during the summer holidays (Scotland's school holidays run from the start of July to mid-August), and there is even more pressure on ferries and car rental availability.

Autumn triggers a mass shift in the wildlife of the islands, with birds either migrating south or fleeing the approaching Arctic winter. The dark days of winter are not for the faint-hearted but bring a sporting chance of seeing the Northern Lights and are a superb time to see hardy wildlife toughing things out. In this season, time your visit for a break in the stormy weather and you may witness some of the most extraordinarily wild and battered landscapes you'll ever see. The low winter sun can also show off the distinctively corrugated appearance of undulating moors and age-old farming furrows.

February and March are the prime time to witness the territorial behaviour of golden eagles, which pair-bond at this time of year, soaring together and locking talons in a breathtaking aerial display.

For walkers and cyclists, the same opportunities and guidance that are relevant elsewhere in the UK apply in the Outer Hebrides: check the weather whatever the season, and acknowledge that a good day out in winter can be as wonderful as anything in summer.

An island climate combined with a location on the northeast edge of the Atlantic mean that extremes of weather can set in at any moment, for good or ill. A late March day may start with a sprinkling of snow only to break later into sunshine and temperatures of 20°C. It's worth bearing in mind that many B&Bs (and even some hotels), most cafés and art galleries close between October and March/Easter, though Stornoway is less affected by this trend than other parts of the islands. Transport runs at a consistent level year-round, and stores stay open, though sometimes with shorter hours.

Older than Stonehenge and just as enigmatic, the standing stones of **Callanish** on Lewis (page 101) are the most popular attraction on the islands. Centred around a single, slender central monolith, they are sited on an elevated promontory that makes a visit a truly haunting experience. On the west coast of Lewis, **Geàrrannan Blackhouse Village** (page 105) is a restored traditional village that provides an insight into how many people lived up to the middle of the 20th century. The distinctive blackhouses – squat, thatched and designed for humans and livestock to shelter together – are open to explore. Stornoway's **Museum nan Eilean** (page 87) represents a technological leap into the 21st century for the islands, with interactive displays firmly oriented towards grassroots culture and first-hand accounts of history. Pride of place goes to the display of a handful of Lewis chessmen. The tale of the Lewis chessmen discovered on a wild beach draws many visitors to **Uig Sands** (page 126). Vast and graceful, the sands are just one point of interest here: others include mountainous skyline, dramatic coastal scenery, some great food, fine walks and important archaeological sites that emerge like apparitions on the marshy moors. **Ness** (page 109), the isolated northwest tip of Lewis (and of the UK), is an elemental place. There is a fine beach, a dramatic lighthouse overlooking towering cliffs, and a community with a strong sense of local identity. The watershed between Lewis and Harris is marked by the **North Harris Hills** (page 145), a range that forms an ancient barrier between the two 'islands'. This is fantastic walking territory. On a clear day, a summit climb affords views of the entire island chain and the west coast of Scotland. In rain, the landscape is transformed into a waterworld. A truly mesmerising array of beaches radiates from the Sound of **Luskentyre** (page 162), with shell-sand bays, shallow lagoons formed by tidal waters and ever-changing dunes. Most remarkable of all is how the colours and patterns of the bays seem to change with the weather and the tides. The waterworld landscape of North Uist, with hills rising from the shores of freshwater and sea lochs, is enchanting, as are the island's north-coast beaches. If you only climb one hill in the Outer Hebrides, make it **Rueval** (see box, page 232). Just 124m (406ft) high, it rises abruptly above the flatlands of Benbecula to give spectacular views of the interplay of land and water that characterises these islands. The thoughtful and low-key **Kildonan Museum** (page 254) gives a fascinating introduction to South Uist island culture and the heritage of song and storytelling.

Often described as the Outer Hebrides in miniature, **Barra** (page 267) has wonderful beaches and rugged inland scenery. The extremely picturesque yet tiny port of Castlebay overlooks medieval Kisimul Castle. Perhaps the most beautiful beach of all the islands – **East Beach, Vatersay** (page 286) – can be found at the southern end of the archipelago. A huge sweep of rectangular sand overlooks a bay with shallow waters that on a sunny day really do look like the Caribbean. Located 40 miles out in the Atlantic to the west of North Uist, **St Kilda** (page 180) is shaped like a South Pacific island and comes wrapped in powerful social history linked to its evacuation in 1930. Home to 1 million seabirds, a visit here is a true once-in-a-lifetime adventure.

SUGGESTED ITINERARIES

The key to exploring the Outer Hebrides is not to overdo things. The island chain may run only 130 miles or so from north to south as the crow flies, but any attempt to 'do' the whole lot in one brief visit is likely to leave you in need of a further holiday to recover from the tiring driving – and you will miss a good deal along the way. In any case, the islands have few 'sights' – such as museums or castles – in the conventional sense. A characteristic of the Outer Hebrides is that the sites are the landscapes, the beaches, the moors and archaeological ruins. The people you meet may also be part of your experience.

Unless you are staying for a good two weeks or longer, it makes sense to focus your time on one section of the islands – either Lewis and Harris, or the Uists and Barra. Here follow some suggestions for how you might prioritise your time.

With one week at your disposal, base yourself on Lewis (days 1–4) and take day trips to Stornoway and Callanish, Ness, and Uig Sands plus the landscapes of the southwest of Uig, such as Mangersta. On days 5–7, explore Harris, taking in the beaches around the Sound of Luskentyre, visiting St Clements Church in Rodel and the Hushinish peninsula and walking up to the golden eagle observatory at Miabhaig. Spend a few hours in the small port village of Tarbert. Take a boat to either the Shiant Isles or Monach Islands (both accessible from Lewis and Harris).

If you have a second week available, spend days 8–10 exploring the beaches of the north coast of North Uist, then hike up Barpa Langass and follow the circular loop around the attractive island of Grimsay. Climb Rueval on Benbecula. Go to the Kildonan Museum on South Uist and explore the lochs and paths around Loch Eynort and Loch Druidibeg. On days 11–14, spend a couple of hours on Prince's Beach on Eriskay and have a drink in the pub there before taking the ferry across the Sound of Barra. Roam or bask on Barra's wonderful beaches, such as Tangsadale or Tràigh Tuath, visit Kisimul Castle and have a coffee overlooking the waters of Castlebay. Go for a walk on Vatersay above the glorious east-facing beach. Watch a flight from the mainland land on the sands at Tràigh Mhòr.

With the luxury of a third week, treat yourself to visiting several additional sites, such as Arnol blackhouse, and Point and the Lochs on Lewis. You could perhaps base yourself for a week in a single location, such as the Valtos peninsula in Uig, the Luskentyre area of Harris or Barra.

TOUR OPERATORS AND GUIDES

It is easy to travel around the Outer Hebrides independently on an itinerary you have worked out yourself. That said, a good tour guide or company will relieve you of the burden of the often long driving times and book you into a gem of a B&B or the right place for an evening meal. Meanwhile, a specialist birder, marine expert or archaeologist can really add to your holiday. Operations marked with an asterisk (*) are Outer Hebrides residents.

Travelling by boat around the coastline of the islands and visiting offshore islands, such as the Shiant Isles (see box, page 98) or the Monach Islands (see box, page 213), can be a real highlight of a trip to the Outer Hebrides. The most adventurous trip of all is to St Kilda, way out in the Atlantic Ocean. Several operators based in the Outer Hebrides run these trips (listed on page 38). Most also offer private charters, where, at a price, you get the boat and skipper to yourselves plus a tailored itinerary. A handful of other, more local boat operators who tend not to go so far afield are listed in the relevant island chapters. Most companies operate from around Easter or April to the end of September.

Dave's Hebridean Archaeological Tours* 📞01851 830777; m 07850 857774; e davesarchtours@gmail.com; w hebrideanarchaeologicaltours.com. Dave

Godwin is a freelance archaeologist & a member of the Institute of Field Archaeologists. Takes you to major & also less well-known sites on Lewis & Harris.

Heb 360* ☎01851 705464; e tours@heb360.
co.uk; w heb360.co.uk. Islanders Derek Murray (a
native Gaelic speaker) & Billy Flower offer engaging
tours, mainly based on Harris & Lewis but also
travelling down the Uists & across to Barra.
Hebridean Hopscotch* ☎01851
706611; e info@hebrideanhopscotch.com;
w hebrideanhopscotch.com. A booked service
that proves popular with many visitors. Essentially,
they build you a self-drive itinerary (including ferry
travel) based on your budget & accommodation
preferences.
Hebrides Wildwatch* m 07747 822417;
e antler130@gmail.com. Bespoke guided wildlife-
watching & walking tours of Harris & Lewis led by
Iain Watson, a former Scottish Natural Heritage
employee, his wife, Ann, &/or colleague Russell
Hird.
Hidden Hebrides* ☎01851 820981; m 07724
150015; w hiddenhebrides.co.uk. Runs guided
tours, including specialist wildlife-watching trips,
max of 8 per group, plus self-guided packages.
McKinlay Kidd ☎0141 260 9260; e hello@
mckinlaykidd.com; w mckinlaykidd.com/scotland/
outer-hebrides; see ad, 3rd colour section. Offers
tailor-made fly-drive holidays up & down the
islands & offers classic & sports car hire as part of
its packages.
Macs Adventure ☎0141 530 3796, (US) +1 844
335 4871; w macsadventure.com. Runs a week-
long self-drive Outer Hebridean Hopscotch through
the islands & provides walking routes.
Magaidh (Maggie) Smith* m 07554 665549;
e maggiesmith@hebrides.net; w magaidhsmith.
co.uk. Island born & bred, Maggie offers excellent
insights into Gaelic culture including ancient
customs & sheep gathering. Her tours of craft
shops & galleries are mixed with stories & even
a spot of wildlife watching. Also offers Gaelic-
language courses.
Out & About Tours* ☎01851 612288; m 07743
507982; e chris@tourguide-hebrides.co.uk;
w tourguide-hebrides.co.uk. Local guide Chris
Ryan is knowledgeable & good company. Offers
customised day tours, multi-day trips & more
energetic hikes around Lewis & Harris.
Rabbies Tours ☎0131 226 3133; e tours@
rabbies.com; w rabbies.com. Offers small-group,
whistle-stop tours in mini-coaches.
Western Isles Wildlife* ☎01876 580619;
m 07867 555971; e steveduffield70@gmail.

com; w western-isles-wildlife.co.uk. Excellent
wildlife tours, focusing on North & South Uist but
also covering the northern islands. Some tours
timetabled, others bespoke & tailored to your
interests.
Wilderness Scotland ☎01479 420020; e info@
wildernessscotland.com; w wildernessscotland.
com. Offers guided walking, kayaking & mountain
bike holidays to the islands.

BOAT TOURS
⚓ **Hebridean Island Cruises** ☎01756
704704; e enquiries@hebridean.co.uk;
w hebridean.co.uk. Runs various itineraries that
take in both the Outer Hebrides & St Kilda aboard
the *Hebridean Princess*. Max 50 berths.
⚓ **Hebrides Cruises** ☎01631 711986;
e info@hebridescruises.co.uk; w hebridescruises.
co.uk. Runs cruises to less-visited island groups
such as Mingulay, the Monach & Shiant islands,
as well as St Kilda, on 2 former naval vessels.
⚓ **Island Cruising** ☎01851 672382;
m 07787 115072; e info@island-cruising.com;
w island-cruising.com. Uses a converted marine
research vessel for a 4–6-day cruise that can take
in St Kilda, Flannen Isles, Scarp or even North Rona
& Sula Sgeir. Approx £800 pp.
⚓ **Kilda Cruises** ☎01859 502060;
e angus@kildacruises.co.uk; w kildacruises.
co.uk. Angus Campbell sends 2 boats out to
St Kilda & has a small booking office & shop on
Main St, Tarbert.
⚓ **Lady Anne Boat Trips** ☎01870 602403;
m 07305 163700; e ningledew@aol.com;
w uistboattrips.com; see also page 203. Departs
from Kallin harbour on North Uist. Offers all-day trips
to Monach Islands & water-based eagle-watching
around shores of North Uist.
⚓ **Northern Light Cruising Co** ☎01599
555723; e info@northernlight-uk.com;
w northernlight-uk.com. Operates multi-day
cruises on a former Norwegian ice-class rescue
vessel to all major & smaller islands, including the
Monachs & Sula Sgeir.
⚓ **Sea Harris** ☎01859 502007; m 07760
216555; e seumas@seaharris.com; w seaharris.
com; see ad, 3rd colour section. Skipper Seumas
Morrison focuses mainly on St Kilda but also runs
RIB trips around East Loch Tarbert, the Shiant
Islands, Loch Tarbert & Taransay. £30–£65 pp,
depending on numbers.

⚓ **Sea Lewis** ✆01851 702303; e sealewis850@gmail.com; w sealewis.co.uk. Runs trips around the east coast of Lewis & to Shiant Isles.

⚓ **Seatrek** ✆01851 672469; e bookings@ seatrek.co.uk; w seatrek.co.uk. Operates out of Miabhaig in Uig on the west coast of Lewis. Runs trips to St Kilda, offshore waters & lochs around Uig, & the west coast of Harris.

⚓ **Uist Sea Tours** m 07833 690693; e uistseatours@gmail.com; w uistseatours.co.uk. Runs trips to the Monach Islands, around the Uists & down to Mingulay, & to St Kilda from Benbecula. Evening boat trips also available.

TOURIST INFORMATION

Your key source of local information is the Outer Hebrides Tourism website (w visitouterhebrides.co.uk). This provides a comprehensive listing of attractions and accommodation and is particularly strong on self-catering accommodation.

In recent years Visit Scotland – to the consternation of many islanders – has closed three of its four information centres in the Outer Hebrides, reducing its presence to a shop in Stornoway and leaving no official national point of information in Harris, the Uists or Barra. The decision was widely ridiculed and seen in some quarters as evidence of a too-metropolitan organisation that simply doesn't 'get' the islands. However, don't overlook the Stornoway Visit Scotland icentre (Visit Scotland Lewis, 26 Cromwell St, Stornoway; ✆01851 703088; e stornoway@visitscotland. com; w visitscotland.com, search 'Stornoway icentre'). It remains one of the best of its kind in the whole of Scotland, its staff are friendly and helpful, and the centre is stocked with guides, special-interest literature and souvenirs.

Islanders have not taken the closures lying down and have responded by setting up a network of six Welcome Points south of Stornoway. These are community-driven ventures that offer information, can book accommodation and give insider tips and up-to-date advice on opening times and local activities. As is the nature of such grassroots operations, they are very much dependent on the personalities of those behind them: most are excellent; a couple can feel like an add-on to an existing small business.

Opening hours of the Welcome Points below are listed in the relevant island chapters.

Borrisdale Tweed Leverburgh (page 171)
Bùth Bharraigh Barra (page 271)
Claddach Kirkibost Centre North Uist (page 209)

Essence of Harris Tarbert Pier, Tarbert, Harris (page 150)
MacGillivrays Benbecula (page 228)
Uist Gifts Lochboisdale (page 240)

MAPS Good road maps of the islands that also identify key sights can be picked up from bookshops and tourist offices in Ullapool (one of the mainland ferry ports for the islands), in Stornoway and across the islands. Whether you are walking, cycling or driving, **Ordnance Survey (OS) Explorer** maps will be extremely useful. Their 1:25,000 scale can give drivers a better idea of the nature of a road than a road atlas or general touring maps. The islands are covered by nine Explorer maps: OS 452 Barra & Vatersay; OS 453 Benbecula & South Uist; OS 454 North Uist & Berneray; OS 455 South Harris; OS 456 North Harris & Loch Seaforth; OS 457 South East Lewis; OS 458 West Lewis; OS 459 Central Lewis & Stornoway; and OS 460 North Lewis, which includes St Kilda. Six **OS Landranger** maps at a smaller scale (1:50,000) also cover the islands: Landranger 8 Stornoway & North Lewis; Landranger 13 West Lewis & North Harris; Landranger 14 Tarbert & Loch Seaforth; Landranger 18 Sound of Harris: North Uist, Taransay & St Kilda; Landranger 22 Benbecula & South Uist; and Landranger 31 Barra & South Uist.

Road signs can take time to work out, mainly because they are generally designed for locals rather than tourists. A typical example is the A859 on Harris. As you drive south, this will be signposted towards Roghadal (Rodel), the small (though historically important) community at the end of the road, whereas most visitors will be looking for a sign to either Luskentyre (Losgaintir) or the ferry port of Leverburgh (which is generally signposted as An t-Ob). You might also be looking for signs for the Sound of Harris ferry, in which case you need to recognise the Aiseag Caolas na Hearadh. Working such matters out over a pint, a glass of wine or a cup of tea is one of the joys of travel but arguably less fun when you have a ferry to catch or are arriving somewhere in the dark.

PLACE NAMES Place names on road signs are usually in Gaelic first, then English. Tourist maps, however, tend to show only the English name, making an exception for some place names that are visited by fewer tourists, in which case only the Gaelic name is used. Attempts to clarify on maps what the feature in question is can occasionally give rise to tautology, such as 'Tràigh Mhòr Beach', which means 'Big Beach Beach'. (A similarly liberal approach to weights and measures also prevails on the islands, and it is not unusual to come across literature including comments such as: 'it takes 1.5 miles to walk to the summit of Clisham (799m)'.) OS maps, meanwhile, give Gaelic place names for almost all locations, with the exception of the larger or more visited communities, where the English name is printed first, as in 'Leverburgh/An t-Ob'. The OS, however, is not entirely consistent, and some major destinations are printed in Gaelic only, such as Losgaintir (Luskentyre) on Harris.

RED TAPE

The Outer Hebrides are part of the UK, so UK, and at the time of writing EU, nationals do not require a visa. Visitors from the United States, Canada, Australia and other countries need only fulfil the procedures required of them at any UK port of entry before freely visiting the islands. After the UK leaves the European Union, documentation requirements for EU citizens may change. Check before travelling.

CONSULATES AND EMBASSIES

The majority of nations, including the USA, Canada, Australia and countries in Europe and Asia, are fully represented by embassies or high commissions (for Commonwealth members) in the national capital of London. No country has an official presence in the Outer Hebrides, though many have consulates in Edinburgh or Glasgow (w visitscotland.com/about/practicalinformation/embassies-consulates). A full list of contact details can be found at w gov.uk/government/publications/foreign-embassies-in-the-uk.

GETTING THERE AND AWAY

A few preconceptions need to be addressed when it comes to travel to the Outer Hebrides, not least of which is the presumption that they are located beyond the back of beyond. Although the islands are one step further than Skye and Mull, the travel is not particularly onerous, and in any case the old adage of the journey being part of the experience certainly applies. The drive to the ferry ports on the mainland is extremely beautiful, especially the northerly routes to Ullapool or through Skye to the port at Uig.

BY SEA The majority of visitors to the Outer Hebrides arrive by ferry. Caledonian MacBrayne, or CalMac (✆ 0800 066 5000; from outside the UK call +44 1475 650 397; e enquiries@calmac.co.uk; w calmac.co.uk), enjoys a monopoly of maritime services. CalMac operates five services from the mainland to the Outer Hebrides (detailed below). For the latest timetables, visit the website. It's worth bearing in mind that while departure times are fixed, ferries do occasionally leave ahead of time to keep clear of incoming bad weather. Travellers with special mobility requirements or parents with young children should inform check-in staff upon arrival. Staff are extremely helpful and will arrange for you to be boarded close to a lift on the ship.

The major problem with ferry services is capacity. This is partly a story of success – more people are visiting the islands – but from May to mid-August you should definitely book any vehicle crossing as soon as you know your plans. Tickets for the summer season (end Mar–mid-Oct) go on sale from the end of the preceding October. There is far less pressure at other times of the year – on occasion you may be forgiven for wondering if you haven't inadvertently hired out the ferry for private use – and the winter frequency on all routes is slightly reduced. A new ferry with greater capacity is due to be introduced, after much delay, to the Uig–Tarbert–Lochmaddy triangular route in 2022.

The cost of travel to and from the islands remains a running sore for locals but, for ferry journeys at least, the picture has improved since the introduction of the Road Equivalent Tariff, a distance-based fares structure that has taken the sting out of the cost of sailing with a vehicle.

Take the **Ullapool–Stornoway (Lewis)** service if your holiday is based on Lewis; it can also be used for reaching Harris overland once arriving in Stornoway. The ferry departs twice daily, including Sunday, between the end of June and early September. Outside this period, the Sunday service drops to a single return journey. The journey time is 2½ hours, and return fares are £19.90 (adults), £10 (children), and £107.60 (standard car, excluding driver). Ullapool is a 1½-hour drive north of Inverness. City Link buses (w citylink.co.uk) connect with ferry departures and arrivals.

The **Uig (Skye)–Tarbert (Harris)** service is ideal for Harris holidays and also convenient for Lewis. Between late June and end August, there are two sailings in each direction on Monday and Saturday; on Tuesday and Thursday, there are two sailings from Uig and one from Tarbert; on Wednesday and Friday, there is one sailing from Uig and two from Tarbert; on Sunday, there is one crossing in each direction. At other times of year, the service is slightly reduced. At 1 hour 40 minutes, this is the quickest crossing to the islands. Return fares are £13.30 (adults), £6.70 (children), £65.20 (standard car, excluding driver). Uig is a good 3-hour drive from Inverness. City Link buses (w citylink.co.uk) connect Inverness to Uig via Portree on Skye but this is not synchronised with crossings and will only get you there in time for some evening departures.

The **Uig (Skye)–Lochmaddy (North Uist)** route is the quickest gateway to the Uists and Benbecula; note there is no land crossing to Harris from North Uist. Between late June and late August there are two crossings from Uig and one from Lochmaddy on Monday and Wednesday; one crossing from Uig and two from

Lochmaddy on Tuesday, Thursday and Saturday; three crossings from Uig and two from Lochmaddy on Friday; and two in each direction on Sunday. Outside these times, the service is slightly reduced. The journey takes 1¾ hours, and return fares are £13.30 (adults), £6.70 (children) and £65.20 (standard car, exc driver).

There is just one daily service each way in summer on the **Mallaig–Lochboisdale (South Uist)** route, taking 3½ hours. Return fares are £22 (adults), £11 (children), £121.70 (standard car, exc driver). By car it takes 3½ hours from Glasgow to Mallaig, from Fort William, it is 1 hour. Shiel Buses (w shielbuses.co.uk/mallaig-fort-william) operates a link between Fort William and Mallaig for the Lochboisdale ferry link. The journey takes 1¼ hours. Note that in winter, many Lochboisdale services depart from Oban (page 239).

The **Glasgow/Oban–Castlebay (Barra)** service runs daily, taking 10 hours from Glasgow and 4¾ hours from Oban (where almost everyone embarks). An additional service runs on Wednesday, from Oban only to Castlebay via Coll and Tiree. Return fares are £31 (adults), £15.50 (children) and £143.40 (standard car, exc driver).

BY AIR There are three airports on the islands: Stornoway (Lewis), Benbecula and Barra, all operated by Highlands and Islands Airports (w hial.co.uk). The only airline flying to the Outer Hebrides from within the UK is Loganair (\0344 800 2855; w loganair.co.uk). Stornoway is reached by direct flights from Glasgow (up to 4 times daily), Edinburgh (1–2 times daily) and Inverness (1–3 times daily). Return fares for all these routes start at around £140–150 but can more than double when demand is high. Other useful routes that Loganair operates that can provide connections to the islands are from Manchester and Bristol to Inverness; from Norwich to Edinburgh; from East Midlands airport to both Edinburgh and Glasgow; and Newquay in Cornwall to Glasgow.

Flights to Barra depart from Glasgow (1–2 times daily); return fares start at £90, but can rise to £160 or more at peak times. Benbecula is served from Inverness (1–2 flights daily, Mon–Fri) with flights stopping en route in Stornoway; and from Glasgow (1–2 flights daily) with one direct flight, the other stopping in Stornoway. Return fares start at around £170 but can be as high as £312.

You can fly with British Airways (w britishairways.com), from Heathrow, Gatwick or London City airport to Stornoway (and on to Benbecula) with a transfer in either Glasgow or Edinburgh. Return fares range from £200 to £350. British Airways does not offer a similar connection to Barra – you would need to book separate tickets for London–Glasgow and Glasgow–Barra. Loganair enjoys a codeshare arrangement with British Airways, so if you fly to Scotland with British Airways and then on with a connecting Loganair flight to the islands, your baggage will be transferred and there is no need to repeat check-in procedures (although not for the flight to Barra).

You can also reach the Outer Hebrides by beginning your journey at regional UK airports that connect to the main Scottish airports. These include easyJet (w easyjet.com) from London Gatwick, London Stansted, Bristol and Manchester; and Flybe (w flybe.com) from Exeter and Birmingham International. Loganair and Flybe have a codeshare so your luggage should be transferred at connecting airports (but always check this is the case). However, there is no codeshare between Loganair and *any* budget airline. In those cases, you must collect your baggage and check in again in Scotland. When it comes to delays, airlines have limited responsibility if you miss a connecting flight on an airline with which they do not codeshare. Therefore, it is best to allow plenty of time between connections.

International flights These are most likely to connect via a London airport to onward flights to Glasgow or Edinburgh, from where you travel the last leg to the islands. In such cases, your luggage should be checked all the way through to the Outer Hebrides, but it is best to confirm this when you check in at your departure airport.

BY RAIL There are no rail services in the Outer Hebrides, but travelling by train to a departure port is a wonderful way to begin your holiday. The **Caledonian Sleeper** (0330 060 0500; w sleeper.scot) departs Sunday to Friday from London Euston and splits en route to travel to Inverness (from where it is easy to travel to the ferry ports at Ullapool or Uig on Skye) and Fort William (for ferries from Mallaig and Oban). Compartments sleep two people, though families can usually arrange for adjacent cabins with adjoining doors. There are also reclining sleeper seats. The buffet car is a jolly place to launch a holiday over a glass or two, and you can order breakfast after waking up with views of the Highland glens. One-way fares start from £40 for a reclining seat and rise to £80 for a bed.

CAR HIRE Hiring a car is handy if you are flying to Inverness or arriving there or in Oban by train.

Companies in Inverness include Arnold Clark (0141 237 4374; w arnoldclarkrental.com), Avis (0808 284 6666; w avis.co.uk), and Hertz (020 7026 0077; w hertz.co.uk). Hire charges on mainland Scotland seem high compared with what you might pay elsewhere in Europe. Book early and you may catch a £300-a-week deal; otherwise, rates escalate quickly. In Oban (where you can join the ferry to Lochboisdale or Barra), contact Hazelbank Motors (01631 566476; w obancarhire.co.uk).

HEALTH

Your risk of contracting a disease or falling ill is the same as on the Scottish mainland. Major hospitals can be found in Stornoway, Benbecula and Barra. All the islands have GP (doctor) surgeries, listed in the individual chapters, and visitors can almost always get a same-day appointment and obtain repeat prescriptions. One difference from the mainland – outside Stornoway – is an absence of pharmacies. You can buy most items such as insect-bite creams, infant paracetamol, eye drops and contraceptives from supermarkets. Prescription medicines are issued and dispensed only by GP surgeries. Attempts to set up independent pharmacies are strongly opposed by local communities since GPs need their pharmacy to make their service viable. For further, and out-of-hours, medical advice, contact NHS 24 (111; w nhs24.scot).

DRINKING WATER Tap water is potable everywhere in the Outer Hebrides. Many walkers like to refill their bottles from streams out on the hills. If you do so, there are general principles you should apply: never drink from water below human habitation, and never from still lochans, only fast-running burns. If you're not confident, consider adding a chlorine tablet to the bottle, as you might elsewhere in the world.

TICKS One animal you should be mindful of is the tick, which is attracted to human blood and lurks in wooded, bushy and moorland areas. Ticks should ideally be removed complete, and as soon as possible, to reduce the chance of infection. You can use special tick tweezers, which can be bought in good travel shops, or failing this use your fingernails, grasping the tick as close to your body as possible, and pulling it away steadily and firmly at right angles to your skin without jerking or twisting. Irritants (eg: Olbas oil) or lit cigarettes are to be discouraged since they can cause the ticks to regurgitate and therefore increase the risk of disease. Once the tick is removed, if possible douse the wound with alcohol (any spirit will do), soap and water, or iodine. If you are travelling with small children, remember to check their heads, and particularly behind the ears, for ticks. Spreading redness around the bite and/or fever and/or aching joints after a tick bite imply that you have an infection that requires antibiotic treatment. In this case seek medical advice.

One nasty surprise ticks appear to be increasingly transmitting is Lyme disease, a bacterial infection often characterised by a circular rash and/or flu-like symptoms, and muscle and joint pain. The incidence of Lyme disease is on the rise across the British Isles, including the Outer Hebrides. North Uist, Benbecula and South Uist are particular hotspots – a 2017 study by the University of Glasgow found the incidence of Lyme disease there was 20 times higher than the Scottish average. The NHS provides good information at w nhs.uk/Conditions/Lyme-disease. The early symptoms of Lyme disease can include a rash and flu-like symptoms. If untreated, more severe symptoms can develop months to years later including neurological disease, heart disease and arthritis. It is worth alerting a health-care professional if you develop the early symptoms as Lyme disease is treatable with antibiotics.

MIDGES Unfortunately, the pesky wee fellas are here, usually from late May until September. That said, they are not as ubiquitous or bothersome as they are in Argyll or the central Highlands. If you sit in an open place for any length of time – they can be infuriating for anglers – then they will certainly descend upon you, but in this part of the world a breeze of some kind or another usually comes along soon enough to keep them bearable. You will rarely need recourse to a head-net of the kind that is so commonly used by walkers on Skye. It may or may not be comforting to know that while at least 35 species of midges have been identified in Scotland, only five species, and only the females, actually bite; that they are at their worst after nightfall or when there is cloud cover; and that they dislike bright sunlight. Repellents of varying effectiveness can be bought from your local chemist or outdoors shop.

SAFETY

The Outer Hebrides is an extremely safe place to visit. Year after year Scottish government crime figures place the islands at, or near, the bottom (ie: least dangerous) of crime league tables, with everything from violent crime to housebreaking statistically very rare indeed. Bigger hazards are likely to be overestimating your **driving** capabilities on some of the narrow roads, overtaking on blind summits or avoiding sheep or deer that dart in front of your vehicle.

Most activities on the islands involve the great outdoors, so you should be mindful of the volatile weather and the often sporadic signal coverage for mobile phones. For **walkers and climbers**, sheer and exposed cliffs have a habit of springing themselves on you, particularly around Ness, Uig, Harris and South Uist, where they can rise up abruptly from sea level with startling contours. You should also take care walking on peat bog, which is far from a constant surface and can conceal eroded channels and buried river courses.

When it comes to **swimming**, basic safety rules apply: do not go into the water alone or, at the very least, have someone watching you from the beach/shore; do not go swimming in a place you are unfamiliar with; check with local groups about the safety of beaches for swimming; remember the water might be colder than you are used to, so go in slowly until you acclimatise.

Rip currents and strong undertows are known on certain beaches on the islands and there are warnings up (but not on all). 'It can be alarming if you're caught in one, but the key is not to panic as they don't take you too far out,' says Norma Macleod of Immerse Hebrides (see box, page 60), a wild swimming operator. 'Do not try and swim straight back into shore. Swimming back in is sometimes futile if you aren't a strong swimmer. Even if you are, it tires you very quickly. Swim parallel to the beach if this happens to get out.'

Generally, on the west side, where beaches are exposed to the Atlantic – and can be good for surfing – it is not safe to swim as there are undertows. Recent years have seen two drownings: one along west Harris, the other off Eriskay. The coastguard does not recommend using inflatable toys in the sea as they can easily be picked up by the wind. If this happens, under no circumstances try to retrieve them.

If **kayaking**, strongly consider going with a guide. The coastguard says that 86% of call-outs on the islands involve visitors. You will occasionally see signs for **quicksand** on beaches, including those at Eoropie on Lewis, Scarista on Harris and at Tràigh Tuath on Barra. The risk from quicksand is not of disappearing into the earth in the style of horror films but of drowning as the tide comes in. The Stornoway coastguard advises that you apply common sense: if you feel sand shifting under your feet, walk swiftly to firmer sand. If you encounter difficulty, call the coastguard on ☏999 immediately.

WOMEN TRAVELLERS

The Outer Hebrides are as safe as any part of the UK for women to travel around, and unwarranted attention is rare. Women can expect to walk in safety and with confidence around the towns and townships at night and to walk with confidence – subject to the same safety measures as men – in the hills. The biggest irritation is likely to be a wayward drunk around Stornoway's boisterous pubs at the weekend.

TRAVELLING WITH A DISABILITY

The historic nature of many houses and other buildings means that the islands are playing catch-up when it comes to accommodating travellers with reduced or restricted mobility and other disabilities. A comprehensive list of accommodation providers that offer facilities for travellers with limited mobility can be obtained by contacting the Outer Hebrides Tourism board (w visitouterhebrides.co.uk/information/contact). Museums and recently built accommodation – particularly new self-catering cottages – and renovated eateries will meet, as they must, the requirements of UK accessibility law. Elsewhere, while many accommodation providers do not explicitly promote disabled access or offer aids or adaptations specifically for disabled guests, they will often be as accommodating as possible. Always phone ahead. Finally, it's not unusual to encounter well-meaning people who still use the term 'handicapped'.

TRAVELLING WITH CHILDREN

With their superb beaches and empty spaces in which to be themselves without making onlookers scowl, the Outer Hebrides make for a perfect holiday for children of any age. If you plan ahead, the entire journey to and from the Outer Hebrides can be enormous fun. If you're travelling from the south of the UK, seriously consider taking the overnight sleeper train from London (w sleeper.scot), which will deliver you by early morning to either Fort William or Inverness. Failing that, a daytime journey north of Edinburgh through the Highlands with a train line such as London North Eastern Railways (w lner.co.uk) is an unforgettable way to start the journey. Look out for dolphins, puffins and gannets during the ferry crossings to the isles.

Once you're on the islands, the Outer Hebrides offer unrivalled opportunities for meaningful family time. Take your pick from huge, empty beaches, wonderful rockpools and welcoming cafés, where you can treat yourselves to delicious cakes without breaking the bank. Wildlife is everywhere: when your children are squabbling over whether they have just seen a golden or white-tailed eagle, you may just feel like a good parent. The island museums and physical visitor attractions, such as the Uig Community and Heritage Centre, the Kildonan Museum on South Uist and the Geàrrannan blackhouses on Lewis, are extremely well interpreted for younger visitors and many have opportunities for dressing up and role play. Finally, when the wind bites, you can snuggle up in your accommodation, playing games or watching a film.

One consideration worth thinking about is the need to soften the impact of long car journeys on narrow roads that can induce motion sickness among those in the back seats.

LGBTQ+ TRAVELLERS

Gay relationships and marriage are legal here, as they are across the UK. The 2011 census indicated that same-sex civil partnerships make up 0.1% of households compared with 0.8% for the UK as a whole. Gay travellers, and indeed any LGBTQ+ visitors, should have no concerns about displaying affection or about how they might be accepted. However, the views of the influential Church can vary, as testified by the split in the Church of Scotland over proposals that gay men and women become ministers.

WHAT TO TAKE

All medicines, sunscreen and clothing you find on the mainland are available on the islands, as are batteries and memory cards for digital cameras. It's wisest to pack warm and waterproof clothing, including hats and gloves, even for a summer holiday. Binoculars are always handy, especially for birdwatchers. Seasickness remedies for choppy ferry crossings across the Minch or to St Kilda are worth considering, as is midge repellent for the summer months. Plugs and voltages are the same as in the rest of the UK.

MONEY AND BUDGETING

MONEY The currency, like the rest of the UK, is sterling (£). Scottish and UK banknotes are both in wide circulation and accepted in the Outer Hebrides. However, be aware that shopkeepers in England appear increasingly reluctant to accept Scottish banknotes: contrary to popular perception there is no legal obligation for them to be accepted. There are plenty of ATMs, usually in the main townships, and these will accept international credit cards. Banking hours are listed in individual island chapters. Note that banks will not cash travellers' cheques, and the only place where you can reliably exchange US dollars and euros for sterling is Stornoway's post office: foreign visitors are best advised to change money on the UK mainland or use ATMs.

BUDGETING The costs of travel are a little higher on the islands thanks to the issue of price premiums (see box, page 27). If you travel by bus, stay in hostels and get your food from community stores or supermarkets, you may spend around £30 per day. It is quite a financial jump from such budget travel to staying at a mid-range B&B, having a picnic lunch and eating a standard pub meal in the evening, which will cost around £80 per day per person (based on two sharing). At the high end, staying at a hotel or top-end B&B and treating yourself to one of the fine-dining options, you'll see your costs rise to anything above £150 per day per person.

If you travel by car, fuel is about 10% higher than on the mainland, and island roads do not lend themselves to economical fuel consumption: typically you might add £20 per day for the fuel needed to travel around the islands.

A main course for a pub meal costs £8–20 (local fish and beef are at the higher end of this scale); a bottle of wine £10; a lunchtime sandwich and coffee £6.

Despite the price premium, most everyday items visitors might want cost more or the less the same as on the mainland. Typical prices include: a litre of water £1.50; a loaf of bread £1.50; take-away sandwich £3.50; Mars Bar 80p; postcard 75p; souvenir T-shirt £25; litre of petrol £1.40.

GETTING AROUND

DRIVING Almost all roads are paved and in generally good condition. A network of main roads, known as the Western Isles spinal route, runs from Stornoway on Lewis all the way south, under different road numbers, to Lochboisdale on South Uist. The islands collectively have 439 miles of A, B and C roads and 302 miles of unclassified roads.

Driving times are listed in the individual island chapters but you should not underestimate how long even seemingly modest distances may take. If you start your day on Barra aiming to reach Stornoway – which is not recommended – you are likely to be exhausted as well as financially poorer from the sizeable cost of petrol and the two ferry journeys.

First-time visitors to the Outer Hebrides are often caught out by the single-track roads, particularly where these abruptly replace stretches of A-road with little or no warning. Single-track roads are always generously sprinkled with passing places, usually at least every 100 metres. The most stress-free way to approach them is to park your ego and maintain a default disposition to yield to oncoming vehicles. Also, be sure to let vehicles overtake you on single-track roads: they may be a doctor or other key worker on call. Never use passing places as parking spaces (if you do pause in one to watch deer, eagles or look at the view, be prepared to move on if a car approaches). If you park up on the side of a road, do so with care and thought for other road users.

Even though the islands are only around 130 miles from north to south, you should keep your fuel tank at least half full. Distances can be further than you think between petrol stations (or filling stations as they are called locally); those on Lewis (apart from Engebret in Stornoway), Harris and North Uist will be closed on Sundays. And while many now have 24/7 credit card payment at the pump, these do seem to play up more often than you would expect. Details of all filling stations are in the relevant island chapters.

Charging points for electric vehicles are appearing across the islands and can be found at the port and Lews Castle in Stornoway and at the ferry terminals in Tarbert, Leverburgh, Lochmaddy, Eriskay and Castlebay, as well as Liniclate School on Benbecula.

Scottish drink-driving laws are stricter than the rest of the UK. In 2014, the legal limit was cut to 50mg in every 100ml of blood, compared with 80mg in the rest of the UK. According to experts, this means that an average man would be limited to just under a pint of beer or a large glass of wine, and women to half a pint of beer or a small glass of wine. The message is clear: just don't drink and drive.

Campervans and motorhomes Berthing your campervan or motorhome overnight and waking up overlooking the machair or a vast beach to call your own is one of the great Hebridean experiences.

People bring their own campervans over from the mainland, but you can also hire locally through Harris Classic Campers (m 07920 748852; w harrisclassiccampers. co.uk; available May–Oct; high season £695/week) based at Seilebost on Harris. Just be mindful, however, of how much diesel you'll need to get your gas-guzzling vehicle up and over the North Harris Hills.

The number of campervans is increasing year on year, with owners lured by the appeal of meandering up or down the island chain and parking either at an idyllic campsite or at designated spots offered by island community trusts overlooking the sea. Drivers should be aware of the potential environmental impacts associated with motorhomes: parking on the machair damages the special plants to be found there; the fact you may see others doing this does not make it OK. The number of motorhomes is also putting pressure on some minor roads such as the narrow and winding single track that makes its way out to Hushinish on North Harris.

Motorhome drivers in particular have a wonderful opportunity not only to enjoy a dream holiday on these islands but to dispel a few perceptions; you can consider regularly allowing overtaking, thinking twice before exploring the narrowest byroads (the roads to Rhenigidale on Harris and between Mangersta and Mealasta in Uig on Lewis are totally unsuitable for motorhomes), and shopping locally rather than stocking up on the mainland. The Outer Hebrides are now responding to the increase in campervans by improving their infrastructure, including chemical disposal points. Useful advice can be found at w visitouterhebrides.co.uk/visitor-info/facilities/motorhomes.

Car hire In recent years, costs have come down and hiring a car on the islands is much more competitive with mainland and mainstream rental companies, particularly when you factor in the cost of the ferry and mileage to get to Uig on Skye, Mallaig, Oban or Ullapool. In addition, all the island companies are family-run, independent businesses and so your money stays in the Outer Hebrides rather than goes outwards to international companies. Details of rental companies can be found in the individual chapters. Some companies now offer electric vehicles (for charging points, see above), which bring significant savings on fuel. You should book well in advance as demand is always high.

BUSES Services are generally reliable but infrequent. They reach every nook and cranny of the islands, from the remote eastern shores of Harris to the lonely townships of Uig on Lewis or the west coast of South Uist. Almost everywhere tourists might want to visit is theoretically accessible by bus. Services are single-decker buses in and around Stornoway and often minibuses in more remote areas.

On the northern isles, buses tend to operate in and out of Stornoway. Further south, on the Uists, Benbecula and Eriskay, routes are geared around the main spinal roads and operate in two zones, from Lochmaddy on North Uist to Balivanich on Benbecula; and from Balivanich through South Uist to Eriskay. Although more intermittent outside Stornoway, services are reliable and, with careful planning, visitors can base days around them with confidence. (The same cannot really be said for locals, who find getting to a hospital appointment on a separate island by public transport is often impossible.) Many routes are tied to the start and end of the school day and so have long gaps between services; others need to be booked the day before by calling the driver or bus company – all numbers are listed in timetables on the website (see below). You can also usually flag down buses, as long as it is safe for the driver to stop. With all journeys, you are strongly advised to check with the driver the time and pickup point for your return journey. A comprehensive summary of all routes can be found at w cne-siar.gov.uk (search 'bus services'). The Visit Scotland iCentre in Stornoway and the Welcome Points (page 39) across the islands will also have details of bus services.

Such is the beauty of many of the bus routes – along the shores of Luskentyre (South Harris) or Rhenigidale on North Harris, for example – that the experience can be akin to that of a tour bus. Bus journeys also take the sting out of the sometimes demanding drives along winding roads where constant concentration on passing places and sometimes startling bends can detract from enjoyment of the scenery. Fares are reasonable, ranging from just £1 for a short hop to £6.80 for the longest trips, such as between Stornoway and Leverburgh. Return tickets offer a minor discount and are valid all day. There are no services anywhere on Sundays, and most routes operate a reduced service on Saturdays.

CAUSEWAYS

Causeways are a dramatic and often photogenic feature of the islands, but they have played an important role in keeping the island communities alive. Over the past century, many communities have vanished because of the problems caused by isolation. St Kilda is the most remote and most famous, but others include Mingulay and Berneray south of Barra, the Monach Islands, Scarp and Taransay. Causeways have been a key way to address the effects of peripherality. The completion of the link between South Uist and Eriskay in 2001 meant that you could finally drive the spine of the southern isles from Berneray, through North Uist, Benbecula, Grimsay and Baile Siar to South Uist and Eriskay, a distance of 60 miles.

That causeways have significantly reduced travel times to the benefit of all is undeniable, but some have pondered on the potential cultural impact. In her illustrated travelogue *An Eye on the Hebrides,* Mairi Hedderwick certainly wondered whether the impact of quicker travel runs deeper, noting that: 'Less than an hour's drive will take you from Lochboisdale in South Uist to Lochmaddy in North Uist without so much as getting your feet wet... Your soul will have been safari-ed through Sunday festivals and football matches, wayside altars of pastel-fed kitsch, smiley priests and a lot of Virgin Marys on mantelpieces, shop counters and mountainsides. Ending finally in Lochmaddy, strait-laced, Sabbatarian and extremely serious. It's quite important for your soul's sake to start at the end that you would prefer not to be the terminus.'

As you travel around, you'll notice unusual concrete bus shelters that somehow echo a Celtic cross. The designs win no beauty contests but are effective and functional as the four walls mean you should be able to find one corner that shelters you from high winds and horizontal rain.

FERRIES CalMac operates two inter-island ferry services. The Harris–Berneray ferry from Leverburgh to Ardmaree is the north–south link between Harris and the Uists. The journey through the Sound of Harris is beautiful and takes around an hour. Further south, a 40-minute ferry ride links Eriskay with Ardmore on Barra. Those connecting from one ferry to another should note that Ardmore is some 15 minutes' drive or 8 miles, about as far as it is possible to be on such a small island, from Castlebay where you will find the ferry port to Oban. For trips planned between Easter and mid-August you should definitely book ahead if you are driving. Usually, foot passengers can just walk on, but the popularity of the Hebridean Way cycle route means that on the busiest days you may not be able to board. It's always worth calling CalMac a few days ahead of time to see how busy things are getting.

THE HEBRIDEAN WAY

The big islands' success story of recent years has been the designation of the Hebridean Way (w hebrideanway.co.uk), a 185-mile cycle route spanning the length of the island chain. The route, or at least the roads along which it runs, has long been in place, of course, but some smart branding has fired the imagination of both casual and more hardcore cyclists. Key to this has been the inviting strapline '185 miles, 10 islands, 6 causeways, 2 ferries'.

The route runs across Vatersay and Barra (13 miles), Eriskay and South Uist (32 miles), Benbecula and Grimsay (13 miles), North Uist and Berneray (32 miles), Harris (33 miles) and Lewis (62 miles). The route finale heads west to the Callanish stones before heading up to the Butt of Lewis.

Just a few years ago, the handful of cyclists you did see along the island roads generally appeared to be of the hardier variety, for whom getting soaked and windblown was part of the appeal. Given the reality of Hebridean weather, that can still apply, but the numbers speak for themselves. From barely a handful of cyclists on the islands in 2010, the launch of the Hebridean Way saw 3,000 undertake the route in 2018, a number that more than doubled in 2019.

Most cyclists take four to six days to complete the route, though the more elite two-wheelers could, at a push and weather permitting, complete it in a day. The appeal is enhanced by the support that cyclists feel they receive from islanders. The risk of being marooned with a puncture is far lower than used to be the case as an ever-helpful cycling support network has burgeoned in line with the increase in cycle traffic. Companies will even transport you back to the start, allow bike drop-off so you don't have to retrace your steps, or pick you up if you do run into difficulty. A useful company is Heb Shuttle (w hebshuttle.co.uk).

Many local businesses, from B&Bs to shops and even artists' galleries, are linked into a pit-stop network that offers free refills, weather updates and, as equally important, companionship and a friendly welcome. The route website contains an up-to-date list of network members.

CYCLING Cycling is a wonderful way to explore the islands. There are good spinal routes through Lewis, Harris and the Uists where it is possible to cover significant distances quickly. A bicycle also allows you to explore the quiet roads and lanes off the main thoroughfares that wind their way through scattered townships and past lochs to the coast. If you don't have a vehicle, a bicycle can be as effective as and more flexible than the bus services. The islands are hillier than many people anticipate, and while the main roads see lighter traffic than the mainland, drivers are not universally any slower or more courteous.

The individual islands all offer limitless opportunities to explore by bike, from the flatlands of Benbecula to circular tours of Barra. A good list of suggested places to explore by bike and cycle hire outlets can be found at w visitouterhebrides.co.uk/see-and-do/activities/cycling.

Cycling from one end of the islands to the other is increasingly popular. It's a logical and glorious route of 185 miles that has been formally waymarked and mapped as the Hebridean Way (see box, opposite). The route is designated as National Cycle Network Route 780 and is commonly undertaken from the south so that the prevailing winds are behind you.

HITCHING Catching a lift is perfectly feasible and, given the friendliness of local people, can be socially rewarding. The islands' reputation for safety means you should expect few issues; nevertheless, always use your judgement and talk to a driver before committing yourself. One factor to bear in mind is the remoteness of townships from one another and the intermittency of traffic off the main roads: you may end up waiting a long time for one of the very few drivers headed for a particular township, and then you have no guarantee they will want to pick you up.

ACCOMMODATION

From modern to traditional, high-end to basic, accommodation on the islands will collectively meet all budgets and tastes. Recent years have seen a scramble for renovation and updating in response to rival new properties that have injected some much-needed higher standards.

The only problem with accommodation is that there is not enough of it, with around 5,200 beds (plus self-catering options) to welcome more than 230,000 people every year. It's also true that some places can divide opinion: traditional can mean cosy and friendly, but it can also mean wonky plumbing or inflexible arrival and departure times, or asking you to keep out of the property during the day.

Always ask ahead whether accommodation providers take credit cards. Many places close between October and March or Easter; even places that advertise as opening all year sometimes close if things are quiet (this also applies to shops). In the *Where to stay* section of each chapter, accommodation that is not open year-round is listed as such. Nevertheless, always check ahead, as many places change their approach from year to year. Just about everyone shuts for Christmas and New Year.

Always keep an eye on the weather. If a storm blows in and the ferries can't put to sea, then accommodation quickly clogs up. In such an event, what usually happens is that most people stay in the same place for an extra night; if not, a bush telegraph seems to come into operation and your hosts will call around for you. The most problematic day and place to be stranded is a Sunday on Harris or Lewis, as the tourist office in Stornoway and most of the Welcome Points will be closed and south of Stornoway, even with masts now covering Uig and South Harris, you can still struggle to get a mobile signal when you need it.

At times, you may also feel that accommodation costs more than you might expect and certainly more than you would pay on the mainland. Undoubtedly, a few providers, aware of the demand for accommodation, try it on; generally though, higher prices reflect the higher costs of materials and provisions that need to be shipped across the Minch. It is very rare to find high prices combined with bad service.

Many guesthouses offer evening meals. These can range from filling – though standard – fare, to increasingly sophisticated and sumptuous offerings, drawing on local produce, that allow your hosts to show off their inventiveness. These meals are also often available to non-residents, though you nearly always need to book ahead. This enables your hosts to rise to the perennial challenge of ensuring they have fresh ingredients.

It's also worth pointing out that you should take online reviews with a pinch of salt, as weather and logistics can sometimes thwart the best of intentions. I once turned up at a wonderful B&B to discover a cracked front window where a wind-assisted golf ball – there wasn't a golf course for miles around – had planted itself during Force 11 winds that lasted for the best part of two days. The owner explained to me that the only carpenter who made replica period windows of the kind required lived on a neighbouring island and did not use email. She had to write to him and wait for a reply; he in turn wrote to mainland suppliers of wood, which often arrived in the wrong specification and had to be sent back. A task that might take three days on the mainland can easily drift into months here.

HOSTELS If you don't mind sharing rooms, toilets and showers, hostels can be both good value and a delight. Many have been refurbished recently in response to what is seen as a growing demand for substantial kitchen facilities and games rooms. They also tend to be passionately and efficiently run by people full of great ideas and suggestions for visits and trips. The Gatliff hostels on North Harris, Berneray and South Uist, in particular, get consistently good feedback. You can, if you wish, stay at hostels every night as you work your way down the entire island chain, following the hostel trail (w ravenspoint.net/hostel-trail).

FAMILIES Many B&Bs are child-friendly, and some can even feel geared more to kids than to adults. It's always best to speak to an accommodation provider in advance as you will get an idea of whether children are fully welcome, or merely expected to be seen but not heard. One bugbear is that many B&Bs and even hotels seem to think that families comprise no more than one – at a push two – children and can demand what feels like punitive charges for extra beds. A family of four can easily be asked to pay £300+ a night for two rooms in an average hotel. Accordingly, many families will opt for self-catering, hostels or camping sites. At the other extreme, some B&Bs can be hugely accommodating, flexible and happily give your family the run of the whole house. Many hosts will also convert a B&B into self-catering or a self-contained family area if you request it. Guesthouses prepared to do this will generally mention this on their websites.

CAMPING The campsites of the Outer Hebrides routinely find their way into UK and even world compendiums of great places to pitch a tent. That's with good reason, though generally this will be more for reasons of location than the quality of facilities, which can – with a few exceptions – be basic or minimal. Some campsites have electric hook-ups but, more often than not, drivers of motorhomes or campervans will need to be self-sufficient. Not all sites have provision for chemical disposal, so ask on arrival or when booking for the nearest location. Bear in mind that campsites are also often a long way from local stores and almost none have a shop on site. There can be few more rewarding experiences, however, than waking up to a view overlooking the Hebridean coast. In addition to the more formal campsites, under Scottish open-access rights (see box, page 58), wild camping is permissible at most locations across the islands. Wild camping does involve some boundaries: it must be done in small numbers and only for two or three nights in any one place. While you can camp in this way wherever access rights apply, you should not camp in enclosed fields of crops or farm animals.

SELF-CATERING Renting a cottage is extremely popular, particularly with families faced with the high cost of eating out every night. Many are wonderfully positioned, overlooking the sea or moors, often enjoy thrillingly isolated locations and are well equipped and characterful. Damp, however, can be a real issue with older properties and you should always check this when booking.

At the other end of the scale, five-star self-catering has definitely arrived in the Outer Hebrides, and 'Grand Designs'-style constructions with floor-to-ceiling windows, built into hillsides or modelled on Iron Age brochs are popping up all over the place.

In contrast to most costs, prices are lower than on the mainland – roughly half what you might pay for equivalent accommodation in Cornwall, for example. A cottage sleeping five people will typically cost £400–£800 per week in high season, although luxury properties can break through the £1,500 mark. A handful of self-catering properties are listed in the *Where to stay* sections of each island chapter of this book; a comprehensive list can be found at w visitouterhebrides.co.uk and the various community-run island websites.

EATING AND DRINKING

It's fair to say that a food revolution is taking place in the Outer Hebrides and that cuisine has come a long way in a short time. Long gone are the days when islanders would catch seabirds and boil them up for soup. While filling and calorific meals of the meat-and-two-veg variety still predominate, recent years have seen the emergence of a trend for fine dining and for using island produce rather than imports from the mainland. Some eateries tend to over-egg matters: there are only so many ways to skin a cat, and you may be left wondering how many more 'towers' or 'gateaux' of Haggis you will encounter (cat or cat skin, just to be clear, are not among the ingredients to be found in Haggis).

On every island, you will have the choice of meat from animals reared locally or fish caught just offshore. **Venison** is common and drawn from island herds of red deer. **Stornoway black pudding** was given Protected Geographical Indication status in 2013 (see box, page 84), putting it on a par with Yorkshire Wensleydale cheese and Cornish sardines. Other dishes you will often come across include *cranachan*, a traditional Scottish dish of oats, cream, whisky and raspberries, and *crowdie*, a soft and crumbly cream cheese with a slightly sour taste that is said to mitigate the effects of drinking too much whisky. **Oatcakes** are another ubiquitous offering, usually served with salmon as canapés or with cheese as a dessert. Several curing and processing outlets have taken the finishing of **salmon** to something approaching an artform. You are unlikely to taste better salmon in the UK than you do on these islands.

Every pub and hotel bar has an extensive selection of **whiskies**. For now, there is just the one single malt, from Abhainn Dearg distillery in Uig on Lewis, which will be followed by a concoction in preparation at the Isle of Harris Distillery in Tarbert. There are also plans in development for distilleries on North Uist and Barra.

Historically, beer and micro-breweries have been curiously underplayed on the islands and, for a brief time, the closure of the Hebridean Brewery Company in Stornoway left the islands without their own ale. The opening of the Loomshed on Harris (page 154) in 2019 filled this niche and looks destined to push the islands successfully into the ever-growing market for craft beer. In addition, craft ales from Orkney and Shetland and organic beer from the Black Isle Brewery (north of Inverness) are commonly found. A frequent misconception that the tourism authority is always eager to correct is the widely reported claim that there are no pubs in the Outer Hebrides. Stornoway has plenty, and although country or roadside pubs that characterise much of the UK are few and far between, you will find one on each of Lewis (near Ness), North Uist and Eriskay. Meanwhile, most hotels have bars that most definitely serve as the local pub. Most places accept credit cards but, as is the case with accommodation, it is worth checking ahead.

Cafés and restaurants are also increasingly upping their game and are geared up for special dietary requirements. On the subject of the former, a curious feature of the Outer Hebrides is that the elemental nature of the landscape is in inverse proportion to the cosiness of its cafés. One of the joyful quirks of the islands is that you can go into the post office to send a postcard only to discover a first-rate café operating out of the back room (such as on Scalpay). This has given rise to the concept of the 'tea-shop safari', whereby you can enjoy salmon pâté and oatcakes to the gentle background melodies of mandolins, bodhrans and pipes. The buildings

EATING-OUT PRICE CODES

The following codes are used in this guide to indicate the average price for a main course in a restaurant or local eatery.

£££	£20+	Expensive
£££	£10–20	Mid-range
£	<£10	Cheap/Cheap & cheerful

Whether it's a cake, a classic fish-and-chip supper or immaculately presented cuisine, high-quality fare is sprinkled across the archipelago. The food trail Eat Drink Hebrides (w eatdrinkhebrides.co.uk) was launched in 2016 and features 35 food producers or outlets offering everything from Hebridean mutton derived from sheep fed on heather moors to seaweed-infused gin and locally caught shellfish. The islands are also excellent for foraging wild foods, just so long as you know what you are doing. *A Guide to Foraging in the Outer Hebrides* is an excellent leaflet that will help you rustle up dinner from a variety of red seaweeds, thyme and three-cornered leeks, all washed down with wine made from the flowers of gorse. Both the local food trail and the foraging guide can be downloaded from the website above.

themselves can often be part of the experience: some are built for dramatic effect, with large windows to take in the views; others are gems hidden within mundane pebble-dash interiors; in many, the interiors seem to be designed along the lines of what might be described as 'garden-shed aesthetics' (and in some cases they are, literally, garden sheds: Mollans, page 100; Croft 36, page 161; and The Hebridean Mustard Company, page 170). Seasonal pop-up cafés are also beginning to appear on the islands. For now, this is a trend in its infancy and they do seem to come and go. Look out for these operators – some of whom offer home-bakes and local fish rather than dismal packaged offerings from the UK mainland – in places such as the west-coast beaches of South Harris and lay-bys in the North Harris Hills.

FESTIVALS AND EVENTS

Many *feisean* (festivals), farming shows and sporting challenges take place throughout the islands, along with *mods* – festivals of Gaelic song, arts and culture. Agricultural shows, with sheepdog trials and farmers' produce for sale, offer good eye-openers into island farming life. The nature of some 'annual' events is that they prove popular for a few years then run out of steam and are quietly dropped from the calendar. An up-to-date list of regular and new events can be found at w visitouterhebrides.co.uk/whats-on. It is worth checking as annual festivals sometimes move from one month to another.

FEBRUARY A welcome addition to the islands' festival calendar is the **Hebridean Dark Skies Festival** (w lanntair.com/creative-programme/darkskies), which runs for two weeks of the month. Events include stargazing at sites such as Callanish, Lews Castle and Gallan Head, while organisers – led by the staff at the An Lanntair arts centre in Stornoway – also put on talks, workshops by leading scientists, film screenings and live music. Details are usually announced the previous autumn.

APRIL The **Donald Macleod Memorial Piping Competition** in Stornoway features some of the world's leading pipers.

JUNE The **St Kilda challenge** is a boat race from Lochmaddy to St Kilda. Half the yachts race, the remainder cruising as a flotilla. The **Barrathon and fun run** is a half-marathon around the island and Vatersay. The **Harris Mod** is held in Tarbert; the **Lewis Mod** is staged in Stornoway.

JULY The waterborne activities of **Sail Stornoway** include a race between working vessels and sailing on sgoth Niseach, a traditional clinker-built fishing boat. The **Hebridean Celtic Festival or Hebcelt** (w hebceltfest.com) is a celebration of Celtic music held in the grounds of Lews Castle. It is sometimes described as Lewis's answer to Glastonbury. **Eilean Dorcha Festival** (w edf.scot) is held on the Liniclate machair on Benbecula and involves two days of live music, workshops and family activities. Held at Askernish, the **South Uist Games and Piping Society Highland Games** include classic events such as tossing the caber and tug of war.

Other events include: **Berneray Week** (w isleofberneray.com/berneray-week.html); **North Uist Highland Games**; **South Uist and Benbecula Agricultural Show** in Iochdar; **South Harris Agricultural Show** in Leverburgh; **Lewis Highland Games** and **Western Isles Strongest Man** in Tong, northeast of Stornoway.

AUGUST Events include the **Lewis Carnival** (floats, music and dances), **Harris Tweed Festival Day** (fashion showcase and performances of waulking songs) and the **Ben Kenneth Hill Race** (a run up the peak behind Lochboisdale on South Uist).

SEPTEMBER An emerging event, held for the first time in 2014, **Hebtember** is a month-long festival of cèilidhs, comedy shows, and arts and crafts. The **Isle of Harris Mountain Festival** comprises guided walks, talks, segway tours, raft races and mountain biking. The three-day Hebrides International Film Festival (w hebfilmfestival.org) is also held this month, with an emphasis on independent drama and documentary. Films are shown at community venues right across the islands and often become something of a social event.

NOVEMBER Marketed as the UK's most remote book festival, **Faclan** (w faclan.org) is held at An Lanntair in Stornoway and regularly features household names.

SHOPPING

Without doubt, the isles are a fertile medium for creative minds and the inspiration for a good deal of arts and crafts of an extremely impressive standard. From hauntingly atmospheric photography through intricate Harris Tweed cushions to paintings of people, birdlife and landscape, the quality of work is high. Other items to look out for include handcrafted patchwork quilts, stoneware from glass collected while beachcombing, driftwood creations and beeswax paintings that capture the islands' ever-changing light.

Tweed is the one medium that is at risk of suffering overkill. While some producers, designers and stitchers are extremely skilled and innovative, do ask about the provenance of the item you want to buy and ask yourself whether you really want a tweed mobile phone cover that may have been woven on the islands but put together in China. Until recently, much of the tweed for sale has been rather conventional and traditional, but a new generation of designers is producing everything from sweaters to hoodies and sprinkling their work with real panache.

Food is another good choice for souvenirs. Salmon can be vacuum packed so stays edible until you reach home, while Stornoway black pudding is another dish with a long shelf life.

When planning shopping trips, be aware that almost all shops are closed on Sundays in the northern islands (Lewis, Harris and North Uist). More generally, shops are open 09.00–17.00, though an infinite number of variations on these times occur across the islands. On a dark, wet afternoon with no prospect of customers, a shop, café or pub may close earlier; conversely, they will often stay open longer if the demand is there. It's also worth bearing in mind that the shopkeeper, or whoever brings your coffee or meal, may be a one-person band, or one half of a couple. There is not an unlimited supply of labour in the Outer Hebrides, as you might find in a city. Often, behind a simple sign that says 'open 9–5' there may be a human being who works an 80-hour week, much of it unseen, keeping their business afloat.

COMMUNITY SHOPS All too often in the UK, rural shops are either rundown or franchised from a dreary national chain where the business plan requires customers to 'take it or leave it' with regard to high prices and desultory service. Your experience in the Outer Hebrides may be rather different. Over the past ten years, several community shops have sprung up; they can be a revelation, stocking fresh local produce, offering take-aways and hot drinks, typically with good-quality rather than low-frills ingredients. Many are punching their weight against fierce competition from online deliveries. What these shops also offer is the knowledge that your money is being reinvested locally. Their business models rely heavily on summer visitors to keep them open for the local community during the more fallow winter months. They work hard to keep their prices competitive with the supermarket chains as they want your custom, and this is reflected in the generally high standard of goods on sale.

ARTS AND ENTERTAINMENT

Major art shows and events tend to take place in Stornoway, simply because the town has by far the largest number of venues and therefore potential capacity. The epicentre of activity is An Lanntair in Stornoway, and the Taigh Chearsabhagh on North Uist is the focal artistic point for the southern isles. Additionally, local activity in the form of cèilidhs and other musical performances is common. Art galleries (which hold regular exhibitions), music performances and shows have an ultra-local character and are hosted in community halls, museums and even schools. Good sources of information about events are w visitouterhebrides.co.uk/ whats-on and w harrisarts.org. Events are also advertised in community shops, or your accommodation hosts should also be able to advise you.

Seeking out the art of the islands is often as much a pleasure as indulging in it. The majority of artists work from home studios, often on remote crofts scattered across the islands. Almost universally, they are happy to talk to visitors and share their tales of island life and how they put their talents to use. They may even offer you tea or coffee; some studios are more formal cafés, where it can be sometimes hard to work out where the coffee stops and the art begins. Many artists are in the Outer Hebrides for the long term, but a good number come and go quite quickly. Look out for the excellent free local guide *Made in the Outer Hebrides*, which includes up-to-date listings of who is around. You'll find it at the Stornoway tourist office, museums and at many sites of interest (it's also available for download from w cne-siar.gov.uk). The guide is good at highlighting local and sometimes ultra-local craftwork.

The Screen Machine (w screenmachine.co.uk; £7.50/£5.50), Britain's only mobile cinema, tours the islands from north to south every six to ten weeks. A show is quite an experience, as the 80-seat cinema is housed in an articulated lorry, complete with soft-back seats and popcorn.

Exploring the landscape of the islands is one of the key attractions and reasons for a visit. Increasingly, every outdoor whim and activity is catered for and comes with an added frisson resulting from the remote locations that are often involved. Watching wildlife (particularly marine creatures), so often a lottery elsewhere, is an activity where the odds are really stacked in your favour here. Kayaking in sheltered lochs and even open seas is a way to not only appreciate the coastline but to haul up on beautiful and otherwise inaccessible beaches. Coasteering, rock climbing, abseiling, wind-karting, scuba diving, powerboating, wild swimming (see box, page 60), photography and much more are all provided for. Thanks to the creation of the Hebridean Way (see box, page 50), cycling has become remarkably popular, not just as a means of getting from A to B but also for using a base to explore a corner of an island (page 51). Individual operators and activities particular to an area are listed in the relevant island chapters. It can always be helpful to know what the tides are doing. A good, reliable source is the World Tides app, while surfers can follow the Wind Finder app.

WALKING From easy beach strolls to strenuous and challenging mountain walks, the Outer Hebrides offer everything a hiker could wish. Several walks are described in the relevant island chapters. Beware, however, that walking in the Outer Hebrides may be different from what you are used to back home. Much of the UK mainland is mapped out with footpaths, permissive paths and fingerpost signs. This is rarely the case in the Outer Hebrides, where many walks take you over open, path-free ground. Sometimes there are waymarker posts leading the way; more often there are not, so a map, a compass and sound judgement are essential.

SCOTTISH OUTDOOR ACCESS CODE

Walking rights in Scotland are less grudging than elsewhere in the UK. The Land Reform (Scotland) Act 2003 established a statutory right of responsible access to almost all land and water, as long as you adhere to the Access Code (w outdooraccess-scotland.com). The code is based on three principles: acting with courtesy, consideration and awareness; looking after the places you visit and leaving the land as you find it; and acting with care at all times for your own safety and that of others.

Very few people would of course deliberately violate the code, but it can be easy to unwittingly have a negative impact on the environment. This is particularly the case with deer and, each year, several pregnant red deer hinds miscarry after they are approached by visitors trying to fill the frame of their camera. 'It can look as though they are ambling away from you naturally,' says Steve Woodhall, manager of the Borve Estate on South Harris, 'but actually they are moving deliberately away, they're anxious, and they can slip their calves. People don't do it deliberately but it can be easy to fall into this trap. We just ask people to be mindful.' In short, if you are uncertain about access, or your impact on an area, ask locally.

Countryside users are also asked to adhere to the crofters' code. This calls upon you to either leave dogs at home or keep them on a leash; to fasten gates behind you and use stiles to cross fences; to leave no litter nor to disturb breeding birds; to protect wildlife and plants; and to avoid damage to archaeological sites.

The tourist board has also produced a series of six walking publications for Callanish, Great Bernera, Rhenigidale, Scalpay, Berneray and Eriskay, which can be downloaded at w visitouterhebrides.co.uk/see-and-do/activities/walking.

A landmark walking route, the **Hebridean Way** (w hebrideanway.co.uk), opened in 2016 and runs from Vatersay to Stornoway. Waymarked throughout, the trail combines existing trails with new paths, peat tracks, quiet roads and open ground. The whole route is 156 miles (251km) long. Generally it is walked south to north so you're not constantly battling with prevailing southwesterlies. Typically, the current walk can be completed in 14 days. For those wanting some peace of mind, the pit stops to which cyclists avail themselves (see box, page 50) are equally open to hikers.

The route through Vatersay and Barra is 15 miles; after taking the ferry it's a further 35 miles through Eriskay and South Uist; Benbecula and Grimsay cover 10 miles; the stage through North Uist and Berneray to the ferry terminal is 22 miles; Harris (south and north) is 38 miles; and from Leverburgh to Stornoway is 30 miles. The toughest section by some distance lies within the hills of Harris; other hilly sections occur in Barra.

There are plans to extend the Hebridean Way to the Butt of Lewis with a spur that cuts northwest, possibly through Garrynahine, and that will then track up the west coast of Lewis (although less direct, this will have the benefit of taking in Callanish, an impressive list of stirring bays and a generally more – though still lightly – populated part of the island).

However, if you are happy with some road walking and are eager for even more plodding along empty moors than you have done already, you can in fact already complete the bottom-to-top trail and walk to the Butt of Lewis along the east coast of the island: from Stornoway make your way out to Tolsta along the B895, a distance of 13 miles; then cross the Bridge to Nowhere and embark on the 16km (10-mile) moorland hike to Port of Ness (see box, page 90).

The Hebridean Way is outstanding: one day you are walking the flatlands of South Uist, the next negotiating the fords and causeways of Benbecula; you step, literally, from the mosaic of colour that is the summer machair, into the inky-peat moorlands. The route in Harris snakes through the passes where the walking can be thrilling. Do be mindful, though, that waymarking is still far from perfect, and make sure you have maps with you (or everything downloaded and a fully charged phone). In some places, such as parts of North Uist and Barra, the route planners appear to have run up against a limited budget and you may feel the route too often hugs the roads rather than taking you deeper into the moors or farmland.

The concept of open access is enshrined in Scottish law (see box, opposite), so you are able, within reason, to roam where you wish. However, the concept of open access is not entirely unfettered and comes with responsibilities. In particular, you should be mindful on the peat moors not to disturb ground-nesting birds. The same applies to the machair (and for the same reason), where you should try to keep to paths, farm tracks and field edges, even if this adds some distance to your walk. You'll soon notice if you do cause disruption, as lapwings and oystercatchers will circle above you, calling noisily, and seabirds may squirt unwelcome deposits in your direction. Remember to never get between a calf and its mother.

When out walking, you should carry clothing for all weathers, even when the forecast appears unambiguously good. It's a good idea to carry a first-aid kit, a whistle and to leave at your accommodation a sketch map of any mountain routes you plan. None of this is designed to put you off: it's just that you are much more likely to be out on the moors and hills on your own than in the Lake District, or even the Cairngorms.

The idea of swimming in a loch or in open water in the Hebrides will sound impossibly romantic to some; and talking to Norma Macleod of Immerse Hebrides (w immersehebrides.com) may entice even those who do a few lengths in their local pool to give it a try.

'Wild swimming in the sea in the Hebrides is exhilarating because it's colder, more isolated and the waters are clearer and cleaner than I've seen in the British Isles so far,' she says. 'It feels like it's always a stolen moment – we go when the weather breaks for the better as we don't know when we'll get to go in again.'

Even if you are familiar with wild swimming, the experience in the Outer Hebrides is quite different. The lochs are peatier than lochs on the mainland and, says Norma, 'can be like swimming in Guinness – which can be challenging and exciting at the same time.'

Norma's favoured spots for wild swimming include the island of Little Bernera, as you can only get to it by boat, kayak or swimming (from Bosta beach). 'There is a ruined temple and cemetery where my ancestors from the village of Carloway were buried,' says Norma, who grew up on Lewis, swimming in the lochs and seas around Callanish. 'It's an uninhabited island (often you're the only person on the island) and has a stunning white, fine-shell beach with the most beautiful sheltered turquoise lagoon to swim around.'

Open swimming between islands can involve swimming from Tràigh na' Beirigh (Reef beach) in Uig traversing the tiny island of Siaram and onwards to Pabbay Mor. The more adventurous could swim from Horgabost beach in Harris to Taransay, but only with boat or kayak support as it's a nearly 2-mile swim.

Basic swimming safety precautions always apply (page 44), but if swimming in lochs you should also be mindful of blue or green algae, which can form when the water temperature rises above 11–12°C.

Norma and her husband, Neil, offer one-to-one beginner courses, training sessions and walk–swim treks. You can be confident of being in safe hands – Norma is a cardiac nurse (don't be alarmed, she points out, she is highly unlikely to need her training while swimming) and Neil was previously full-time RNLI coxswain of Stornoway Lifeboat so has extensive knowledge of the coastline and waters.

The particular circumstances of crofting ownership also throw up some unique access difficulties when planning walking routes. Crofters can exercise their right to graze common land under a system known as apportionment. 'It can be hard to know where land is apportioned as it can look unused,' says Johanne Ferguson at Scottish Natural Heritage. 'You can plan the route, but when you get there you find a fence right where you want to go.' Should this happen, you should not damage the fence but, in the absence of a gate within sight, look for stones that will give you the elevation to clamber over.

Smartphones and GPS It's true that the latest GPS devices and smartphones can provide highly accurate grid references, right down to within 5m in areas of forestry or narrow valleys, where they have previously been unreliable. But the Mountaineering Council of Scotland points out that a GPS device cannot read and interpret a map for you. Heavy rain may make a burn impassable, snow may suggest a ridge or a terrace on a mountainside is wider than is actually the case, so you need to be able to work out and adjust routes as you go along. Moreover, batteries may run out. Mountain rescue on the islands gets calls from people in difficulty who can give a grid reference but have no idea what to do with that knowledge.

FISHING The isles have more than 2,000 fishable lochs. May–June and September are the best months for brown trout, while those in pursuit of salmon and sea trout should come from late June, when the salmon run, until October. The island watercourses are regarded locally as better than rivers in mainland Scotland for gillnetting for salmon. Other species include Arctic char, pollock, saithe, haddock and whiting.

Harris and the Uists are the main areas for loch fishing, with brown trout found in the highly fertile waters of South Uist. The lack of fish farms in the western watershed of South Uist has kept the gene pool so pure, according to locals, that it can be traced back to the Ice Age.

'This is simply a unique area,' says Donnie Maciver, angling promotion officer at the Outer Hebrides Fisheries Trust. 'You can come here, fish the sea lochs for a week and not see anyone else. You can fish in wild, remote and scenic places, such as the hills of Harris, or fish the trout lochs on the machair of South Uist and take in all the flora and fauna at the same time.'

It is not uncommon for visitors who have never fished in their lives to be beguiled by the prospect of doing so here. If the spell is cast on you, then you'll find the local fishing fraternity welcoming and happy to share their passion, basics and knowledge with you.

The right to fish any fresh water in Scotland is covered by Civil Law. In practice, this means the right belongs to the owner of the bank from which you fish. In short, you must seek approval from the owner of the land where you wish to fish, usually secured in the form of a permit.

There are two key – and excellent – sources of information on permits and where to fish. Fish Hebrides (☏ 01573 470612; w fishhebrides.com) and the Outer Hebrides Fisheries Trust (☏ 01851 703434; w outerhebridesfisheriestrust.org.uk).

MEDIA AND COMMUNICATIONS

MEDIA The venerable *Stornoway Gazette* (w stornowaygazette.co.uk) is the main source of news and continues to hold a degree of respect among the community, something long lost by many mainland newspapers. *Am Pàipear* (w ampaipear. org.uk), a community monthly newspaper distributed on the southern isles, has a similar reach and tone. The *West Highland Free Press* (w whfp.com), based on Skye, also covers news from the islands. Two good online sources of news are w hebrides-news.com and w welovestornoway.com (the latter is an often bouncy read offering insights into local matters and useful for short-notice listings of events). A magazine worth looking out for is *Scottish Islands Explorer* (w scottishislandsexplorer.com), which comes out every other month and includes a consistently good range of ultra-local features in the Outer Hebrides and, as the name suggests, beyond.

Isles FM 103 Community Radio (w isles.fm) is a mixture of local news, chat and music. BBC Radio Scotland (92.4–94.7FM; w bbc.co.uk/radioscotland) is the national station. All UK TV channels are available. Of less practical use to English speakers but perhaps of interest is that BBC Alba, the Scottish-language digital TV channel, has a major base in Stornoway. Some programmes the channel broadcasts are actually in English with Gaelic subtitles. The BBC Gaelic radio station, Radio nan Gàidheal, has its headquarters in the town.

2

INTERNET Many cafés and an increasing number of guesthouses and most hotels offer free Wi-Fi, although internet cafés themselves are a rarity.

Due to the population being widely distributed across a number of islands, traditional methods of providing broadband are impractical and leave those at great distances from their exchanges without a service. Instead, high-performance wireless is being used. Schools, health centres and council offices already receive a high-speed connection, and other parts of the islands are slowly gaining access to the network.

In practice, much of the time, Wi-Fi is 'island speed', which means that it can be intermittent and certainly slower than you may be used to back home. Hebnet is the island broadband service, providing connections of up to 2mbps through wireless antennae. Where accommodation providers offer Wi-Fi, they may request you not download films or large files so as to avoid clogging up the service for other users.

THE REVIVAL OF GAELIC IN THE OUTER HEBRIDES

It would be easy – and mistaken – to assume that Gaelic, like many minority languages the world over, is spoken only by the older population and shunned by younger generations. While visiting the Na Geàrrannan blackhouses on Lewis, I noticed the young staff taking orders for soup and souvenirs talking to each other in Gaelic. It turns out that Iain Murdo Macmillan had just graduated in Gaelic from the University of the Highlands and Islands, while his sister Kathryn was a school-leaver with similar plans. After finishing his summer job at Na Geàrrannan, he was to begin work as a primary school teacher in a school where only Gaelic is spoken for the first two years.

'I was brought up in a Gaelic household – my grandparents spoke it, my aunties too – and my parents insisted that only Gaelic was spoken in the house,' he says, before elaborating on why Gaelic is important to him. 'Gaelic is in our ancestry, it's the language of the croft, of the community. It's in my identity, it's more than just something that's spoken.'

A key driver has been the 2005 Gaelic Language Act, which gave the language a legal status it hadn't enjoyed in the past. Gaelic-medium primary schools are increasing, as are more regionalised Gaelic-focussed secondary schools. Just over half of all children in the Outer Hebrides go to Gaelic-medium schools, where they speak and learn Gaelic exclusively in their early years.

An additional curiosity gives Gaelic supporters hope that the language may yet truly thrive: the willingness of incomers, particularly those from England, to send their children to Gaelic schools. 'A lot of people who come into the islands are actively trying to learn it – especially the people who move in from England who are making such an effort to learn the language and the culture,' says Iain. Other simple measures could give Gaelic a boost among younger generations, he suggests. 'You don't have Gaelic on Facebook, or in Microsoft Word; we need that,' he says.

Bill Lawson of the Seallam! Visitor Centre on Harris (page 167) says that well-intentioned support for the language in isolation will not be enough. 'There are jobs opportunities in Gaelic, and learning it may keep you here. But the question, the problem, is how many children will stay here long enough to learn it on the islands? If there are no jobs for their parents, the pay is poor, and housing is expensive, they will leave for the mainland. You can't make a living or own a house just by cleaning a holiday home on a Saturday changeover.'

The picture is slowly changing as high-speed fibre broadband infrastructure is slowly rolled out across the Hebrides, initially along the main spine of the islands. Communities off the main route – of which there are many – are being upgraded by different means, as funding permits.

MOBILE PHONES Getting a signal can be a vexing and frustrating process, although coverage is improving all the time. You will have no problem in Stornoway but, elsewhere, many popular tourist destinations have little or no signal. New masts and 4G coverage have improved matters in Uig (in southwest Lewis), the Pairc (southeast Lewis) and both the west coast of South Harris and the eastern Bays area. Where coverage remains defiantly non-existent, you can sometimes snatch a signal on the brow of a hill, but things are often still hit and miss.

POST You will find small community post offices spread across the islands, often inside community shops and sometimes even in guesthouses. For such a rural location, they can have impressively long opening hours and retain their role as social and community hubs, where people come to do more than just buy stamps.

CULTURAL ETIQUETTE

The Gaelic name for the Outer Hebrides is Na h-Eileanan Siar, a title that cannot be rattled off by non-native tongues but instead must be enunciated carefully and slowly, reinforcing in a more literal sense the slow ethos that runs throughout the island chain. This means that a museum, shop or café may not always open at the very nanosecond it is supposed to. 'People rarely turn up late – it's just that we don't always turn up on time' is how one shopkeeper put it to me. You adjust quite quickly: there's no need to rush, you learn, they'll open up soon enough. One morning on Lewis, I woke up thinking it was a Tuesday. That evening, I realised it was actually a Wednesday. Not only was this the first time in my life that I had muddled up my days, I had missed a meeting with a senior politician in Stornoway. Rather than contrive a mishap, I admitted my sin, and awaited the deserved dismissive response. Not to worry, he laughed down the line, he too had overlooked the meeting as he had been busy helping his brother do some gardening.

That experience sums up how a relaxed approach to life runs through the Outer Hebrides. For there's an independent resilience, a phlegmatic pragmatism to the Western Isles, a good humour and a preparedness to take their environment, if not themselves, seriously. Time and time again, other local people have made the same point to me; comments that elsewhere might sound clichéd, but in the Outer Hebrides are said with meaning: 'the pace of life is different here', 'we have different values to the big cities', or 'our culture is distinct and alive'.

THE SABBATH Sunday observance is a part of the unique culture of the northern islands (Lewis, Harris and North Uist). Only partly in jest are self-catering visitors asked not to hang washing out on a Sunday; and tales persist about separating roosters from hens on a Saturday evening. While there has never been official confirmation of the story that the Free Church of Scotland successfully campaigned to stop NATO jets conducting training manoeuvres on Sundays, it is true that commercial flights from the mainland on a Sunday were only permitted in 2002 and that ferries have only sailed on Sundays since 2009.

The reality is that almost everything on the three islands is closed on Sundays. Even play parks are either locked or have signs requesting families to respect the

Sabbath. In recent years, universal closure has been slowly chipped away at the edges – a decision to allow a single petrol station to open on Sunday afternoons in Stornoway did not pass uncontested – but there is no sense that the tradition is under genuine threat. Sunday trading laws apply to larger supermarkets, but there is nothing to stop a small shop or café trading: generally, they choose not to, whether out of choice or to respect the sentiments of their community. Finally, the island council has a policy that all its properties be closed on Sunday, something that supporters of Sabbath observance say has been breached by the opening of a café in 2016 at the Museum nan Eilean in Stornoway.

That said, every year or so, another café on Lewis, Harris and even North Uist seems to nudge its door ajar on Sunday; meanwhile, Stornoway's An Lanntair arts centre now opens its doors and hosts cinema screenings on the last Sunday of the month and has tentatively mooted plans to open every Sunday. One concern in this regard is that staff at any venue are not pressurised to work on Sundays. Another minor but socially significant event has been the decision to enable 24-hour automated petrol pumps (where they exist) to operate on Sundays on Lewis and Harris.

There is still a way to go, however, for those pressing for more places to open on Sunday. Proposals to open Stornoway's golf club on Sundays were recently turned down flat, while a local campaign group, Families into Sport for Health, has met a similar impasse in persuading the island council to open its swimming pools on the Sabbath. A decisive shift may come in 2022 or thereabouts, when the deepwater port in Stornoway opens, providing greater access to the islands for cruise passengers and placing further pressure on outlets of all kinds to open their doors should an ocean liner arrive on a Sunday.

GRAVEYARDS A striking feature about the Outer Hebrides is the stirring location of many graveyards, many of them dramatically perched on headlands, all but pushing out into thin air above the ocean. Sometimes, the desire to capture an atmospheric image on camera can get the better of some visitors; again, you are asked to treat such places with respect by being discreet.

TRAVELLING POSITIVELY

It takes a certain kind of person to live in the Outer Hebrides; the corollary is that it also takes a certain kind of person to visit. The islands' popularity is only going to increase in years to come, and their future to a great extent depends on visitors, not just in the form of the tourist shilling but in the attitudes those tourists bring.

You can make a difference – give something back – by how you choose to shop. Online supermarket shopping has made it here, with delivery vans making the

PLAYING OUT ON A SUNDAY

On a visit with my three young children to Leverburgh one Sunday, I found the playground locked. It would have been easy to lift the children over the low metal perimeter fence but, before doing so, I thought it best to ask. Approaching the first person I saw, it was explained to me, patiently and politely, that it would be seen as deeply disrespectful. The elderly lady – who was on her way to church – thanked me for asking. We took our children to the beach instead: playgrounds are everywhere, Harris's beaches are rare and beautiful.

It's not unusual for visitors to the Outer Hebrides to get the bug and want to make a lifestyle change. House prices are significantly lower than on the mainland, or if you want to build your own property then Scotframe (w scotframe.co.uk) provide kit packages for bespoke house designs from your own architectural drawings. You will also need to understand the procedures relating to de-crofting. This is when agricultural land held by the crofter is re-zoned, allowing it to be used for purposes other than crofting, most commonly to build a house on. Island estate agents will advise you on this process.

Any decision to relocate here should follow a sojourn for the whole of January to see what you make of things out of season. It takes a certain kind of person to put up with barely 5 hours of daylight and gales that can last a week at a time. You can expect to be intermittently without a mobile phone signal or a landline, thanks to the vagaries of weather. In winter, there can be precious little open, and it helps to be comfortable in your own skin. As Margaret Fay Shaw once put it: 'It is difficult not to put one's house in the path of every storm that rages.'

There are certainly jobs to be had: key worker posts in the NHS and schools are regularly advertised; good, trusted builders will find themselves in high demand; and on the tourism front, a well-run B&B will be kept busy. The improving broadband picture means that working remotely (not just in the literal sense) is more feasible in the Outer Hebrides than it has ever been.

I once shared my own dreams of escape here with Lewis Mackenzie, who operates the Hebrides Fish 'n' Trips boat tour company, as we pulled up creels with crabs to take home for supper. Lewis smiled and spoke diplomatically. 'We see a few families that come here, have a wonderful holiday and decide to sell up and relocate,' he says. 'After the first winter most of them leave. A few stay on, saying that perhaps the first winter was unusually bad, that they were just unlucky. After the second winter, they go home.'

journey from Inverness. Visitors have a great deal of influence on whether or not local community-run stores stay open.

If you are in search only of a holiday comprising day after day of sunshine, where everything works like clockwork, your crisp bed linen is replaced daily, just so, then the Outer Hebrides are not for you. If you want to stay permanently connected to the rest of the world, to make video calls to friends on demand, download films to watch of an evening, be prepared for disappointment. Some visitors are also really challenged by this landscape of bare moorland and sometimes extreme weather; they have never seen anything like it.

The islands are not perfect, but if you come expecting them not to be perfect, then you will avoid disappointment. Places can have a bad day. If a restaurant has a limited menu, it may be because the ingredients are on a ferry cancelled on account of bad weather; a guesthouse may have to explain away a leaky roof because there is a shortage of builders. This is, remember, the northwestern extremity of the UK.

But if you fall in tune with the Outer Hebrides, the world has few places more enchanting to offer. Chris Ryan, who runs Out and About Tours, argues that 'there is nowhere else in the British Isles that matches this place. If you are interested in unspoilt places, this is truly wonderful. The culture sets it apart; it is so important here. There is an unhurried pace of life. There is no better place for wonderful scenery and to escape the rat race.'

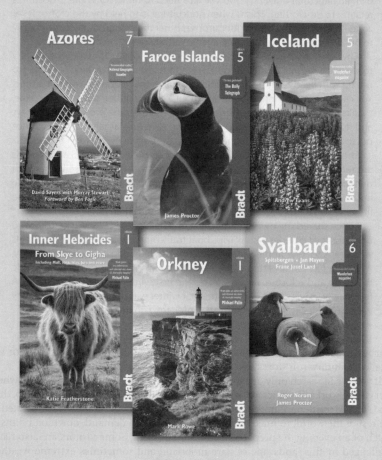

Part Two

THE GUIDE

3

Lewis (Leòdhais)

Lewis (Leòdhais in Gaelic) is the largest of the Outer Hebrides islands and by far the most populous, something that can seem improbable among the empty upland moors that dominate much of the island. The name derives from *leogach*, the Gaelic word for 'marshy', and that is certainly one of the words that springs to mind when you gaze across the phenomenally stark interior of this island.

Yet this is far from a monotonous and unpopulated landscape: the coastline is stupendous, with cliffs collapsing into bays along the west and east flanks. The coast is also where the vast majority of the population is found, most of them in the port of **Stornoway (Steòrnabhagh)**, the remainder in the many townships that inscribe the coastal contours of the island.

Much of the rest of Lewis consists of atmospheric moorland, dotted with sparkling freshwater lochans and bleak, seemingly endless bog. The dominant colours of this landscape of peat are hues of grey-green and russet-brown, occasionally speckled with tufts of wavy white bog cotton. Settlement mounds, cairns and long boundary walls that represent ancient township grazings seem to stretch out to vanishing points in the mires of the middle distance.

HIGHLIGHTS

Stornoway is the de facto capital of the Outer Hebrides and the only population centre that remotely fits the description of a town. It merits more time than most people tend to allow and has some good textile and art shops, a handful of fresh-faced, bright and breezy cafés, and the outstanding **island museum (Museum nan Eilean)**, which opened in 2016, documents the history of the Outer Hebrides and daily life. The most-visited site on Lewis – and the Outer Hebrides – is the collection of standing stones at **Callanish (Calanais)** on the west coast, which dates back 5,000 years and provides a haunting spectacle that arguably surpasses that of Stonehenge. Other major sites dot the west coast, including the broch of **Dùn Chàrlabhaigh** at **Carloway**.

Along the west and northwest coast, you will also find two **blackhouse** sites well worth visiting, at **Na Geàrrannan** and **Arnol**. The landscape here fractures into dramatic bays, geos (narrow, steep-sided clefts) and beautiful beaches at **Dalmore (Dail Mhòr)** and **Dalbeg (Dail Beag)**. The island tapers to a dramatic finale at the **Butt of Lewis** and the sprawling communities of **Ness (Nis)**, where sea stacks and startling cliffs create an edge-of-the-earth atmosphere.

The northeast of the island is Lewis's 'Empty Quarter', with a remote coastline and a littoral road that simply runs into the soil at the **Bridge to Nowhere**, north of **Tolsta (Tolastadh)**, a crushing testament to the failed dreams of Lord Leverhulme, who had planned to build an east-coast road linking Stornoway to Ness on the northern tip of Lewis. The interior here is bleak and comprises little more than blanket bog and moorlands, inlaid with peat cuts; it off... and is a birdwatcher's delight. Along the... townships such as **Back (Bac)** are rarely... walking and wildlife spotting. The same... also find the ruins of the **church of St C**... burial ground of the Macleod chiefs.

To the southeast of Stornoway lies o... **and South Lochs**, and the **Pairc**, a medie... to watch wildlife and sprinkled with a...

The southwest of Lewis is attache... **Bernera (Beàrnaraigh)**, a wildly rugg... and scattered with gorgeous locha... western Lewis lies **Uig (Ùig)** – not t... truly wild and remote atmosphere of Lewis is a...

The vast spectacle of **Uig Sands (Tràigh Ùige)** is nothing less than... is home to the enigma that is the **Lewis chessmen.** Further south, Uig fragments int... an elemental hotchpotch of cliffs, geos, hills and tiny townships such as **Mangersta (Mangarstadh)** that can feel more like Patagonia than the British Isles.

HISTORY

Lewis has been occupied by humans for 9,000 years and, over time, both the landscape and the way people have eked an existence from it have changed significantly. The 'peat-scapes' of Lewis are a relatively recent phenomenon in the island's geological timeline, developing only during the past 5,000 years. The interior was once more fertile, the climate drier. The first settlers of Lewis are thought to have been of Mediterranean origin; they were probably responsible for the building of the standing stones of Callanish (page 101).

Then Neolithic farmers began to clear areas of forest on a large scale and this, combined with grazing and a wetter climate, prevented trees from re-establishing and instead encouraged peat to form. At first, peat grew in small hollows but by

LEWIS

For listings, see from page 97, unless otherwise stated

🛏 **Where to stay**

1	Achmore Cottage	E5
	The Blue Bothy	
	(see Blue Pig Studio)	D4
2	Borve Country House	F2
3	Broad Bay House *p87*	G4
4	Callanish Camping Pods	D5
5	Clearview *p93*	E6
6	Creagan B&B	D5
7	Cross Inn	G1
8	The Decca	G1
9	Doune Braes	D4
10	Galson Farm	F2
11	Gealabhat Callanish B&B	D5
12	Glen House *p93*	F6
13	Lewis Longhouse *p88*	G4
14	Loch Erisort Inn *p93*	E6
15	Loch Roag Guest House	D5
16	Moorpark Cottages	F3
17	Na Geàrrannan	D4
18	Ravenspoint Hostel *p94*	F6
19	Ravenstar B&B *p88*	G4
20	Taigh Chailean *p93*	E6
21	Tigh Na Bruaich *p94*	E6
22	Whitefall Spa Lodges	D5

✖ **Where to eat and drink**

23	Bernera Community Café *p113*	C5
	Borve Country House	(see 2)
24	The Breakwater	G1
25	Café Roo	G5
26	Callanish Visitor Centre Café	D5
	Comunn Eachdraidh Nis Café	
	(see Ness Historical Society Museum)	G1
	The Decca	(see 8)
	Geàrrannan Blackhouse Café	(see 17)
27	Mollans	D3
	Morven Gallery (see Morven Gallery)	E3
	The Old Barn Bar	(see 7)
	Oystercatcher Tearoom	
	(see Coll Pottery Craft Centre) *p88*	G4
	Ravenspoint Café	(see 18)
28	Wobbly Dog of Lewis	G1

Flannan Isles

Roaireim
Eilean
a' Ghobha

A
1

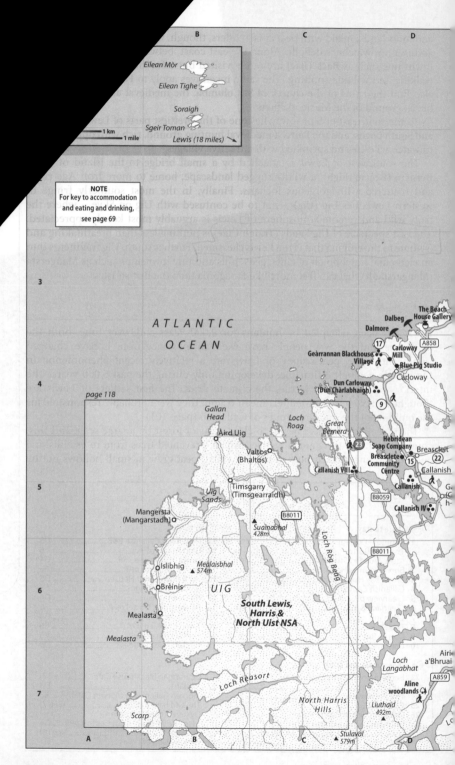

NOTE
For key to accommodation
and eating and drinking,
see page 69

B   **C**   **D**

Eilean Mòr

Eilean Tighe

Soraigh

Sgeir Toman

1 km

1 mile

Lewis (18 miles)

3

ATLANTIC

OCEAN

Dalbeg

The Beach
House Gallery

Dalmore

Geàrrannan Blackhouse
Village

17

Carloway
Mill

A858

Blue Pig Studio

4

Dun Carloway
(Dùn Chàrlabhaigh)

Carloway

page 118

9

Gallan
Head

Loch
Roag

Great
Bernera

Àird Uig

Hebridean
Soap Company

23

Valtos
(Bhaltos)

Breasclete
Community
Centre

15

Breasclete

22

Callanish VIII

Callanish

5

Uig
Sands

Timsgarry
(Timsgearraidh)

Callanish

B8059

Callanish IV

Mangersta
(Mangarstadh)

B8011

Suainabhal
428m

B8011

Islibhig

Mealaisbhal
574m

6

Brèinis

UIG

Mealasta

South Lewis,
Harris &
North Uist NSA

Mealasta

Airi
a'Bhruai

Loch
Langabhat

A859

Aline
woodlands

7

Loch Reasort

North Harris
Hills

Liuthaid
492m

Scarp

Stulaval
579m

A   **B**   **C**   **D**

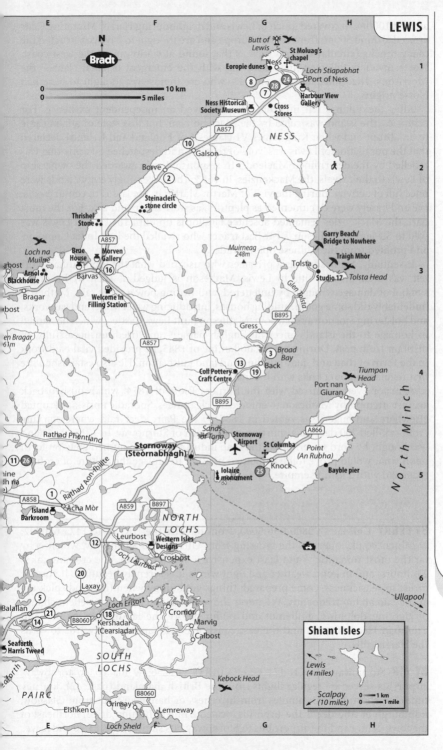

N

Bradt

0 _____ 10 km
0 _____ 5 miles

Butt of Lewis

St Moluag's chapel

Eoropie dunes

Ness

Loch Stiapabhat
Port of Ness

(8)

(28)

(24)

(7)

Harbour View Gallery

Ness Historical Society Museum

Cross Stores

NESS

A857

(10)

Galson

Borve

(2)

Steinacleit stone circle

Thrishel Stone

Muirneag 248m

Garry Beach/ Bridge to Nowhere

Tràigh Mhòr

Loch na Muilne

Brue House

Morven Gallery

A857

Tolsta

Studio 17   Tolsta Head

abost

Arnol Blackhouse

Barvas

(16)

Bragar

Welcome In Filling Station

Glen Tolsta

bost

en Bragar
61m

A857

Gress

B895

Tiumpan Head

Coll Pottery Craft Centre

(13)

(19)

3   Broad Bay

Back

Port nan Giuran

Rathad Phentland

B895

Sands of Tong

Stornoway Airport

St Columba

Point (An Rubha)

North Minch

(11) (26)

Stornoway (Steòrnabhagh)

A866

Knock

Bayble pier

nine
h na
e)

A858

(1)

Island Darkroom

Acha Mòr

A859   B897

Iolaire monument

(25)

NORTH LOCHS

(12)

Leurbost

Western Isles Designs

Crosbost

Loch Leurbost

Ullapool

(20)

Laxay

Balallan

(5)

(21)

(14)

B8060

(18)

Kershadar (Cearsiadar)

Loch Erisort

Cromor

Marvig

Calbost

Seaforth Harris Tweed

eaforth

SOUTH LOCHS

PAIRC

B8060

Kebock Head

Eishken

Orinsay

Lemreway

Loch Sheld

Shiant Isles

Lewis (4 miles)

Scalpay (10 miles)

0 ___ 1 km
0 ___ 1 mile

around 1000BC, it covered much of Lewis and neighbouring Harris. Migrating Celts arrived around 500BC from central Europe and are thought to have constructed the many brochs (circular towers) such as that found at Carloway on the west coast. Norse invaders followed, intermarrying with the emergent original clans – the Morrisons, Nicolsons and MacAuleys – who are themselves thought to have had Norse origins.

After the Vikings left in 1266, Lewis enjoyed an independent existence. For centuries, the island was ruled by the Macleod clan, but this state of affairs came to an abrupt end when King James VI (James I of England and Ireland) declared that the population of Lewis was 'void of religion' and despatched an army that was repelled by the determined Macleods. In response, James awarded the ownership of Lewis to their rivals, the Mackenzies, in 1613. These seemingly empty lands were once full of activity: during the visit of Martin Martin in the late 17th century, oats, rye and barely were documented as plentiful, as were hemp and flax. For the most part, the Mackenzies remained absentee landlords up until 1844 when Lewis was sold to Sir James Matheson, a Far East trader who rivalled the East India Company and profited from the Chinese opium trade.

Essentially, Matheson was a privateer who usurped what the island inhabitants felt was their historic title to Lewis. Matheson is judged as such by history, a symbol of damage wrought by unfettered landowning power. That said, Matheson undeniably did some good: building houses, introducing waterworks and gasworks, and bolstering Stornoway's harbour. Matheson built Lews Castle – which he named in homage to the island's ancestral English name – and tried, unsuccessfully, to distil tar from peat. During the potato famine of 1845, he provided vital paid work in the form of road and quay building and land cultivation. He also established the first regular shipping links with the mainland.

A major event occurred with the Bernera Riots of 1874, which pushed back against attempts by Matheson to enforce the clearances. Sporadic uprisings erupted elsewhere and anger was vented in 1887 by the Pairc deer raid where starving crofters killed 200 deer on a sporting estate south of Stornoway. In 1917, the island was bought by Lord Leverhulme, the soap industrialist, who immediately set forth upon what would prove to be a doomed mission to replace the culture of crofting (page 26) with a fishing empire.

GETTING THERE AND AWAY

BY FERRY CalMac (☎ 0800 066 5000; from outside the UK ☎ +44 1475 650397; w calmac.co.uk) operates the crossing from Ullapool to Stornoway, which is by far the most romantic – and least expensive – way to arrive. The crossing takes 2½ hours, and in good weather and light winds it is serenely beautiful. If you are prone to seasickness, come prepared: things get bumpy when the winds pick up, as they do all too frequently. Whatever the weather, you have an excellent chance of sighting dolphins, guillemot and puffin before the landmasses of Bac and Tiumpan Head emerge, and the east coast of Lewis tapers southwards towards the Harris hills.

BY AIR Stornoway Airport [71 G5] (☎ 01851 702256; w hial.co.uk/stornoway-airport) is served by regular flights from the British mainland (page 42). Journey times are short: just 40 minutes from Inverness or barely an hour from Glasgow, Edinburgh or Aberdeen. The airport is located 2 miles (10mins' drive) northeast of the town centre and the airport **bus** to Stornoway bus station costs £1.20 and leaves

Flying across the highlands and islands to Stornoway, depending on your attitude to flights in small aircraft, is either sensational or hair-raising. The small Dash-8 or de Havilland aircraft (and occasionally the larger Embraer) that ply this route mean you are almost guaranteed a window seat and, weather permitting, glorious views across northwest Scotland, including the Cuillin on Skye, Assynt, Wester Ross, Torridon and even as far north as Cape Wrath. Landfall on Lewis has its own beauty, too, as the aircraft crosses low over the isthmus by Loch Bràigh na h-Aoidhe and skirts above the beach at Mhealaboist. Nervous fliers should bear in mind that flights are delayed or cancelled only in extremely high winds (flights seem to depart even when storms confine the ferries to port). This means you may well experience the infamous sideways landing that enables small aircraft to combat crosswinds: the pilot will descend towards the runway at what seems like a right angle, turning the nose of the aircraft only at the very last moment. Look up these landings on the internet and they may give you the collywobbles; onboard, however, things can actually feel better than they appear from outside.

every other hour (no service on Sundays), which means the service does not always coincide with flights. A **taxi** costs £8–10 to the centre. There is usually a handful of cabs on the rank, but it's probably best to book in advance. Companies include A1 Taxis (m 07818 216970), Stornoway Taxi Services (☏01851 704444) and 24:7 Taxis (☏01851 702424), whose modest fleet includes a hybrid electric car.

The airport has a good café, the **Island Kitchen** (⊕ 07.00–19.00 Mon–Fri, 07.00–13.30 Sat, noon–17.30 Sun; £). Hot food is served until 30 minutes before closing time and includes large breakfasts, sandwiches, homemade soup and daily specials such as fajitas or chicken curry.

GETTING AROUND

BY CAR Lewis's roads are good, and you are likely to use three main thoroughfares regularly, all of which have one lane in each direction. The **A857** heads northwest from Stornoway across the moors to the west coast and gives you a good sense of how the land gently lifts and peels away northwards and upwards. The A857 merges with the **A858** at Barvas (Barabhas) just inland from the west coast and then (still the A857) heads up the coast for 18 miles to Ness and the Butt of Lewis. For southerly journeys out of Stornoway you'll use the **A859**, which runs all the way through Lewis and Harris to Leverburgh and Rodel, though for much of Harris the route becomes a single track with passing places.

The A858, meanwhile, can be confusing. In practice, though it is not signed as such, it peels off west from the A859 at Leurbost (Liurbost), 5 miles south of Stornoway, passes the turn-off for Uig (the **B8011**) at Garrynahine (Gearraidh na h-Aibhne) and veers north at Callanish along the west coast to Barvas.

Journey times are always longer than you expect. From Stornoway to the northerly tip of Lewis takes the best part of an hour; the sands of Uig are a 50-minute journey; if you travel all the way down the coast of Uig past Mangersta, you should allow the best part of 1½ hours. It is 51 miles from Stornoway to Leverburgh, which takes around 1½ hours.

Lewis (Leòdhais) GETTING AROUND

3

Two other single-track roads across the heartland of Lewis are worth using if you are not in a rush. The **Rathad Phentland** leaves Stornoway and gives wonderful views as it threads through the moor and cuts between the hills of Eitseal Bheag (to the south) and Beinn Bharabhais (to the north). After 3 miles, **a single-track spur of the A858**, the Rathad Aon-fhillte (translating as something approximate to 'the single, or simple, road'), forks left from the Rathad Phentland and cuts southwest over the moors for 5 miles to merge with the main A858 at **Acha Mòr**. Both these narrow roads pass lochs, old shielings (summer huts), and neglected crofts being overwhelmed inexorably by deergrass. In fine weather, the roads also give stirring views south of the hills of Harris and Uig. Towards its end, the Rathad Phentland splits, with a left fork heading to **Breascleit** and on to **Callanish**; the other track continues ahead and eventually tumbles off the moors and down into **Carloway**.

Car hire

🚗 **Car Hire Hebrides** [map, page 77]
📞 01851 706500; e bookings@carhire-hebrides. co.uk; w carhire-hebrides.co.uk; see ad, page 131. Operates out of Stornoway Airport &, for a fee, allows you to drop off in the southern isles out of Stornoway airport, and also has a base by the ferry terminal (📞 same number).

🚗 **Stornoway Car Hire** [map, page 77] 18 Inaclete Rd, Stornoway; 📞 01851 702658; e info@ stornowaycarhire.co.uk; w stornowaycarhire. co.uk. Can also collect & drop off at airport.

Petrol

Engebret is 1 of only 3 places on Lewis where you can buy petrol on Sun – the others are in the Lochs (page 95) & in Timsgarry in Uig (page 123).

⛽ **Engebret filling station** [map, page 77] Sandwick Rd; 📞 01851 702303; w engebret.co.uk; ⏰ 06.00–23.00 Mon–Sat, 10.00–16.00 Sun. Located on the A866 airport road & a 5min walk from the centre.

⛽ **Welcome In Filling Station** [71 F3] Lower Barvas (Barabhas); 📞 01851 840343; ⏰ 07.00–22.00 Mon–Sat. Adjacent to the junction of the A858 & A857.

BY BIKE Cycling around Lewis is entirely plausible and – given the right weather – enjoyable. If you plan to cycle the Hebridean Way (see box, page 50), try and save some energy, for that route, while spectacular, traverses only a limited slice of Lewis. Drivers are generally courteous and will give you a wide berth, and roads are in good condition. Easy day trips by bike from Stornoway include Tolsta and the Bridge to Nowhere, as well as Callanish. The flat, gently undulating roads that cut through Lewis's moorlands and up the island's west side towards Ness (where the road represents the Hebridean Way) also make for relatively easy cycling, though headwinds will slow you down. The Lochs' quiet roads and unending opportunities to pause for views are ideal for two wheels, too (though their unimproved lanes mean you'll be comforted by that puncture repair kit you remembered to bring). The casual cyclist may find Uig's sweeping valleys and abrupt hills harder work, but the paybacks include stunning coastal views around Uig Sands and the blissful solitude of Mangersta and Mealasta.

Cycle hire
See also Bike Hebrides (opposite).

🚲 **AD Cycle Centre** [map, page 82] 67 Kenneth St, Stornoway; 📞 01851 704025; w stornowaycyclehire.co.uk

🚲 **Bespoke Bicycles** [map, page 77] Willowglen Rd, Stornoway; m 07876 570932;

⏰ 09.00–18.00 Mon–Sat. Owner Alistair Glover is immensely helpful, will repair bikes & has reciprocal drop-off arrangements with Barra Bike Hire (page 271), which is of great help to those hiring bikes for the Hebridean Way, saving you the return journey. Runs the Hub Café (page 81) on the same site.

BY BUS Just about all buses run to and from Stornoway or go through it en route to their destination. Most services run daily, apart from Sunday when there is no public transport. Services **W2** and **W10** are the ones visitors are most likely to use. W2 is known as the Westside Circular and travels west from Stornoway to Callanish via Barvas, Shawbost and Carloway. The W10 links Stornoway to Tarbert and Leverburgh, a journey of around 3 hours; this takes longer as the journey is broken in Tarbert. From Stornoway to Tarbert the journey time is 1 hour and from there to Leverburgh and Rodel is a further ¾ hour.

Of other lines, the W1 travels from Stornoway all the way up to Port of Ness. The W3 links Stornoway to Bosta at the northern tip of Great Bernera. The W4 runs from Stornoway to Uig and Uig Sands then goes all the way down to Brenish (Brèinis) at the bottom of the B8011. Tolsta and the airport are served by the W5, the Lochs area by W8 and W9. For the latest timetables, visit w cne-siar.gov.uk/roads-travel-and-parking/public-transport/bus-services/bus-services-overview.

BY TAXI There's usually a short line of cabs waiting for business by the Perceval Square car park in Stornoway; they serve both short and longer journeys, though for the latter you should book ahead just to be sure.

🚗 **Quick Cabs** 📞01851 701234; w taxistornoway.co.uk

🚗 **Stornoway Taxi & Courier Service** 📞01851 704444; w stornowaytaxis.co.uk

TOURIST INFORMATION

The **Visit Scotland Stornoway iCentre** (26 Cromwell St, Stornoway; 📞01851 703088; w visitscotland.com; ⊕ Jun–Sep 09.00–17.45 Mon–Sat, Oct–May varying times Mon–Sat – call ahead or check website). The centre has a good selection of guidebooks, related literature and souvenirs, and staff are helpful and knowledgeable.

FESTIVALS AND EVENTS

You'll find a steady stream of festivals and activities throughout the year that can shed light on island life or make use of the landscape and elements. February sees the **Hebridean Dark Skies Festival** (w lanntair.com/creative-programme/darkskies), while April visitors can catch the Donald Macleod Memorial Piping Competition. July brings the Hebridean Celtic Festival or Hebcelt (w hebceltfest.com), a celebration of Celtic music held in the grounds of Lews Castle in Stornoway. Book festival Faclan (w faclan.org) is held in Stornoway in November.

TOUR OPERATORS AND ACTIVITIES

Bike Hebrides m 07775 943355; w bikehebrides.com. Rents bikes & kayaks, advises where to go & offers excursions by bike & kayak.

✳ 🛶 **Hebrides Fish 'n' Trips** 📞01851 871165; m 07778 786901; e hebfishntrips@yahoo.co.uk; w hebridesfishntrips.co.uk. Run out of Keos (Ceos) in the Lochs by Lewis Mackenzie. Mackenzie runs trips around the eastern waters of Lewis, primarily between Loch Erisort & Loch Shell, looking for white-tailed eagles & seals, & doing a spot of mackerel fishing. Prices are £150 for 2hrs/£220 for 3hrs, max 3 passengers. Mackenzie is licensed by RSPB & Scottish Natural Heritage to interact with the eagles, allowing passengers to see & photograph these huge birds at close range.

Immerse Hebrides m 07920 111390; e info@immersehebrides.com; w immersehebrides.com. Qualified instructors offer guided wild swimming in lochs & along the shores of both Lewis & Harris. Options for both beginners & more experienced open swimmers wanting to swim between outer islands (see box, page 60).

◢ **Sea Lewis** ☎01851 702303; e sealewis850@ gmail.com; w sealewis.co.uk. Runs trips around the east coast of Lewis & to the Shiant Isles.

◢ **Seatrek** ☎01851 672469; e bookings@ seatrek.co.uk; w seatrek.co.uk. Based in Miabhaig on Uig. Offers boat & RIB trips mainly to the southwest coast of Lewis, including trips around Gallan Head, into Loch Roag to look for otters & to nearby islands such as Pabbay, which has a striking natural arch & lagoon that can only be seen by boat. A 2hr or half-day trip typically cost the same (adults £42, children £32). Also runs trips to St Kilda (page 186).

◢ **Stornoway Seafari** ☎0800 246 5609; e stornowayseafari@gmail.com; w stornowayseafari.com. Runs trips to Shiant Isles & other excursions down to the lochs along the eastern shores of North Harris.

Surf Lewis m 07920 427194; e info@surflewis. co.uk; w surflewis.co.uk. Offers lessons for beginners & advanced surfers off beaches, reefs & headlands across Lewis & Harris. Rents boards & wetsuits. Also offers paddleboards, coasteering & snorkelling.

STORNOWAY (STEÒRNABHAGH)

For most people, Stornoway is their first and usually fleeting port of call in the Outer Hebrides. The majority of visitors drive off the ferry and disappear into Lewis's hinterland but there is certainly enough to keep you here for a day, perhaps more. An excellent museum of island life, inaugurated in 2016, has added to the town's appeal: there's a working quayside, shop-lined streets overlooking the marina and a Victorian pedestrian quarter. Much of this modest bustle is overlooked by the mock-Tudor Lews Castle, around which the River Creed meanders its way into the Minch.

Stornoway's population was precisely 8,038, according to the 2011 census, which accounts for almost a third of the entire population of the Outer Hebrides. This represents a 5% increase on 2001 and reflects a wider trend of the islands' population concentrating in the town. Construction, transport, storage, public administration, and health and social work are major employers. The Job Seeker's Allowance claimant rate across the Outer Hebrides is just 3.3%, slightly below the Scottish average. All streets in Stornoway are signposted prominently in Gaelic, with the English translation usually given in smaller print, which can be hard to pick out if you are driving; despite this, almost everyone uses the Anglicised names. The main streets you are likely to encounter are Cromwell Street (Sràid Chrombail), Church Street (Sràid na h-eaglaise), Kenneth Street (Sràid Choinnich), Point Street (Sràid an Ruibha) and Francis Street (Sràid Fhrangain). Cromwell Street, Point Street and the intersection between the two is where most interest and shops are to be found.

Apart from the hotels, just one shop and the occasional café or baker's open on Sundays. For some visitors this can be frustrating, for others – and not just those of a religious disposition – it represents a rare chance to experience the sound of silence in a town.

Stornoway's sleepy atmosphere may change as the town's port authority progresses plans to convert the harbour into a deepwater port. Mindful that cruise ships are unable to dock in the port – instead they must land passengers by tender – the harbour authority hopes that a new deepwater berthing facility along the quayside will attract a further 40 cruise ships to the island every year. The development would also enhance the existing marina and provide more berths for visiting yachts. The deepwater component of the plan is scheduled for completion by 2022 and has aroused mixed feelings among residents: while the economic case for attracting cruise passengers who generally head for Orkney

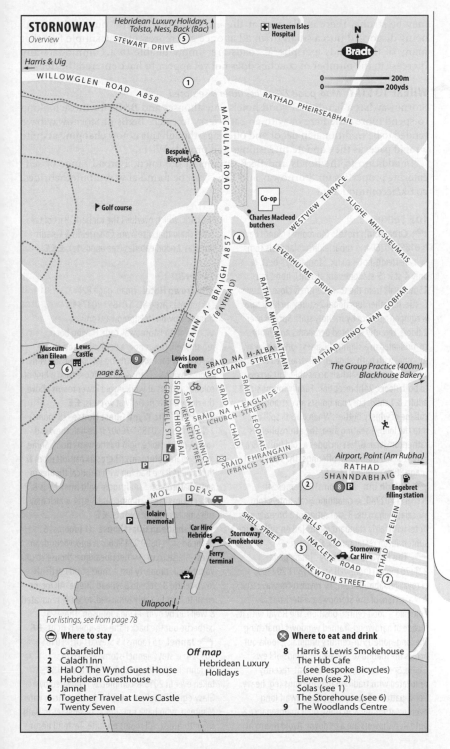

For listings, see from page 78

Where to stay

1 Cabarfeidh
2 Caladh Inn
3 Hal O' The Wynd Guest House
4 Hebridean Guesthouse
5 Jannel
6 Together Travel at Lews Castle
7 Twenty Seven

Off map
Hebridean Luxury
Holidays

Where to eat and drink

8 Harris & Lewis Smokehouse
   The Hub Cafe
   (see Bespoke Bicycles)
   Eleven (see 2)
   Solas (see 1)
   The Storehouse (see 6)
9 The Woodlands Centre

may be strong, there is disquiet at the intrusion that several hundred tourists being disgorged into a small town all at once can represent. The simple fact that many of the islands' peripheral roads are simply unable to accommodate any increase in the number of coaches does not yet appear to have entered the debate.

🏠 WHERE TO STAY *Map, page 77, unless otherwise stated*

Stornoway has a handful of good hotels, guesthouses and B&Bs for those looking to spend more time here or with an early ferry to catch. B&Bs in Stornoway have tended to be traditional in décor and offerings, though this is now changing at quite a rapid pace, as they update furnishings and provide Wi-Fi.

In addition to the hotels and B&B options in the town, a broad range of self-catering properties for Stornoway and Lewis can be found at w visitouterhebrides. co.uk/accommodation.

Top range

🏠 **Cabarfeidh Hotel** (46 rooms) Manor Park; ☏ 01851 702604; e cabarfeidh@calahotels.com; w cabarfeidh-hotel.co.uk. Stornoway's best, & only 4-star (5-star ones are absent), hotel is a 15min walk from the town centre & close to Lews Castle. Its rather functional 2-storey architecture is compensated for by friendly staff. Spread over 2 floors, recently updated bedrooms are colour co-ordinated in a slightly business-oriented way. All come with bath, shower, toiletries, tea & coffee. 1 twin room is wheelchair accessible. Lift access to both floors; 24hr reception. Family rooms suit 2 adults & 1 child. Cosy bar boasts an extraordinary collage of whisky bottles. When guests spill out into the lobby's seating area, the atmosphere is rather convivial. B/fast includes a cold buffet & à la carte cooked traditional offerings. The restaurant (page 80) is excellent. **£££**

🏠 **Caladh Inn** (69 rooms) 11 James St; ☏ 01851 702740; e caladhinn@calahotels.com; w caladhinn.co.uk. 3-star rating in a breezily run hotel with fairly standard rooms (all en suite). Fine, subterranean restaurant. **£££**

🏠 **The Royal Stornoway** [map, page 82] (26 rooms) Cromwell St; ☏ 01851 702109; e royal@calahotels.com; w royalstornoway.co.uk. A real fixture of the Stornoway waterfront, & enjoying a good central position, the Royal with its façade of hardwood-framed windows (matching the long-gone 19th-century originals), looks out across the marina to the leafy grounds of Lews Castle. Some rooms, mainly at front, recently renovated with traditional furnishings (eg: heavy, floral-patterned curtains); others await long-overdue attention & in these poor maintenance & outdated showers are a letdown. Avoid rooms at

the back, which overlook the car park. Part of Cala hotel chain that also owns Cabarfeidh & Caladh Inn. Has 2 good eateries (see opposite). **£££**

Mid-range

🏠 **Crown Hotel** [map, page 82] (16 rooms) Castle St; ☏ 01851 703734; e info@crownhotelstornoway.com; w crownhotelstornoway.com. Having been refurbished, this is now a perfectly good choice, particularly for those arriving late or leaving early. Rooms swish & clean, & there's more than a hint of colour schemes at work. Avoid lower rooms above the noisy bar, especially at w/ends. **££**

🏠 **Hal O' The Wynd Guest House** (5 rooms) 2 Newton St; ☏ 01851 706073; w halothewynd. com. A good choice right by the waterfront. Some rooms share bathrooms. There's a cosy loft room & the owners have had fun with nautical themes in some bathrooms. Family room with bunk beds & 2 other rooms can accommodate 3 sgls, which may suit small groups of cyclists. **££**

🏠 **Hebridean Guesthouse** (11 rooms) 61 Bayhead St; ☏ 0800 054 9866; e info@hebridean-guest-house.co.uk; w hebrideanguesthouse.co.uk. Voluminous property just a short stroll north of town centre & close to Bayhead Bridge. All rooms en suite. Comfortably furnished, recently renovated & well run by owner Linda Johnson. There's a barbecue out the back if the weather is right. **££**

🏠 **Jannel** (5 rooms) 5 Stewart Dr; ☏ 01851 705324; e stay@jannel-stornoway.co.uk; w jannel-stornoway.co.uk. A charming B&B, taken over in 2013 & completely renovated by Glaswegian Paul Ramsay & his South African wife, Maureen, who have run similar businesses in Bath & South Africa. All rooms en suite. Tasteful décor throughout, including Harris Tweed curtains, local art & Paul's own landscape photography. The biggest & brightest room is number 4 (in the loft), but you can't go wrong here. The very friendly owners give good advice on places to visit across the islands. Located a 15min walk north of the town centre, near Cabarfeidh Hotel. The unusual name is an amalgamation of the name of the previous owner, Nelson, & his sister, Janet. **££**

🏠 **Stornoway B&B** [map, page 82] (5 rooms) 29 Kenneth St; m 07917 035295; e stay@ hebgroup.co.uk; w stornowaybedandbreakfast. co.uk. Housed in a 175-year-old building & recently renovated, with Harris Tweed trimmings, to 4-star standard by hosts Graham & Rachel McLellan. 'We used the renovation to make things a bit arty,' says Graham. Rooms over 3 storeys. All are en suite, with TV & Wi-Fi. The attic room with dormer feels particularly secluded. Behind the property, there's also a cosy self-catering flat with a mezzanine level, kitchenette, private decking & patio (sleeps 2; 2-night min, £170 in total). **££**

🏠 **Twenty Seven** (4 rooms) 27 Newton St; ☎ 01851 701782; e stay@ stornowaybedandbreakfast.com; w stornowaybedandbreakfast.com. All rooms overlook the harbour. Private showers. Recently modernised with clean lines & snug guest lounge. **££**

Budget

✳ 🏠 **Heb Hostel** [map, page 82] (4 bunkrooms) 25 Kenneth St; ☎ 01851 709889; e christine@hebhostel.com; w hebhostel.com. This popular hostel is well run & has a guest lounge with TV, computer & Wi-Fi. There's a kitchen for

guest use with basics such as bread & cereals provided & cooking facilities for hot meals. The women-only bunkroom has a standalone en-suite bath that adds an unexpected touch of luxury. There's a men-only dormitory, a mixed room & a family room in the loft which sleeps 4. There's also a laundry, bike lock-up, small garden overlooked by a tree house (the latter sadly for hosts' use only) & a grotto-like summerhouse that conceals an indoor barbecue (hugely popular in dry weather). Family owners live on the premises & contribute a great deal to the welcoming feel. **£**

Self-catering

🏠 **Hebridean Luxury Holidays** m 07917 035295; e stay@hebgroup.co.uk; w hebrideanluxuryholidays.co.uk. The first 5-star self-catering on Lewis is tucked away in the suburb of Laxdale, 1.2 miles north of town. This collection of 4 lodges includes 2 with hot tubs & spa baths with star ceilings. 2 are suited to families & larger groups; 2 are ideal for couples. A 5th property, a beautifully renovated croft house 1 mile east of town in Sandwick, has recently opened & is of equally high standard. From £999/ week. **££/£££**

🏠 **Together Travel at Lews Castle** (23 apts) Lews Castle; ☎ 01625 416430; e info@ togethertravel.co.uk; w togethertravel.co.uk/ destinations/scotland/lews-castle. Luxury international & environmentally prescient group Together Travel (formerly Natural Retreats) has converted the upper 2 storeys of Lews Castle into apts to an extremely high specification. From £879/week. **££/£££**

✗ **WHERE TO EAT AND DRINK** *Map, page 82, unless otherwise stated*
The food-and-drink scene in Stornoway is changing quickly, with a smattering of new cafés and restaurants heralding a challenge to the rather humdrum offerings that used to typify the town. You can describe some experiences as 'fine dining' without a trace of irony, and decent, fresh coffee is readily available. You will need to plan ahead for Sundays, however, when only the hotels and a couple of cafés are open for food.

Expensive

✗ **Boatshed Restaurant** Royal Stornoway, Cromwell St; ☎ 01851 702109; w royalstornoway. co.uk/slider/boatshed-restaurant-2; ⊕ noon– 14.30 Fri–Sat, 17.30–21.00 Mon–Sat, Apr–Sep also noon–15.00 & 17.00–21.00 Sun. The formal

dining offering of the Royal Stornoway (see opposite), overseen by head chef Dahi from Nepal, has the same creative bug as its rivals, serving starters of scallops with chargrilled polenta or seafood tacos & meaty mains such as poached venison with puff pastry, as well as monkfish wrapped in smoked bacon. Desserts range from orange & marmalade pudding to a good regional cheeseboard. £££

✳ ✖ **Digby Chick** 5 Bank St; ☎01851 700026; w digbychick.co.uk; ⏲ noon–14.00, 17.30–18.30 & 19.00–21.00 Mon–Sat. The original recognisably high-end restaurant in Stornoway is still by some distance the best, not only here but in the entire Outer Hebrides, with an eye-catching menu that ranges from guinea fowl lollipops (in reality, swish kebabs) to pigeon breast with black pudding & turbot caught in the Minch served with langoustines. Save space for dessert such as brioche, peanut butter & white chocolate pudding or coconut crème brûlée with citrus shortcake. Presentation by chef/proprietor James Mackenzie is stunning & you may be left wondering if *The Great British Bake Off* has decamped to these islands. Also offers a set lunch for £16.50 & a 3-course early dinner menu (⏲ 17.30–18.30) for £26.50. £££

✖ **Solas** [map, page 77] Cabarfeidh Hotel, Manor Park, Perceval Rd South; ☎01851 702604; e cabarfeidh@calahotels.com; w cabarfeidh-hotel.co.uk/restaurant-in-stornoway; ⏲ noon–14.00 & 17.00–21.00 Mon–Sat, 12.15–14.30 & 18.00–21.00 Sun. Another good choice with excellent steaks, venison & shellfish, puddings such as rhubarb crumble with blood orange ice cream or coconut & mango tapioca. Good picks include salmon & lemon crab cake with squid ink (£16.95), mussels from Leurbost down the road with smoked paprika & chorizo cream (£7.25) & Lewis lamb (£19.50) for a main. Also offers a fixed-price à la carte menu ⏲ 17.00–21.00 Mon–Sat (3 courses for around £30). Sun menu includes traditional roasts. Extensive wine list. 'Solas' is Gaelic for 'light' – the architects matched the name with the large windows & an open feel, though they could do little about the view over the hotel car park. The chef's provision of take-away explanatory notes for a dish of the day is a nice touch. ££/£££

Mid-range

✖ **Eleven** [map, page 77] Caladh Inn, 11 James St; ☎01851 702740; e caladhinn@calahotels.com; w caladhinn.co.uk; ⏲ noon–14.00 daily, 17.00–21.00 (inc fixed-price early dinner 17.00–19.00) Mon–Sat, noon–16.00 & 17.00–20.00 Sun. Popular buffet lunches: dishes range from chicken with haggis to stir fries. For a restaurant attached to a 3-star hotel, food is of a commendably high standard. ££

✖ **Harbour Kitchen** 5 Cromwell St; ☎01851 706586; f HarbourKitchenSTY; ⏲ noon–14.30 & 17.00–21.00 Tue–Sat. Hearty meals in a bistro-style atmosphere. Choices range from ½kg (1kg if you can manage it) of mussels in cream sauce to salmon salad with mango & chilli. ££

✖ **Harbour View Restaurant** Crown Hotel (page 78); ⏲ noon–20.00 daily. The restaurant has come on in leaps & bounds in recent years & is now a good choice for dinner. Mackerel salad & smoked crab are among the picks, plus buttermilk waffles with bacon. Strong on gluten-free & vegan options. ££

✖ **Harris & Lewis Smokehouse** [map, page 77] Sandwick Rd; ☎01851 619238; e info@harrisandlewis.co.uk; w harrisandlewis.co.uk; ⏲ 08.00–22.00 Mon–Fri, 09.00–22.00 Sat. As the name suggests, smoked salmon is at the heart of this new venture, with fish prepared in the adjacent smokery (you can see the fish being processed through a large window at the back of the open kitchen). Mains include fish tacos, duck salads & rib-eye steaks. Save room for puddings that include lemon pavlova & apple zefir (a sponge with seasonal jam). Also serves b/fast until 11.00. Mezzanine floor seating adds another touch of style. ££

✖ **An Lanntair (Lantern arts centre)** Kenneth St; ☎01851 708480; e info@lanntair.com; w lanntair.com; ⏲ 10.00–late Mon–Sat (b/fast 10.00–noon, lunch & dinner noon–20.00), 13.30–17.00 last Sun of month. This modern airy café & restaurant in Stornoway's vibrant arts, music & film centre sells cakes, coffee, beer, wine & cocktails. For more substantial meals, they serve excellent main courses such as chowder of local haddock & salmon (£7.50) along with pasta dishes, risotto, gourmet burgers, salads & a traditional cooked b/fast. Fri evenings is steak night & good value: 2 steaks & bottle of wine for £35. In addition to hosting regular exhibitions & displays, An Lanntair houses a cinema showing the latest releases. £/££

✳ ✖ **Artizan** 12 Church St; ☎01851 706538; ⏲ 10.00–17.30 Mon–Sat (lunch noon–14.30). This combined café, wine bar & art gallery is a delight: truly original & something Stornoway has long been crying out for. The ground floor is a licensed café serving light meals such as tapas, platters of ricotta cheese & Parma ham, ciabattas & soup, accompanied by a good wine list, craft ales

& Harris gin. 'We've sort of grown arms & legs as we go along,' laughs owner Alison Cunningham, summing up the place nicely. 'We didn't want to do bacon rolls & supermarket bread, we wanted to do something different, something nicer,' she says. 'We'd gone on holiday many times & seen cafés that did things well. We tucked things away in our heads then finally got round to it.' The colour scheme – pastels & shades of ocean blue – are, Alison says with admirable candour, lifted from the colour scheme of the settings dial of her washing machine. Artwork hangs on the walls & upstairs there is also a showroom for small independent Scottish designers. £/££

✖ **HS-1 Café Bar** Royal Stornoway, Cromwell St; ✆ 01851 702109; w royalstornoway.co.uk/hs-1-cafe-bar-in-stornoway; ⏱ noon–late Mon–Sun. Located on the other side of the entrance to the hotel, this bistro-café is usually bustling & bright: something of an evening social centre for families & groups. Dishes are eclectic to say the least, with something for everyone, though the food you eat can be less creative than the menu suggests, such as a tower of black pudding & haggis. Pizzas & curries are particular strong points. Name comes from the postcode of the hotel. £/££

✖ **The Storehouse** [map, page 77] Lews Castle; w lews-castle.co.uk; ⏱ 09.00–16.00 daily; whisky bar ⏱ until 23.00 Sun–Thu, until 01.00 Fri–Sat. Hot drinks, cakes, bacon rolls & seafood platters. Run by the Together Travel group just across the lobby from the museum. The decision to open on Sun was fiercely criticised by those keen to preserve the Sabbath but, judging by how busy it gets, most locals & visitors clearly think otherwise. On a wet & windy Sun morning it's a lifesaver for visiting families in particular. Whisky bar is rather stately in design & has a wide range of tipples. £

Cheap and cheerful

✖ **The Blue Lobster** Cromwell St Quay; m 07909 728548; ⏱ 09.30–17.00 Tue–Sat. Friendly, light & airy café with good views over the marina. Excellent coffee & formidable range of homemade bakes & cakes including banana, pineapple-&-passionfruit or raspberry-&-white chocolate friand. Small gift shop including mix of local artwork. £

✖ **Cameron's Chip Shop** 33 Point St; ✆ 01851 703200; ⏱ 11.30–21.00 Mon–Sat. Boasts a clutch of regional & national awards. Stornoway has few vantage points with benches for you to sit & gaze out to sea as you munch & the quayside mooring posts behind the tourist office are your most atmospheric bet. £

✖ **Church Street Chip Shop** 6 Church St; ✆ 01851 288020; ⏱ 11.30–14.30 & 16.30–21.00 Mon–Thu, 11.30–22.00 Fri–Sat, 16.30–19.30 Sun. This chippie tucked away in Church St is also hugely popular & marginally cheaper than its rival. £

✖ **The Hub Café** [map, page 77] Willowglen Rd; m 07876 570932; ⏱ 10.00–17.00 Mon–Sat. New venture by local cycle shop owner offering hot rolls, cakes & hot drinks, with plans for more substantial dishes. £

✖ **Kopi Java** 87 Cromwell St; ✆ 01851 700477; e kopijava1@gmail.com; ⏱ 08.00–18.00 Mon–Sat. Run by local islander Alana & her Indonesian husband, William Poernomo, who met when William travelled solo around the Hebrides – presumably one of the very few Indonesians to do so. The coffee is their own blend sourced from several countries. They also serve homemade cakes & quiches. £

✖ **The Woodlands Centre** [map, page 77] Castle grounds, Lews Castle; ✆ 01851 706916; ⏱ 09.30–17.00 (lunch 13.00–15.00) Mon–Sat. Run by the Stornoway Trust on the site of an old sawmill. Good coffee & cakes plus lunches of the quiche & panini variety. Friendly staff recently added excellent pizzas (£6.95) to their repertoire to eat in or take away. Comfy sofas on the mezzanine level & tables carved from trees from the surrounding castle grounds. If weather is favourable, there is a pleasant outside seating area by the River Creed, overhung with mature woodland. There is also a small gift shop selling local crafts, other souvenirs & booklets. £

ENTERTAINMENT AND NIGHTLIFE It's fair to say that few of Stornoway's pubs are oriented to the tourist trade. Some can reasonably be described as 'rough and ready' come Friday and Saturday evenings, and can be dominated by huge sports screens. It's also true that very few visitors indeed come to the Outer Hebrides for the sole purpose of seeking out Stornoway's pubs. That's not to say that you should give up on an evening tipple altogether: just by sticking your nose in the door you'll be

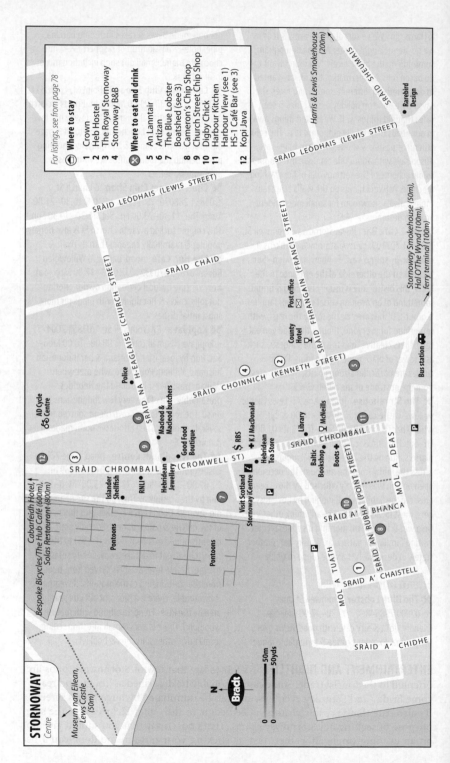

STORNOWAY

Centre

Museum nan Eilean,
Lews Castle (50m)

Bespoke Bicycles/The Hub Café (50m),
Cabarfeidh Hotel (600m),
Solas Restaurant (800m)

Stornoway Smokehouse (50m),
Hal O'The Wynd (100m),
ferry terminal (100m)

Harris & Lewis Smokehouse (200m)

Rarebird Design

SRÀID SHEUMAIS

SRÀID LEÒDHAIS (LEWIS STREET)

SRÀID LEÒDHAIS (LEWIS STREET)

SRÀID CHAID

SRÀID FHRANGAIN (FRANCIS STREET)

SRÀID NA H-EAGLAISE (CHURCH STREET)

SRÀID CHOINNICH (KENNETH STREET)

Police

AD Cycle Centre

Madeod & Madeod butchers

Good Food Boutique

County Hotel

Post office

SRÀID CHROMBAIL (CROMWELL ST)

Islander Shellfish

RNLI

Hebridean Jewellery

KJ MacDonald

RBS

Hebridean Tea Store

Visit Scotland Stornoway iCentre

Library

McNeills

Baltic Bookshop

Boots

SRÀID CHROMBAIL

SRÀID AN RUBHA (POINT STREET)

SRÀID A' BHANCA

MOL A DEAS

Bus station

MOL A TUATH

SRÀID A' CHAISTELL

SRÀID A' CHIDHE

Pontoons

Pontoons

For listings, see from page 78

Where to stay

1. Crown
2. Heb Hostel
3. The Royal Stornoway
4. Stornoway B&B

Where to eat and drink

5. An Lanntair
6. Artizan
7. The Blue Lobster
   Boatshed (see 3)
8. Cameron's Chip Shop
9. Church Street Chip Shop
10. Digby Chick
11. Harbour Kitchen
    Harbour View (see 1)
    HS-1 Café Bar (see 3)
12. Kopi Java

N

Bradt

0   50m
0   50yds

able to gauge whether a place is for you. **McNeills** [map, opposite] (11 Cromwell St) currently has a good reputation and boasts an open fire; it featured in *The Blackhouse*, part of the Peter May Trilogy (page 33). The Harbour Bar at the back of the **Crown Hotel** (page 78) has benefited from a refurbishment and sells regional craft beers. Another decent choice is the cocktail bar at the **County Hotel** [map, opposite] (12–14 Francis St; ✆ 01851 703250; w countyhotelstornoway.co.uk). In truth, though, **An Lanntair** (page 80), while veering towards the arty rather than the distinctively local, is, along with the bar at the Crown Hotel, by some distance your best option for an evening drink.

SHOPPING Stornoway has a good choice of places for **food shopping** where you can put together a picnic or stock up for self-catering. Everywhere, though, you'll notice the impact on local prices of importing fresh fruit and vegetables. For a large all-in-one shop, head for the substantial **Co-op** (Macauley Rd; ⊕ 06.00–23.00 Mon–Sat) on the A857 to the north of town, a 10-minute walk from the centre. Nearby is a good independent butcher, **Charles Macleod** (Ropework Park, Matheson Rd; ✆01851 702445; e sales@charlesmacleod.co.uk; w charlesmacleod.co.uk; ⊕ 08.00–17.00 Mon, 08.00–17.30 Tue–Fri, 09.00–17.00 Sat). In the town centre is another good butcher's, **Macleod & Macleod** (17 Church St; ✆01851 703384; e littlefatbutcher@btinternet.com; w macleodandmacleod.co.uk; ⊕ 07.30–17.30 Mon–Sat, closed 13.00–14.00 Mon–Wed). They have another outlet (45 Westview Tce; ⊕ 07.30–13.00 & 14.00–17.30 Mon–Tue, 09.30–17.30 Wed, 07.30–17.30 Thu–Sat) just behind the Co-op. All these butchers sell Stornoway black pudding (see box, page 84), which now enjoys protected domain status, along with white and fruit variations. Ask and they will wrap it up for you in a natty branded canvas bag.

You'll find the best bread in Stornoway at the **Blackhouse Bakery** (Plasterfield; ✆01851 702804; w blackhousebakery.com; ⊕ 08.00–20.00 Mon–Fri, 09.00–18.00 Sat, 10.00–16.00 Sun). Their French bread, bloomers, different varieties of grains and filling hot rolls are all excellent. The location, in a suburb a good mile's (1½km) walk from the town centre and at the back of the airport, makes it tricky to get to unless you're in a car, in which case, stock up. On Sundays it can feel as though half the town is in there.

The most accessible local bread in Stornoway – from a visitor's point of view – is made by **Stag Bakeries** (w stagbakeries.co.uk). While they bake at a factory in town, they do not have a retail outlet but instead supply supermarkets and other shops. You'll see their bread and other innovative products, such as seaweed-infused breadsticks, all over the island. For take-away sandwiches, the go-to place is the **Good Food Boutique** (59 Cromwell St; ✆01851 701394; e thegoodfoodboutique@gmail.com; w thegoodfoodboutique.co.uk; ⊕ 08.30–17.30 Mon–Sat), a deli selling a good range of bread, baguettes and rolls with imaginative fillings such as lentil pâté or beef and blue cheese for around £4.50. Run by self-confessed foodie Emma Campbell-Macleod, this is also a useful place for last-minute shopping for salmon and island-themed oatcakes, biscuits and other snacks to take home.

If you're self-catering and looking for fresh fish, head for **Islander Shellfish** (Cromwell St Quay; ✆01851 706772; ⊕ 08.00–17.00 Tue–Fri, 08.00–13.00 Sat) at the quayside (just below the RNLI shop). There is a huge range of white fish, from skate wings to hake, available here along with prawns, scallops and mackerel. Staff won't say it to your face, but they are quietly pleased to have seen off competition from the town's major supermarket fish counters, which have both recently closed.

THE PROOF IS IN THE PUDDING

It's hard to avoid black pudding in the Outer Hebrides as it seems to pop up on every menu, appearing in both basic pub grub and fine dining, where it is served in 'towers' alongside seared scallops. Occasionally it gets crumbled, in the manner of croutons, on soup and salads.

That butchers in Stornoway took the trouble to apply – successfully – for protected designated status for their black pudding may strike the outsider as curious, but the move tells you two things: it is wildly popular with customers; and there's money in it. Several thousand signatories supported the case for the protected status that was achieved in 2013.

Marag-Dhubh, to give the pudding its Gaelic name, comprises beef suet, vegetable fat, oatmeal, onion and salt. To these are added pork blood, to give it its distinctive dark colour, and spices – any self-respecting Stornoway butcher has a 'secret recipe' for these. There are no artificial flavours or colours, bulking agents nor added water. The resultant mixture is boiled for 90 minutes and sold in sausage-shaped plastic casings weighing in at around 1.3kg (full size) or 600g (half). You can also buy white pudding, which comes blood-free (the grey colour comes from the oats), and there are even gluten-free white puddings.

The origins of the Stornoway black pudding lie in the traditional crofting way of life, wherein no part of an animal could be wasted. Accordingly, pigs' blood and intestines (to encase the pudding) were put to good use to provide protein through the winter months.

When it comes to polarising foods, Stornoway black pudding is right up there with Marmite. It's not an acquired taste: the ability to eat solidified pigs' blood, reinforced by conspicuous white globules of fat staring back at you, is something you are either born with or not.

One of the questions Stornoway's butchers are most asked is: can it be eaten without further cooking? To which the answer is yes, but generally the preference is to grill or fry it for around 8 minutes. On no account should black pudding be confused with haggis, which comprises a mixture of sheep's organs.

Baltic Bookshop 8–10 Cromwell St; ☎01851 702082; ⏲ 09.00–17.30 Mon–Tue & Thu–Sat, 09.00–17.00 Wed. Thoughtfully stocked bookshop that has operated on this site for more than 50 years. The name, with its far-flung connotations, is a nod to the original store here, a shoe shop – the Baltic Boot Store – run by an Estonian émigré. You'll also find a decent range of books at the An Lanntair arts centre (⏲ same hours as centre).

Engebret filling station Page 74. The only place in Stornoway for general food supplies on Sun (should you need more than the bread & pastries of the Blackhouse Bakery). Also sells hot food.

Hebridean Jewellery 63 Cromwell St; ☎01851 702372; w hebrideanjewellery.co.uk; ⏲ 09.00–17.30 Mon–Sat. Retail outlet for the South Uist-based jewellery company. Offers a large range of thoughtfully designed jewellery, including Celtic brooches & earrings in clan crests, & necklaces with lattices in patterns of Norse longships.

Hebridean Tea Store 22 Cromwell St; ☎0800 228 9294; w hebrideanteastore.co.uk; ⏲ 10.00–17.00 Mon–Sat. An exquisite little shop, packed with fine loose teas, run by a German family. The emphasis is on tailored local brews that include Fisherman's Friend, a black tea mix from Assam, Rwanda & Sumatra; Machair, another Assam tea mixed with cornflowers & mallow blossom; & An Taigh Dubh, a Hebridean Blackhouse tea that combines Chinese black tea with heather blossom.

Rarebird Design 1 Bells Rd; ✆01851 709974; e hello@rarebirddesign.co.uk; w rarebirddesign. co.uk; ⏱ 09.00–17.30 Mon–Sat. Another contemporary take on Harris tweed, producing tops & purses in bold colours – think sky blues & light green & an engaging orange-brown that, unfairly, is technically called 'drab'. As owner & designer Paulette Brough notes, 'even brown tweed is colourful because you need to mix so many other colours to make it'.

OTHER PRACTICALITIES
Bank
$ Royal Bank of Scotland 47 Cromwell St; ✆01851 763806; ⏱ 09.30–16.30 Mon–Fri. Has ATM.

Library
Cromwell St ✆01851 822744; ⏱ 10.00–17.00 Tue–Wed & Fri–Sat, 10.00–19.00 Thu

Medical
✚ **The Group Practice** Springfield Rd; ✆01851 703145
✚ **Western Isles Hospital** Macauley Rd; ✆01851 704704

Pharmacies
✚ **Boots** 4–6 Cromwell St; ✆01851 701769; ⏱ 09.00–17.30 Mon–Sat
✚ **K J MacDonald** 29–31 Cromwell St; ✆01851 703131; w kjmpharmacy.co.uk; ⏱ 09.00–17.30 Mon–Sat

Police
Stornoway Police Station 18 Church St; ✆101; ⏱ 07.00–midnight daily

Post office
✉ **Stornoway Post Office** 16 Francis St; ⏱ 09.00–17.30 Mon & Wed–Fri, 09.30–17.30 Tue, 09.00–12.30 Sat

WHAT TO SEE AND DO Running from the ferry terminal to the Bayhead Bridge just north of Cromwell Street, Stornoway's quayside and marina repay a short stroll around the water's edge. This is a working harbour, so fishing boats or supply vessels chug back and forth. There are a handful of places to grab a coffee or a sandwich. Here and there, you come across statues to the Herring Girls, women who spent their summers processing fish up and down the Outer Hebrides right up to the middle of the 20th century.

Just behind the ferry terminal is Shell Street, Stornoway's oldest surviving street and home to **Stornoway Smokehouse** (✆ 01851 702723; e info@ stornowaysmokehouse.co.uk; w stornowaysmokehouse.co.uk; ⏱ 08.30–17.00 Tue–Fri), a father-and-son business run by Alasdair and Ranald Fraser. This is the last traditional smokery in the Hebrides, and one of only a handful in the UK. Before the ferry complex was built on reclaimed land, Shell Street opened out on to the harbour and, until the mid 20th century, more than 20 smokeries operated here, the street lined with barrels of fish being unloaded or exported. Behind the retail counter you can step back to a past era. The Frasers have two kilns, a 100-year-old kipper trough and a Tardis-like curing room where up to 1,000 fish – salmon, haddock, squid, mackerel, herring – can be hung and smoked. The pungent tar on the back wall of the curing room is an inch thick. 'How would you prefer your smoked fish?' asks Ranald, pointing to the curing room. 'This way, or the more sanitised way with lots of shiny metal? I think things have gone too far down that road. This place has character, it has a story; it is not what people expect to see. We have a sense of pride that we are carrying on a tradition in Stornoway. We're grateful that there's a demand for it.' Call in advance and the Frasers will happily give you an informal tour.

If you continue along the waterfront with the ferry terminal on your left, you will come to the **memorial to the *Iolaire* disaster** (see box, page 91), in which a ship bringing troops back from World War I sank a mile offshore. The tribute takes

6½km (4 miles); 2hrs
Start/finish: Bayhead Bridge, Bayhead/A857

The landscaped grounds of Lews Castle are a delight, not least because they are home to that rare thing on wind-blasted, peat-dominated Lewis – a mature woodland. A walk through the western and southern reaches of the estate is well worth the time; pick up a map with various walks at the Woodlands café. The woods were planted by Sir James Matheson after he acquired Lewis from the Seaforth family, using seed from the Far East and the New World, and planted in soil imported from the mainland.

This circular walk begins at the bridge that crosses the River Creed by the Bridge community centre off Bayhead, 5 minutes' walk north of the town centre. Turn left along the paved track, following signs for 'Cuddy Point' and 'Circular walk', enjoying pleasant views up towards the castle and across the river to the harbour. Pass the Gardener's Cottage and after the jetty at Cuddy's Point, continue through a set of gates to follow the track as it hugs the coastline. Up to your right you'll see what at first glance you may mistake for a statue of the Virgin Mary (an improbable spectacle on Presbyterian Lewis) but is in fact a statue of Lady Matheson.

The path flicks inland, following the River Creed. As it does, take the first track on the right, which immediately leads to a circular track around the small hill. This mound, Gallows Hill, was where capital punishment was meted out to errant islanders. The summit gives good views over the harbour, but better ones await: follow this circular track anti-clockwise to pick up the main path once again and keep going along an obvious paved track as it winds its way up to the highest point around. As you reach elevated ground, the moors of Lewis and the North Harris Hills appear. Just below the enormous summit cairn, there are some benches where you can sit and take in the view of the harbour and river. Ravens often perch in the trees here. The easiest return route is to retrace your steps.

The castle grounds are undergoing redevelopment until 2022, with improved landscaping and waymarking central to the work. New signage is already in place indicating mountain bike trails (though the off-road cycle trails look tempting, walkers are strongly advised to avoid them as cyclists will simply not be expecting to see you on them), with walking routes promised too. Ask for details at the Visit Scotland office.

the form of 359 posts – 280 representing those who died; the remaining 79 the survivors – assembled on the harbour bed in the exact shape and size of the stricken ship. They are, in tandem with the tides, submerged or exposed. At night they are illuminated. Along the adjacent sea wall the numbers of those who survived or died from each township on Harris and Lewis are displayed. It's hard to think of a more intensely thoughtful or apt memorial.

Just back from the quayside is **An Lanntair** arts centre (page 80), which regularly puts on good displays by local artists or themes of island life. There is a small but good bookshop here too.

For an unconventional take on the Harris Tweed industry, take a peek inside the **Lewis Loom Centre** (3 Bayhead; ⏲ 10.00–17.00 Mon–Fri), a couple of minutes' walk up Cromwell Street from the quayside, tucked away in an unprepossessing alley. Entering this former grain store is like being whisked back into the pages of a Dickensian novel. This is a warren of a place, an old curiosity shop heaped high with tweed scarves, socks, clocks and offcuts, where you will stumble upon whalebones and an 80-year-old order book containing £4 million of orders for tweed from across Europe. The client list of proprietor James R Mackenzie ('Spell it with a capital or a small *k*, I don't care,' he says), better known as Ronnie, includes HRH Prince Charles. Talk to Ronnie about looming and you get a sense of what it was like to work in the industry before modern mechanisation and outsourcing to Asia came along. 'You would throw the material on to the road to be picked up by the lorry in the morning and taken to the mill,' he laughs.

Across a tidal stretch of the River Creed and a 15-minute walk from the centre is Stornoway's island museum, **Lews Castle Museum and Archive (Museum nan Eilean)** (Lews Castle grounds; \ 01851 822746; w lews-castle.co.uk; ⊕ Apr–Sep 10.00–17.00 Mon–Wed & Fri–Sat, Oct–Mar 13.00–16.00 Mon–Wed & Fri–Sat; free entry, charge for special exhibitions). Based on the ground floor of the castle, the museum opened in 2016 and, despite the rather unimaginative name, represents a quantum leap for Stornoway. A series of galleries and interactive displays tells the history and present of the islands. With its emphasis on humanising the stories of fishing, farming and song, it strives successfully to bring the island landscapes to the fore. Centre stage is given to six Lewis chessmen, on long-term loan from the British Museum in London. Captions are in Gaelic and English. Deliberately and intriguingly, they do not always say the same thing, as the intention is to appeal to two distinct audiences – Gaelic speakers and English speakers. The building also houses a genealogy and archive centre (\ 01851 822750), which operates on an appointment basis.

The castle building, which glows a gentle honeyed colour on a sunny evening, has had something of a mixed history. When Lord Leverhulme offered Lewis for sale, Stornoway and the castle were the only parts that the community were in a position to buy (though a handful of crofters took the opportunity to buy their land in further-flung parts of the island). The town spent several decades working out what to do with the castle – it served as a further education college for many years – while it sat cloaked in woodland.

AROUND STORNOWAY

BACK (BAC) Back is the generic name for the east-coast communities of Lewis that straggle north for 11 miles from Stornoway along the dead-end B895. The road courses alongside the vast Broad Bay, an expanse of water that hovers somewhere between open sea and a sea low (its alternative name Loch a Tuath reflects this), and concludes in dramatic fashion at the **Bridge to Nowhere** [71 G3], an extraordinary testament to the failed dreams of Lord Leverhulme.

↱ **Where to stay, eat and drink** A handful of good accommodation options make a stay along or off the B895 a viable alternative to staying in Stornoway; you'll find both a café and a useful community shop out this way too.

✳ 🏠 **Broad Bay House** [71 G4] (4 rooms) Back; \ 01851 820390; e stay@broadbayhouse. co.uk; w broadbayhouse.co.uk. A really excellent guesthouse with stirring views over beach &

Minch. Rooms are fitted to an extremely high standard & feature commissioned artwork. 1 is designed for wheelchair users. All rooms have patio doors opening on to enclosed decking areas;

room 4 has sea views. Hosts Tom & Sue Reid, who relocated in 2018 from the Cotswolds, are welcoming hosts and offer a choice of 3-course dinners (£40 pp) & light platters (£55 for 2 people) Tue–Wed & Fri–Mon. Imaginative dishes include chicken & whisky pâté or pan-fried cod with beetroot purée. Lounge has superb views across the bay & the honesty bar is well stocked with whiskies, wine & beer. Wood-burning stove makes the lounge even snugger in winter. Fish & meat is sourced locally & recognition for the food's quality has come with a 5-star rating from Visit Scotland. Access to the beach is via a gate at the foot of the garden – bear left & follow the track across the brow for 100m. **£££**

⌂ Ravenstar B&B [71 G4] (3 rooms) 24 Vatisker, Back; ☎ 01851 820517; e dave@ ravenstar.co.uk; w ravenstar.co.uk; ⊕ May–Sep. Comfortable rooms, attentively furnished. Family room has 3 beds & cot. Owners Dave & Jane Eastwood are very much into self-sufficiency & produce delicious chutneys & jams. If you're not already relaxed – by dint of being on these islands – Jane offers therapies including Reiki, reflexology & Indian head massage. Dave also works as a blacksmith at his nearby forge. **££**

✗ Oystercatcher Tearoom [71 G4] Coll; ☎ 01865 820475; e collpotterycraftcentre@gmail. com; w collpottery.co.uk/tea-room; ⊕ Apr–Sep 10.00–17.00 Mon–Sat, noon–16.00 Sun. Good range of cakes & hot drinks including vegan options. Housed in the grounds of the Coll Pottery Craft Centre (see below). **£**

Self-catering

⌂ Lewis Longhouse [71 G4] ☎ 01425 483078; e stay@lewislonghouse.com; w lewislonghouse.com. The name of this striking property, located above Broad Bay in Back, doesn't lie & the Viking design is delivered with some brio. High-end trimmings include open-plan living area, oak floors, ground-to-ceiling windows, balcony & outdoor deck. Plenty of green credentials. Sleeps 4. £1,100–1,950/week. **£££**

Shopping The **community shop** (Bùth Tholastaidh; w buththolastaidh.co.uk; ⊕ 10.00–17.00 Mon–Sat) in Tolsta is yet another of these islands' well-stocked rural outlets, and you can pick up anything for a picnic here.

What to see and do The townships along the B895 are not of great interest, but the lagoons and saltings are a paradise for birdwatchers, and there are several good beaches. The first wildlife hotspot is the large inlet, the **Sands of Tong** [71 F5], by the township of **Tunga**. Arctic terns congregate here in large numbers, along with skylark, shelduck, oystercatcher and ringed plover. In winter the saltflats are often full to bursting with waders, ducks and geese. Eiders generally winter in large numbers in the next inlet up the road behind the beach at **Coll (Tràigh Chuil)**, where you may even spot a Slavonian grebe. The geology here is unusual, comprising solidified shingle and sand, in contrast with the gneiss that dominates everywhere else on Lewis.

A good place to stop hereabouts is the **Coll Pottery Craft Centre** [71 G4] (☎ 01851 820475; e collpotterycraftcentre@gmail.com; w collpottery.co.uk; ⊕ same as Oystercatcher Tearoom), a small craft centre with workshops and studios that house potters, artists and a blacksmith. The venture is driven by the highly creative Whittle family. In a previous incarnation Stella Whittle ran Solus Glass on South Uist and has relocated her eye-catching glasswork here. Meanwhile her husband, Alan, produces ceramics, her blacksmith son Aidan has a forge on site and daughter Angharad runs Sidheil Design, producing chainmaille and polymer clay jewellery. The family plans to offer space to other artists. They also welcome visitors and are more than keen to talk about their work and the landscape in which they live. 'I'd wanted to be a glassblower,' says Stella, 'but growing up on a council estate in southern England, the opportunity never came along.' Instead, she turned to glass design and found inspiration in both the Uists and the northern isles. 'Anybody who is creative has a mind that is always open,' she says. 'Everything about the Outer Hebrides is inspirational. The colours of the sea are what really do it for me – you see so many different colours depending on the depth of the water. Colours rather than realism inspire my work.' The centre also houses a small but pleasant tearoom, the Oystercatcher (see opposite).

The scattered township of **Back (Bac)** overlooks the vast sands of **Gress (Ghriais)** and the appositely named **Broad Bay** [71 G4]. **Bac saltings**, just south of Gress, is another good spot to linger: you can park up by the memorial to the land struggle, then scrutinise the machair and river estuary. Look out for grey and harbour seals along the coast. Arctic and great skuas nest here and are a thrilling sight, but if they have laid eggs they often dive-bomb fearlessly should you get too close.

The road then empties out and ploughs a lonely furrow towards Tolsta. A couple of miles north of Back, and a mile south of Tolsta, the road sweeps and bends through **Glen Tolsta (Gleann Tholastaidh)**. Just as the road rises out of the glen, you'll see a minor lane signposted on the right. This route merits a short diversion as it gives the opportunity for a short and beautiful – if boggy – walk through the glen ✳. Follow the road for almost a mile to its end in a small communal car park. You'll need boots from here for the walk down to the glen because the ground is sodden, even during those rare spells of extended dry weather. Take the small gate in the middle of the car park and head downhill, following the line of the small burn and fence. There is a path but it is so muddy that you may choose to walk along its edge. After 150m you reach another gate. Go through this and cross over open – and again, boggy – ground for 150m to the gate by the river on the far side of the field. Go through this and turn left, walking down the glen with the river on your right for a further 100m until a small, secluded cove opens up. This is a delightful spot, the sort of place where you may find a flock of oystercatchers, or look up and see a couple of buzzards circling overhead. It's the kind of hideaway where you can feel briefly but deliciously cut off from the rest of the world. Look up at the surrounding flanks of the glen and you may be able to pick out individual rowan and aspen trees. These are native species and propagated cuttings taken from here are forming part of the plan to re-wood parts of the Outer Hebrides with native species (see box, page 6).

Back on the B895 the road narrows to a single track as you enter Tolsta. Where the road drops down towards the beach, look out on the right for Studio 17, the workshop of Tom Hickman (w tomhickman.org.uk). Tom's unique work is intensely esoteric and ranges from embroideries of biblical scenes to what could be described as naive folk art and assemblages created from seashells. If the sign is up, Tom is at home.

Keep going through the township; after a cattle grid, the road winds its way above **Tràigh Mhòr** [71 H3], a vast expanse of sand stretching for almost 2 miles. There is parking here, enabling you to explore the beach. If you have children, or fancy something different, Tràigh Mhòr Pony Trekking (✆ 01851 890453; e minions@ tolsta41.com; w tolsta41.com) offers rides along the beach, as well as moorland treks and picnics.

You can carry on by road over the brow above Tràigh Mhòr until the road skirts above another headland to drop you above **Tràigh Ghearadha** ✳, popularly known as **Garry Beach** [71 G3]. This is a delightful small bay. A wooden bridge leads across to the beach, where there are sea stacks at the southeast end of the sands, which you can walk around at low tide.

High above the beach is the **Bridge to Nowhere** [71 G3]. As part of Lord Leverhulme's plans to transform the Outer Hebrides' economy, he commissioned a road up the east coast from Stornoway to Ness. His idea was to build three

🚶 FROM THE BRIDGE TO NOWHERE... TO NESS

16km (10 miles); 4–5hrs
OS Explorer 460 North Lewis
Start: car park at Garry beach (Tràigh Ghearadha; ◈ NB533499)
Finish: Port of Ness harbour (◈ NB538637)

You can if you wish walk all the way to Ness up the east coast of Lewis. This is a tough trek across open moorland following the waymarker posts. The route is generally clear but whittles down to barely a goat's track in places. An information board in the Garry Beach car park tells you how to navigate your way. The one-way walk involves some planning as you must arrange to be collected at the other end or check bus timetables. A less ambitious walk would be to follow the track while it remains in good condition for 2½km (1½ miles) past the waterfall at Abhainn na Cloich to the enthralling sea stack of Dùn Othail, which is home to nesting fulmars in season, and then retrace your steps. As you continue along the coast towards Ness, you enter the domain of Arctic and great skuas, whose prowling flight will add a frisson to your ramblings. Also look out for mountain hare, which sport white coats from October to April.

huge farms to provide dairy for the canning factory workers on his hoped-for fish empire that would replace what he saw as the antiquated pastime of crofting. Garry Beach is where the dream, in the literal sense, crumbled. Leverhulme's ambitions foundered on the post-World War I desire for land ownership from returning soldiers, whereupon he cut his losses and put Lewis up for sale; the road was halted some 10 miles short of completion. History is judging Leverhulme increasingly more kindly; certainly he was more patrician and philanthropic than he is sometimes given credit for and today you will find a handful of crofters in Lewis who are grateful that their parents or grandfathers took up his offer to sell them the land they lived on.

Leverhulme's legacy is a serendipitous one for the walker, as the bridge marks the start of a dramatic walk along the east coast (see box, above). The bridge traverses the Stone River, which winds its way dramatically under the arches, while the road proper stops some 10m the other side. This is no longer exactly the 'bridge to nowhere': the stony track is occasionally accessed by peat cutters for a short distance further around the headland. Don't try to emulate them, as places to perform a three-point turn are scarce, and the rocks will make a painful dent in any hire-car insurance excess.

POINT (AN RUBHA), THE EYE PENINSULA Known colloquially as Point, the Eye peninsula (the name is a corruption of *eidh*, a Norse word meaning neck of land) is connected by a membrane of land to the rest of Lewis. Although barely 10 miles in length, the peninsula is worth exploring, with more interest than a glance at a road map of the islands would suggest. The peninsula is home to a small population of 2,600, spread across 14 townships, and it has been given vibrancy by the decision to build a new primary school here, which consolidated – and compensated for – the closure of other nearby schools. The community shop at Knock, Bùth an Rubha [71 G5] (⏰ 09.00–20.00 Mon–Sat), is well stocked and houses the cake-heavy Café Roo (⏰ 09.00–17.00 Mon–Sat; £), which also offers toasties, jacket potatoes and burgers. They make a fine brew of proper coffee, too. A useful leaflet detailing walks and other points of interest can be picked up at the shop and at Stornoway tourist information centre (page 75). The A866 runs the length of the peninsula and gives fine views of the North Minch.

What to see and do Leaving Stornoway and before you reach the airport, a turning to the right leads across farmland and winds past a water treatment plant to reach a dead end by a stone plaque dedicated to the *Iolaire* disaster (see box, below). A narrow gravel path leads over the headland to **Rubha Thuilm**, where there is a cairn and monument [71 G5] to the tragedy. There are fine views here north towards Tolsta and south along the indented coastline of Lewis.

Back on the A866, you pass the airport and cross an isthmus barely 100m wide, where a curved sea wall mirrors the shape of the graceful beach and keeps the Minch at bay. Behind here is **Loch Branahuie**, which gets lots of salt spray in storms and is a good place to spot large charismatic birds such as red-throated, black-throated and great northern divers.

Immediately to the north of the sea defences stand the remains of the **church of St Columba** [71 G5], or **Eaglais na h-Aoidhe**, one of Lewis's great unsung treasures. The ruins are dramatic, the exposed stones weathered after 600 years of brutal winds and rain. This is the burial ground of the Macleod chiefs, and 19 are said to lie here. The tombs in the western part of the chapel are astonishing: reflecting their importance, the bodies were interred with slabs on which detailed images and effigies have been chiselled. The grave of Roderick Macleod is designed with a bas-relief effigy of a warrior, while the single Mackenzie tomb features a *cabarfeidh* (stag's head) and symbols of mortality such as a skull, coffin and an hourglass. A restoration project is bringing a change of fortune for the church, with its western chapel now covered from the elements. The sense of history here is intensified by the more recent and adjacent high double-cairn monument to the **Aiginis farm raiders** of 1888. During this appalling episode, men and women facing starvation and poverty rebelled and raided the farm. The authorities' response was to imprison 13 of them. It was only a matter of time before the wrongs were, to some extent, put right. After more intermittent turbulence, the farm was finally turned over to crofts in 1905.

The A866 threads east, and it is worth turning off on to the single-track road to **Pabail Uarach**. Keep straight ahead on this road until you reach the sea and the

THE *IOLAIRE* DISASTER

During a gale on New Year's Day 1919, a makeshift troop ship, the *Iolaire*, hit Holm rock, known as Blastan Thuilm or the Beasts of Holm, just outside Stornoway harbour. In the UK's worst peacetime shipping disaster of the 20th century, 280 men drowned; all were returning from World War I and had celebrated the Armistice barely six weeks earlier. Thanks to John Macleod, a boatbuilder from Ness who swam to shore with a line that acted as a handhold, 79 survived. In order to encompass the tragedy, the World War I memorials in Stornoway and Tarbert are dated 1914–19 – only a handful of similar memorials can be found elsewhere in the British Isles. The centenary of the tragedy has galvanised plans to build an *Iolaire* visitor centre on the Stornoway quayside. The centre will tell the story of the tragedy and the lives of those involved, and will also serve as a centre for Hebridean and Gaelic culture. You can follow developments at w iolaire.org.

small slipway of **Bayble pier**. This is a lovely spot, and you will often see shoreline birds as well as gannets diving into the waters. The nearby island, Eilean Mòr Phobail, is home to colonies of seabirds. To get the best vantage point of this pleasant and little-visited slice of Lewis, you can stomp out over open ground and ascend Bayble hill.

Journey's end on Point is **Tiumpan Head** [71 H4], reached by a single-track road that turns off from **Port Bhelar (Phort Mholair)**. The road passes Loch an t-Siumpain, which is a good place for all sorts of birdlife, including whooper swan. The road then sweeps uphill rather like a ski jump, and for a second you may wonder if you are about to leap into the sea. Over the crest is Tiumpan Head and the lighthouse, decorated in cream and light brown. You can stroll over the open land here, though be mindful of cliffs, particularly near the kittiwake colony that gathers between April and July. This is an excellent place to watch for Minke whale and Risso's, white-beaked and common dolphins, and the location is rightly on the new Hebridean Whale Trail (see box, page 16). You can explore the headland further in both directions. Just above the lighthouse you can go through the gate and follow a peat-cutter's path that winds uphill for 200m to yield fine views across Broad Bay, all the way to Ness. Alternatively, climb over the stile on the coastal side of the lighthouse and, bearing right, follow the various tracks that meander along the coast. If you allow yourself to be herded by the rather forlorn waymarkers, you will eventually come to another stile that leads you back on to the road, some 450m further south.

EAST COAST: THE PAIRC AND LOCHS Much of southeast Lewis is given over to a vast expanse of land known as the **North** and **South Lochs** and the **Pairc**. The South Lochs have some of the most attractive small villages on Lewis, a traditional and vibrant Gaelic-speaking community and great wildlife-watching opportunities. They comprise many freshwater lochs and two large sea lochs, **Loch Leurbost (Loch Liurboist)** [71 F6] and **Loch Erisort (Loch Eireasort)** [71 F6]. The Pairc's vast emptiness, meanwhile, is one of the unsung jewels of the island.

The North Lochs are reached along the B897, 7 miles south of Stornoway where a 'scenic route' sign invites you to take a circular route via **Crosbost** [71 F6]. The South Lochs, meanwhile, are serviced by the B8060, which turns off the main A859 some 13 miles south of Stornoway at **Balallan (Baile Ailein)** and winds its way deep into the eastern hinterland of Lewis. Less than a mile south of the B8060, an unclassified road turns off the A859 into the Pairc. From a cursory glance at a road map of Lewis, it looks as though the area is just off the A859 and you might infer that you could 'do' the Pairc and South Lochs in a couple of hours. Don't fall into that trap: it's 16 miles (40mins' drive without stopping) each way between the A859 and the end of the B8060 at **Lemreway (Leumrabhagh)**; while the journey through the Pairc may only be 8 miles but will take you a good half an hour in each direction. Combining your exploration with a visit to the Ravenspoint Centre at Kershadar (see box, page 96) will take the best part of a day.

History The Pairc and the Lochs were originally a deer park for the Lords of the Isles and later Lord Seaforth. The area was heavily populated until the 1850s when – unusually for the highlands and islands – they were cleared on a reasonably amicable basis. The population is documented to have moved fairly happily to the coast, where the land and opportunities were better, and the Pairc was turned over to sheep. In November 1887, however, several hundred crofters from the Pairc staged a raid in protest at their treatment by James Matheson, then landlord of the Lewis estate. Prior to the raid, many Pairc townships had been systematically cleared to give greater access to land that was regarded as deer-hunting ground. Crofters working the land for survival were regarded as a hindrance to sporting pleasure and treated accordingly. The raid was planned by six men who alerted sympathetic journalists on the mainland with what became an iconic three-word telegram: HUNT IS UP. In protest at the loss of their ancestral lands they killed a large number of deer, which they handed out to destitute and hungry families. The men were arrested and sent for trial in Edinburgh where they eloquently disabused city folk of preconceived ideas of savage and ignorant Hebrideans. They were acquitted but it took a further seven years for the grievances to be addressed with cuts to the amount of land given over to deer forest. Today, however, most of the Pairc remains a sporting estate in private hands. A large cairn commemorating the raids stands proud by the A895 on the edge of Balallan.

Where to stay and eat Accommodation in the Lochs area is often along the A895 Stornoway Road and provides a good base, equidistant between Lewis and Harris and usually with fine views over Loch Erisort. The establishments' proximity to the main road is not as intrusive as might be the case in other parts of the UK.

Clearview [71 E6] (3 rooms) Balallan; 01851 830472; e stay@clearview-lewis.co.uk; w clearview-lewis.co.uk. 1 dbl & 1 twin en suite, 1 dbl with private facilities. Cosy, homely rooms provided by Irene Mackay, but the USP is the elevated position with superb views over Loch Erisort. **££**

Glen House [71 F6] (4 rooms) 77 Leurbost; 01851 860241; e leurbost77@yahoo. com. Located 2 miles off main road at Leurbost. Mixture of dbls & twins, 2 with adjoining doors that can provide family accommodation sleeping 5. **££**

Loch Erisort Inn [71 E6] (5 rooms) Sheildinish; 01851 830473; w locherisortinn. co.uk; ☉ Apr–Oct. Located approx 1 mile

along the B8060, & recently refurbished. Rear rooms have views over Loch Erisort; front rooms overlook Eishken & Pairc hills. Family room has a dbl & bunk beds. Cosy bar sometimes sells real ale & has a wood-burning fire. Restaurant offers filling food that doesn't try to be too clever: salmon in a mussel stew & crab & leek pasties (**££**). **££**

Taigh Chailean [71 E6] (2 rooms) Laxay; 01851 830315; e info@lewisbedbreakfast.co.uk; w lewisbedbreakfast.co.uk. A spruce & modern feel to this B&B run by the welcoming Marion Maciver, with dbl & twin both with patio doors opening towards the loch (reached by a 10min walk through the croft). Both rooms have ground-floor level access; ramp at front door. **££**

🏠 **Tigh Na Bruaich** [71 E6] (1 room) 8 Balallan, Lochs; 📞01851 830742; e tighnabruaich@tiscali.co.uk. The solitary room here is actually a suite with a large dbl – effectively you get the run of the first floor – that can accommodate a family. Friendly owners Debbie Cullis & Paul Smith manage the B&B on a traditional croft. DBB options available (££). The couple also runs the adjacent Island Arts, a small gallery of Debbie's art, & coffee shop, both open year-round (inc Sun). **££**

🏠 **Ravenspoint Hostel** [71 F6] (3 dbl rooms, 15-bed bunkroom) Ravenspoint Centre, Kershadar; 📞01851 880236; w ravenspoint. net; ⊕ Mar–Oct. This lovely & immaculately maintained community-owned hostel offers good levels of quality & comfort. Added bonus is that residents get after-hours use of the café area & its stupendous views. **£/££**

✖ **Ravenspoint Café** [71 F6] ⊕ year-round 11.00–17.00 Mon–Sat. Beautifully positioned, with comfy sofas & wide windows that overlook Loch Erisort. The Lochs region has more breeding pairs of white-tailed eagles than anywhere else in the Outer Hebrides – & indeed anywhere other than Mull – & Loch Erisort serves as something of an avian runway for them, so you have a fighting chance of seeing one as you sip your latte or munch a slice of mint cake. Otters also scuttle around the foreshore. **£**

What to see and do

The North Lochs Although the B897 is well maintained for only a few hundred metres from the A859 – making exploration a little wearisome for both cyclists and drivers – the compensatory payback is the pleasant views over Loch Leurbost. The road meanders over the moors and, just as it turns west back towards the main A859, you reach the tiny community of Crosbost, hard above Loch Leurbost. Crosbost is mission control for an excellent new Harris Tweed venture, **Western Isles Designs** [71 F6] (m 07833 335186; e crossbostweavingco@yahoo.com; w westernislesdesigns.co.uk; ⊕ Apr–Sep 10.00–18.00 Mon–Sat, by appt Sun & rest of year). Drop by and you'll find weaver Miriam Hamilton either working on her loom or happy to chat and show you around her small studio and shop. Miriam is candid about the fact she is living her dream. Having grown up in the Forest of Dean in Gloucestershire, she relocated in 2017 and has put to good use the knitting and design skills she has been picking up since early childhood. Miriam holidayed in the Hebrides as a child. 'I always dreamt about moving up but thought it wasn't something I would ever be able to do,' she says. 'For me Harris Tweed weaving had been a childhood dream but I always thought you had to be born into it, that I would never be able to do it. When I was offered the chance, I jumped at it.' Miriam's range includes tweed bags, girls' clothing, waistcoats and women's tunic dresses along with a sideline in jewellery. 'Tweed is special for me as it is a beautiful tactile cloth, has its wonderful history and heritage, and is still made in the same way that it has been for hundreds of years.'

South Lochs An area that feels as if it's on the up, South Lochs offers an insight into how rural life continues away from the tourist gaze that is for the most part focussed on the west coast of Lewis. The coastline is spectacularly rocky, indented with deep lochs that have something Norwegian about them. Inland, the landscape is dominated by loch-studded blanket bog.

The lochs are dominated by Loch Erisort, a graceful finger of sea water that cuts deep into the coast and that is home to Arctic char (a rare fish). This loch and others, such as Loch Odhairn to the southeast and Loch Sealg in the south, are extremely scenic. They are also home to a good deal of marine life; otters, porpoises, dolphins, seals and even minke and long-finned pilot whales, basking sharks and orcas turn up. The lochs are good for great northern divers (in winter), the rarer black-throated diver, which breeds on larger freshwater lochs and the smaller, mallard-

The huge low-lying northern part of Lewis is one of the largest undisturbed expanses of blanket bog in Britain. A forbidding 80% of Lewis north of the A858 Leurbost–Garynahine road is covered by peat, supporting dense colonies of nesting divers and waders such as dunlin and golden plover. At first glance, this peat-scape can look formidably monotonous, but for such a bleak landscape it can be remarkably full of colour. Look closer and it yields an extraordinary range of colours, from golden tormentil to the violet flowers of butterwort and the rich red and purple tones of ling and marsh orchids, the pink of ragged robin, the yellow of bog asphodel, the pink-white heath spotted-orchid and the grainy white of cottongrass.

sized red-throated diver. You can expect to hear corncrakes and spot spiralling lapwings. Despite the vast, open and empty lands, determined clumps of willows, rowan, aspen and birch hang on here and there.

The hub of the South Lochs area is the township of **Kershadar (Cearsiadair)**, 6 miles from the A859. This not only has an excellent museum, café and visitor centre, but that rarity in the Outer Hebrides: a petrol pump (two, in fact) that takes credit cards and therefore operates on Sunday.

Linked to the café of the same name (see opposite), the **Ravenspoint Visitor Centre** ✳ [71 F6] (w ravenspoint.net; ⊕ year-round 11.00–17.00 Mon–Sat) in Kershadar houses a small and emotionally powerful museum. The collection is eclectic, ranging from possessions that emigrants from the Lochs took to Patagonia, to a harpoon from the area's whaling days found in a back garden. The centrepiece is a mobile pulpit that was wheeled from stump to stump during the 1870s and from where the minister would dispense his sermons. The pulpits were deployed while churches were being built in order to avoid the appalling prospect of the population going without religious instruction until the minister had a roof over his head. One extraordinary photograph from the late 19th century shows the pulpit positioned in a glen, with several hundred people sitting on the banks.

The Centre has a good community shop, stocked with provisions and books, and has some good walks and cycle routes on its website. If you're walking, contact Centre volunteer John Broom via the website in advance. John has walked almost every square inch of the Lochs and Pairc and is an excellent source of advice on where to go and what to look out for. 'It's just a fabulous place to come. You can walk for days here and not see anyone,' he says, conveying the sense that this is what he loves about the place. The centre will also give you advice on trout, salmon and sea fishing. The lochside here is a good place in summer to catch mackerel, laithe and pollock.

The Ravenspoint Centre is also home to the **genealogy archive of Angus Macleod**, who in the late 20th century compiled an extraordinary compendium of more or less everyone who had ever lived in the area, going way back when. Volunteers at the Centre have digitised the whole archive. An Australian woman who traced her ancestors back to the village of Crowder got married in the ruins of her forefathers' croft after tracking his roots down through the centre and the wider Hebridean Connections website (w hebrideanconnections.com).

Southeast of Kershadar, a couple of minor roads peel off east to explore the communities around **Marvig** and **Calbost**, or northeast to **Cromor** where you get perhaps the best view of Skye. At the very bottom of the South Lochs, and well

The empty roads of the Lochs make for easy exploration by two wheels. The Ravenspoint Centre website (w ravenspoint.net) lists several suggested routes, including the Ring of Pairc, which leaves Kershadar and follows an anti-clockwise 14½km (9-mile) loop up to Marvig and Calbost.

The same website also details several good walks. A short walk from Orinsay is waymarked with posts over open ground for 1½km (1 mile) to Steimreway (Stiomrabhaigh), a village deserted in 1942 which has an evocative nature to its ruins, field walls, cultivation beds and a well, all in a scenically beautiful location. There's a bewitching narrow channel between the freshwater loch and the sea here, where sea water flows in and out according to the tides. This is a good place to spot otters.

At low tide, from Cromor on the northeast coast of the South Lochs, you can also walk across to the island of Chaluim Chille. The route takes a minor track for just under 2km (1 mile) to the shoreline at Crobeag and you have a good hour either side of low tide to get across (and back!). The island cemetery was described graphically as far back as 1876 by John Sands who wrote of coffins piled ten feet high and where the graveyard swarmed with rats that devoured each body as soon as it was left.

worth the journey, a minor road leads west for a mile or so to the attractive village of Orinsay (Orasaigh), where a smattering of houses picturesquely perch on sloping moor above the sea with views across to the uninhabited Shiant Isles.

The Pairc The word *pairc* means 'an exposed area' in Gaelic. The district, predominantly lying southeast of Loch Sheld, comprises an incredible 168,000 acres almost entirely free of humans and roads. The single unclassified road that winds through the Pairc is one of the most depopulated moorland tracks you will encounter in the UK. It's a slightly stomach-churning, uneven and up-and-over route but scenically it is dramatic, particularly as it runs above the narrow headwaters of Loch Seaforth (Loch Shìphoirt) where it passes a monument to the Pairc raiders. Blanket bog makes up a sizeable chunk of the landscape and among it you will find ling, bell heather and cross-leaved heather, along with purple moor grass, deergrass and bog cotton. Specialist plants here include carnivorous, midge-loving sundews. White water lilies make for an unexpectedly exotic-looking spectacle, though they are in fact native to the islands (and indeed, the UK).

The narrow road heads south, passing two sets of four rather grandiose pillars 3 miles apart before ending rather abruptly at a set of electrified gates at **Eishken** (**Eisheradh**), a private hunting lodge.

Back on the A859, a mile or so south of Balallan, you arrive at the village of Airidh a'Bhruaich (postcode HS2 9LE). As you drive through, a short turning (to your left if heading towards Tarbert, to the right if you're Stornoway-bound) leads down to the croft of **Seaforth Harris Tweed** ✳ [70 D7] (5 Airidh A'Bhruaich; m 07876 727000; e iainm4665@hotmail.com; ⊕ year-round 09.30–late Mon–Sat). This appealing workshop is home to Harris Tweed weaver Iain Martin. A visit here can be as short or as long as you wish – and you may well be captivated by Iain's gently engaging passion. Steeped in the history of Harris Tweed, Iain will give you a down-to-earth, from-the-heart insight into its importance to the island. Iain's great-grandmother, grandparents and father were all involved with weaving and you may well find Iain hard at work on one of two traditional Hatterslay domestic looms, or the 100-year-old bobbin winder. Iain will show you how colours are made, such as the auburn-browns of crotal from lichens scraped off the moors, and explain the intricate, laborious process of warping the yarn that is destined to become tweed.

'I grew up on this croft and from the age of five I was winding the bobbin, 2 hours before school, 2 hours afterwards,' he recalls. Rather than make items from tweed, Iain sells fabric for you to take away. If you want a tweed lampshade or mobile phone cover, go elsewhere. Depending on the time of year you visit, you could also learn about – and help out with – peat-cutting, lambing, sheep-shearing or sheepdog demonstrations. As Iain puts it, 'This isn't all about tourism. It's the real deal. It matters because this is the iconic cloth; the crofting way of life was so dependent on it. The looms were the backbone of communities. I'm seeing so much more interest – perhaps because this involved hand work, hard work, it's the opposite of the single-use approach to making things.'

Some 6 miles south of Balallan and before you cross the invisible boundary into Harris, a handful of short walks has been put together to let you explore the coniferous plantation of Aline woodlands. The walks range in distance from about ½km (0.3 miles) to 1½km (1 mile). Two of them are along level boardwalks and are wheelchair accessible. There is also a good children's play park.

THE WEST COAST – FROM CALLANISH, NORTH TO NESS The west coast of Lewis is the most visited part of the Outer Hebrides, visitors flocking – a relative term here – to the island's chief attraction, the standing stones of Callanish (Calanais). Archaeology is a dominant theme, as blackhouses, brochs and other standing stones are scattered along a coastline also characterised by beautiful secluded beaches. At the end of the A857, Lewis tapers to a conclusion in the sprawling township of Ness (Nis), with its landmark lighthouse and edge-of-the-world atmosphere. The most handy petrol station out this way is the Welcome In Filling Station (page 74), which also has a decent shop. As elsewhere, distances may not look great on the map but travelling can eat up your time. From Callanish to Ness is around 25 miles and takes 45 minutes. The driving time from Stornoway to Ness is about 1 hour.

Where to stay
Callanish

Creagan B&B [70 D5] (2 rooms) Callanish; 01851 621200; e ann@creagan-bedandbreakfast.co.uk; w creagan-bedandbreakfast.co.uk; Mar–Oct. A twin & a dbl, the latter with views to the standing stones, which are within easy walking distance. Run by friendly local couple Angus & Ann Smith. **££**

Gealabhat Callanish B&B [70 D5] (2 rooms) 9 Callanish; 01851 621467; w 9callanish.co.uk. Comfortable en-suite dbl & twin rooms with views of the stones & the Harris hills, in a restored & modernised croft house on high ground just a short stroll from Callanish. Tastefully furnished with Harris Tweed features & a stone floor in the small guest lounge. **££**

Loch Roag Guest House [70 D5] (5 rooms) 22a Breasclet; m 07889 884112; e info@lochroag.com; w lochroag.com; Mar–Oct. Smart bedrooms & hearty b/fasts make this a good choice, just 2 miles from Callanish. 4 rooms en suite, 1 with private shower. Good views across Loch Roag towards Callanish & Great Bernera, particularly from the b/fast room. **££**

Self-catering

Whitefall Spa Lodges [70 D5] Breasclet; m 07789 802260; e stay@whitefalls.co.uk; w whitefalls.co.uk. 2 luxurious boutique lodges built from cedar on high ground with floor-to-ceiling windows making the most of the views of the Lewis moors. Sauna, private spa, underfloor heating & much more. Run by the owners of Loch Roag Guesthouse. Correctly marketed as suiting special occasions. £1,595–1,940/week. **££££**

Visible to those arriving by ferry to Stornoway and lying 4 miles off the southeast coast of Lewis, the Shiant Isles are well worth a day trip on account of their wildlife. These are one of the great bird stations of the northern hemisphere, with an estimated 250,000 seabirds nesting here, including puffin, guillemot, razorbill, shag and great skua. Many people say that the puffin colony here is even more spectacular than that of St Kilda. The Shiants comprise three main islands: Gairb Eilean, Eilean an Taighe and Eilean Mhuire. The cliffs are spectacular and their basalt rock columns, rising 150m high, rival those of Staffa off Mull. A magnificent sea arch adds to the drama.

The last permanent residents left at the beginning of the 20th century but shepherds still occasionally visit, staying in the bothy once owned by the author Compton Mackenzie, who wrote some of his novels here. The islands (pronounced 'shant') came to prominence in 2002 with the publication of *Sea Room* by Adam Nicolson. Adam inherited the islands from his father at the age of 21 (and later passed them on to his own son, Tom, at the same age) and the book tells of the emotional and practical relationship between the family and the islands.

Until recently the islands have been plagued by (non-native) black rats – in 2012 they were estimated to number more than 3,500 – to the detriment of nesting seabirds. Following an RSPB rat-eradication scheme (the Shiant Isles Recovery Project), the islands were declared rat-free for the first time in more than a century in 2018. Storm petrels have already begun to nest again on the island (the rats would eat their eggs) and the RSPB hopes that other birds, including Manx shearwaters, will be similarly – and quickly – encouraged.

You can, at a push, stay on the islands, in the old house. The Nicolsons candidly admit the house is extremely basic and has no electricity, running water, telephone or toilet. For up-to-date details on staying there, visit w shiantisles.net. Most of the boat operators listed on page 38 will take you out to the Shiants or tour around their waters. Dropping you there and picking you up will set you back around £700.

⋏ **Callanish Camping Pods** [70 D5] (3 wooden pods) m 07809 330971; e callanishfarmtrust@ gmail.com; w callanishcamping.co.uk; ⏲ Apr–Sep. Located by a jetty 5mins' walk south of the stones. Each pod sleeps 3 adults/2 adults & 2 children. All have double glazing, electricity, heating, kettle & microwave; a separate wash pod has hot showers. A 4th pod houses shower, toilet & washroom. Plans to open year-round. **££**

West coast

🏠 **Borve Country House Hotel** [71 F2] (9 rooms) Borve; ☎01851 850223; e info@ borvehousehotel.co.uk; w borvehousehotel. co.uk. Good-sized bedrooms, all en suite, large bar & conservatory. Good food in both bar (**£/££**) & restaurant (**££/£££**). **£££**

🏠 **Doune Braes Hotel** [70 D4] (16 rooms) Carloway; ☎01851 643252; e hebrides@doune-braes.co.uk; w doune-braes.co.uk; ⏲ Mar–Oct, enquire ahead in winter. A decent mixture of simply furnished if tired dbls, twins, sgls & family rooms. 3 rooms suitable for travellers with mobility problems. There are 2 bars, & both restaurant (**££**) & bar (**£**) meals are available to non-residents. **££/£££**

🏠 **Cross Inn** [71 G1] (5 rooms) Cross, near Ness; ☎01851 810152; e crossinn@protonmail. com; w crossinn.com. Mix of dbls, sgls & trpl, all en suite. Tidily & freshly decorated rooms with views of machair or moor make this a good-value choice. Cycle-friendly: owners Alice Bagley & Duncan Phillip store bikes overnight & recharge electric bikes. **££**

✳ 🏠 **The Decca** [71 G1] (10 rooms) Lionel, Ness; ☎01851 810571; e louise@thedecca; w thedecca.co.uk. Converted from an old radio navigation station, The Decca offers a heart-warming welcome to those who make it out this far. Mix of dbls, twins & family options, but whatever you need, the owners will make it work. The upstairs dbl with jacuzzi bath should top your list. A warm, informal & friendly atmosphere sets this place apart. Accessible toilets & access ramp. New arrivals are requested to arrive after 16.00. **££**

✳ 🏠 **Galson Farm** [71 F2] (4 rooms) South Galson; ☎01851 850492; e galsonfarm@yahoo. com; w galsonfarm.co.uk. Located on an 18-acre working croft off the A857, 8 miles south of Ness. Excellent B&B run by Elaine Fothergill & Richard Inger. Comprises 4 comfortable en-suite bedrooms across a quirkily designed 18th-century farmhouse with 2 separate flights of stairs. 2 guest lounges have views across fields to the coast. Everything feels just right here, from the tasteful décor & thoughtfully furnished rooms to the position of the farmhouse & outbuildings on a small rise that affords views all the way up the coast to the lighthouse at the Butt of Ness. Whatever the weather, try to leave your bedroom window open so as to catch the sound of waves making landfall along the coast. Good, Aga-cooked evening meals, with local meat. Home-grown veg will follow as soon as owners' polycrub (a wind-proof plastic greenhouse) is up & running. Set dinner £25 for 2 courses. The farm's hinterland is worth exploring with the distinctive grassy mounds thought to be Neolithic & Bronze Age cairns. The path behind the farmhouse invites a 350m stroll down to the beach. Your helpful hosts are good company & full of ideas for local walks & things to do. As Elaine says, 'I used to be a hairdresser so I'm quite good at chatting.' They also run an adjacent 6-bunk hostel (£22 pp), which also works well for a family. **££**

🏠 **Na Geàrrannan** [70 D4] Garenin; ☎01851 643416; e info@gearrannan.com;

w gearrannan.com. For a unique experience, stay on a self-catering basis in restored blackhouses at Geàrrannan. 4 cottages with solid fuel stoves, some with underfloor heating: 1 suitable for a couple, 2 that can take families of up to 5 & a hostel-style bunkhouse that sleeps up to 14. There's also a hostel that sleeps 13, including a separate family room for 3. All the properties are named after a family that once lived in them; for example, Taigh Dhonnchaidh (Duncan's House), which was occupied 1861–1940. Staying here is a wonderfully atmospheric experience & you might have to suppress the mischievous thought that, had blackhouses been this comfortable 150 years ago, the history of the islands would be very different: the cosiness, warmth & high-quality construction of the renovated houses are far removed from the historical reality of soot, disease & even semi-squalor. By definition of the original purpose of the buildings, views & natural light are at a premium. Rates vary depending on length of stay & time of year, but blackhouses typically £142–296 for 2 nights, hostel £20 pp/night. **££**

🏠 **The Blue Bothy** [70 D4] ☎01851 643225; w bluepigstudio.co.uk. 2 simple bothies, each sleeping 1–2 on the croft of the Blue Pig Studio (page 104). **£**

Self-catering
🏠 **Moorpark Cottages** [71 F3] (2 cottages, sleep 4) Barvas; ☎01851 840225; e info@ moorparkcottages.co.uk; w moorparkcottages. co.uk. Just north of the intersection between the A858 & A857. Striking larch-clad properties, airy & spacious. £800/week. **££**

🏠 **Achmore Cottage** [71 E5] (Sleeps 4) Acha Mòr; ☎01851 612288; e info@lewiscottages. com; w lewiscottages.com. Faultlessly furnished cottage, with cosy sitting room with stove & superb views of Uig & Harris hills. Owner manages 2 other cottages in Uig (see website). £480–860/week. **££**

✗ Where to eat and drink
✗ **Borve Country House Hotel** [71 F2] Borve; ☎01851 850223; e info@borvehousehotel. co.uk; w borvehousehotel.co.uk; ⊕ noon–21.00 Mon–Sat, 18.00–20.00 Sun (guests only). Excellent food in both bar & restaurant. **£/££/£££**

✗ **The Breakwater** [71 G1] Port of Ness; ☎01851 811001; ⊕ noon–18.00 Mon–Tue, noon–

21.00 Wed–Sat. Decent range of toasties & build-your-own pizzas & ice cream. Popular with locals, which is always a good sign. Superb location right above the harbour & appropriately named for the eponymous breakwater. Worth visiting in bad weather just for the spectacle of waves overtopping the sea wall – in the highest winds they can crash over the grassy headlands on the far side of the bay. **£**

✕ Callanish Visitor Centre Café
[70 D5] Callanish; ☎ 01851 621422;
w callanishvisitorcentre.co.uk; ⏰ Apr–May
& Sep–Oct 10.00–18.00 Mon–Sat, Jun–Aug
09.30–20.00 Mon–Sat, Nov–Mar 10.00–16.00
Tue–Sat. Cakes & hot drinks plus more substantial
main meals in high season. Wonderful location
with views over Loch Roag. £
**✕ Comunn Eachdraidh Nis (Ness Historical
Society Museum) Café** [71 G1] Sgoil Chrois,
Ness; ☎ 01851 810377; w cenonline.org;
⏰ 11.00–16.00 Mon–Fri. Good coffee, cakes,
bacon rolls & toasties. £
＊ **✕ The Decca** [71 G1] Lionel, Ness; ☎ 01851
810571; e louise@thedecca; w thedecca.co.uk;
⏰ 19.00–21.30 daily inc Sun. Open to non-guests
but must book in advance. Excellent fixed menu
offered at this popular eatery using local meat (the
pork comes from the croft across the road) & fish.
Owners' kitchen garden provides onions, spinach &
herbs. Save room for Louise's raspberry cheesecake.
2 courses £22. Unlicensed but no corkage fee.
Keep an eye out for their occasional tasting menu
evenings (£40) & meals that include talks by
local wildlife guides or performances by island
musicians. Part of The Decca B&B. £
✕ Geàrrannan Blackhouse Café [70 D4]
Geàrrannan; ☎ 01851 643416; e info@gearrannan.
com; w gearrannan.com; ⏰ Mar–Oct 09.30–
17.30 Mon–Sat. Good café & hot soup within snug
stone walls. £
✕ Mollans [70 D3] Shawbost; ☎ 01852 710230;
m 07985 233723; e acrorats@gmail.com;
w mollans.com. Good take-away food served out
of a wooden shack. Freezer meals include curry
pasties & rhubarb crumble; there are traybakes
too, all paid for by an honesty system. Owners
Julie & Rachel Child will also cook fresh meals,
such as chilli con carne & bacon rolls, to order.
The venture represents quite a change in career

for Julie, who used to breed rats & sell related
items – 'rat furniture', she says – such as wheels
& rat hammocks for a living. 'Rats are amazing
creatures,' she says. 'If you take 2 good-natured
rats, their offspring will also be good-natured.
They are hugely popular pets.' Fortunately for
environmentalists right across the Outer Hebrides,
Rachel has left her trade behind, acknowledging
that they are regarded as vermin here. Incidentally,
the name of the shack is a homage to one of the
croft's previous owners: Mollans means 'eyebrows'
in Gaelic. 'The family was known for their
amazingly bushy eyebrows,' says Julie. 'The crofter
himself was called "Murdo Mollans" by everyone.'
✕ Morven Gallery [71 E3] Barvas;
☎ 01851 840247; e morvengal@gmail.com;
w morvengallery.com. Located just north of
Bragar, it serves good coffee & cakes. Check
website or contact ahead of visiting to check if
open. £
✕ The Old Barn Bar [71 G1] Cross Inn, Cross;
☎ 01851 810152; e crossinn@protonmail.com;
w crossinn.com; ⏰ noon–23.00 Mon–Wed,
noon–01.00 Thu & Fri, noon–23.30 Sat, food
served noon–16.00 & 18.00–21.00 Mon–Sat.
Attached to the Cross Inn. Homemade pub grub
for under £10 (scampi & chips, macaroni cheese).
In good weather, the small garden comes into its
own. Popular with cyclists in de-mob mood as they
finish the Hebridean Way. Owners have plans to
open additional seasonal restaurant with a gastro-
pub feel in the inn itself. £
✕ Wobbly Dog of Lewis [71 G1] Lionel;
☎ 01851 810838; w wobblydogoflewis.com;
⏰ 10.00–17.00 Mon–Fri, 10.00–17.30 Sat.
Homemade cakes & teacakes & hot drinks from this
friendly – & dog-friendly – shop run by Mark &
Sheila Firth. Run out of the long-gone village shop,
it retains the 1940s till & original counter. Shelves
are stacked with Ness-made souvenirs.

Shopping Cross Stores [71 G1] (☎ 01851 810241; ⏰ 09.00–18.00 Mon–Fri, 09.00–
19.00 Sat) lies 2 miles south of Ness harbour and is signposted off the A857. Excellent
grocers and general stores. Inside you'll find The Scullery (⏰ same hours as stores),
a take-away deli/café selling substantial meals such as curries. The shop also stocks a
good range of Ness-themed souvenirs, as well as chocolates locally made by Paul and
Emma Moorby of Galson, which are among the best you will find anywhere in the
Outer Hebrides.

What to see and do Everybody headed to Lewis's west side is bound for the
stone circle at Callanish. If you're travelling via the A858, then about 3 miles west

of the turning from Leurbost you'll find the **Island Darkroom** [71 E5] (5c Acha Mòr; m 07599 217064; e info@islanddarkroom.com; w islanddarkroom.com; ◷ Apr–Sep 10.00–17.00 Wed–Sat, Oct–Mar by appt), the photographic studio of Mhairi Law. Mhairi sells her work on site and specialises in striking black-and-white images of Lewis and the adjacent region of Uig.

Callanish (Calanais) [70 D5] Evocative, haunting and believed to be older than both Stonehenge and the Pyramids of Giza, the standing stones of Callanish are by some distance the most visited site in the Outer Hebrides. Hewn from otherwise undentable Lewisian gneiss, a central monolith some 3½m high is surrounded by a circle of 13 stones, while lines or avenues of other stones lead away to all points of the compass. There's a graceful symmetry to the site, enhanced by the patterning of the gneiss visible on the rough-cut surfaces of the stones. Their texture is mesmerising, the gneiss stones fine-grained, pea-green and as thin as a finger in places but – and please don't try this, just in case – utterly unsnappable.

HOW TO MAKE A MICHELIN-STAR CHILLI CON CARNE IN THE OUTER HEBRIDES

In another life, Alan MacRitchie, until recently the chef at the Borve Country House Hotel, would be a philosopher-poet. I notice the menu features a dish called *ceann cropaig*, which translates literally as 'head stuffing'. Alan explains: 'It's a meal I remember my grandmother making when I was a child. You just stuff all sorts of fish into a fish head. Whether they thought there was lots of good flavour in the head or the head was the only vessel they had to use, it was delicious.' The version served up at Borve is presented more prosaically, as Alan acknowledges that guests may baulk at the dish appearing in a real fish head.

While guests slumbered, Alan would famously (notoriously, say some staff) wake in the small hours pondering just what would make a good meal, then go down to the kitchen to try out an idea. 'The best time to be in a kitchen is 4am,' he recalls. 'At the moment everything is "artisan this, artisan that", but it will go full circle,' he forecasts. 'If you put time, effort, love, care and attention into your cooking, you end up with a good meal.'

Which is where the Michelin-star chilli comes in. 'I can make a damned good chilli if someone wants it – a Michelin-star-quality one – but how do you judge whether one dish is better than another because of the way it's presented? A lot of people here say the best cup of tea they ever drink is while they are out cutting peat. Is it the tea, or the fact they're cutting peat, or the heather blossom or drowned midge in the tea that makes it great?'

The hotel menu features a *clootie* dumpling (a traditional Scottish steamed fruit pudding) that draws heavily on Alan's childhood memories. 'I remember cycling to my grandmother and she'd just pull a clootie out of the oven, freshly baked. How can I take the memory of that cycle ride and put it into a clootie? I can't just throw a dumpling on the plate. So I present it as a slice, with the skin on one side. I want the golden syrup my grandmother used but you can't just ladle that on, so I make a sorbet out of it. It took four attempts to get it right. That's what I try to do with my food – make it great by bringing something else, part of me, into it.' Alan still occasionally drops by – if he's around, he's worth talking to if you want to learn about how chefs in remote locations go about their business.

The stones were erected around 4,500–4,900 years ago but the site is known to have been cultivated by farmers planting barley even earlier, around 3500BC. At the time, the climate was less wet and windy. A ring of stones with the monolith was erected around 2900–2600BC. Around 2600BC, a small burial cairn was placed in the stone ring and the rows of stone that run north from the central site may have been added at this time. By 2000BC, the chamber was encased in a cairn with cremated bones and pottery placed inside. Significant changes happened from 1500BC onwards: farmers ploughed the area and peat smothered the site and by the time it was excavated in 1857, the peat had settled 1½m deep.

You can take your pick from the many ideas put forward to explain what Callanish represented; the current prevailing view is that the site is tied into lunar events. Research shows how, at certain points in its cycle, the moon skims along the silhouette of the skyline of hills that make up Uig and Great Bernera to the southwest, an outline known as Cailleach na Mointich, the Old Woman of the Moors, which is thought to depict a sleeping woman.

Patrick Ashmore, former principal inspector for Historic Scotland, who excavated the site in the 1980s, calculated that every 18½ years the moon skimmed especially low over the southern hills 'like a great god visiting the earth'. He suggested that knowledge and prediction of this 'heavenly event' gave 'earthly authority to those who watched the skies'.

In 2016, Ashmore published what is widely regarded as the definitive report on Callanish, in which he revealed that, when a small burial chamber surrounded by a cairn was made in the ring, rituals were carried out in an enclosure built just outside. He described the depth and complexity of the archaeology in the ring as 'exceptional'.

Even the etymology of the name 'Calanais' is of uncertain origin. The first recognisable recorded reference to the name today is to 'Classernish', by traveller Martin Martin in 1703. What the name might mean, though, has proved hard to unpick. It may possibly be a phonetic rendering of a Gaelicisation of a Norse name ('nish', or 'ness', is a common Norse word for promontory or headland). One theory suggests the name translates as 'promontory from where one calls for a ferry boat across a sound'.

Remarkably, up to 20 smaller, satellite, sites have been identified in the surrounding landscape. Quite how these interacted with the central stones is unclear – some of them probably did not – but collectively they testify to a landscape that was of huge ritual importance to Neolithic peoples. Two of these sites, **Callanish II** and **Callanish III**, are substantial and worth visiting, as is **Callanish IV** [70 D5], an elliptical ring of five standing stones. Callanish II and III can be inspected on a pleasant walk from Callanish I (see box, opposite); Callanish IV (✪ NB229304) is located across Loch Ceann Hulavig in a magnificently featureless slice of moorland, 1½ miles south of the main site and accessed via a gate just to the west of the B8011. Another ensemble of gneiss, Callanish VIII, comprises a half-circle and is to be found on Great Bernera (page 114).

As impressive as anything else about the stones is the near absence of commercial activity. Infrastructure is low key: there is no entrance fee, no timed ticket, no gate locked after hours, though there is a car park with spaces for coaches and a modest **visitor centre** and café (✆ 01851 621422; w callanishvisitorcentre.co.uk; ☉ Apr–May & Sep–Oct 10.00–18.00 Mon–Sat, Jun–Aug 09.30–20.00 Mon–Sat, Nov–Mar 10.00–16.00 Tue–Sat), all tucked away out of sight.

Barely 2 miles up the A858 from Callanish is the township of Breascleit, home to the workshop of the **Hebridean Soap Company** [70 D5] (25 Breascleit; ✆ 01851 621306; e hebrideansoapco@gmail.com; w hebrideansoap.co.uk; ☉ Feb–Dec 10.00–

3¼km (2 miles); 1½hrs
OS Explorer 458 West Lewis
Start: rear (northern) gate of main Callanish site
Finish: Callanish Visitor Centre

Of the 20 or so related sites that surround the central Callanish stones, the two nearby satellite assemblages of stones and plinths, known as Callanish II and Callanish III, are worth visiting, both for their own interest and for the perspective they offer on the main site. While short, this walk can be boggy. Leave the main site through the back gate and turn right down the lane. At the bottom, turn left and follow the main road for 200m to a sign for Callanish II, or Cnoc Ceann a' Ghàrraidh. Go through the gate or over the stile. Five main stones from an original ten stand here, one resembling an upturned molar, another an incisor that curls and tapers to a sharp point. They are believed to have surrounded a small burial chamber overlooking Loch Roag. The view back towards the main site is striking, with the stones clearly delineated on a high ridge. Follow the boardwalks and marshy ground east to Callanish III, or Cnoc Fhillibhir Bheag, which comprises a double ring of 20 stones, of which 12 are still standing. Head to the main road and turn left to return to the main site. Fork left after 50m and again after 400m to reach the visitor centre.

16.00 Mon–Fri, 10.00–13.00 Sat). In a land once owned by the soap magnate Lord Leverhulme, there is an irony that the company making a viable business from the product is run by a woman from a small stone-clad building across the road from her croft. In her previous life Linda Sutherland was an overloaded systems programmer for a major German bank, managing, as she puts it, 'a dozen other stressed-out and sweaty programmers'. She fled for the hills, taking a holiday on Lewis – and stayed here ever since.

'I sat down with a piece of paper and waited for an idea to come,' she laughs. Linda taught herself how to make soap and draws heavily on local sources such as heather, plants from the machair, and peppermint and comfrey grown in her garden to make 16 different scents. Her company, which employs two part-time staff, produces 16,000 bars of soap per year. Linda will happily show you around the workshop and the yard-long slabs of soap, each weighing 14kg and cut into 120 bars. When the mixture of oils is heated and poured into trays, she places it in a sleeping bag to ensure everything expands fully before cooling and solidifying. You'll see Linda's soap all over the islands, and she has a small shop at the studio, but purposely does not sell on the mainland. 'I made a decision to stay small,' she says and has even declined commissions to make soap moulds of the Callanish stone circle.

The next point of interest, 3 miles further north, is **Dun Carloway (Dùn Chàrlabhaigh)** [70 D4], one of the best-preserved Iron Age forts in Scotland. Visually stirring, the fractured lichen-mantled ruins sweep upwards like a half-collapsed volcano. The broch is thought to have been the home of a tribal leader but its actual purpose remains unclear: too small to be a defendable fort, theories suggest that it may have been a status symbol, a means of showing the power you were able to wield by calling on the substantial labour required to construct it. Exploring the *dùn* involves a lot of ducking under small lintels. Be wary with children here as the staircases front thin air. The site is open year-round and the adjacent subterranean **Doune Broch Centre** (☉ Apr–Sep 10.00–17.00, 'or thereabouts' says the sign, Mon–Sat; free) offers excellent interpretation.

Further up the A858, you cross over the 19th-century Carloway Bridge, which locals, tongue in cheek, claim is one of Scotland's oldest flyovers. A turning here signposted for Na Geàrrannan first takes you past the **Blue Pig Studio** [70 D4] (11 Upper Carloway; ℡01851 643225; w bluepigstudio.co.uk; ☉ Mon–Sat, visitors welcome any time of day). Artist Jane Harlington deploys a captivating use of colour and bold abstract streaks that capture the shifts and changes of light across the islands. A formally trained artist who has exhibited with the Royal Scottish Academy, Jane also offers pottery classes. She retrained as a deacon, divides her time between painting and ministering, and is happy to give you thoughtful insights into the role religion plays up and down the isles. She and her partner Peter have turned part of their studio into a creative space, where visitors can either draw or just talk; they have also landscaped a small quiet garden as a place for reflection.

🚶 THE BONNET LAIRD TRAIL: A WALK IN THE MOORS

13km (8 miles); 4–5hrs
OS Explorer 459 Central Lewis
Start: Callanish Fank (✛ NB224330)
Finish: Carloway School (✛ NB205424)

The Lewis moors keep visitors company all the way up the west side of the island. Yet it can sometimes feel as though they sit in your blind spot, an intangible backdrop to the glories of the west coast. Or perhaps it is just that they look so forbidding and empty: you rarely see anyone other than a peat-cutter on the skyline.

An excellent new moorland walk now allows safe access to these moors and offers a fascinating perspective on this landscape. Running parallel to (but a distance from) the A858, the Bonnet Laird Trail is easily walkable over a day and takes in a mixture of open ground, tracks and small township lanes. The entire route is well waymarked with posts.

The route begins at Callanish Fank (sheep pen), across the main road from Callanish III, and leads up on to the moor proper. Highlights include Braescleit Falls and sweeping views from hills such as Beinn Bheag just north of Braescleit that take in the Flannan Islands.

The walk has been compiled by the Carloway Estate Trust and has been a community-led project from start to finish with schoolchildren designing the waymarkers and helping with groundwork. The name 'Bonnet Laird' is actually a Scottish lowlands term, for people who were not lairds but owned a small amount of land, and is used by those on the estate trust to describe themselves.

The walk can be undertaken in either direction (at its southern end you can walk across to the Callanish visitor centre for food; towards its north end you could break the walk at the Doune Braes hotel for lunch). You can park at either end and use the W2 bus to travel back, or take the bus from Stornoway and pick it up in Carloway as it makes its circular route back to town via Barvas. Pick up a detailed leaflet on the walk from either the tourist office in Stornoway or Callanish visitor centre, or visit w carlowayestatetrust.co.uk.

Continue along the road towards the coast and you reach **Geàrrannan Blackhouse Village** ✱ [70 D4] (◯ 01851 643416; **e** info@gearrannan.com; **w** gearrannan.com; ⊕ Mar–Oct 09.30–17.30 Mon–Sat; £4/£3.80/£10). Blackhouses were the most common living quarters for islanders right into the 20th century and a collection of restored buildings is huddled together here either side of a winding track. Constructed of stone or turf-faced protruding walls with an earthen core and covered with further layers of turf and a straw thatch, blackhouses face the wind and their thatched roofs are pegged down with boulders and ropes made from heather.

One blackhouse contains the admission desk, a good bookshop and a small café but the centrepiece is blackhouse 6, a reconstruction of a modernised 1960s blackhouse that was inhabited until 1972. The design is that of a longhouse and inside the space is divided into two areas. At the top end are box beds for communal sleeping and a hearth of beaten clay which provided warmth and heat for cooking; smoke drifted upwards into the open rafters of the roof before filtering out through the thatch. An enclosed fire would appear to be a health hazard but it did have advantages: it killed bugs, the tar coated the roof timbers, thus preserving them, and, of course, meat and fish could be smoked. The soot-impregnated thatch was also a useful fertiliser once its waterproofing qualities had expired. The 'peat-reek' of the fire is retained for visitors.

Blackhouses were always constructed on a slope and the lower end typically housed a byre, so that cattle slurry did not encroach into the human quarters. Keeping the animals in the same house made it warmer and saved on the labour required to build a barn. A documentary runs in a loop in another house along with other useful interpretation. The remaining blackhouses are offered as holiday lets (page 99).

Close to both the blackhouses in Garenin and the Blue Pig Studio is **Carloway Mill** [70 D4] (◯ 01851 643440; **w** thecarlowaymill.com; **e** sales@thecarlowaymill.com tours; ⊕ 10.30 & 14.00 Tue & Wed, £10 but book in advance; shop ⊕ 09.00–17.30 Mon–Thu, 09.00–13.00 Fri). One of the world's three Harris Tweed textile mills, this is the place to learn more about Harris Tweed. Tours last 20 minutes or so and can be engaging as you watch staff using traditional machinery in what comes across as a family atmosphere. The shop sells finished products such as shawls and purses, as well as yarn and fabric.

Further north, successive turnings wind their way down to two wonderful beaches, first **Dalmore (Dail Mòr)** and then **Dalbeg (Dail Beag)**. Just a few

5½km (3½ miles); up to 3hrs
OS Explorer 460 North Lewis
Start: gate at bottom of Geàrrannan Blackhouse Village (❀ NB192442)
Finish: car park at Dalbeg (❀ NB228458)

A gorgeous, if sometimes tough, walk links Na Geàrrannan to the beaches of Dalmore (Dail Mòr) and Dalbeg (Dail Beag) with thrilling views of towering sea stacks. Yellow waymarkers guide you all the way over open ground though they wander around and are sometimes quite spaced out. Go through the gate at the bottom of the blackhouse village and turn right uphill towards Àird Mhòr. The path drops to Fivig burn, then climbs to the next headland, Àird Mheadhonach. Scattered around, though tricky to find, are the remains of three whisky stills uncovered by archaeologists. A superb sea stack, known as *stac a' chaisteil*, remains tethered – just – to the cliffs here, and is smothered in spring and summer with kittiwakes and fulmars. With binoculars you should be able to pick out a cairn and remains of an Iron Age fort on the stack.

Just beyond the sea stack is Àird a Ghobhann, the last major headland on this route. From here, a grassy bluff zigzags through turf terraces down to a fence which you cross and then follows more waymarkers beneath the hill of Beinn Bheag to the beautiful beach of Dalmore. This is the beach where an oil rig was blown in during a storm in August 2016 (page 10). At the top of the bay is a lonely sand-blown cemetery, featuring many grand tombstones. The path heads northeast between a fence and a stone wall, beneath the hill of Creag an Taghain and cross another fence by a stile. Then keep ahead beneath the hill of Cleit Dalbeg, cross a small stream and then turn right with a fence on your left. After 150m, turn left over the fence to a minor road. Turn left again to reach Dalbeg, a true gem of a beach. You'll pass Loch Dhailbeag, which enjoys a mournfully quiet pond-like setting, fringed with seaweed, where sand blown up from the beaches adds a shimmer to the dark, peaty waters. In summer white lilies cover the water. If using public transport, walk up to the A857 to catch the W2 either to Stornoway or Callanish.

hundred metres up the main road is a **restored Norse mill** and reconstructed kiln barn housed in two thatched buildings on the bank of a small river valley, a short walk from the car park. Nearby in **Shawbost (Siabost)** is Harris Tweed Hebrides (📞01851 700046; e shop@harristweedhebrides.com; w harristweedhebrides.com; ⏰ 10.00–17.30 Mon–Sat), where the shop should satisfy any remaining tweed needs you may have. Just a short way further up the A858 – and still in Shawbost – you'll see the turning to the west that leads down to the township's small but sandy and dune-backed beach.

Dalbeg is home to **The Beach House Gallery** ✳ [70 D3] (m 07500 113872; w thebeachhousegallery.co.uk; ⏰ 'most afternoons'). This recently opened art space will be welcomed by aficionados of Hebrides Art, a gallery in Seilebost in Harris that closed a few years back. The new gallery is run by the same couple, Lesley and Alisdair Wiseman, and boasts a fine collection of their hauntingly evocative seacapes, often painted in intense colour tones. Alasdair's work is more

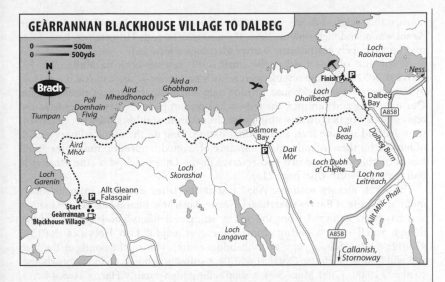

GEÀRRANNAN BLACKHOUSE VILLAGE TO DALBEG

detailed and tends to be pen and ink, while Lesley's paintings are more abstract and capture the different layers of light you see along the coast. The custom-built gallery is integrated into a house of *Grand Designs* proportions and stunningly located above the bay. 'I've always loved this part of Lewis, it's particularly beautiful,' says Lesley. Self-taught, Lesley only returned to painting when she moved to the Outer Hebrides ('we were bringing up children in a small space in Leeds; we had to do work that brought money in'). Her original works, painted on silk, are particularly eye-catching and draw on her observations of fabrics being dyed and dried in Bali.

The adjacent **Loch Dhailbeag**, fringed by both sandy shores and peatland, is exquisitely beautiful. The loch is more nutrient-rich than its counterparts found deeper into the moors. Lime-rich sand is blown into the loch and neutralises the acidic peaty waters that tumble down from inland, fertilising the sediment; this enables white lilies to flower in a striking display in June and July. Eels, sticklebacks and brown trout have been found in its waters. Teal, a colourful, jigsaw-patterned duck, are often around to add to the visual feast.

A mile or so north, the headland at **Labost** is excellent for watching the offshore passage of skuas in spring and skuas, shearwaters and petrels in autumn. On the boundary between South and North Bragar, look out for the **whalebone arch** on the seaward side of the road, complete with harpoon. This 6m-high jawbone of a blue whale was washed up in the 1920s and the harpoon only exploded when it was removed by the local blacksmith, who was seriously wounded.

The **Arnol Blackhouse** [71 E3] (✆ 01851 710395; w historicenvironment.scot, search 'Arnol Blackhouse'; ⊕ Apr–Sep 09.30–17.30 Mon–Sat, Oct–Mar 10.00–16.00 Mon–Tue & Thu–Sat; £6/£3.60/concession £4.80) is located at the end of the road through the township of the same name, just off the A859. To describe it as more authentic is to do the blackhouses at Na Geàrrannan a disservice, but there is something about its unprettified structure that gives you a sense of the rawness involved in living here. A single, long building, it was constructed around the beginning of the 20th century; the roof timbers were insulated with turf and thatch made from oat straw, though the part above the fire was left unturfed to allow smoke to escape. Ropes made from heather were laid over the roof like a hairnet and weighed down with anchor stones to safeguard against bad weather. Arnol was abandoned only in 1966. If your luck's in your Historic Scotland guide may be the hugely enthusiastic Barney Macphail, a local lad.

At the end of this road is the small RSPB reserve **Loch na Muilne** [71 E3] (✆01851 703296; w rspb.org.uk, search 'Loch na Muilne'). You can reach it on foot by heading past the blackhouse, turning right and going through a gate after 750m. During spring and summer, the red-necked phalarope is the key species here and represents a big tick on any birder's list. In autumn, southbound whooper swans from Iceland use the loch as a feeding station. Despite the extraordinary wealth of birdlife on these islands, the dominance of crofted tenureship means the RSPB has been able to secure just two reserves in the Outer Hebrides (the other is at Balranald on North Uist; page 213).

The A858 merges with the A857 just as the latter descends from its lonely moorland route at **Barvas (Barabhas)**. Nearby **Loch Mòr Bharabhais** is very shallow and has been dammed from the sea by shingle. It offers good salmon fishing, though you'll need a permit: contact the ever-helpful Fish Hebrides (✆ 01573 470612; e info@fishpal.com; w fishhebrides.co.uk). Just to the south of the loch you will find Brue House (✆01851 840706; e info@bruehouse.co.uk; w bruehouse. co.uk; ⊕ 10.00–17.00 Mon–Sat), a shop selling high-quality Harris Tweed items, ranging from lampshades to cushions and diary covers. The shop is run by Lyndsey and Nick Stansfield, who have turned a spare room in their house into a shop front for their sewing and creative skills.

The landscape and the road empty out north of Bragar. The first place worth stopping at is the **Morven Gallery** ✳ [71 E3] (✆01851 840247; e morvengal@gmail. com; w morvengallery.com; ⊕ Easter–Sep 10.30–17.00 Tue–Sat). This beautifully designed art gallery run by Janis Scott has a central loft-style exhibition space and conscientiously promotes local contemporary artists. There's also a small café. Check ahead to ensure both gallery and café are open.

Just beyond the gallery, look out on the coastal side of the road for a signpost to the **Clach an Truiseil**, or **Thrishel Stone** [71 E3], a 6m-high monolith thought to be the tallest single stone in Scotland. It has a distinctive sideways tilt and is thought to have been used as a beacon since Norse days, a theory backed up by more recent reports from the sea of the stone lit up by bonfire. Other perspectives suggest that a stone circle of the stature of Callanish once stood here with the stone at its centre; or that it was erected by the people of Ness to celebrate a victory over their rivals, the MacAuleys, from Uig.

Another mile up the road in Siadar, this time on the right, is a signposted turn-off for the **Steinacleit stone circle** [71 F2]. The lane leading there is in poor condition but there's space to park at its end where a gate leads on to open ground to reach the stones. They're hardly dramatic but it's a pleasant short walk that gives views across the open landscape. You may find the fractured remains of the *dùn* in the loch behind you; these may date back 2,000 years and are easier on the eye. Further up the coast at **Borve (Borgh)** and clearly signposted is the Borgh Pottery (✆01851 850345; e borghpottery@yahoo.co.uk; w borghpottery.co.uk; ⊕ Easter– Oct 10.30–17.30 Tue–Sat, Oct–Easter 10.30–17.30 Sat), a studio run by Alex and Sue Blair. Their focus is on ceramics and they have a distinctive and sometimes subtly Norse take on design; their ornamental-pottery garden is a pleasant place to linger.

A mile north of Borve, the road passes through the township of **Galson (Gabhsann)**, where fine views open up and the peaty moors that have accompanied you all the way up the coast finally begin to yield to grassland. The community-run

The Flannan Isles, 20 miles off the west coast of Lewis, are home to an unsolved and tragic tale. The miniature archipelago is also known as the Seven Hunters after the seven isles they comprise, but it gets its common name from a ruined chapel dedicated to St Foannen on the main island, Eilean Mòr. Work on a lighthouse, designed by David Alan Stevenson, began in 1899, but it was only a year later that tragedy struck. The first sign that something had gone awry emerged on 15 December 1900, when a passing steamer recorded that the light was not working. A severe storm prevented the relief lighthouse tender from sailing to the islands until Boxing Day. The keepers alighted on shore and entered the lighthouse only to find an untouched meal on the kitchen table, an overturned chair and a set of oilskins. The last entry in the log book was 09.00 on 15 December. A search of the island and waters found no trace of the three keepers. A poem by Wilfred Wilson Gibson captured the mood of the mystery:

Though three men dwell on Flannan Isle,
To keep the lamp alight,
As we steer'd under the lee, we caught,
No Glimmer through the night.

Tour operators (page 38) occasionally run trips out to the Flannan Isles from Uig with gannets, puffins, storm petrels and mountain hares to watch out for. Landings can be difficult. A small memorial to commemorate the lives of the lighthouse keepers was unveiled in Breasclete in 2017, while a modest exhibition telling the tale can be found in **Breasclete Community Centre** [70 D5] (⊕ Apr–Oct 14.00–16.00 Mon–Sat).

Galson Estate Trust is very active and every year runs Dùthchas, the Galson Estate heritage week (w galsontrust.com). This enjoyable event actively welcomes visitors and features food and drink, walks, music and dance, storytelling by the fireside, workshops on Gaelic, and traditional skills courses such as rope work.

Ness and the Butt of Lewis Ness is the name given to a large and sprawling collection of communities which amalgamate in the northwest corner of Lewis. Home to 1,100 inhabitants, it's a surprisingly busy part of the island that runs for 3 miles both north–south and (in a grand arc over an expanse of machair) east–west. The main places of interest are found around the harbour at **Port of Ness (Port Nis)** [71 G1] in the north and the community of **Eoropie (Eòropaidh)** to the west. Thrilling coastal walks are a highlight, along with a lonely lighthouse, an even lonelier church and sweeping views to the horizon in all directions. In addition, Ness can offer you a swimming pool, ten-pin bowling and a social club.

Ness is somewhere that draws you in quite quickly. It's not just the spectacle of dramatic cliffs and the palpable sense you get of the northwest extremity of the British Isles tilting into the sea; it's also the piercing clarity of the light, which, as it bounces off Ness's many rocky promontories, seems to absorb and refract the machair of the sandy grasslands and the tapering edges of the Lewis peatlands. The cliffs, rocks, even the pebbles on the beaches, add to the atmosphere: made from Lewisian gneiss, they have all been pummelled and contorted into striking shapes and contours.

Lewis (Leòdhais)   AROUND STORNOWAY

3

Visually, the area can be slightly confusing for the first-time visitor, but essentially a looping ring road knits everything together and runs west from Port of Ness to Eoropie and back to the A857 via **Loch Stiapabhat**. Ness can be incredibly windy, so much so that you wonder how people have ever made a living here.

The sturdy harbour in Port of Ness is tucked down a slope and looks as postcard-pretty as anything in Cornwall, except that you will often have it, and the beach beyond, to yourself. The concrete walls of the breakwater, assembled in dog-leg fashion like Herculean blocks of Lego, reflect the matrix of buttresses needed to keep at bay the savage waves that heave up here in the wildest winds. The harbour is the place from where each year the men of the area set sail to conduct the annual Guga (gannet) Hunt on **Sula Sgeir**, 45 miles northeast of the Butt of Lewis (see box, opposite). Archaeological remains are regularly found on the exposed dunes of the west coast of Ness.

Follow the road from Ness anti-clockwise as it curves around to reach Eoropie, where you'll find tiny **St Moluag's chapel (Teampull Mholuaidh)** [71 G1] tucked away, 300m down a narrow footpath squeezed between field fences. The church was built during the 12th–14th centuries on the site of a much earlier chapel that had associations with pre-Christian rituals that paid homage to the sea god Shony. Some pagan elements are believed to have survived into the 19th century. Inside, a beautiful stained-glass arch of blue and yellow above the altar is hemmed in by thick-set stone walls. In 1999 the church yielded a surprise when the sacristy was forced open to reveal a late 18th-century chalice of French origin.

If you have children, your luck is in as the **Eoropie dunes** [71 G1] have one of the most wonderful play parks you could hope to find, with swings, slides, a pirate ship and roundabouts built on the sandy grass that overlooks the wider dunes. One

AN ARTIST IN NESS

Just above the harbour is **Harbour View Gallery** [71 G1] (℡ 01851 810735; e info@abarber.co.uk; w abarber.co.uk; ⊕ Mar–Nov 10.00–17.00 Mon–Sat, other times by appt; see ad, page 131), the studio of Anthony J Barber. You are likely to see Anthony's watercolour and acrylic landscape paintings, which often portray the captivating sands of Luskentyre on Harris, for sale and on display around Lewis and Harris. 'It sounds a bit cheesy but the minute I arrived in the Outer Hebrides, they felt like proper islands,' he says. 'They just struck a chord.' Anthony began with eight prints that were well received and has gone from strength to strength. He will head with his sketch book for the hills and beaches, the light and contrast of colours catching his eye. 'You will often see something you haven't seen before simply because the light has changed. Some days I have a vague idea of what I'll paint, on others I flick through the sketch books and pick out something from years ago.' Luskentyre is his favourite area. 'It's the change of light that gets you there,' he says. Conveying this on canvas is a challenge. 'I don't try and paint every blade of grass and sometimes I'll add a colour that isn't there because it can bring out other colours. It's a challenging landscape. I will pick up certain colours and magnify them eight or nine times. For that reason, I tend to paint on acrylic as it dries at the same intensity as you go along, so you don't lose the colour as can happen with watercolours.'

Look out for Anthony's small book of sketches, complete with field notes, available from his studio and at bookshops in Stornoway.

Every August, ten men from Ness set sail from the harbour and head 40 miles almost due north to the island of Sula Sgeir. There, over the course of two weeks, they catch, kill, skin, gut and smoke 2,000 young gannets (*guga*). Working around the clock, the men live in stone bothies first constructed by monks more than 1,000 years ago. They return home laden with the processed bird carcasses. While the hunting of seabirds in the UK was outlawed in 1954, the community of Ness has been granted an exemption under UK and EU law.

The tradition is certainly not to everyone's taste and is challenged from time to time by animal welfare organisations. Yet supporters of the hunt will not be shifted: in an age when Gaelic culture is at risk of being submerged by that of incomers – even if those incomers are well-intentioned – the hunt seems to have crystallised into a symbol of local identity and pride. Furthermore, the entire quota of 'harvested' gannets is spoken for before the men have even set sail from Ness. The earliest written evidence suggests the hunt dates back to at least 1549, and advocates point out that, when crops and potatoes have failed, or fish depleted, the guga were always there to provide protein.

For many years, the hunt was a closely guarded secret with few details in the public domain. Wariness prevails, but in 2011 a BBC film crew was allowed to document the hunt and produce a captivating film, *The Guga Hunters of Ness*. The definitive book on the tradition, *The Guga Hunters*, was published in 2008 by Ness-born writer Donald S Murray.

Sula Sgeir, meanwhile, attracted further national attention in the spring of 2005 when a black-browed albatross turned up there. Inevitably named Albert, the bird returned for the following two summers. Thought to have wandered off course from his natural habitat in the South Atlantic, the bird may well live out its life somewhere in Scotland.

Boat trips are occasionally organised to Sula Sgeir, usually by Lewis-based operators (page 75). These trips may also take in **North Rona**, which lies 10 miles east of Sula Sgeir. North Rona is so small that even when the weather is clear it is rarely seen from afar. One tale claims that, in a race to gain ownership of the island, a man from Ness cut off his own finger and threw it on to the rocks to beat the claim of rivals from Sutherland. The island has a tiny drystone chapel of distinctive Celtic appearance, dating to the 7th or 8th century AD; it may be the oldest intact Christian chapel in Britain. Clustered around it are a small number of abandoned houses and a walled graveyard.

time while my own children were playing here, a hen harrier coasted over the pirate ship and flapped its way across the moors. Around the dunes, warm days bring out meadow brown and common blue butterflies. Port of Ness beach, just by the harbour, is another vast and empty playground for little people. Meanwhile, wildlife watchers can keep an eye out here for Arctic terns and gannets in summer and, year-round, red-throated, black-throated and (highly unusually for the UK) great northern divers.

A signposted track near to St Moluag's points to the **Butt of Lewis (Rubha Robhanais)** [71 G1]. You can drive a mile to this, the most northwesterly point of the British Isles and of Europe; alternatively it's a 30-minute walk or a short cycle ride. The Butt is an exposed and elemental place, just how you might imagine the

CIRCULAR WALK FROM EOROPIE TO THE BUTT OF LEWIS

6½km (4 miles); 2hrs
OS Explorer 460 North Lewis
Start/finish: car park & play park at Eoropie dunes (⊕ NB518647)

Be prepared for wind: I began this walk anticlockwise and hit powerful headwinds, whereupon I turned tail and walked it clockwise – yet still felt as though I was walking backwards.

Begin at the Eoropie dunes play park and walk up on to the machair towards the sea with the over-high dunes to your left, following the Ness Coastal Walk waymarkers (a footprint on purple and aquamarine). The rhubarb-like leaves of the butterbur plant add an unexpectedly lush sheen to the landscape around the dune edges. The dunes themselves are enticing but extensive, so, if you're doing this walk, they are probably best left to explore another time.

There is a gentle reminder about quicksand at the top of the beach. Go through the gate and along the right side of the beach, passing a large stone bench, and up through the gate to the right. You pass a monument to the Cunndal drowning, a fishing disaster that claimed 12 local lives in 1885. The tragedy somehow managed to be even more distressing as it unfolded in broad daylight, just offshore. A dangerous undercurrent prevented rescuers from reaching the men.

Follow the waymarker posts as they sweep down towards the shore and then cut above a geo. Up above, the headland simply collapses into the sea above Cundill Bay. Here – and indeed along all the cliffs of Ness – is a good place to look out for birds of prey, including white-tailed and golden eagles, along with darting peregrine falcons and the smaller merlin. The path rises once more across a wide strip of pronounced lazy beds, which resemble turfed polytunnels, but are in fact a form of arable cultivation that involves distinctive manmade ridges designed to improve the soil and help drainage. Cross a stream by stepping stones and walk up to a gate below a conspicuous cairn. The path sweeps west and upwards with views down the west coast of Lewis.

The waymarker posts begin to nudge you east towards the lighthouse – its tip now visible – but it's worth persevering due west, a little further towards the coast, across the huge open machair headland. This is an exposed part of the universe, but the scenery is breathtaking.

Turning back towards the lighthouse, there is a spot some 550m before you reach it that, on a fine day, gives a truly magical view; to the west you can see Àird Uig headland, while to the east you can pick out Cape Wrath on the mainland. Including the land you are standing on, you have three of the most dramatic coastal points in the UK in one view.

Walk through a gate towards the lighthouse. Then, if you don't have a head for heights, take the right-hand, inland path to reach the lighthouse while avoiding the sheer cliffs. The transmitter mast here is one of the most astonishing places to witness a starling roost at dusk. During such a spectacle, the whole place feels like a stage set for Alfred Hitchcock's *The Birds*. From the lighthouse, there is a paved track that winds its way up and over the headland back to Eoropie.

edge of a map should look, with sheer cliffs, seabirds slicing through punishing headwinds and sea stacks weathered by a broiling sea. Towering above this natural drama, at 58°30'92N and 6°15'71W, is the **lighthouse** [71 G1]. Standing 36.8m (121ft) high, the lighthouse's red bricks have resisted the weather despite never having been painted since it was completed in 1862 by the Stevenson family.

Heading south from Eoropie on the road that passes Ness Football Club you reach the township of Lionel and the easiest access point for **Loch Stiapabhat** [71 G1]. The signposted path is across the road from The Decca guesthouse (page 99) and the giant sports centre, Spòrsnis (📞01851 810039; e info@sporsnis.co.uk; w sporsnis. co.uk) with its ten-pin bowling alley and swimming pool. Loch Stiapabhat is among the most fertile on Lewis as it lies on glacial soils carried across the Minch from the mainland during the last Ice Age. Its name is said to mean 'the loch of immersing or soaking' and is thought to relate to the practice of soaking flax prior to spinning. The loch lies on the main flyway from and to the Arctic and is consequently a magnet for ornithologists with regular flurries of excitement as unexpected birds are blown off course. The loch also has archaeological secrets that it only sparingly reveals; it's thought, for example, that the ballast of a Viking ship rests in the loch. In summer, the machair around the loch becomes a carpet of colour with bird's-foot trefoil, eyebright, clovers and orchids. Keep an eye out here for some of Ness's six species of bumblebee: their healthy populations are generally attributed to the near absence of pesticides and insecticides, and the abundance of vetch, clover and thistle.

The Galson Estate Trust (w galsontrust.com) provides a ranger service for the loch, and indeed the whole of Ness, offering programmes of seasonal walks. You can learn more about the natural environment in this extremity of the British Isles on the first floor of the Spòrsnis complex, where there is a useful and free ongoing exhibition, 'Wild About Ness'.

Back on the A857, 3 miles south of Ness harbour, is the **Comunn Eachdraidh Nis (Ness Historical Society Museum)** [71 G1] (📞01851 810377; e office@cenonline. org; w cenonline.org; ⊕ 10.00–16.30 Mon–Fri) in North Dell, which houses the chalice found in the sacristy of St Moluag, plus genealogical records. This excellent small museum has recently been renovated and converted into an impressive public space with slate flooring and Douglas fir seating.

GREAT BERNERA (BEÀRNARAIGH)
Located southwest of Callanish and reached off the Uig road, the island of Great Bernera is wild and empty. An Iron Age fort is the single 'sight' here, but the moorlands and quiet roads are excellent for yomps over open ground amid undulating scenery of hills and lochs. The long loch of **Tòb Bhalasaigh** dominates the hinterland of the island, starts deep inland and then narrows and tapers before reaching the open sea at Loch Roag. The loch and adjacent coastline are good places to look for otters. In spring and early summer this is an excellent place to see and hear cuckoos.

Great Bernera is tied to the 'mainland' of Lewis by a small single-track metalled road bridge known locally as 'The bridge over the Atlantic'. This was opened in 1953, following great pressure from local communities, who had threatened to blow up rocks and create their own causeway if they did not get their way. The opening ceremony was documented by the *Stornoway Gazette*, which reported how: 'On that day Bernera ceased to be an island and became part of Lewis. Or perhaps it would be more accurate to say Lewis ceased to be an island and became part of Bernera.'

✖ Where to eat and drink The **Bernera Community Café** [70 C5] (Breacleit; 📞01851 612311; ⊕ Jun–Aug noon–16.00 Mon–Fri, other times 13.00–15.00 Tue &

In 1874 a land dispute brought to a head the sizzling tensions between crofters and the despised factor Donald Munro, who squeezed rents and evicted those who failed to pay. When 54 crofters refused to comply with demands to restrict their summer grazings they were served with a summons. A riot ensued, forcing the sheriff to retreat from the island. One rioter was subsequently arrested in Stornoway, whereupon 400 men and women from Great Bernera marched on the house of the landlord James Matheson. Given his record and reputation, Matheson was unexpectedly sympathetic and pledged to take no further action. Munro had other ideas and three ringleaders were arrested, though they were later acquitted. The movement led to the Crofters Act and greater security of tenure. The small monument at the junction of the Bostadh and Tobson roads is dedicated to the rioters and was built from stones from every croft on the island. It's an excellent vantage point from which to look west towards the coast and Uig.

Thu; £) inside the community centre, which also houses the museum (see below), serves sandwiches and hot drinks.

What to see and do The first site you encounter on Great Bernera offers proof that the island has a long, shared history of rituals with its larger neighbour Lewis. Immediately after you cross the bridge from Lewis, follow a short path up to the left for about 50m to reach a striking semicircle of stones (✪ NB164342), standing on the lip of a 12m cliff. This is **Callanish VIII** [70 C5], comprising four stones and overlooking Loch Roag. Despite the name, it remains unclear if the site is actually one of the more remote outliers of the main Callanish stone circle (which is out of view). A theory of a link between the two sites is sustained by various lunar alignments that can be made from this location. Whatever the provenance, the site's elevated lochside position, isolation and the singularity of its stones, creates a special atmosphere, particularly as dusk approaches on a clear, still day. If you're driving, there are parking places by the Great Bernera side of the bridge.

Bostadh Iron Age House [118 G1] (⊕ mid-May–Sep noon–16.00 Mon–Fri; £3/£1) lies at the northern tip of the island. In 1992 a severe storm exposed the dunes and beach at Bostadh, allowing archaeologists to uncover five Pictish houses, dating to AD400–800. The houses quickly suffered from exposure to the elements and defied preservation, so what you see today is a reconstructed Iron Age house, known locally – because of its shape – as the 'jelly baby house' with a subterranean entrance and small chamber.

The small **Bernera Museum** [map, page 116] (⊕ same hours as café, page 113; £2/ free) is housed in the community centre in Breacleit (Breaclete) and has displays from the island's fishing heritage and information on social history.

UIG Tucked away – if such a large area can be hidden – to the southwest of Lewis, Uig is one of the island's great secrets. Its remoteness can make it easy to overlook and even the otherwise pedantic Ordnance Survey omits the name Uig from the title of the sheet that covers the region (OS Explorer 458 West Lewis, Callanish & Great Bernera).

Much hillier than Lewis, Uig has a bit of everything: a mountainous skyline, staggeringly beautiful beaches, some great food, fine walks and important

11¼km (7 miles); 3hrs
OS Explorer 458 West Lewis
Start/finish: Bernera Community Centre & Café at Breacleit (✪ NB159368)

This walk tackles the northern half of Great Bernera, following the coast northwards, above a series of geos that cut into the rocky shore. Vantage points along the way offer excellent views of a large part of much of Lewis and Harris. Begin by taking the minor road behind the Breacleit community centre signposted for Tacleit and Bhalasaigh. After a hairpin bend, you reach a house on the right. Immediately after the house, turn right down a minor road, signposted to Bhalasaigh. Just beyond a sign advising 'no parking' you reach an arched footbridge across Tòb Bhalasaigh with a footpath sign saying 'Tobson 2¾km'. Cross the footbridge via a gate at its eastern end, following signs and waymarkers for Bostadh. At the point where the waymarkers fork, keep to those by the coast.

The path goes to the west of Loch Veiravat then cuts inland across a short marshy section. This brings it closer to the waters of Tòb Bhalasaigh, with a cairn up to your left. The waymarkers continue down to the road at Tobson. Turn left uphill at the T-junction and after 150m head right through a gate, signposted 'Bostadh 2km'. Here waymarkers lead across the summit of Beinn am Toib and then across the head of Loch a' Sgail. The route heads north up a cleft in the hill, then descends the valley to Bostadh beach. Follow the road behind the Iron Age settlement back to Breacleit along the shores of Loch na Muilne, passing the monument to the Bernera rioters along the way.

archaeological sites that emerge like apparitions on the vast marshy moors. For generations, Uig has been a place visited only by those 'in the know'; it has long been a popular summer holiday destination for inhabitants of Stornoway. While this is broadly still the case, the secret of Uig's magnificent landscape and coastline is getting out and every year that passes now brings a smattering of new places to stay or eat.

Places to explore include the **Valtos (Bhaltos) headland** and the stunning beaches at Cnip (Kneep), **Uig Sands** (scene of the discovery of the Lewis chessmen), the isolated and often violent scenery around **Gallan Head** on the **Àird peninsula**, and the **southerly reaches of the B8011**, which drift away through a series of scattered townships and breathtaking cliffs around **Mangersta (Mangarstadh)** to the road's remote end at desolate **Mealasta**. Here and there you will catch sight of wild North Ronaldsay sheep that were introduced here and live (like their counterparts on the Orcadian island whence they came) for the most part on seaweed, which gives their meat a delectably subtle salty flavour. Services are focussed around the township of **Timsgarry (Timsgearraidh)**. Plan ahead for Sunday when – apart from the Edge Café at Gallan Head (page 121) and the Uig Sands restaurant (page 121) – everything is closed. A new mast at Islibhig means that 4G is now widespread in Uig and the region is no longer the mobile-phone black hole it once was.

History Scandinavian influence is evident from around AD800, and many villages of that time are thought to lie unidentified, concealed under subsequent habitations. Norse names predominate and the word 'Uig' itself comes from 'takeVig', the Norse

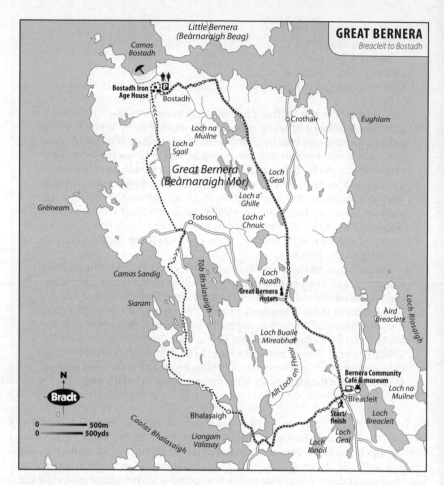

word for bay. Elsewhere you will see Norse name influences such as Mangarstadh (Mangus's farm), as well as geographical features such as 'nis' (headland), 'shader' (shieling), 'ay' (island), 'vat' (loch) and 'val' (hill). Historically, Uig has never been anything other than a tough place to live. The Seaforth Mackenzies were the feudal lords here from the middle of the 17th century until they sold it in 1844 to James Matheson. By the 1850s, sporting estates had taken hold of much of the landscape.

The clearances in Uig were as devastating here as anywhere. It can be hard to take on board what it means when you read time and again how several thousand people were evicted from the Outer Hebrides; yet the grassroots impact becomes more tangible when you learn that 22 families were evicted from the village of Capadail in Uig, or that 12 families were evicted from Carnais. Matheson saw to it that 28 families at Reef were evicted even though they had no rent arrears. By the late 19th century, the remaining population on Valtos was crowded together in two villages with no access to the land surrounding them.

Today, the region faces the same challenges as the rest of the Outer Hebrides. One by one schools have closed, some converted into teahouses or outdoor centres. Deserted blackhouses from the mid 20th century dot the landscape. Elsewhere, salmon cages stud the sea lochs, hinting at one of the few industries that is thriving.

In theory, things should be looking up for Uig: improvements to the road network have cut travel times to Stornoway while the internet should encourage the kind of younger blood that can base their work anywhere. Time will tell. It's worth seeking out the excellent booklet *Discovering Uig*, available in the Uig Community and Heritage Centre and the community shop in Timsgarry, which gives a great deal of background to the region, history and offers excellent suggestions for places to visit.

Getting there and away Getting to Uig is much easier thanks to the steady upgrading of the B8011, which threads its way through the canyon of Glenn Bhaltois to Timsgarry (Timsgearraidh). The turning for the B8011 is at Garrynahine on the A858, 4 miles west of Acha Mòr. The road keeps you on your toes, however: funding for the highway seems to expire halfway along the shores of Loch Ròg Beag. The consequence is that a run-of-the-mill A-road, which invites people to hit the speed limit (60mph here), suddenly shrivels to the width and sometimes the quality of a cattle track. As you travel further along, the B8011 splutters back to a double-width road for brief and seemingly random interludes. It's easy to underestimate driving times: it will take around 50 minutes to reach Timsgarry from Stornoway and a further 30 minutes or so to the end of the B8011 at Mealasta. If you're based anywhere else on Lewis or Harris then a visit to Uig that takes you as far as Mealasta involves a long day trip.

The W4 bus links Stornoway to Uig and runs all the way past Uig Sands down to Brèinis at the bottom of the B8011. Note there are usually only two services a day and for some services you need to book in advance.

Where to stay, eat and drink Uig is a curiosity. There's not much out here in the way of sleeping or eating, but the few places you come across are, without exception, of an extremely high standard. This is particularly the case with food: if fine dining in the wilds of the Celtic fringe – mainly at mid-range prices – is for you then Uig is the place to come. Instead of taking the easier approach of disappointing a captive audience, the scarcity of food and accommodation outlets has been turned into a virtue by all who offer them. As Marianne Campbell at Loch Croistean puts it: 'I just fell in

> ## ROPE-GROWN MUSSELS
>
> You can hardly pick up a menu anywhere in the Outer Hebrides without being offered rope-grown mussels, and this has been one of the most successful island industries of recent years. When you look at what you think are salmon farms and cages on lochs, what lurks below the surface is often in fact a mussel farm and this is the case on Uig. Upon discovering that 'mussels feed themselves and come in their own packaging' Hebridean Mussels Ltd was founded by 'Jock' Mackenzie in 1992 for the purposes of cultivating mussels on suspended ropes in West and East Loch Roag. The mussels require no feeding or supplements to maintain their health and development. Each spring, 'spat' ropes are suspended from floating long lines in sea lochs where wild mussel spat (spawn) are present. After drifting in currents for two weeks, wild spat attaches to these ropes and feeds on plankton. The spat reach market size in about 30 months. This method contrasts to the principal method of obtaining mussels in the UK, which is to dredge the bottom; supporters of the Uig method say their approach means less disturbance to the ecology of the waters and seabed.

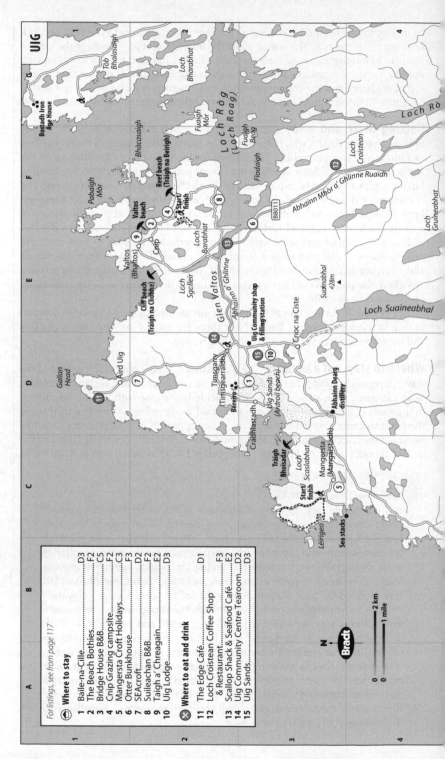

For listings, see from page 117

① Where to stay

1	Baile-na-Cille	D3
2	The Beach Bothies	F2
3	Bridge House B&B	C5
4	Cnip Grazing campsite	F2
5	Mangersta Croft Holidays	C3
6	Otter Bunkhouse	F3
7	SEAcroft	D2
8	Suileachan B&B	F2
9	Taigh a' Chreagain	E2
10	Uig Lodge	D3

✕ Where to eat and drink

11	The Edge Café	D1
12	Loch Croistean Coffee Shop & Restaurant	F3
13	Scallop Shack & Seafood Café	E2
14	Uig Community Centre Tearoom	D2
15	Uig Sands	D3

118

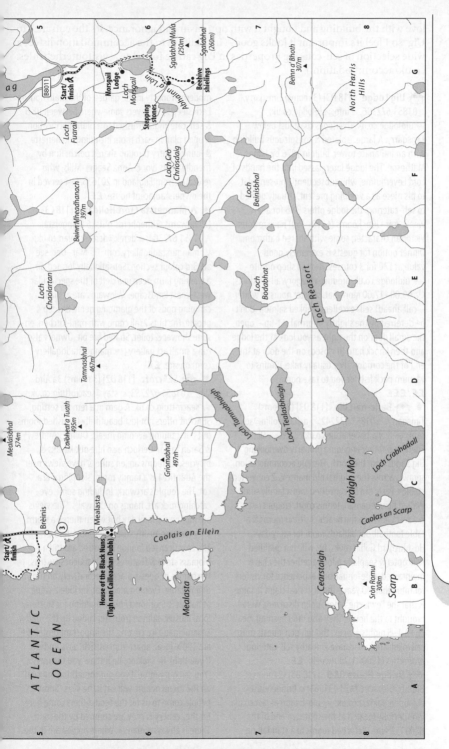

ATLANTIC OCEAN

Start/ finish

Brèinis

Mealasta

House of the Black Nuns
(Tigh nan Cailleachan Dubh)

Caolais an Eilein

Mealasta

Mealaisbhal
574m

Taibheal a Tuath
495m

Griomabhal
497m

Loch Chaolartan

Tamnasbhal
467m

Loch Tunnabhaigh

Beinn Mheadhanach
397m

Loch Crò
Chrìosdaig

Loch
Fuarail

Start/ finish

B8011

a g

Morsgail
Lodge

Loch
Morsgail

Stepping
stones

Abhainn a' Loin

Sgalabhal Mula (250m)

Sgalabhal
(260m)

Beehive
shielings

Loch Beinisbhal

Loch
Bodabhat

Loch Rèasort

Loch Tealasbhaigh

Behn a' Bhoth
307m

North Harris
Hills

Bràigh Mòr

Loch Crabhadall

Caolas an Scarp

Cearstaigh

Sròn Romul
308m

Scarp

love with the building and bought it with optimism and ignorance. It's the entrance to Uig, so I feel it's important it looks good.' (In addition to the accommodation listed, a wide selection of self-catering properties in Uig can be found at w visitouterhebrides. co.uk/accommodation.)

Uig Lodge [118 D3] (3 rooms) Timsgarry; 01851 672396; e info@uiglodge.co.uk; w uiglodge.co.uk. Overlooks coast just below Timsgarry. A large, isolated & conspicuous building with an Italianate tower, built in 1876 by James Matheson. The lodge later passed into the hands of Lord Leverhulme, who subsequently presented it to his niece as a wedding present. Usually geared to self-catering, the lodge offers B&B for a few weeks Apr–Jun. Rooms (£110–150) have restored Victorian character; some with shared bathroom. Dinner option for guests is extremely good value at £30 for 3 courses. A small shop on site (w uiglodge.co.uk/product-category/all-products; 09.00–17.00 Mon–Sat, shorter hours in winter – call ahead) sells excellent smoked salmon; don't be deterred by the slightly informal set-up – open the small door on the right as you look at the lodge and then knock hard (if closed) on the door at the end of the corridor. They usually take 10mins to vacuum pack fish for you to take home. **££/£££**

Baile-na-Cille [118 D3] (8 rooms) Timsgarry; 01851 672242; e richardgollin@aol. com; w www.bailenacille.co.uk; May–Oct. Friendly & rather engaging property overlooking Uig Sands from the north. Flexible accommodation sprawls across the original old manse & 2 converted stables. Parts can be converted into a family suite. Walled flower garden, tennis court, croquet lawn & a track down to the beach. 3 sitting rooms & a table football/bar billiards room for rainy days. Host Richard Gollin cooks; his wife is a qualified helicopter & seaplane pilot. Together they have maintained a life-enhancing experience for visitors for more than 40 years. The historical claim to fame is that the Lewis chessmen, upon discovery, were brought to the house. They also offer evening meals (££) 4–5 nights a week, though non-guests must call in advance. Also have 2 nearby self-catering properties (£900–1,200/week). **££**

Bridge House B&B [118 B5] (2 rooms) Brèinis, Uig; m 07423 431961; e bridgehouse@ uig-bedbreakfast.co.uk; w uig-bedbreakfast.co.uk. Wonderfully located at the southern end of the B8011, 2 semi-detached rooms in a standalone

modern property in the garden of the main house. Each sleeps 2 & hovers somewhere between B&B & self-catering. Furnished to a high specification & open plan in each room including kitchenette & lounge. Entry through shared porch. Run by friendly hosts Ivor & Anna Seager-Mills, who relocated from England in 2016. B/fast served in the owners' adjacent house. **££**

Mangersta Croft Holidays [118 C3] (2 wigwams, 2 shepherds' huts) 5 Mangersta; 01851 672384; e derek@derekscanlan.co.uk; w mangurstadhgallery.com; Mar–Dec; see ad, 3rd colour section. Sensationally located on a working farm deep in a cleft of the spectacular west-coast landscape. 'Wigwams' are actually camping pods of the glamping genre & sleep 4 people, the huts 2; all come with mini-kitchen, en-suite shower & toilet. Shared fire pit. Owners also run a small art gallery (w mangurstadhgallery. com) on site. **££**

SEAcroft [118 D2] (3 rooms) 3a Àird Uig; 01851 672753; e stay@seacroftuig.co.uk; w seacroftuig.co.uk. A gem in a remote setting, SEAcroft offers not just beautifully furnished rooms but outstanding evening meals. Owners Andrew & Sarah Taylor-Gerloch also hire out kayaks & bicycles. All rooms are en suite & have views over the Atlantic. 1 is a family room, sleeping 4 & a cot. The couple's artwork, including some eye-catching rock art, hangs on the walls. 'The views are nice on a sunny day but when there's a storm they really come into their own,' says Andrew. The cosy licensed lounge is centred around a biomass stove & features lovely touches such as the names of guests placed decoratively on the dining table. Evening meals can include a crêpe of haggis & Stornoway black pudding for starters, local lobster, salmon from Uig Lodge up the road & homemade ice cream. 'The important proteins are 100% local, apart from ostrich,' says Andrew. If you think he's joking, he'll show you the menu. 'You can guarantee if you put something unusual on the menu people will eat it,' he says. 'Some people come to us for the food, others come here for the scenery & they are stunned by the food. There is always a market, wherever you are in the

above   The lonely moors and lochs of South Uist give way to the dramatic Beinn Mhòr mountain range on the island's east coast (JG/S) page 260

below   The rocky moonscape around the townships of Borsham and Finsbay in The Bays on the east coast of South Harris yield bewitching colours at dawn (CW) page 173

left The restored blackhouse village at Na Geàrrannan on Lewis shows how islanders lived as recently as the 1960s (KL/VS) page 105

below The spectacular broch at Carloway (Dùn Chàrlabhaigh) remains an enigma — no-one knows for sure who built it, or why (KL/VS) page 103

bottom An avenue of stones on elevated land leads up to the central circle of Callanish on Lewis (PB) page 101

right   Lews Castle in Stornoway is home to the new island museum, while its grounds offer pleasant woodland walks (SS) page 87

below   Like other blackhouses, Arnol on Lewis squeezed bedchambers into living quarters while livestock overwintered in the next room (LC) page 107

bottom   Many traditional blackhouses have been restored and make for wonderful self-catering holidays (LQ/D) page 105

above The island 'capital' of Stornoway has a clutch of good cafés and a working harbour (DM) page 76

below left Crofting remains central to cultural and economic life on the islands (LC) page 26

below right A replica of a Lewis chessman in woods in Stornoway — see the (much smaller) originals in the nearby island museum (S/D) page 127

bottom Time for the author to take a break with some local food at the superb Croft 36 on Harris (SM) page 161

top   Peat remains an important source of heating fuel, and peat cuttings are a common sight (ML) page 8

above   Harris and Lewis are home to Harris Tweed, and you can buy anything from tweed scarves to handbags, hoodies and offcuts (BTIH and CW) page 175

below   *Feisean* (festivals) take place throughout the year and often include traditional lilts played by piping bands (PB) page 55

top left   Eider ducks, with their green nape and distinctive 'coo', can be seen in large numbers (LC) page 14

top right   Around 80 pairs of golden eagles inhabit the islands' mountains, often darting down after prey on the machair and lochs (LC) page 14

above   Frequently heard, sometimes seen, the corncrake and its rasping song thrive on North Uist and Benbecula (LC) page 14

below   Puffins can often be the first birds you see as you cross to the islands by ferry in May and June (LC) page 14

above   Look out for red deer just about anywhere — even by the roadside (LC) page 11

right   Grey seals can be seen right along the islands' Atlantic shorelines, especially around the Monach Islands (LC) page 15

below   Some locals claim that the Highland cow first emerged here before moving to the mainland (PB) page 12

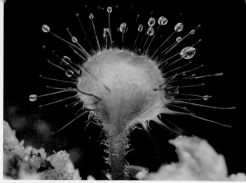

above left   Bog asphodel often brings a dash of colour to the bleak moors of the Outer Hebrides (LC) page 95

top right   The mighty Hebridean midge meets its match when faced with one of its predators – the carnivorous sundew (LC) page 96

above right   A walk across heath, bogs or moorland will reveal many colourful plants, including the cross-leaved heather (LC) page 9

below   The sea meadows known as machair are transformed in summer with up to 45 species of wild flowers in any square metre (JS) page 16

world, to make people feel special.' Dinner (££).
Also recently built 2 'seapods' (high-end en-suite
wooden camping pods), each sleeps 2 & are
stunningly located a short walk from the house &
overlooking the sea (£). **££**

🏠 **Suileachan B&B** [118 F2] (3 rooms) 15
Reef; 📞01851 672370; e samuig@hotmail.co.uk;
w spanglefish.com/suileachanbandb; ⏰ Apr–
Oct. All rooms have sea views at this welcoming
B&B on the south side of Valtos. Helpful owners are
happy to set up 2 rooms for families of 4 or 5. The
striking monument to the land struggles on Uig
stands just across the road. **££**

✳ 🏠 **Taigh a' Chreagain** [118 E2] (3 rooms)
15 Valtos; 📞01851 672209; e kilbride101@
hotmail.co.uk; ⏰ Apr–Oct. Lovely, peaceful B&B
with comfortable rooms, all overlooking Loch Roag
from a pine conservatory & veranda with similar
views, perfect for sunsets. Small walled garden is
a lovely suntrap in good weather. Owner Catriona
Macleod will welcome you with scones, crowdie &
jam, & will also reconfigure house for self-catering
(£500/week). **££**

🏠 **The Beach Bothies** [118 F2] (sleeps 3)
Cnip; 📞01851 672403; e stay@thebeachbothies.
co.uk; w thebeachbothies.co.uk. 2 high-end
camping pods wonderfully positioned above
the beach at Cnip on the Valtos peninsula with
uninterrupted views of Loch West Roag. Includes
king-size bed, shower, kitchenette & decking area.
Also provides cots, making this a perfect spot for a
small family. **£/££**

🅧 **Cnip Grazing campsite** [118 F2] Tràigh na
Beirigh (known as Reef beach), Cnip, Valtos; 📞01851
672332; ⏰ Apr–Oct. Superb position for tents &
popular with caravans overlooking the sands. Basic
facilities but includes showers & toilets. **£**

🏠 **Otter Bunkhouse** [118 F3] (1 bedroom,
8 beds) Carishader; m 07942 349755;
e otterbunkhouse@gmail.com; w otterbunkhouse.
com. Beautifully located on Loch Roag just before
the turning for Valtos. Hot showers, each bed has its
own light & there's a good kitchen. Private access to
the loch for kayakers. Also runs the adjacent Otter
Bothy (small cabin), which sleeps 1–2 & has basic
cooking & en-suite facilities (££). **£**

🏠 **Mangersta Bothy** [not mapped] (sleeps
3) w lindanorgrovefoundation.org/mangersta-
bothy. If you want to sleep on the edge, this
magnificently located stone shelter is unbeatable.
Built hard into the cliffs above the sea, there is

nowhere more elemental for you to lay your head
on the entire island chain. Must be booked in
advance via the Linda Norgrove Foundation, who
will give directions. Free.

✖ **Uig Sands** [118 D3] 📞01851 672334;
e info@uiglodge.co.uk; w www.uigsands.
co.uk; ⏰ May–Aug noon–14.00 & 18.00–21.00
Tue–Sat, noon–16.00 Sun, shorter hours at other
times. Note that all times can change (this is the
Outer Hebrides) & that booking is essential; this
is a restaurant rather than somewhere for coffee
& cake. Excellent food includes Lewis mussels or
crab & coconut risotto for starters, followed by
cod fillets or Stornoway cheddar smoked pudding.
Stunning location overlooking the bay is enhanced
by wide floor-to-ceiling windows. **£££**

✳ ✖ **Loch Croistean Coffee Shop &
Restaurant** [118 F3] Loch Croistean; 📞01851
672772; ⏰ Mar–Dec noon–20.00 Tue–Sat. A
wonderful haven of a café/restaurant on the B8011
opposite the loch of the same name. Run by the
indefatigable one-woman band that is Marianne
Campbell in a converted former schoolhouse.
Serves up delicious homemade triple-chocolate
biscuits, elderflower & lemon drizzle cakes, soups
& evening meals including spiced Moroccan
chicken. People travel a long way to eat here.
'I often get people turning up for lunch at 4pm.
They've underestimated just how big Uig is & how
much there is to see, how far you can walk,' says
Marianne. 'When I bought the building it had most
recently been a warehouse & it looked so sad. I felt
the house was a gateway to Uig & had sent a very
poor message to visitors.' Internal décor is part of
the experience & involves heavy curtains & tables
decorated with Chinois lacquer. A small range
of exquisite handicrafts is also on sale, including
eye-catching prints of the traditional Hebridean
alphabet. Marianne runs cinema evenings
offering food & a film. 'I like watching films & I like
company,' she laughs. She has no website 'because
I just don't seem to need it,' she explains honestly,
&, in her case, correctly. **£/££**

✖ **The Edge Café** [118 D1] Gallan Head, Àird
Uig; m 07977 883215; w gallanhead.org.uk;
⏰ year-round 11.30–17.30 Mon–Tue, Thu–Fri &
Sun; early evening meals until 18.30 by appt only.
Excellent tearoom on northern edge of Gallan Head
township. Run by Fiona L'Estrange, the café serves
scones, cakes, soup & more substantial meals such
as chicken salad & hugely popular fish pie. Offers

themed talks on issues such as permaculture. Also promotes local crafts & local artists who lack a studio, & usually has work by up to 20 artists on display. 'There is so much creativity here waiting for the chance to flourish,' says Fiona. She also has a telescope to help pick out whales offshore & there are plans for a sonar link to be installed so that you can hear cetaceans & seabirds while you munch. £

✗ Scallop Shack & Seafood Café [118 E2] Valtos; ☎01851 672403; e uigseafare@gmail. com. Located in a sheltered cove at Miabhaig by the turning for Valtos, this enterprising outlet sells delicious scallops from the Scallop Shack. If owners are not around, or are out diving for scallops in

Loch Roag or off Tarbert, there's an honesty box for payment. Also operates an excellent seasonal café on the same site (⊕ Jun–Aug noon–15.00). All run by the same couple who own the Beach Bothies at Cnip (page 121). £

✳ ✗ Uig Community Centre Tearoom [118 D2] Eireastadh, Uig; ⊕ Apr & Sep noon– 16.00 Mon–Sat, Jun–Aug noon–17.00 Mon–Sat. A truly excellent café high above Uig Sands & a short walk from Timsgarry. Offerings include soup & delightful light meals such as oatcakes with salmon, homemade ice cream & carrot cake. Don't be deterred by the dour pebble-dash exterior. Remarkably low prices. £

Shopping The excellent **Uig Community shop** [map, page 126] (Timsgarry; ☎ 01851 672444; e info@uigcommunityshop.co.uk; w uigcommunityshop.co.uk; ⊕ 09.00–17.00 Mon–Wed & Sat, 09.00–18.00 Thu & Fri; Post Office ⊕ noon–16.45 Mon–Tue & Thu–Fri) is extremely well stocked with everything you need

---

🚶 TO BEEHIVE SHIELINGS   *Map, page 119*

10km (6 miles); 3–3½hrs
OS Explorer 458 West Lewis
Start/finish: small car park at gate to Morsgail Lodge at the head of Loch Ròg Beag (⊕ NB139238)

Important note This walk involves crossing the river Abhainn a' Lòin by stones at ⊕ NB133213. These are not manmade stepping stones and can only be crossed when the river is not in spate. If the river is in spate you should not proceed any further and be prepared to retrace your steps. Wear suitable clothing and footwear. Do not attempt to wade across. Only do this walk in clear weather as there are few features on the moor apart from a faint track and the distant Morsgail Lodge.

This is a magical walk that can you leave you feeling that you are hiking deep not only into Uig's hinterland but also its Neolithic past. The destination is a small collection of beehive shielings (summer dwellings) [119 G6], which resemble stone igloos deep among the remote peat-squelch of Uig's moors.

Uig is home to several beehive dwellings, the true origins of which are not yet fully understood. They are named for their distinctive shape: a double skin of stone walling with a corbelled dome built up from a height of around 1m and meeting in a beehive shape at the copestone. Their original function is obscure as no evidence of cultivation has been found in the areas around them, but they are thought to have been devised in Neolithic times, perhaps as primitive seasonal dwellings. During the Iron Age, they may have provided refuge from slave raiders. Later, Celtic monks seeking solitude beyond what Uig already had to offer adapted them into cells. More recently – and well into the 20th century – they are thought to have functioned as a summer camp away from the coastal winter quarters.

for picnics or self-catering. If you're renting a cottage in Uig, you can order ahead and they'll deliver to your accommodation. A minuscule relaxation of the Sabbath opening hours means that the petrol pumps here now take cards 24 hours a day Monday to Sunday (they had previously been disconnected altogether on Sundays). Bought by the community in 2003, the shop has proved extremely popular and has won national awards for its role in community regeneration. The map of Uig designed to imitate the London Underground is eye-catching: one day they'll get around to selling it as wallpaper.

What to see and do Empty landscapes of moors and lochs are the order of the day as the B8011 passes the turning for Great Bernera and skirts around the Scaliscro Estate. The road cuts through a forbiddingly bleak interior, marked only by a scattering of beehive shielings (see box, below), drably beautiful lochs and a backdrop of glacial hills and weather-battered escarpments.

It then loops around a hairpin bend at the headwaters of Loch Ròg Beag and scoots past a smattering of tiny townships including Giosla and Einacleite. Accompanied by a bustling river, the Abhainn Mhòr a' Ghlinne Ruaidh, it makes for the small community of Miabhaig (the name is Norse for narrow bay). The sheltered pier and natural harbour here were important for unloading cargo from steamers well into the 20th century.

Women and girls were released from household and township chores to chat, play and entertain visits from courting young men away from the scrutiny of parents. Other examples have been found on the Flannan Isles and Sula Sgeir.

The most accessible – relatively speaking – beehive dwellings are found in the southeast of Uig, south of the headwaters of Loch Ròg Beag. Take the turning for Kinloch Roag off the B8011 and follow the road to the gates of Morsgail Lodge in front of a bridge. Park with care here and walk along the road for about 1½km (1 mile) to reach Loch Morsgail. Cross the bridge and walk clockwise around the loch's east shore, keeping to the narrow track right by the shoreline. Walk around the head of the loch and cross a footbridge on the far side (⊕ NB136216) to begin heading north on the west side of the loch.

About 200m beyond the bridge, by a small stretch of beach and parallel with the nearest islet in the loch, look out for a path going back in the opposite direction in a sharp 'v'. Follow this as it tracks the Abhainn a' Lòin upstream past a weir and to a collapsed bridge (⊕ NB133213). About 100m further upstream you should be able to find enough stones to step across the river, so long as it is not in spate. On the other side, return downstream to the collapsed bridge to pick up the track which heads southeast and then south.

The path is usually exceptionally boggy and sometimes indistinct but never disappears; in places tyres from agricultural vehicles have been laid down to keep the boggy terrain at bay. For reassurance, keep the low hills of Sgalabhal Mula and Sgalabhal to the east at hand. Continue along the path for 1½km (1 mile). You only see the beehives when you are perhaps 50m from them. They are positioned down a slope by a burn, until then inconspicuous and swallowed up by the landscape (⊕ NB132200). On your return, keep Sgalabhal Mula and Sgalabhal on your right and use Morsgail Lodge in the distance as a locator to keep you confidently on the path.

Valtos (Bhaltos) Comprising the communities of Cliff (Cliobh), Valtos, Cnip, Reef (Riof) and Uigean, Valtos is a gorgeous peninsula jutting out into **Loch Roag (Loch Ròg)** [118 F2]. The name is Norse and means 'sheep fold on the mouth of the river'. Served by a circular road, it has views across towards Great Bernera and Lewis. Many of the people who base their Hebridean holiday in Uig, straying no further for the duration, do so on the Valtos peninsula, which has it all: dreamy lochs, stunning beaches, walks and wildlife. Valtos is community owned, bought for £75,000 within months of going up for sale in 1998.

A clockwise route around Valtos gives the best views; if you have the time and inclination, you can walk around it as the road is quiet and the total distance is just 9½km (6 miles).

Heading northwest you pass alongside Loch Sgalleir, whose waters cut north in the shadow of rocky uplifts. At the head of the loch, the road climbs in a stirring sweep high above **Cliff beach (Tràigh na Cliobhe)** [118 E2], which in turn is reached along a downhill fork in the road. Open to the full force of the Atlantic, the swells are popular with surfers, who seem undaunted by a fierce undertow that makes it unsafe for bathers.

The main road curves to the sprawling scattered village of **Valtos** and its panoramic views across to Great Bernera. **Valtos beach** [118 E2], reached by a turning just after the red telephone box, is beautiful, remarkably shallow and safe for swimming with wonderful opportunities for rockpooling. If you have children with you, they may recognise the jetty here, as it was used for scenes from the TV series *Katie Morag*.

The machair to the southeast of Valtos beach hides the even more striking **Reef beach** [118 F2], or **Tràigh na Beirigh (Beach of the Fort)**, best reached by driving a little further clockwise to the village of Cnip. This vast crescent-shaped bay is one of the best beaches in the Outer Hebrides for collecting seashells, and wind-battered, wave-hammered pigments of shell the colour of lapis lazuli crunch gently under your feet. On the northern headland is a jumble of ruins that have yielded pottery dating to both Iron Age and Viking burials. Traditionally, this is where families from Stornoway would decamp for the summer holidays. Like Valtos beach it is safe for bathing. An exquisitely small beach, Tràigh Teinis, lies just to the south of Reef beach. Walk to the far (east) end of Reef beach and then turn south over open ground through the small valley for 550m to reach the beach.

The hinterland behind Reef beach is of great archaeological interest and the location for four Norse watermills that are regarded as the finest set of watermills on the coast of Lewis by Christopher Burgess, author of *Ancient Lewis and Harris*. Finding them involves a short walk from the campsite at Reef beach [118 F2]. Heading clockwise along the circular road look for a stile about 200m beyond the toilets (⊕ NB103359). Head across the open grassland and pick up the clear narrow track that leads to a gate in the left-hand corner, with the marshes to your right. Go through the gate and follow the stony track to quickly reach another gate. Then follow the path with the marshes still on your right for 200m to reach the first watermill at the bottom of a narrow, steep and lush valley. Ascend the narrow valley, passing the other mills to emerge on a small, marshy plateau by Loch Bharabhat. This is an exquisite, Narnia-like spot, with an Iron Age fort in the loch easily accessed by a semi-submerged causeway. The whole walk there and back is little more than 1½km (1 mile) and with the short clamber uphill should take an hour in total.

Timsgarry (Timsgearraidh) The descent through Glen Valtos (Gleann Bhaltois) to Timsgarry may be short and swift but is one of the most dramatic routes in the Outer Hebrides: think Cheddar Gorge without the tat and people.

The glen runs for 1½ miles and was formed by glacial meltwater that carved through the tough rocks, eroding sand and gravel, and – as a sideshow – also created the vast Uig Sands and its adjacent machair. During heavy rainfall, the cascading waterfalls on either side are breathtaking, bouncing off the angular debris of stratified scree.

Emerging from the gorge you get a first sighting of the extraordinary spectacle of Uig Sands. High above them is the important township of Timsgarry, home to Uig's only shop, post office and petrol station.

A signposted turning to the right just above Timsgarry leads to the **Uig Community and Heritage Centre** [map, page 126] (w ceuig.co.uk; ⏰ Apr–Sep noon–17.00 Mon–Sat; £2/free). One of the world's great miniature museums is housed in this rather unpromising building, including replicas of the chessmen, the tale of their discovery and reconstructions of crofting communities. An excellent café is here too (page 122).

Àird Uig and Gallan Head A single-track road drills 3 miles due north from Timsgarry to Àird Uig through stark and empty scenery. Shortly after Timsgarry, a fork left off the Àird road leads for a mile to the township of Cradhlastadh, which has dramatic views over Uig Sands. Time your visit between June and September and you may see salmon jump as they come in on a fast tide, heading upriver to spawn. Here, by the saltings of Tràigh nan Sruban are the remains of the deserted village of Bereiro, abandoned in the late 18th century when the grounds of the local manse were expanded. Remnants of four blackhouses and a corn-drying kiln are tucked away behind the small rise on the east side of the loch and can be visited by walking east around the north shore of this small bay.

Back on the road to Àird Uig, the track cuts through a ravine before emerging in the small but scattered township of Gallan Head, where houses open right on to the road. The place has the feel of a film set with nothing but open country behind the single row of houses. The drystone walls on the hills are even more vertical than those in the Yorkshire Dales, clambering up steep hillsides like aircraft contrails. The fields they divide are narrow and known as runrigs: each year every croft shifted along to the adjacent plot, thereby ensuring no-one hogged the sunniest slopes for too long.

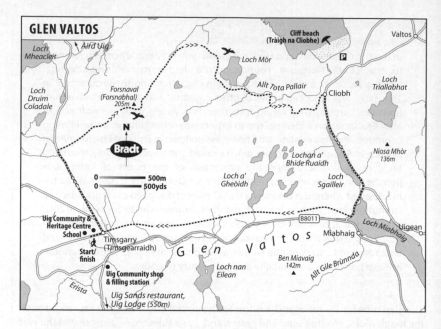

The green blocks and other housing on the tip of the peninsula are a hangover from the brief time Àird Uig was home to an RAF station with 200 serving staff. After the RAF pulled out in the 1960s, the site lay derelict for some 30 years, but over the past decade houses have slowly been bought up. In early 2016, a long-running community campaign to buy the headland was successful; a key motivation for the community trust (w gallanhead.org.uk) was to make public access to the sensational headland of Gallan Head easier and less forbidding. You can park up by the Edge Café, walk up through the gate along the old military road, pass the last of the outbuildings and on to the headland. Some of the shallow lochans here are inlaid with black sand. You can meander out for about a kilometre (½ mile) over open ground to the cairn and old lookout post, the latter serving as an excellent wind shelter. From here, you have views of geos, a blur of headlands and the lighthouse at the Butt of Lewis. Along the way, look out for two talking telescopes positioned near the cliffs which provide a chance to zoom in on any passing cetaceans and learn about what might be out there at the same time.

South of Timsgarry; Uig Sands (Tràigh Ùige)
Some 1½ miles south of Timsgarry, you'll spot a turning south off the B8011 at Cnoc na Ciste. This track – you must walk it rather than drive – is something of a 'cheat's access' to Uig's remote interior, leading after 2km (1½ miles) of easy walking to lonely Loch Suaineabhal, which, at the remarkable depth of 66.7m, is the deepest lake on any offshore island in the British Isles. The loch is geared up for anglers staying at local estates, but you are fully entitled to enjoy the views from the shore.

Many people will have heard of **Uig Sands** [118 D3] as the place where the Lewis chessmen are said to have been uncovered; perhaps fewer are aware of the spectacular beauty of this monumental landscape. Visible for miles around, the vast sands of Uig boast an extraordinary tidal range. The distance between the highest and lowest spring tide can be almost a mile, and at low tide it feels as though you

11¼km (7 miles); 3hrs
OS Explorer 458 West Lewis
Start/finish: Uig Community & Heritage Centre (✿ NB057344)

This is a classic Hebridean yomp across open moorland, bouncing off sprigs of heather and skipping across the boggier bits with views across Glen Valtos and Uig Sands. From the community centre, walk up the road to the small junction and turn left by the Eireastadh road sign. After almost 1km (½ mile), turn right up the paved track and through a gate towards the telecommunications infrastructure on the summit of Forsnabhal. At the summit, there are wonderful 360° views of the seemingly infinite Uig Sands, the lonely Àird peninsula poking northwards, the hills of Uig and Harris, the west coast of Lewis, the Flannan Isles and, on a good day, St Kilda. Descending the hill towards the Valtos peninsula requires a little navigation, but you're aiming northeast for a quarry track nearly 1½km (1 mile) distant (✿ NB067366) from the summit. You need to negotiate a 1m-high fence on the lower, eastern flanks of Forsnabhal; there's no gate, but you should be able to clear it by using one of the boulders at its base. Continue down through the valley for 650m over open ground, keeping lochs at a good distance on either side. Just over halfway down the valley a burn emerges – keep it close to your left to be guided down to the track. Turn right and follow the track southeast past Loch Mòr and then the hidden, smaller Loch Beag. Descend the hairpins above Cliff beach to meet the road and turn right alongside Loch Sgailleir and later Loch Miabhaig to your left. Just by a triangular sign for a cattle grid, there are what appear to be steep goat tracks uphill on your right. Follow these; the land quickly levels off and you are walking along the top of Valtos Glen. Keep the fence close to your right, as the edge of the glen cuts in from time to time. The Uig Community and Heritage Centre returns to view. Go through a gate, with the fence now on your left and continue ahead. After another gate, cross the road and return to the centre.

can walk towards the sea for ever. During the equinox, the high water can even cover the low-lying part of the machair behind the high dunes.

Also known as **Ardroil beach**, and signposted as such, the sands are most easily accessed from the south side of the bay at Eadar Dha Fladhail, 2 miles south of Timsgarry and signified by a 3m-high wooden Lewis chessman piece perched by the sandy track. The chessmen are said to have been uncovered just behind this giant woodwork figure. Close by the car park is a useful information board.

The chessmen were brought ashore in the 16th century from a wrecked ship on the coast between Uig and Harris. The sailor who carried them is believed to have been murdered by a herdsman who later buried them. Embellishments and contradictions to the tale are plentiful but ill fortune is said to have befallen the herdsman who was later hanged at Gallows Hill in Stornoway, having confessed to the murder and given the location of the pieces. The story goes that the chess pieces were then uncovered in 1831, either by a fierce storm or by a cow rubbing against a sand dune. Either way, nature exposed the 12th-century Viking pieces carved from walrus ivory, including kings, queens, bishops, knights, warders and pawns. The complete find comprised 78 chessmen, 14 tables-men and a buckle to secure a bag and is thought likely to have come from a collection of four chess sets. Eleven of the chessmen are owned by National Museums Scotland and the remaining 82 pieces by the British Museum in London, though six of the British Museum's collection are on long-term loan at the Lews Castle Museum and Archive (Museum nan Eilean) in Stornoway. The figures are believed to be Scandinavian in origin and probably made in Trondheim in Norway during the late 12th or early 13th centuries. They range in height from 6cm to 10cm. Despite their intricate detail and skilled carving, it is thought they were intended for practical use, for *hnefatafl* (a Viking chess-like board game that involved two unequal sides) and/or chess. Four of the wild-eyed warders are biting the tops of their shields; these are berserkers, fierce Viking warriors who worked themselves into a frenzy before heading into battle without armour. More of the tale of the Lewis chessmen remains to be unpicked, as other stories claim the chessmen were in fact found far from Uig Sands, an argument that unsurprisingly gets short shrift locally.

On the southern side of Uig Sands, the B8011 crosses a bridge over the Red River (Abhainn Dearg, pronounced 'jerrak') at Carnish (Carnais) and immediately forks. The left-hand turn, flanked by a wooden Lewis chessman, leads to **Abhainn Dearg distillery** [118 D3] (✆01851 672429; w abhainndearg.co.uk; ⊕ 11.00–13.00 & 14.00–16.00 Mon Sat, closed Sat in winter; tours on the hour, £10). The most westerly whisky distillery in Scotland and, until the Tarbert (page 151) and Barra (page 277) distilleries deliver their first malts, still the only whisky producer in the Outer Hebrides. In 2011, the distillery produced the first single malt on the islands since 1929, bringing to an end centuries of illegal stills. The wonderful thing about Abhainn Dearg is that it *looks* just how you would imagine a bootleg rig operating under the radar should: a handful of what appear to be farm outbuildings overlooking a sprawling river that clatters over glacial boulders on its way to the sea. The farmhouses are actually home to a professional, if small-scale, industry producing just 10,000 bottles a year – peanuts for major distilleries – and now includes a ten-year malt. Founder Mark 'Marko' Tayburn will keep you entertained and tells a good story or three. As he cryptically points out: 'the Outer Hebrides has long been famous for its whisky, even though ours was the first legal distillery.' He is also lyrically passionate about his produce. 'We don't have the shiny, brassy kit that is all the rage,' he declares. 'All our products are from the Outer Hebrides, from the plough to the bottle. If I'm giving you a bit of the Outer Hebrides, it should come from here. The ground we plant the barley in, the air the barley takes in are important. Maybe I'm a snob but a single malt whisky should be entirely from the region it says it comes from.'

Across the road from the distillery, a small track peters out above **Tràigh Bhoisadar** [118 C3]. Park with care anywhere along the grassy track before the final couple of houses and follow the signpost to the beach along a grassy track that winds down to the beach, avoiding a private road. The attractive cove-like beach is usually sheltered by weather-flattened skerries.

Further south: Mangersta (Mangarstadh) to Mealasta

The B8011 clambers over the northern outliers of the Uig hills before suddenly opening up with a full view of the Atlantic. The 12-mile stretch from Timsgarry to Mealasta is worth persevering with: where the road hugs the coast tightly, sea spray can erupt suddenly a few feet away; on a clear day you can see the Flannan Isles and the Bali-Hai outline of St Kilda. The views south to the Harris hills are uplifting and the Atlantic Ocean backdrop is infilled with small battered islands along with the larger and uninhabited island of Scarp. Towards the road end, even the passing places disappear and drivers must pull on to the machair to yield to oncoming vehicles.

Fishing, crofting and tweed have intermittently sustained livelihoods here. Migration, though, has characterised the fortunes of the villages, with families sailing to the New World. Some sailed all the way to Patagonia, where they would have arrived at a coastline as desolate and remote as the one they left behind. The elemental setting is arguably enhanced – rather than detracted from – by the ugly detritus of Army and RAF installations from World War II.

Mangersta Another turning off the B8011 takes you over moorland and down to the community of Mangersta. The cliffs along here are violently serrated, brutal and breathtaking. Travelling through this landscape – where geology, exposed rock faces, dips and rises, cairns and random fragments of age-old pottery collide – can give you the feeling of being inside the earth, an observation that may possibly sound less pretentious when you're here. The vertical cliffs are the highest on mainland Lewis or Harris and plants such as lovage and roseroot cling tenaciously to the rocks. In spring, the headland is a good place to catch the passage of pomarine and other skuas.

Ambitious plans are afoot for Mangersta, given that its striking cliffs and birdlife arguably offer a flavour of St Kilda without the need to brave the high seas. A St Kilda visitor centre is planned, housed in what is promised to be an iconic building, and will contain memorabilia and archives from St Kilda and be linked to a cliff-top walkway and nature trails. Plans to open the centre by 2020 to coincide with the 90th evacuation of St Kilda were thwarted by funding problems. A downscaled centre, which has a price tag of £2 million, is now inching closer to the building phase, though financial support remains an issue. You can keep up to date with developments at w ionadhiort.org.

Brèinis represents the 'full stop' for human habitation in Uig, but the track staggers on for a further 3¼km beyond the rocky outcrop of Mealasta, a deserted

---

🚶 ABOVE MANGERSTA   Map, page 118

3¼km (2 miles); 1hr
OS Explorer 458 West Lewis
Start/finish: 1st gate on minor road north of & above Mangersta (✚ NB008319)

A fine 3¼km (2-mile) circular walk explores the coastal scenery west of Mangersta. As you drop down through the village take the right turn uphill in front of a garage. (It may not be immediately obvious that this is a T-junction; look for the prosthetic arm sticking out of the grassy bank, clasping a wine bottle with a stream of water running through it.) A jolly signpost directing you 'this way' and 'that way' and 'dead end' will confirm whether you're in the right place. After 50m or so park either side of the gate with care. Walk for 1½km (1 mile) to the end of the paved road and turn left along the cliff edge. Continue southwest along the coast and turn left again when you reach a fence to return to the gate. The coastline is considered one of the best places on Lewis to view seabirds travelling back and forward from their breeding colonies on St Kilda while the deep waters off the Uig cliffs here are favoured by whales, porpoises and basking sharks. The elemental spectacle of the rock faces at Lèirigeo, just before you turn back to the road, is truly breathtaking. Offshore islands in the bays here were used as recently as the 1980s for winter grazing. Extraordinarily, yearlings were swum across the waters, coaxed with oars from rowing boats.

4km (2½ miles); 2hrs
OS Explorer 458 West Lewis
Start/finish: southern end of Islibhig (✷ NA993273)

A pleasant circular walk from Islibhig to Brèinis gives a good feel for the coastal landscape and attractiveness of this part of Uig and leads past a spectacular blowhole. *Note: You should under no circumstances attempt this walk in poor visibility as the blowhole is some distance inland, precipitous and unfenced.*

Park up just to the south of the last house in Islibhig and strike out west across open ground, keeping roughly in parallel with the fence on your right. The going is boggy to begin with and there are several small streams to negotiate. This is territory for good boots.

Just before the land rises up towards the coast, you cross a larger stream via stepping stones. Keep your eyes peeled for wildlife as this stretch of moorland is favoured by young bucks kicked out of the red deer herd which often loiter here rather like desultory teenagers on a street corner. Arctic skuas like to pounce on terns offshore as they rise out of the water with fish, forcing the smaller bird to drop their quarry, whereupon the skua swoops below and snatches it just above the ocean.

Having clambered up the slope, the going becomes much easier as you enter a magical world of flatlands pitted with dozens of lochans and surrounded by a carpet of faded mossy green. The sea spray seems to hang in the air and creates a truly ethereal haze. At the coast, look out for geos that cut deep inland and bulge with surging water. Turn south and follow the coast, making for the two yellow warning boards that provide a rather low-key guard to the blowhole. Sheep in pursuit of unnibbled plantings seem happy to graze at what is more or less the angle of repose on the western side of the blowhole. Continue across open ground and undulating moorland along the coast for another 1½km (1 mile). You should see three conspicuous cairns to follow. Ahead you are looking deep into the hills of Harris. At the third cairn, turn inland and pick up the track just to the right (south) of the first houses in Brèinis. Possibly uniquely, Brèinis was overcrowded a century ago, to the extent that the overspill of families was used to repopulate adjacent cleared villages. This long lane leads to the B8011, where you turn left to return to your starting point.

village that has not been resuscitated since its last inhabitants were forced out in 1838. There are three beaches almost side by side here, wonderfully isolated but nevertheless popular with those in the know for barbecues. The waters are safe for swimming and potatoes are still grown on the lower machair. Between the road and the second beach is Tigh nan Cailleachan Dubha ('House of the Black Nuns'), a crumpled pile of rocks thought to be the site of a pre-Reformation nunnery and chapel. Intriguingly, some argue that this is the true site where the Lewis chessmen were discovered: the case for this being the fact the area was inhabited and is believed to have been an important trading post. The third beach, near the end of the road, has a grave on its northern slope of an unknown seaman whose body was washed up here.

4

Harris (Na Hearadh)

Named from the Old Norse for 'High Land', Harris looks and feels like an ancient island and boasts some of Scotland's most remote and rugged terrain. This is a landscape of imposing hills and peaks, formed from some of the oldest rocks on the planet. If you've come from Lewis, Harris will immediately seem startlingly empty of people; heading north from the Uists, meanwhile, Harris is a sharp topographical shock to the system.

A glance at the map will reveal that Harris is not an island but part of the same landmass as Lewis. The boundary between the two runs west–east from Loch Rèasort to Aline on the shore of Loch Seaforth (Loch Shìophoirt) at the foot of the North Harris Hills. In truth the borderlands are sometimes blurred, and certainly the lands around the dividing point between the two islands are visually indistinguishable. The North Harris Hills may fall short of being Munros (a Scottish term for a hill more than 914m (3,000ft) high) but they still form a substantial barrier, representing not just the Harris side of the boundary but also a watershed

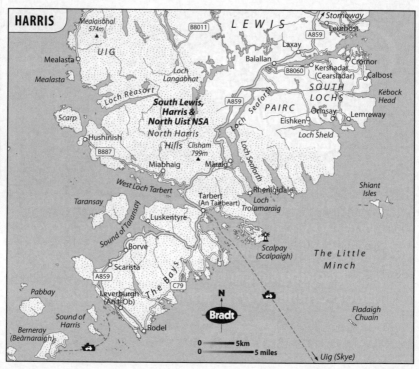

and a weathervane – often keeping one part of Harris wet while another is bathed in sunshine. Any cyclist will tell you that these mountains can be a heartbreaker after the flatlands you encounter elsewhere.

Harris is divided again into North and South Harris. The northern half is rugged, mountainous and populated with a handful of scattered and minuscule townships. The south is almost as hilly but has, around Luskentyre, a clutch of stunning showcase beaches. North and south are conjoined by the thinnest of geological membranes, a narrow isthmus, at the tiny port of Tarbert (An Tairbeart).

HIGHLIGHTS

The beaches, seascapes and hills of Harris combine to create one of the most spectacular landscapes in the British Isles, with mile upon mile of vast sands backing on to a hinterland that can be both extraordinarily lush and austere. The centre of this natural majesty is **Luskentyre (Losgaintir)**, a small township that has come to lend its name as an umbrella term to the succession of beaches sweeping along the southwest coast of Harris. You are likely to end up in the small port of **Tarbert (An Tairbeart)** for essential shopping but the township also has some good places to stay and eat. East of Tarbert lies the island of **Scalpay (Sgalpaigh)**, which offers some good walks and a distinctive culture combining families that have been here for generations as well as incomers. The **North Harris Hills** attract walkers for the breathtaking wilderness they offer, along with the chance to climb **Clisham (An Cliseam)**, the highest mountain in the Outer Hebrides. West of Tarbert is the lonely peninsula of **Hushinish (Huisinis)** reached by a road that passes the front door of **Amhuinnsuidhe Castle** (pronounced '*AVIN-sooee*'). Radiating east from Tarbert is the dramatic swooping road to the remote outpost of **Rhenigidale (Reinigeadal)**. Further south, the port of Leverburgh (An t-Ob) has a forlorn air and is really a place to pass through while waiting for the ferry across the Sound of Harris to the southern isles. Southeast of Leverburgh, where the island roads converge and meet the sea, is the wonderful **medieval church of St Clements** at **Rodel (Roghadal)**. With exposed sheets of Lewisian gneiss scoured by glaciers during the last Ice Age, and boulders burping up through the ground, it's hard to believe that the moonscape around the southeast coast of Harris known as **The Bays (Na Bàigh)** belongs to the same island as the lush, softer western fringes.

HISTORY

Human occupation of Harris had begun by at least 3000BC, during the Neolithic or New Stone Age. Some settlements have been identified on the machair around present-day Northton in the south, where the grazing would have been good and the soil easily cultivated – as remains the case today. Middens (rubbish pits) have revealed tools from antler bones and broken pottery, which suggests that these early people were not merely hunter-gatherers but also the first farmers on the islands who established settlements on the machair.

In Norse times, Harris became a separate seat of power from Lewis. The west side of Harris was heavily populated under the Lordship of the Isles between 1266 and 1494 and subsequently under its Macleod owners, with most villages located where the fertile machair could be farmed. In summer, animals would be grazed on higher land and along the coast of the east bays.

The Macleods of Harris and Dunvegan on Skye retained ownership of parts or all of Harris for 500 years. In 1779, Harris was sold by the Dunvegan Macleods to Alexander Macleod of Berneray who set upon a mission that might nowadays be described as well-meaning philanthropic autocracy: he provided land and rent-free crofts, established a spinning factory, built a school and an inn, and laid the skeleton of the road network that exists today. His main motive, however, was to make money from the land to subsidise his extravagant lifestyle. Sheep and deer replaced active communities along the west coast. The clearances were continued by Macleod's descendants and most of the farmsteads on the west coast were cleared between 1828 and 1853 to make way for large sheep farms.

During this time, hundreds of families from Harris migrated to Cape Breton in Nova Scotia and the Carolinas.

To add insult to injury, traditional blackhouses were demolished and their materials used to build the drystone walls that marked the extent of the new sheep farms. Those pushed out made their way to The Bays, the indented and unforgiving coastline along the east coast south of Tarbert. Here, in an attempt to eke out a living, resilient farmers would ingeniously gather the shallow soil into raised beds, mix it with seaweed, potash and old straw to grow potatoes and grain on small furrows of land whose ridges can still be seen today. These rolling humpbacks of land, known incongruously and ironically as 'lazybeds' – a misnomer if ever there was since this involved back-breaking work – remain visible today. When the potato blight struck in 1845, farmers were horribly exposed, being left with few options other than emigration or grimly trying to see things through.

By the 1850s, however, The Bays were recovering: the potato blight was history and Harris Tweed had been revived as a commercial concern by Lady Dunmore (see box, page 175). The demographic consequences are still seen today, with a lopsided population, the majority on the gneiss-based rocky eastern fringes, rather than the fertile machair of the west coast.

After becoming exasperated with his experience on Lewis (page 89), Lord Leverhulme purchased Harris in 1918 and shaped its destiny almost as much as he did its northern neighbour. He faced similar problems here, however, as crofters and soldiers returning from World War I sought to redress the unfair land deals imposed on them after the clearances. Leverhulme expanded the road system, introducing a further spinning mill and purchasing a Norwegian whaling station (page 143). He died in 1925 whereupon his dreams withered, lacking any local appetite to see them through. The post-war period saw the break-up of the farms on the Harris machair into crofting villages which were settled mainly by families from The Bays. Today, fishing and increasingly tourism are the mainstays of the industry, with lobsters, scallops and prawns hauled out of the waters off Scalpay and Leverburgh.

GETTING THERE AND AWAY

Road and ferry are the only direct transport options into and out of Harris. Stornoway Airport is a good 2 hours' drive from Leverburgh. If arriving from the south, the ferry route across the Sound of Harris is truly one of the world's great unsung sea journeys (page 179).

BY FERRY CalMac (☎0800 066 5000 or, from outside the UK, ☎+44 1475 650397; w calmac.co.uk) runs services from Uig on northwest Skye to Tarbert. This gives the most immediate access to Harris but if crossings are busy you could also consider taking the ferry from Ullapool to Stornoway as it's only a 20-mile (30min) drive from Stornoway to Harris. A smaller ferry links the port of Leverburgh on the southern tip of Harris to Ardmaree on Berneray through the Sound of Harris, a journey that takes an hour; this is the gateway to the Uists and Benbecula. Tickets cost £14.35 for a standard vehicle (one way) and £3.80/£1.90 for foot passengers.

BY ROAD The A859 runs from Stornoway through the southern third of Lewis and all the way through Harris to Leverburgh and Rodel. It's a 37-mile (50min) drive from Stornoway to Tarbert and a further 20 miles (30mins) to Leverburgh.

BY AIR Flying to Stornoway from mainland airports is a perfectly feasible option for those staying on Harris. Stornoway Airport lies just a couple of miles east of town, and getting across to the A859 and down to Harris is quick and easy. See page 42 for details of flights and airport services.

BY BUS The W10 links Leverburgh and Tarbert with Stornoway, though the trip takes a lengthy 3 hours as the journey is broken in Tarbert. From Stornoway to Tarbert takes 1 hour and from there to Leverburgh and Rodel is a further 45 minutes. The service is reliable but bear in mind there are no more than five a day in each direction and none on Sunday. For up-to-date timetables, visit w cne-siar. gov.uk and use the menu to find 'bus services'.

GETTING AROUND

BY CAR Newly laid two-lane roads are steadily removing the single-track stretches of the A859. Unlike Lewis and South Uist, where you must generally get off the main roads to see anything, on Harris the A859 cuts thrillingly through the hills and around the west coast, affording sensational views of the beaches around Luskentyre. The minor roads on Harris are just that: almost exclusively narrow, single-track routes with passing places. They are, however, almost universally paved and kept in good condition.

Car hire
🚗 **Isle of Harris Car & Bike Hire** m 07483 161159; e carhireharris@outlook.com; w carhireharris.co.uk

Petrol
⛽ **An Clachan Filling Station** Leverburgh; ☏01859 520370; ⊕ 09.00–18.00 Mon–Thu,

09.00–19.00 Fri–Sat; automatic car payment 24/7. Run by the Harris Community Shop.
⛽ **Ardhasaig Filling Station & Stores** Ardhasaig; ☏01859 502066; ⊕ 08.00–18.00 & 20.00–21.00 Mon–Fri, 09.00–21.00 Sat
⛽ **Harris Garage** Tarbert; ☏01859 502441; ⊕ 08.30–18.00 Mon–Sat

BY BUS Services tend to radiate out from Tarbert. The W11 runs from Tarbert north and east to Rhenigidale, while the W12 runs west to Hushinish. The Rhenigidale service only runs twice a day and must be booked the previous day (m 07769 159218, 07769 698306). The W14 runs between Scalpay and Stornoway via Tarbert. Typical single fares include Stornoway–Tarbert £4.80; Tarbert–Scarista £2.30 and Tarbert–Leverburgh £3.20. For up-to-date timetables, visit w cne-siar. gov.uk and use the menu to find 'bus services'. Study these carefully as changes are often made, and a route, or even just a single departure or stopping point, may require booking on one day of the week but not another.

BY TAXI For local service, try **Harris Taxis** (m 07500 450387; w harristaxis.co.uk). A trip from Tarbert to Leverburgh costs £35–40; they will also take you up to Stornoway for £60 but you need to book ahead.

TOURIST INFORMATION

Tarbert no longer has a tourist information centre because Visit Scotland closed its premises. Notionally, this service has been reallocated to Essence of Harris (in Tarbert; page 150), but it is most definitely a sideline there. Hotels also provide local advice. See also the island website w explore-harris.com.

FESTIVALS AND EVENTS

For a lightly populated island, Harris gives its inhabitants an active social life: look out for the South Harris agricultural show in July and the Harris Tweed Festival Day in August. A highlight of the year is the Harris Mountain Festival in September, which includes a range of excellent guided walks.

SHOPPING

There are three good local stores on Harris: a small but well-run shop and petrol station at Ardhasaig (page 135) just **south of the turning for Hushinish**; a community-run shop in Tarbert (page 150); and the Harris Community Shop in Leverburgh (page 170). They work hard to put the typical, tired, regional stores you see all too often on the mainland to shame. There are no national supermarket chains on Harris.

SPORTS AND ACTIVITIES

Harris offers outstanding opportunities for outdoor sports and activities, such as photography in dramatic locations. If experienced, you can strike out for a walk, kayak trip or mountain-bike ride by yourself, but bear in mind that the weather in these parts is as changeable as it can get in the UK. In particular, strong tides and rapidly changing sea conditions mean that Harris is not the place to make an unaccompanied debut at an adventure activity. Several operators not only hire out equipment but offer excellent experiences under their guidance. These can range from mountain hikes to coasteering and rock climbing. Kayaking is increasingly popular, with operators leading trips in both the sheltered conditions in the eastern sea lochs in the east and more challenging conditions on the exposed west coast. North Harris is also a great base for longer kayaking expeditions to offshore islands such as the Shiant Isles or into remote areas around Loch Rèasort on the Harris/Lewis border. If you want to snorkel in secluded inshore waters, download the North Harris snorkel trail at w scottishwildlifetrust.org.uk/things-to-do/snorkel-trails, which lists six excellent sites to nose around underwater (Loch Mhàraig is particularly good) and details what you might encounter, from seagrass to velvet swimming crabs.

One event to look out for in July is the Harris half-marathon (w harrishalfmarathon. org), one of Britain's most picturesque, which runs from Borve, just south of Luskentyre sands, along the A859 to just north of Tarbert. There's also a 3-mile fun run, which is popular with locals; visiting families are welcome to join in.

Mike Briggs Sports Bun-na-Gille, Bunavoneadar (Bun Abhainn Eadarra); ☎01859 502376; e mike. briggs1@virgin.net; w mikeandpeggybriggs. co.uk. Based in the remote Hushinish peninsula, Mike offers guided hillwalking (£180/day, 2 people). A qualified yoga teacher, Mike holds courses on the beaches or in the glens (from £45/ hr, up to 4 people) & also hires out his tennis court (£20, 2hrs).

Scaladale Centre Ardvourlie; ☎01859 502502; e info@scaladale.co.uk; w scaladale-centre. co.uk. This adventure & outdoors charity has branched out from its core market of youth clubs into the wider tourist trade. It offers coasteering, scrambling, climbing, mountain biking, abseiling, hillwalking & boat trips on Loch Seaforth. Prices vary but typically £45/£35 for 2hrs. Good for families looking for taster experiences.

OTHER PRACTICALITIES

BANK
$ **Bank of Scotland** Pier Rd, Tarbert; \01859 502465; ⊕ 09.30–12.30 & 13.00–16.30 Mon & Fri, 10.00–12.30 & 13.00–16.30 Wed. ATM.

MEDICAL
Always phone ahead if you need a GP as surgery hours can vary (eg: if a doctor is making house calls). For 24hr & emergency care, you'll need the Western Isles Hospital.

✚ **South Harris Medical Practice** Leverburgh; \01859 520278; ⊕ 09.00–10.00 Mon & Wed, 09.00–noon Tue & Thu, 09.00–11.00 Sat, closed Fri & Sat
✚ **Tarbert Medical Practice** Tarbert; \01859 502421; ⊕ 08.00–17.00 Mon–Tue & Thu–Fri, 08.00–18.00 Wed
✚ **Western Isles Hospital** Macauley Rd, Stornoway; \01851 704704

POST OFFICE
✉ **Tarbert** ⊕ 09.00–17.30 Mon–Tue & Thu–Fri, 09.00–13.00 Wed, 09.00–12.30 Sat

NORTH HARRIS (CEANN A TUATH NA HEARADH)

A largely treeless terrain free of manmade structures, North Harris is sparsely populated with around 700 inhabitants, roughly half of whom live in Tarbert with the remainder in small crofting townships scattered along the coastline. The North Harris Estate comprises 29,500ha of croft land, common grazing and open hill ground including Clisham.

The ascent into North Harris from Lewis along the A859 is nothing less than a sensational experience – one of the most dramatic entrances to a region you could ever hope to make. The road emerges from the Aline woodlands and sweeps south of Alt Linne and through Bogha Glas (Bowglass), giving huge views across Loch Seaforth (Loch Shìophoirt) before clambering up two huge hairpin bends as it passes through the heart of the Harris hills. At this point, far below, what looks part of the mainland of Harris is in fact the phenomenally large bulk of the island of Shìophoirt rising up from the loch's waters. There are barely half a dozen public roads on all of North Harris: in addition to the A859, the lonely B887 pushes west to Hushinish, much of it single track; meanwhile, an unclassified road meanders east of Tarbert to the causeway for Scalpay, while another peels away further north of Tarbert to Rhenigidale.

GEOLOGY North Harris is a landscape moulded by textbook glaciation, the evidence of which is everywhere – terrain littered with huge rocks, known as erratics, deposited by receding glaciers. The hills are rugged and mountainous despite their modest altitude, and are dissected by valleys and lochs that have been scoured by glaciers. Peat has formed in many valleys and on hillsides. On the more exposed ridges and summits, however, soils are thin or non-existent and bedrock, predominantly made up of Lewisian gneiss, is exposed at the surface.

WHERE TO STAY *Map, page 138*
There are a number of accommodation options in North Harris. In addition to those listed, further self-catering options can be found at w visitouterhebrides.co.uk.

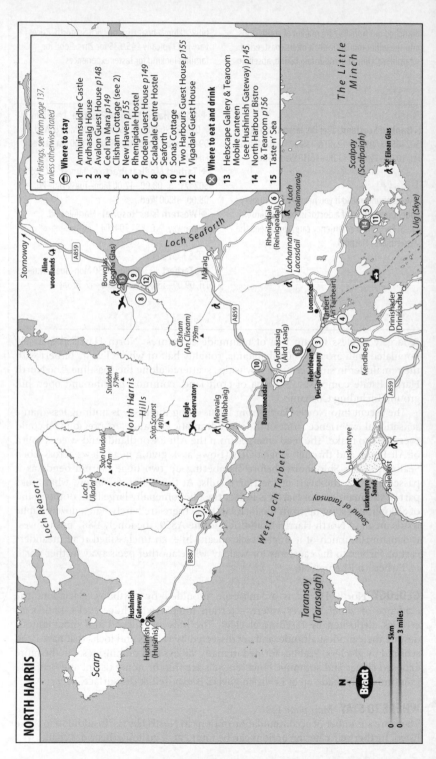

NORTH HARRIS

The Little Minch

Stornoway

A859

Aline woodlands

Bowglas (Bogha Glas)

Loch Seaforth

Rhenigidale (Reinigeadal)

Loch Trolamaraig

Lochannan Lacasdail

Scalpay (Scalpaigh)

Eilean Glas

Uig (Skye)

Clisham (An Cliseam) 799m

A859

Maraig

Loomshed

Tarbert (An Tairbeart)

Drinishader (Drinisiadar)

Ardhasaig (Àird Asaig)

Hebridean Design Company

Kendibeg

Stulabhal 579m

North Harris Hills

Sròn Scourst 491m

Eagle observatory

Meavaig (Miabhaig)

Bunavoneadar

Luskentyre

Luskentyre Sands

Seilebost

Sgòn Uladail 442m

Loch Ulladail

Loch Rèasort

West Loch Tarbert

Sound of Taransay

Hushinish Gateway

Hushinish (Huisinis)

Scarp

Taransay (Tarasaigh)

B887

N

Bradt

0   5km
0   3 miles

Amhuinnsuidhe Castle (12 rooms) Amhuinnsuidhe Castle Estate, near Hushinish; \01859 560200; e info@amhuinnsuidhe.com; w amhuinnsuidhe.com; ⏲ Jun–Oct. An extraordinary sight, this baronial-style castle sits right on the B887 as it bumps & winds its way out to Hushinish. It's a grand pile with all the features you would expect from a castle: a Teutonic-looking turret, atmospheric library, even a resident ghost & 150 years of history. The pick of the rooms overlook Taransay & include the Voshimid suite (named for a nearby loch) & Sir Sam's room. On a point of principle, there are no locks on bedroom doors. Rates start at around £370 for a dbl & include afternoon tea & 4-course *table d'hôte* evening meal. Typical dishes include crab cakes for starters, venison in a port & masala sauce for main, followed by Hebridean fudge cheesecake. The 18-seat dinner table commits you to communal dining, which, perhaps refreshingly given the surroundings, is not as formal as you might expect. The interior style is conservative & in tune with the wider ambience of the building: chandeliers, heavy curtains, grand staircases, period furniture & portraits. Antique furniture & fine art are everywhere but the showstopper is arguably the life-sized bronze cast of a 29kg salmon, the largest caught in the British Isles. **£££**

Ardhasaig House (6 rooms) Ardhasaig; \01859 502500; e accommodation@ardhasaig.co.uk; w ardhasaig.co.uk; ⏲ Easter–end Oct. Dramatically located on the southern descent through the Harris hills just off the A859, 2 miles north of Tarbert with views across West Loch Tarbert to Ben Luskentyre & Taransay. A welcoming place to stay with a small bar. Guests are greeted with a hot drink or glass of wine & a slice of cake. Rooms include a family room. Outside in the lodge is a dbl room with stone, timber & beamed ceilings. The excellent restaurant (**£££**) is open to non-guests & comprises a 4-course set menu. Look out for lobsters caught in the loch 100m away, cauliflower & saffron soup, local lamb with a port gravy, & desserts including pear tart with walnut ice cream. 'Nothing comes from the deep freeze,' says owner-chef Katie Mackaskill. 'I'm proud of the food of these islands & I want our guests to have good local food.' The conservatory overlooking the loch is an excellent place for a sundowner. **£££**

Seaforth (1 room) Ardvourlie; \01859 502031; e croftercampbell@btinternet.com; w ardvourliebandb.co.uk; ⏲ Apr–Oct. Just 1 dbl at this working farm beautifully positioned by Loch Seaforth. A well-run B&B & a good place for watching deer & birds of prey. A stay here will immerse you in farm life: autumn guests are invited – but not obliged – to help gather sheep in from the hills. Owners can give good advice on local walking tracks; this is a good stopping point if you are walking the Hebridean Way (see box, page 50), which goes past the front door. 2-course evening meals £15 pp by prior arrangement. **££**

Vigadale Guest House (3 rooms) Bogha Glas; \01859 502024. Superb location, pretty much on the border of Lewis & Harris in the shadow of the Harris hills. 1 dbl, 1 sgl & 1 family room (sleeps 3). Cosy & neatly furnished. Friendly & helpful host Cristina McAvoy gives you run of the guest kitchen, too, if you fancy cooking for yourself. **££**

Rhenigidale Hostel (2 dorms with 5 beds, 1 with 2 beds) Rhenigidale; e ghht@gatliff.org.uk; w gatliff.org.uk. Perched on the far flanks of the sheltered cove that frames the village, the hostel has a cosy common room & kitchen with a multi-fuel stove. Toilet & shower with hot

DEER STALKING

Deer stalking (culling deer) is an important business in North Harris for both commercial and environmental reasons. It takes place from July through to mid-February. The North Harris Trust does not close any part of the estate while deer stalking takes place, so it asks that you are mindful of the responsibilities for stalkers, walkers and cyclists alike. Where possible, keep to obvious footpaths. If you see deer, avoid approaching or deliberately disturbing them. If you notice a deer-stalking party, do not approach, call, or wave to them, and, if at all practical, do not walk in front of them unless you are on a footpath, in which case, stick to the path.

THE NORTH HARRIS TRUST

North Harris was transferred to community ownership in 2003 and makes up one of the largest community-owned estates in Scotland. 'The spark for us was that the land came up for sale,' says Alistair Macleod, manager of the North Harris Trust (w north-harris.org). 'There was no resentment in the community regarding the landlord. But you had no idea how a new landlord might behave – they could be worse, or there could just be benign neglect. It was an opportunity for us to take the future into our own hands. It gave the community an incredible sense of optimism.'

The North Harris Trust paid £2.2 million for the estate and oversees all its affairs, investing in projects for wind and hydro energy, managing around 90km (55 miles) of paths and opening the golden eagle observatory. It also set up the Harris Stalking Club to manage the 1,000 or so red deer that graze the estate and implemented a home-insulation programme. The trust has been supported along the way by the John Muir Trust, which has offered financial, practical and staffing assistance. 'Control of what happens is a good thing,' says Macleod. 'There's an increase in confidence that comes with control of your own destiny. We have put the North Harris area up for display in a better way than was perhaps done before.'

water. Note you cannot book a bed in advance but the managers say the hostel never operates to capacity. **£**

🏠 **Scaladale Centre Hostel** (4 dorms with 4 beds (2 en suite) & 2 dorms with 6 beds) Ardvourlie; ☎01859 502502; e info@scaladale. co.uk; w scaladale-centre.co.uk. Good kitchen & common room, picnic benches outside. **£**

Self-catering

🏠 **Sonas Cottage** (sleeps 2) Bunavoneadar, Hushinish peninsula; ☎01415 330117;

e sonascottages@btinternet.com; w sonas-cottages.com. Roll-top bath, sauna, cinema room & popcorn machine make this a cottage with a difference. £600–980/week. **£££**

🏠 **Clisham Cottage** (sleeps 6) Ardhasaig; ☎01859 502066; e stay@harriscottage.com; w harriscottage.com. Immaculately furnished. Superb position among the North Harris Hills with wonderful views of the mountain range. Ground floor suitable for people with impaired mobility. Owned by the Macaskill family who run Ardhasaig House. £300–600/week. **££**

✕ WHERE TO EAT AND DRINK *Map, page 138*

Remarkably, from the Lewis–Harris border, right down until you reach Tarbert, there is just the one permanent and one mobile (but excellent) café. Fortunately, both are really excellent and popular, something that leaves you thinking that a few more such enterprises should be bold enough to make a go of things in the wilds of Harris.

✕ **Hebscape Gallery & Tearoom** Ardhasaig; ☎01859 502363; e info@hebscapegallery. co.uk; w hebscapegallery.co.uk; ⏱ Apr–Oct 10.30–16.30 Tue–Sat. Located on the A859 just a couple of miles north of Tarbert. Offers a superb combination of photography, coffee & cake, all presented by Darren Cole, whose breathtaking landscape images hang from every wall (originals & prints are available for sale). A former lecturer

at the University of the West of England, Darren moved to Harris in 2013 with his partner Chris Griffiths. While Darren & his camera explore the island in all weathers & seasons, Chris – a master baker & confectioner – prepares salmon & oatcake lunches, excellent brownies & coffee. **£**

✳ ⬛ **Taste n' Sea** Bogha Glas; m 07444 729113; f tastensealochseaforth; ⏱ usually Apr–Nov 11.00–19.00 Mon–Sat, times can vary so check their social media. A trailer located on a stunning brow above Loch Seaforth in the foothills of the Harris hills right on the Harris–Lewis border, run by local couple Irene & Alasdair Morrison. The location is actually part of their croft. If you thought trailer vans equate to greasy burgers & fries, think again: top-notch fish & chips, scampi & cullen skink, plus langoustines, crab, lobster, & occasionally cod, all caught by Alasdair from Loch Seaforth. Also cakes & what walkers & cyclists may consider to be life-enhancing hot chocolate. **£**

SHOPPING **Amhuinnsuidhe Castle** operates an honesty shop (⊕ Easter–Sep 24hrs daily) where you can pick up a range of goods, from meats to ice creams. A mile or so north of Tarbert, on the main road and 350m south of Hebscape, you will find the **Hebridean Design Company** (✆ 01859 502644; e info@ thehebrideandesigncompany.com; w thehebrideandesigncompany.com; ⊕ Apr–Oct 09.30–17.00 Mon–Sat, Nov–Mar 10.00–16.00 Mon–Sat). Also trading as Ardhasaig Glass & Arts, this engaging little craft shop is home to Kate and Doug Blake. The embroidery work, such as tea towels and prints of the Lewis chessmen, is done by Kate, while Doug works at producing eye-catching glasswork that frequently captures the extraordinary island light.

WHAT TO SEE AND DO Odd as it may sound, the main road – the **A859** – is one of North Harris's chief attractions. An impressive feat of engineering sees the road climb via a series of dramatic switchbacks from just 15m (50ft) above sea level to more than 180m (600ft) inside 2 miles. The road then straightens to head south and gives truly dizzying views down through Harris with the land to the east – and very adjacent to the road – falling away towards Loch Seaforth. This is tremendous scenery in all weathers. In mist, it is moodily atmospheric; in heavy rain the water seems to spring out of the peat, creating spurting, gushing waterfalls that splatter down the bare rock like an overflow from supersized guttering. High winds combined with rain bring the rare phenomenon of reverse waterfalls, with streams of water being blown back up the mountainsides. If the skies are clear, the views will stay with you for ever. Convenient parking bays allow you to pull over and take in the spectacle.

Just south of the watershed, a minor road peels off left and dips dramatically via more hairpin bends towards the hamlet of **Màraig**, overlooking the diminutive and sheltered loch of the same name. A left-hand fork here leads to the hamlet and, just around the corner behind the smattering of houses, is another of the Outer Hebrides' exquisite cemeteries. It is divided into two parts: one modern, and the other truly ancient, with fallen, weathered headstones staggered over a rugged uneven hillock of turf. Returning to the fork, the road continues east down a series of loops for a further 4 miles. At the road end is the tiny community of **Rhenigidale** overlooking an embryonic headwater for Loch Trolamaraig. The bay here is secluded and has views across the Minch to Skye. The village's main claim to fame is that it is believed to have been the last community to be linked up to the UK road network. Until barely 20 years ago, the village could only be reached on foot over a pass from Tarbert, or by sea. Before the clearances of the early 19th century, Rhenigidale supported just two shepherds, as wisdom held that this was all the poor soils could sustain. But as people were forced off the fertile machair on the west coasts, the population swelled to 100 and people turned to fishing, focussing on the herring catch, to eke out a living. This proved unviable for most and emigration saw the population drop to just ten by the 1980s. At that point, Rhenigidale looked poised to join the lengthy list of abandoned villages. Instead, a vigorous campaign was launched to have the road built, with supporters arguing that this would encourage people to move in. A road was somehow drilled through the obdurate blocks of gneiss and opened in 1989. The population now stands at 20, and there is a popular hostel here (page 139) and, more remarkably, the doughty W11 provides a daily bus service, squeezing and groaning its way down and up from the A859.

Hushinish (Huisinis) It's a mighty 14 miles along the single-track B887 that explores the Hushinish peninsula. The journey's end is the beach and tiny community of the same name. The road twists and rises simultaneously, tightly following the

𝕩 FROM RHENIGIDALE TO TARBERT ALONG THE POSTMAN'S TRAIL

Map, opposite

11km (7 miles); 3hrs
OS Explorer 455 South Harris
Start: fingerpost sign on road, 500m west of Rhenigidale (⊕ NB224017)
Finish: Tarbert (⊕ NG156999)

For centuries, the only way for the outside world to reach Rhenigidale was by boat, or by a narrow path that threaded its way over the hills from Tarbert. This age-old track, known as the postman's trail, makes for a wonderful walk, with mountain and coastal scenery and an abandoned village. The walk can be completed in either direction but is described here from Rhenigidale, simply because it allows you to round off the walk at a café.

The walk is signposted all the way, either for Urgha or Tarbert. Walk up the lane from Rhenigidale and follow the fingerpost sign to the left that leads around Loch Trolamaraig and the mournful remains of the abandoned village of Gearraidh Lotaigear, which clung on here until the late 19th century. The most striking feature is the pair of chimney breasts that simply front thin air, thereby resembling an uncompleted Lego building. Beyond here, the trail is lovely, undulating above the shore, passing waterfalls and little burns, and crossing footbridges. The gullies here are home to a species of aspen that is thought to have taken root thousands of years ago.

Then comes the daunting climb from sea level all the way up to 274m (900ft) and the col between the twin peaks of Beinn Tharsuinn and Trolamul. The route ascends the notorious 'zigzags', 12 thrilling hairpin turns that take the edge off the gradient. The views are just as breathtaking. While you climb, spare a thought for the postmen (and possibly women) who lugged their packages this way. For their sake, one hopes the letters and parcels were worth the effort: perhaps a love letter, tremulously accepting a proposal of marriage; or insults traded between two families who had long fallen out? At least the road opened before the advent of junk mail.

Finally, the track levels off at the col, amid rocky, boggy moorland. Both golden and white-tailed eagles nest around here. The descent is straightforward, the path clear as it drops to the waters of Lochannan Lacasdail. As you descend, you'll pass a curious plaque that reads 'Duncan Macinnes 1827–1908, Duncan Macinnes 1908–1982'. The name is that of a postman who did this walk, but the inscription and the symmetry of the dates remain something of a riddle. From here, it's a further 3¼km (2 miles) along the road to Tarbert, via the minuscule hamlet of Urgha.

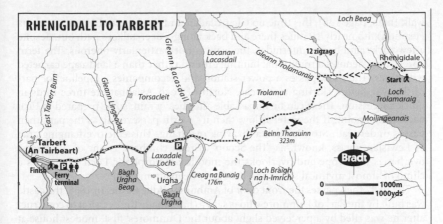

contours of the land as it runs along West Loch Tarbert (Loch a' Siar). This feels like a road to the end of the world, the kind you might expect to encounter at the bottom of Patagonia. Just a mile or so along the road, you pass the old Norwegian whaling station of **Bunavoneadar (Bun Abhainn Eadarra)**, built in 1912. The station was operational until the outbreak of World War I and then again from 1918 until 1922. Then – that man again – Lord Leverhulme stepped in and bought the station with well-intentioned plans to create employment. Although the machinery was overhauled in 1923 and three new vessels purchased to catch whales in the Atlantic, the scheme haemorrhaged money. This was due to Leverhulme's unusual business plan: he intended to produce oil but, turning his eye to the traditional smokeries of the islands, mused on whether smoked whale meat and whale sausages could be exported to the interior of Africa. Unsurprisingly, Leverhulme soon thought better of it and the station collapsed. The most conspicuous reminder of the whole bizarre affair is the rather elegant, terracotta square brick chimney.

Almost as unexpected as a whaling station, perhaps, is the Bunavoneadar tennis court you pass a mile or so further west along the road (page 136). This presents the unlikely opportunity of playing on what is claimed to be the world's most remote tennis court. The surface is good-quality artificial grass, and you can hire the court along with racquets and balls. Should rain stop play, you may even shelter in the small wooden pavilion.

Five miles from turning off the main road is the minuscule township of **Miabhaig**. This is the location for a gorgeous and spectacular walk, due north up the glen to the **North Harris Eagle Observatory** ✳ (w north-harris.org/north-harris/the-north-harris-eagle-observatory; ⊙ year-round). Built by the North Harris Trust, the observatory lies in golden eagle territory. This is a delightful walk on a good track that follows the course of the River Mhiabhaig. This is also a fine walk for children, and there's a bridge for them to play on and streams to play in along the way. In spring and early summer, you may well be accompanied by the constant song of cuckoos. After 1½ miles (around 45mins) you reach the hide, a small hut with a view further up the glen towards a peak and promontory known as Sron Scourst. With 20 pairs of golden eagles, Harris has one of the highest densities of the bird in Europe; look upwards and you may spot them, albeit as dots high in the sky. With careful planning, you can extend the walk into an epic traverse of the glens of the central Harris hills all the way to Bogha Glas (see box, page 151).

Some 4 miles further west along the B887, immediately before reaching Amhuinnsuidhe Castle, a turning to the right leads to a track and another stunning walk [map, page 138], this time up Glen Uladail and the Forest of Harris (Frith na Hearadh). It's nearly 10 miles there and back along a deerstalker's path but, despite a few rocky and boggy interludes, the walk is not particularly onerous. The term 'forest' here denotes a traditional hunting ground rather than a landscape carpeted with trees. The track passes a power station and accompanies a pipeline for part of the way before skirting two lochs. North of Loch Asiabhat are three fords in quick succession. These can be impassable after heavy rain, so be prepared to turn back at this point. If the water is low, then it's worth persevering as the path then passes underneath Sron Uladal, a dizzying overhang. This epic overhanging crag of Lewisian gneiss, known as 'The Scoop' to rock climbers, is one of the largest overhangs in Europe and overlooks the moodily atmospheric Loch Uladal. It's a climb of almost mythical status and has rarely been attempted.

The B887 then passes the front door of **Amhuinnsuidhe Castle**. In 1868, the castle was built by the Earl of Dunmore who is said to have made the decision to construct after he was riled by a perceived slight about the Dunmores' first, modest house at Rodel. The comment was made by the prospective bride of the Earl's son: joining the long list of people who put their foot in it with prospective in-laws, the daughter of MacDonald of Sleat had observed that her father owned bigger stables than those at the Earl's house. The castle was later owned by Thomas Octave Murdoch Sopwith, of Sopwith Camel aircraft fame. A weir with crashing falls is located just beyond the

SCARP AND THE ROCKET POST

The island of Scarp was settled in 1803, and at its height the population reached 200, but numbers dwindled, and the last crofting family left in 1971. A major factor in this decline was the heavy seas, which could cut off the island for several days, even though it is barely 350m from the 'mainland' of Harris. The challenges were highlighted in January 1934, when Christina Maclennan, pregnant with twins, went into extended labour. An 85-year-old midwife delivered Mary, the first of the babies, but insisted the mother be ferried across high seas to the mainland to deliver the second twin. She was driven to Tarbert and on to Stornoway. She finally gave birth to Jessie two days later, on a different island.

Meanwhile, Gerhardt Zucher, a German rocket scientist, had persuaded the British government to fund a research project to deliver mail rather than babies to the island. The plan was to attach mail to a rocket and launch it across the waters. If all went well, Zucher maintained, the scheme might be rolled out across remote islands and communities around the British Isles. Sadly, things didn't work out. In July 1934, a rocket stuffed with thousands of letters marked 'Western Isles Rocket Post' spectacularly failed to deliver, exploding at the first attempt. A second trial was an equal failure. The British then deported him to Germany, deeming him a 'threat to the income of the post office and the security of the country'. He was arrested in his homeland on suspicion of spying for the British but later served in the Luftwaffe. He spent the rest of his life failing, again and again, to launch mail rockets commercially, or even safely, an endeavour he pursued until the end of his days. The whole saga is captured in the engaging 2002 film *The Rocket Post*. It goes without saying that while the option of wading across to Scarp may look tempting at low tide, it is in reality a wildly reckless and dangerous thing to attempt.

castle lawns. From June to September, you have a realistic chance of seeing salmon leap here as they head upstream to spawn.

The terminus of this road is the community of Hushinish with its glorious shell beach and views across to South Harris. The sand settles far inland and environmental groups have made the claim – difficult to refute – that the beach has a higher percentage of shell fragments (92%) than any other in Scotland. The machair here is a bewitching khaki-mustard colour and flowers with creeping willow and Scottish bluebells, or harebells, in late summer. This and the rockpools at the western end of the beach will keep children entranced for many an hour.

Here, a modern wooden building, known as the **Hushinish Gateway**, serves both as a community centre and a sheltered viewing point in which to eat packed lunches. It has toilets, and adjacent to the building is a mobile canteen (⊕ Apr–Sep 09.30–18.00 Mon–Sat; £), which serves hot food and drinks.

Walking in the North Harris Hills
The majority of the hills of note in the Outer Hebrides are clustered together in the north of Harris, and their northernmost limit demarcates the boundary with Lewis. While Clisham is the highest and offers simply stunning views from its summit on a clear day, many walkers argue that the hills to the west are even more impressive with swooping overhangs and textbook glacial valleys. The whole area is now managed by the North Harris Trust, which has moved quickly in the early years of its ownership to make the mountains more accessible and leave walkers less subject to the vagaries of high river flows. An extensive network of paths through the estate covers some 50km (30 miles) along the coast, through glens and overpasses. The North Harris ranger service (\01859 502222; e ranger@north-harris.org; w north-harris.org) runs guided walks from April right through to the deer rut in October. See the website for the schedule of walks and details of the annual Isle of Harris Mountain Festival, usually held in the first week of September.

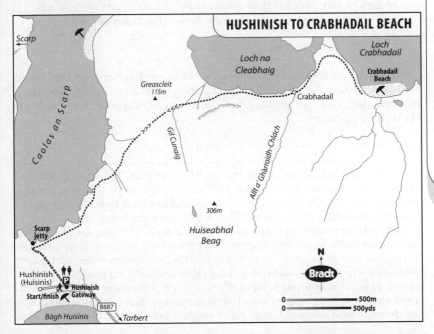

HUSHINISH TO CRABHADAIL BEACH

Scarp · Caolas an Scarp · Loch na Cleabhaig · Loch Crabhadail · Crabhadail Beach · Greascleit 115m · Gil Cunaig · Crabhadail · Allt a' Ghàrraidh-Chlach · 306m · Huiseabhal Beag · Scarp jetty · Hushinish (Huisinis) · Start/finish · Hushinish Gateway · B887 · Bàgh Huisinis · Tarbert · N · Bradt · 0 — 500m · 0 — 500yds

7¼km (4½ miles) return; 3hrs
OS Explorer 456 North Harris & Loch Seaforth
Start/finish: car park at Hushinish (⊕ NA993121)

In a land not short of glorious beaches, one of the best on Harris can only be accessed on foot. This walk from Hushinish edges around the flanks of the hill Huiseabhal Beag to reach the small beach at Crabhadail. This is a tough little hike, mainly on account of the first 1½km out of Hushinish, which involves boggy ground and some clambering. The easiest way to begin is to walk west past the Hushinish Gateway and, after 100m, turn right along the sandy track towards the Scarp jetty. When you see the pier, turn right and walk above the beach, heading for the clear path that winds its way along the coast.

Watch your step as in places the path edges close to a gully above a geo. Look out above, too, for an extraordinary gully that drops almost perpendicular down the side of the hill, the water rushing through a gutter below your feet. The views of the island of Scarp improve as you move along, and you can soon see the dozen or so houses that remain on the now abandoned island. The beach ahead is Tràigh Mheilin, not the target of this walk. The path becomes rocky as it drops downhill towards two iron posts. Take the right-hand path where the track forks, following the clear route that rises gently uphill through the glen and away from the sea. At the top of the pass, the views open up dramatically. Below is Loch na Cleabhaig, overlooked by two small lochans. Beyond, to the north, are the southernmost islets of Uig on Lewis (a distance of some 4 nautical miles across Loch Rèasort but 75 miles by road); to the east are the western outliers of the central massif of the Harris hills. The path squeezes tight between the southern shoreline of the loch and the hill of Huiseabhal Beag, past a lonely cottage, and only when you are almost upon it do you see the beach at Crabhadail. Return the same way.

Three walks are described here: the ascent of Clisham (see box, page 148); Bogha Glas to Miabhaig (see box, page 151); and Tarbert to Abhainn Sgaladail via Màraig (see box, page 153). For all three, you should use OS Explorer map 456 North Harris & Loch Seaforth.

TARBERT (AN TAIRBEART)

The main township of Harris and the island's chief port, Tarbert, is positioned on the narrow isthmus that connects North and South Harris ('Tairbeart' means 'isthmus' in Gaelic). The location between west and east Loch Tarbert is stirring, the main road funnelling down through high hills to the water's edge.

Tarbert is very small, with just two roads that form a 'T' shape – Main Street running across the top of the village and Pier Road running down to the quayside. Its one-way system, however – designed to ease the pinch points of the comings and goings of the ferry – can make it seem larger than is actually the case. Nevertheless, it's easy to form the impression that Tarbert is simply somewhere that visitors must negotiate before dispersing into the Harris hinterland. That sense is reinforced by the defiantly local-oriented feel of many shops which makes it clear that, unlike

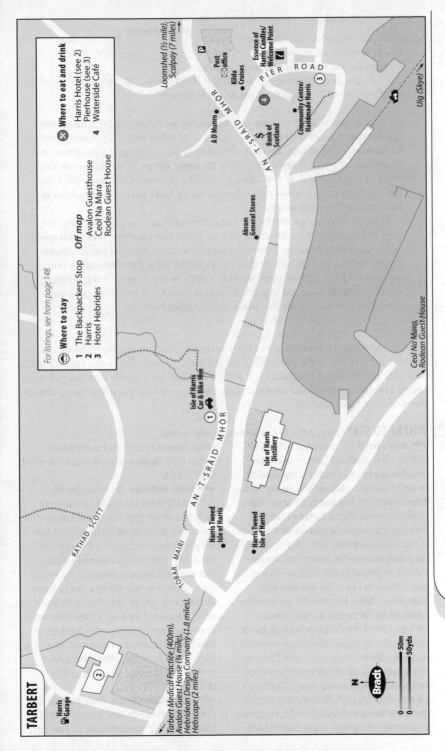

TARBERT

P Harris Garage

RATHAD SCOTT

Tarbert Medical Practice (400m),
Avalon Guest House (¾ mile),
Hebridean Design Company (1.8 miles),
Hebscape (2 miles)

LOBAR MAIRI

Isle of Harris Car & Bike Hire 🔧 1

AN T-SRAID MHOR

Isle of Harris Distillery

Harris Tweed
Isle of Harris

Harris Tweed
Isle of Harris

Loomshed (½ mile),
Scalpay (7 miles) ↑

P

Post
office
✉ Kilda
● Cruises

PIER ROAD

A D Munro ●

AN T-SRAID MHOR

Bank of
Scotland
$

Essence of
Harris Candles/
Welcome Point ℹ

Community Centre/
● Handmade Harris

4

3

Akram
General Stores ●

Ceol Na Mara,
Rodean Guest House ↗

Uig (Skye)

For listings, see from page 148

🏠 **Where to stay**
1 The Backpackers Stop
2 Harris
3 Hotel Hebrides

Off map
Avalon Guesthouse
Ceol Na Mara
Rodean Guest House

⊗ **Where to eat and drink**
Harris Hotel (see 2)
Pierhouse (see 3)
4 Waterside Café

N

Bradt

0   50m
0   50yds

A WALK UP CLISHAM (AN CLISEAM) *Map, opposite*

9½km (6 miles) return; 4hrs
OS Explorer 456 North Harris & Loch Seaforth
Start/finish: small parking places on the A859 at ✦ NB174056 (the most southwesterly of the 4 parking areas on the high pass)

Clisham is the highest summit on the islands at 799m (2,621ft). Relatively speaking, it is an easier hike than a number of other peaks on either Harris or South Uist. That said, there is still open ground and pathless ridges to negotiate along with some proximity to sheer drops. What follows is the most straightforward of the various ascents; it saves time and effort by starting high up in the hills rather than at shore level. Even so, it should only be attempted in good weather.

From the road, walk northwest along the path up the glen, keeping the river to your right. The path then peels away left from the river and becomes much steeper and fainter. Where it disappears altogether, the key is to keep the ascent towards Clisham as direct as possible. Near the summit, the ridge narrows and the path returns, leading a little painstakingly to the summit, which is entirely wrapped in a stone wind shelter. From here, you can survey the entire chain of islands that make up the Outer Hebrides.

ports in the Inner Hebrides such as Portree on Skye or Tobermory on Mull, tourists are still not yet the main event. Galvanised buckets and sheep dip are as readily available in Tarbert as postcards and a slice of cake. It's a gentle reminder that the Outer Hebrides retain local communities that have yet to prostrate themselves in front of the tourist shilling.

 WHERE TO STAY *Map, page 147, unless otherwise stated*

Harris Hotel (23 rooms) Scott Rd; 01859 502154; e info@harrishotel.com; w harrishotel. com. Rooms are a mix of modern & traditional but be sure to ask for one that overlooks the bay. The bar is the kind of classic Highland snug that you might expect to see more often in the Outer Hebrides. It even claims to harbour the most extensive selection of malt whiskies anywhere in the Hebrides. A plaque sits proudly above the bar quoting Louis MacNeice – poet & contemporary of W H Auden – from his book *I Crossed the Minch*: 'The hotel has a very original bar – dark as bars should be (no decent bar admits the light of the sun).' A window in which J M Barrie, author of *Peter Pan*, etched his initials, is now ensconced in a glass cabinet by the entrance to the lounge. The restaurant (££) is good & open to non-residents. Starters include Hebridean scallops with black pudding & parsnip purée (£10) & haggis pakora with chutney (£7). While mains go through the traditional range of meats (£16–22); vegetarians could opt for the vegetable haggis croquettes with

neeps, tatties & cream (£13). Creative desserts include gin & blueberry jelly with a cucumber sorbet (£5.95). **£££**

Hotel Hebrides (21 rooms) Pier Rd; 01859 502364; e stay@hotel-hebrides.com; w hotel-hebrides.com. 1 family room. From the outside, this looks like a business hotel, but the interior has a much warmer feel with smart furnishings, fresh décor & patterned wallpaper that give the rooms a contemporary feel. Plenty of nice smellies in the bathrooms. Run by Angus Macleod, who took on the business from his father & renovated the hotel in 2009, & his wife Chirsty, who grew up in Borrisdale, southeast of Leverburgh. Also contains a restaurant (page 149). The couple manage the Kirklee Island suites, 4 serviced apts sleeping 2–4, just across the road (£££). **£££**

Avalon Guest House [map, page 138] (3 rooms) 12 West Side, West Tarbert; 01859 502334; w avalonguesthouse.org; ⊕ Apr–Sep.

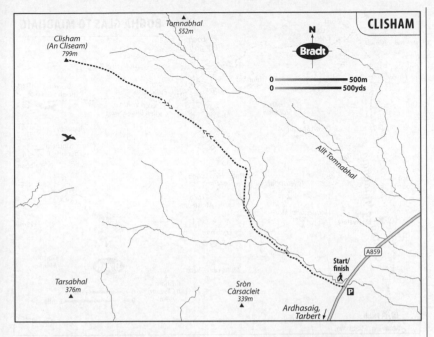

A family croft located off the A859 ¾ mile north of Tarbert & overlooking Loch West Tarbert (Loch a' Siar). 2 rooms have loch views, as does the dining room. Good-sized rooms, thoughtfully decorated & furnished with colour co-ordinated bedding & curtains. **££**

Ceol na Mara [map, page 138] (4 rooms) 7 Direcleit; 01859 502464; w ceolnamara.com; mid-Mar–mid-Oct. Located ½ mile south of Tarbert & just off the A859, this light & airy guesthouse has 3 spacious en-suite rooms & 1 with private bathroom. Thoughtful touches include organic toiletries & a large sundeck overlooking Loch Caenn Dibig, as well as an honesty bar. The house name translates as 'choir of the sea' & was suggested by the daughter of the former owners, for when the weather is rough you can hear

the tide & the river clashing. New owners Dave & Jane Loomes have retained the same restful atmosphere. Both are former primary school headteachers who relocated from England and who chose, as Dave puts it, 'to pursue a life-long dream to live in an area we love'. **££**

Rodean Guest House [map, page 138] (3 rooms) Kendibeg, just south of Tarbert; 01859 502079; e famorrison@hotmail.co.uk. Wonderful position above Loch Kindebeg looking across to Scalpay. A dbl, a twin & a sgl, all en suite, & guest lounge. **££**

The Backpackers Stop (22 beds) Main St; m 07708 746745; e bpackers_stop@hotmail. com; w backpackers-stop.co.uk. Clean & simple hostel accommodation in 2 single-sex dorms & 1 mixed. Shared toilets & showers. **£**

✕ WHERE TO EAT AND DRINK *Map, page 147*

✕ Pierhouse Restaurant Hotel Hebrides, Pier Rd, Tarbert; 01859 502364; w hotel-hebrides. com/dining; Easter–Oct bar menu noon–16.00 daily, evening dining 18.00–21.00 daily. Specialises in fish, striving to offer a fine-dining experience with dishes such as Lewis scallops with beetroot carpaccio & fillet of megrim (a species of flatfish) with samphire. Window seats are prized as it's quite something to watch a CalMac ferry steadily loom

up to fill the entire window before disgorging its passengers. In winter, the restaurant is replaced by a more informal café/diner arrangement (noon–18.00 daily) serving warming food such as pizzas & jacket potatoes, & cakes, The hotel's adjacent Mote lounge bar (noon–21.00 daily) serves burgers, nachos & similar offerings for around £7–12.50. The bar is always busy with locals; if you've spent some time on Harris, it

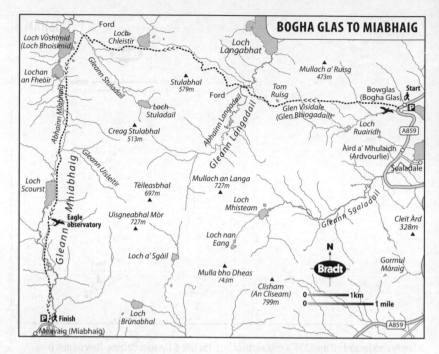

can seem unexpectedly lively of an evening. The ambience of both bar & restaurant is deliberately cultivated, according to co-owner Chirsty Macleod. 'We didn't want a place where locals did not feel welcome, or give the impression we were only for visitors. I think it's nice that visitors can sit & drink in a bar with local people & talk.' ££

✗ **Waterside Café** Pier Rd, Tarbert; 📞01859 502439; ⏰ 10.00–16.00 Mon–Sat. Located just above the harbour, this is a lovely café decorated in pastel shades of blue, with a small lawned outdoor seating area & excellent cakes & coffee. Owned by local couple John Cook & Mary Shaw – Mary was born in the building. £

SHOPPING For an authentic insight into how Tarbert serves its local community, take a peek inside, **Akram General Stores** (Main St; 📞 01859 502474; ⏰ 09.00–18.00), an emporium that has something of the air of Grace Brothers and Mr Benn combined, and which is full of yesteryear crockery, hosiery for ladies of a certain age, and traditional home furnishings. Down by the pier, housed in the old Visit Scotland building, you'll find the **Essence of Harris** candle shop (📞 01859 502768; e info@essenceofharris.com; w essenceofharris.com; ⏰ 09.30–16.30 Mon–Sat). The shop produces elegantly packaged and delicately scented candles, many named after Harris beaches: Horgabost comprises lemon and ginger, while Luskentyre features bergamot, vanilla, coconut and almond. The shop also offers candle-making workshops.

If you are self-catering or just stocking up for the day, Tarbert has two good local stores. The larger is A D Munro (📞01859 502016; ⏰ 07.00–18.00 Mon–Sat), at the top of Pier Road, a licensed community shop that also sells fresh meat and fish plus local oatcakes and breads. A smaller alternative is John Morrison newsagents (Main St; 📞01859 502319; ⏰ 08.30–18.00 Mon–Fri, 08.30–20.00 Sat), which is also home to Park View Stores. If you're seeking souvenirs, a seasonal craft market (⏰ 10.00–16.00 daily) is held in the community hall immediately above the Hotel Hebrides.

FROM BOGHA GLAS TO MIABHAIG

Map, opposite

16km (10 miles) one way; 5–6hrs
OS Explorer 456 North Harris & Loch Seaforth
Start: Bogha Glas car park (⊕ NB187116)
Finish: Miabhaig car park (⊕ NB100062)

This dramatic walk is one of the longest you can undertake on Harris and takes you through staggeringly wild and remote scenery. This is a linear walk, so you'll need to arrange transport at either end.

Leaving from Bogha Glas (Bowglass), strike out west up Glen Visidale (Glen Bhiogadail) before turning left under the shadow of Clisham and heading due south, passing the North Harris Eagle Observatory (page 143) and bringing you out on the Hushinish road. Established by crofters, fishermen and deerstalkers, the path has been improved and is now accessible for fit hikers. For the most part, this is a hill trail, though the last stretch is much easier as the path approaches the eagle observatory.

For many years, the major obstacle for walkers was two fords that walkers must negotiate (at ⊕ NB148120 in Gleann Langadail and at ⊕ NB108132 by Loch Voshimid), which can become impassable after heavy rain. However, bridges now cross these waters, making the walk much more accessible.

Along the way you'll notice infant deciduous trees, including alder, rowan, downy birch, hazel and willow that have been planted as part of a landscape regeneration project. Such trees were the area's native land cover, particularly Gleann Mhiabhaig – remnant seeds of the native trees that used to populate this area have been easy to identify in the peat – but they have been historically cleared to allow grazing for sheep and deer. The hope is that their presence, once limited to gullies and crags, will expand and, in turn, attract more bird species into the area. If you're into your mosses, there's plenty to keep you interested, including woolly fringemoss on the ridges and bog mosses in the hollows. The carnivorous sundew and butterwort are here, feasting on the all-too-abundant midges in season.

WHAT TO SEE AND DO Although Tarbert has few sights as such, wandering around the handful of shops, having a lunchtime meal or a slice of cake and coffee, and watching the coming and going of the ferry can still hold your attention for a few hours.

The rich variety and quality of Harris and Scalpay's artistic folk is on display at **Handmade Harris** (Tarbert Community Centre; f Handmade Harris; ⏲ Easter–Oct 10.00–16.00 Thu & Fri & occasional days before Christmas, check social media). Tucked away, immediately behind the Waterside Café, this small but high-quality craft fair showcases wares such as the artwork of Lorna Wheeler, who deploys driftwood, shells and even animal bones, as well as the fine tweed work of Jayne and Richard Green from Pink Sheep Studio (w pinksheepstudio.com), who fashion tweed lamps, cushions and foot stools.

The village's landmark attraction is the **Isle of Harris Distillery** (📞01859 502212; e info@harrisdistillery.com; w harrisdistillery.com; ⏲ 10.00–17.00 Mon–Sat; tours £10), a warehouse-like, whitewashed building opened in 2015 that now exerts a supersized dominance on a diminutive quayside. The distillery has been universally welcomed, with the hopes fulfilled that it would draw visitors – more than 200,000 have visited since it opened – and boost the local economy. It also

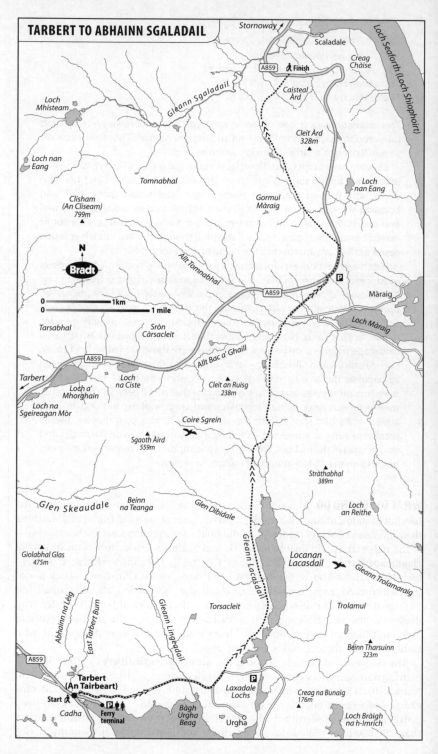

TARBERT TO ABHAINN SGALADAIL

Stornoway

Scaladale

A859   Finish

Creag
Chàise

Loch
Mhisteam

Gleann Sgaladail

Caisteal
Àrd

Cleit Àrd
328m

Loch Seaforth (Loch Shiophoirt)

Loch nan
Eang

Tomnabhal

Gormul
Màraig

Loch
nan Eang

Clisham
(An Cliseam)
799m

Allt Tomnabhal

N

Bradt

P

0 ——————— 1km
0 ——————— 1 mile

Màraig

Loch Màraig

Tarsabhal

Sròn
Càrsacleit

A859

Allt Bac a' Ghaill

Tarbert

Loch a'
Mhorghain

Loch
na Ciste

Cleit an Ruisg
238m

Loch na
Sgeireagan Mòr

Coire Sgrein

Sgaoth Àird
559m

Stràthabhal
389m

Glen Skeaudale

Beinn
na Teanga

Glen Dibidale

Gleann Lacasdail

Loch
an Reithe

Locanan
Lacasdail

Gleann Trolamaraig

Giolabhal Glas
475m

Torsacleit

Trolamul

Abhainn na Lèig

East Tarbert Burn

Gleann Lingeadail

Beinn Tharsuinn
323m

A859

Tarbert
(An Tairbeart)

Start

Cadha

P
Ferry
terminal

Bàgh
Urgha
Beag

Laxadale
Lochs

P

Urgha

Creag na Bunaig
176m

Loch Bràigh
na h-Imrich

13½km (8½ miles); 4hrs
OS Explorer 456 North Harris & Loch Seaforth
Start: Tarbert
Finish: A859 at Abhainn Sgaladail (⊕ NB186096; marked by a small well-shaped monument). The W10 bus can be flagged down at the end of the route.

The route heads east out of Tarbert along the main road, passing the turn-off for Urgha and descending to the dammed waters of Lochannan Lacasdail and a small car park (⊕ NB177004) by the loch. There is some interpretation here about the Harris Walkway (Frith na Rathaid na Hearraidh), a network of paths that links North Harris to the west-coast bays of South Harris and wildlife. Take the footpath that heads northeast along the west side of the loch. The route rises gently through Gleann Lacasdail, the silence likely to be broken only by birdsong and the gurgling of unseen burns. You may spot red grouse, stonechat and raven along the way, and in good weather Clisham will loom large. Once over the pass, the track leads to a small footbridge to reach the hairpin of a minor road (⊕ NB187058). Walk uphill to reach the main island road, the A859, above the tiny hamlet of Màraig, with gorgeous views of Loch Shìophoirt, a vast sea loch that opens out into the Minch.

At this point, 9½km (6 miles) in, you can choose to cut short the walk and flag down the W10.

To continue, head north along the road verge for 450m (conveniently, much of this stretch is taken up by a large lay-by). Then cross the road with care to pick up the Harris Walkway as it pulls away northwest (⊕ NB194069).

The route here contours its way gently around the side of the peaks Cleit Àrd and Caisteal Àrd and drops steadily towards the valley floor. It's a thoughtful example of planning and contrasts with the road route's tight hairpin bends.

The striking fractured columns of basalt that emerge at the brow of the hill are those of Creag Mò and the course of the River Sgaladail is clearly visible, with its tributaries twisting and turning in textbook fashion. The path meets the A859 by a small well-shaped monument that commemorates the creation of the Harris Walkway.

has a small licensed café (⊕ 10.00–16.00 Mon–Sat; £) selling cakes, seafood platters and coffee, though this suffers from that rare thing in the Outer Hebrides: the whiff of presumption and off-hand service that comes with knowing you merely have to open your doors to make a profit. The gift shop sells gin-based infusions and other souvenirs, with whisky to follow once the malt arrives. The first malt – the Hearach, named after the Gaelic word for an inhabitant of Harris and nurtured in Bourbon barrels from Kentucky and sherry butts from a Spanish bodega – has been pencilled in for 2020, but the vagaries of distilling mean this may slip a little; in the meantime, gin production has proved hugely popular. The distillery has been eager to position itself as part of the community and has trained up five islanders as distillers.

The entire enterprise is adjacent to Tarbert's new pontoon, which received funding from the Scottish government. The combination of whisky and yachts is rapidly injecting both money and a modest bustle into Tarbert's sleepy backwater character.

Across the car park from the distillery is the **Harris Tweed Isle of Harris storeroom and retail outlet** (✆01859 502040; e info@harristweedisleofharris.co.uk; w harristweedisleofharris.co.uk; ⊕ 09.00–17.30 Mon–Sat). This is the place to buy anything in tweed you might ever wish for, from tablet covers to ties. In truth, this is as close as the Outer Hebrides come to mass tourism: the shop is firmly aimed at cruise ship passengers and travellers seeking last-minute gifts before catching the ferry. The owners also run the Clò Mòr exhibition in Drinishader (page 176) in The Bays.

If you travel half a mile east of Tarbert on the Scalpay road, you will find the **Loomshed** (w loomshed.scot; ⊕ 13.00–17.00 Mon–Fri, tastings 13.00, booking recommended), Harris's new – and the Outer Hebrides' only – brewery. Three beers are concocted here (others, including seasonal beers, are in the offing): Crofter (an island pale ale with a peaty, malty flavour); Iasgar (a craft lager); and Poacher (a brown ale). As well as tours of the small brewery, there's a gift shop and a tap room. The owners plan to expand the Loomshed to include the production of other locally made food and drink. Localism is at the heart of this enterprise, with the raw materials including the soft water of Harris (the rock is so hard, the rainwater bounces off the land and doesn't pick up any minerals on its journey to the brewery). Head brewer, Calum Bennett, intends to source Hebridean rye to use in the brewing process and support local crofters to nurture it as a purpose-grown crop. 'We can't compete on quantity with the big brewers, but we can compete on quality,' he says.

SCALPAY (SGALPAIGH)

East of Tarbert the road winds its way for 7 miles to the island of Scalpay (a Norse name meaning 'Ship Island'). In terms of interest and character, Scalpay, just 2½ miles wide and long, punches above its size. It's an island of little bridges, tight turns and intensively farmed crofts with an intriguing community that mixes residents who go back many generations and more recent incomers.

A *dùn* (fort) in Loch an Duin provides the earliest evidence of settlement in Scalpay, and Norse names, such as Sgorabhaig (Scora's Bay) date to around AD800. The population peak came in the mid- 19th century while a thriving herring industry kept going right up until the 1980s: in the 1960s Scalpay was home to at least five 'fish millionaires'. The author Gavin Maxwell, of *Ring of Bright Water* fame, came through here on a shark-hunting expedition in the 1950s. Basking sharks were the recipients of Maxwell's unwelcome attention – something of an irony given Maxwell's later conservationist credentials.

Scalpay has a sense of a world apart, due in part to the fact that until 1997 you could only reach it by ferry. The bridge that now connects Scalpay to the world came with what seems an astonishingly low price tag of £7 million. Its clean lines and main span of 170m are something of a landmark when viewed across the lochs from the A859; Scalpay's oldest resident at the time, Kirsty Morrison (103 years), led the way for the first drive across the bridge. The object that looks like a concrete boat in the water as you cross the bridge is just that – a concrete boat, the *Cretetree*, built during World War II when steel was at a premium.

This may not feel like a large island, but the township houses are scattered across 2 miles or so, and the last census put the population at 290 (about one-sixth of all people on Harris). Even though the school closed in 2012, Scalpay feels like a

BONNIE PRINCE CHARLIE AND HIGHLAND HONOUR

Like many places in the Outer Hebrides, Bonnie Prince Charlie pops up on Scalpay, hiding here as a fugitive while awaiting transfer by boat to Stornoway and onwards to Orkney and France. Arriving on 30 April 1746, he spent four nights as the guest of Donald Campbell, the tacksman – a middle-ranking land holder – of Scalpay. The prince had Campbell to thank for his escape. Campbell took his role as host and Highlander seriously and declined a bribe to hand over the prince to government forces despatched from Stornoway. The Bonnie Prince meanwhile failed to make it north and instead returned to North Uist and Benbecula, sailing from there to Skye. A codicil to the tale concerns the decidedly mixed fortunes that subsequently befell Campbell. When rents were increased on Scalpay in 1774, Campbell was persuaded by his son Kenneth to move to North Carolina. He was none too pleased to later learn that his son had promptly taken on the lease at Scalpay. Furthermore, Campbell had barely arrived in North Carolina when the American Revolution began and another of his sons was killed by loyalist troops. Wisely, Campbell elected not to fight himself, citing 'too many memories of the trouble I got into when I sheltered Bonnie Prince Charlie. I was never a Jacobite but what else could I do when he arrived and claimed my hospitality on Scalpay?' Campbell's last will and testament can be found at the Seallam! Visitor Centre at Northton (page 167).

buoyant place. The island became community owned in 2014 when the previous owner, Fred Taylor, gifted it to the inhabitants, who promptly moved to become part of the North Harris Trust.

The fact that you may hear Harris referred to as 'an island off Scalpay' is indicative of a particular world view that says much about the pride that you find here, just as the oversized penguin rubbish bin that has long been a feature in the bus shelter says something about the character of the place. This is a township where a stern notice advises that the large play park is closed on the Sabbath, a day when many people attend church twice. For some, the strictures of Presbyterianism can be frustrating; for others, it represents a gratifying handbrake on the trend to homogenise every day of the week and safeguards Scalpay against becoming just another trendy coastal destination where a metropolitan crowd might otherwise dominate. The visitor may leave with the impression that Scalpay demonstrates how the duty of neighbourliness works in practice, with mutual tolerance to the fore.

➡ **WHERE TO STAY** *Map, page 138*

🏠 **New Haven** (3 rooms) 15 Ardinashaig; 📞 01859 540325; e newhaven@hebrides.net; w newhavenscalpay.com. Another excellent guesthouse. All rooms thoughtfully decorated to a high standard & there's a comfortable guest lounge. Patio overlooks the harbour. **££**

✳ 🏠 **Two Harbours Guest House** (3 rooms) 📞 01859 540329; e twoharboursharris@hotmail. co.uk; w twoharboursharris.co.uk; ⊕ Easter–Sep. All rooms of this outstanding guesthouse are on the 2nd floor with modern furnishings & sofas;

2 have harbour views & on a good day Clisham fills their window frames; the 3rd overlooks the garden. All are spacious, light & en suite. This was the original house on the island at a time when Scalpay was managed as a sheep farm & it stands on the Campbell house site where Bonnie Prince Charlie took refuge in 1746 before fleeing to France (see box, above). There is a pleasing edge to the way it has been sympathetically restored by Jacqui & Shaun Hayes. A pink erratic boulder broodingly stands guard outside the front drive,

making the house hard to miss. The owner's son, Trix, is a street artist in the vein of Banksy & his highly individual spray-can art of Callanish, the Lochs & other landscapes hangs on the walls of the house. It's also welcome to find, on a group of islands where floor-to-ceiling windows appear to be the must-have for any new development, that the owners have retained the feel of the old house. The restored open hearth with its exposed ½m-thick walls of Lewisian gneiss in the dining room is dramatic. 'We wanted to work with the geology of the island,' laughs Jacqui. It helps that Shaun is a builder by trade, so has applied his own high-end finishes, including reproducing the original mouldings, with coving in the same style as Amhuinnsuidhe Castle, which was built around the same time. **££**

✖ WHERE TO EAT AND DRINK   *Map, page 138*

✳ ✖ **North Harbour Bistro & Tearoom**   Harbour, Scalpay; ☎ 01859 540218; ▪ NorthHarbourBistro; ⏰ 10.00–20.00 Mon–Tue & Thu–Sat. This hugely popular bistro run by chef George Lavery serves everything from fish & chips to roast salmon with Parisian potatoes, Tandoori-

---

🚶 TO EILEAN GLAS LIGHTHOUSE

3¼km (2 miles); 1hr, if returning along the gravel path/5km (3 miles); 2hrs, if returning via south coast
Map: OS Explorer 455 South Harris
Start/finish: Outend (⊕ NG232949)

A relatively new gravel path has made Scalpay lighthouse much more accessible. This walk begins and finishes in Outend, a tiny hamlet at the southeast tip of Scalpay, 3¼km (2 miles) from the shop and bistro. If driving, park in the spaces gifted from the croft of weaver Sheila Roderick. The gravel track leading to the lighthouse is clear and easy to follow, and zigzags across high ground before dipping towards the coast with striking views down to the lighthouse. This will take most people about 25 minutes. You can return the same way, but a slightly longer and a little more rugged route loops south from above the lighthouse to Outend. On a clear day, this walk offers some outstanding views. To the north, you can pick out a whole host of jagged peaks on the mainland, from Assynt to the Torridon range and Skye where the terraced geology of Macleod's Tables looks just a stone's throw away. To the south, much of the southern half of the Outer Hebrides pulls away across the water. As you cross the moorland, look out for some charismatic bird species, including wheatear (the male with its distinctive 'robber' mask). From April to June, you will rarely be out of earshot of a cuckoo. On higher ground in summer, you'll see foxgloves and meadowsweet, while reeds and bogbean sprout in the freshwater lochs.

A little patience is required to follow this optional return along the south coast. The problem is that the walk is over open ground and it is not always possible to see the next waymarker ahead; the posts are part of the Hebridean Way (see box, page 50), and their slightly ad hoc nature here could charitably be described as a snagging issue. Keep a keen eye out and be prepared to walk a few metres in the wrong direction before you pick up the posts; in any case, the scale of this walk is small and as long as you keep the coast on your left you really cannot go astray. Eventually the posts lead through a gate and up a final stretch of high ground before returning to the road at Outend.

baked sole & chocolate *pavé*. The quality of the food is way beyond what you might expect on such a small island in such a rural location. To be sure of one of the 10 tables in summer, you need to book 3 or 4 months ahead. The owner has plans for an outdoor decking area which will expand capacity in good weather. The local licensing committee steadfastly refuses to approve an alcohol licence on the island, so the bistro is bring-your-own – so don't forget to buy your booze in Tarbert as you pass through on your way. ££

SHOPPING With the sad demise of the Scalpay Community Shop in 2017, you must now shop in Tarbert.

WHAT TO SEE AND DO Scalpay's twin harbours are pleasant places to linger, and enjoy the birdlife and any sunshine that may be going. **Cottam Island** in the North Harbour is home to a colony of terns and is also used as a pit stop by curlew, turnstone, redshank, geese and gulls. The new 120m-long pontoon berths on the North Harbour have begun to add another dimension to the island, encouraging arrivals by sea. It may not be immediately apparent but Scalpay has a strong artistic community. The geology of the island has thwarted the desire of many to expand on their own croft, and local laws, rather inflexibly applied, require any retail outlet to have space for six cars. In the absence of dynamite to blow up the ubiquitous rocks, smooth out the tight contours and clear sufficient space for visitors, these artists can be found at the twice-weekly craft fair in Tarbert (page 151).

Other than simply enjoying the shores and creeks of the Scalpay shoreline, the island's main attraction is Eilean Glas lighthouse. For years, the lighthouse was seen almost exclusively by passengers on board the Uig–Tarbert ferry – the structure had been an extraordinarily large light hidden under a bushel: arguably, this is the most dramatic and picturesque of all the lighthouses in the Outer Hebrides. Positioned on an outcrop of lower headland on the east coast, the backdrop includes the Uig peninsula on Skye and the shark's-teeth silhouette of the Cuillin skyline. With the new access track (see box, opposite), the lighthouse is easily accessible for most walkers.

SOUTH HARRIS (CEANN A DEAS NA HEARADH)

The west coast of South Harris is the poster child of the Outer Hebrides: it comprises a mesmerising succession of beautiful beaches and bays of all sizes and shapes that push out into the Atlantic Ocean from a crenulated coastline that rises sharply to craggy hills and strikingly stern moorland. The east coast should not be overlooked: here you will find **The Bays**, an area of astonishing starkness, where vast swathes of land are all but stripped to bare rock, and boulders are separated by red deergrass or by ground underfoot that can best be described as black peat-squelch. Further south, the A859 winds its way to the tiny communities of **Leverburgh** and **Rodel**, the southerly full stop of Harris. A minor road, the C79, clings to the east coast.

WEST COAST: FROM LUSKENTYRE (LOSGAINTIR) TO NORTHTON (TOABH TUATH)
Where to stay In addition to the hotels and campsites listed below, South Harris is home to some innovative self-catering properties that have been ingeniously designed to blend into the coastline with great success. While far from cheap, they represent a unique experience and prove popular choices for special occasions.

✷ 🏠 **Scarista House** [158 C4] (3 rooms) Scarista; ☎01859 550238; e bookings@

scaristahouse.com; w scaristahouse.com; ⊕ Mar–mid-Dec. This beautifully maintained

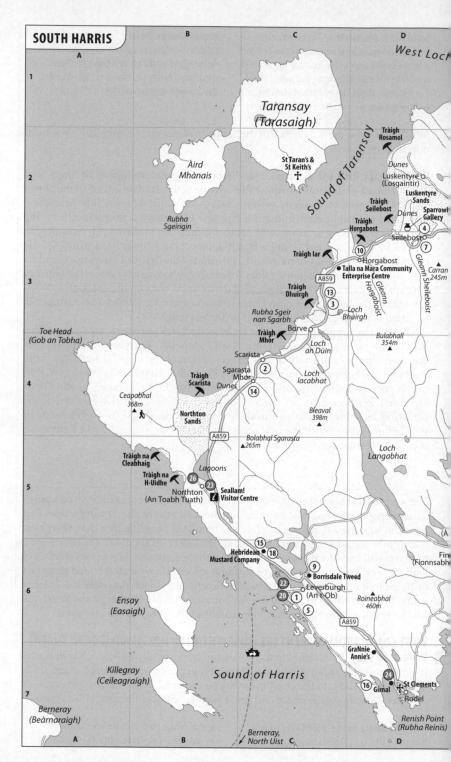

A   B   C   D

1

West Loch

Taransay
(Tarasaigh)

Tràigh
Rosamol

2

Àird
Mhànais

St Taran's &
St Keith's ✝

Dunes

Luskentyre
(Losgaintir)

Luskentyre
Sands

Rubha
Sgeirigin

Sound of Taransay

Tràigh
Seilebost

Dunes

Sparrow
Gallery

Tràigh
Horgabost

Seilebost

④

⑦

Tràigh Iar

⑩

Horgabost

Gleann Sheileboist

3

Talla na Mara Community
Enterprise Centre

Toe Head
(Gob an Tobha)

Tràigh
Dhuirgh

A859

⑬

Gleann Horgaboist

Carran
245m ▲

③

Loch
Bhuirgh

Rubha Sgeir
nan Sgarbh

Barve

Tràigh
Mhòr

Loch
an Dùin

Bulabhall
354m ▲

Scarista

4

Tràigh
Scarista

Sgarasta
Mhòr

②

Loch
Iacabhat

Ceapabhal
368m ▲ 🚶

Dunes

⑭

Northton
Sands

Bleaval
398m ▲

Loch
Langabhat

A859

Bolabhal Sgarasta
▲265m

Tràigh na
Cleabhaig

5

Tràigh na
H-Uidhe

㉖

Lagoons

㉓

Seallam!
Visitor Centre

Northton
(An Toabh Tuath)

ℹ

⑮

Hebridean
Mustard Company

⑱

(A

Fin
(Fionnsabh

⑨

Borrisdale Tweed

6

Ensay
(Easaigh)

㉒

㉑

Leverburgh
(An t-Ob)

①

Roineabhal
460m ▲

⑤

A859

GraNnie
Annie's

Killegray
(Ceileagraigh)

Sound of Harris

⑯ Gìrnal

㉔

St Clements ✝

Rodel

7

Berneray
(Beàrnaraigh)

Renish Point
(Rubha Reinis)

A   B   Berneray,
North Uist   C   D

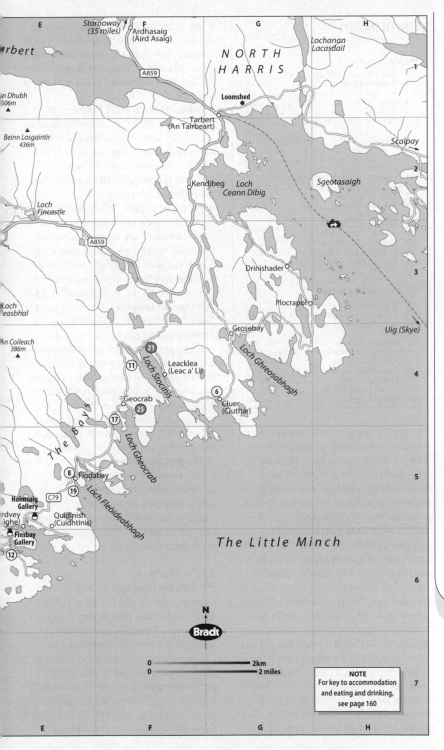

NOTE
For key to accommodation
and eating and drinking,
see page 160

SOUTH HARRIS

For listings, see from page 157, unless otherwise stated

19th-century Georgian manse overlooks the hauntingly drifting sands of Scarista. All rooms have sea views & en-suite bathrooms, & are traditionally furnished with features such as handmade replica Georgian windows. No TV. Run by Patricia & Tim Martin; Tim also leads the local mountain-rescue team. Despite its large size, the house feels small & intimate; the library is a cosy place to retreat to at the end of the day, with comfortable sofas to sink into by an open fire. If you stay here, pull *A House by the Shore* off the library shelf. This is a piercingly honest account of the experience of the previous owners of Scarista, who converted the manse into a guesthouse. It includes vignettes about potatoes that self-seed between the floorboards, the time Prince Charles arrived by helicopter & memorable guests such as Major Chimp & Major Baboon. The Martins serve excellent evening meals (3 courses £49.50, 4 courses £57; £££; available to non-residents, booking essential). The drinks list includes, perhaps unexpectedly given where you are in the world, 50 fine French wines ranging in price all the way up to £120. More accommodation, in the form of 3 suites (each with its own private sitting room), is located in the adjacent Glebe House, one of which has a kitchenette & can sleep a family of 5. ££££

🏠 **Buel na Mara** [158 D2] (4 rooms) 12 Seilebost; ☎ 01859 550205; w beulnamara.co.uk; ⏰ Mar–Oct. Wonderfully located B&B, right on the shores of Luskentyre, just off the A859. 2 dbls, a twin & a family room that sleeps 3. The conservatory looks out over the bay & must have one of the best views on Harris. ££

🏠 **Pairc an t-Srath** [158 C3] (4 rooms) Borve; ☎ 01859 550386; e info@paircant-srath.co.uk; w paircant-srath.co.uk. Superbly positioned on a small hill overlooking Luskentyre sands & the Sound of Taransay. There's even a sauna available for chillier days. Owners offer 3-course dinner for non-guests (£38; £££; booking essential). ££

⛺ **Horgabost campsite** [158 D3] Horgabost beach; ☎ 01859 550386. It's easy to see why this campsite regularly gets listed in UK & global compendiums of the world's best places to pitch a tent: positioned on a raised bank above a beautiful beach & with wonderful views. Toilets & showers based in an old shipping container, which also houses a small seasonal shop. Only drawback is that this is an exposed spot in high winds. Mobile van serves hot food including fish & chips, most days end May–Sep. No advance bookings. £

⛺ **The West Harris Trust** [158 D2] ☎ 01859 550457; e admin@westharristrust.org; w westharristrust.org/camping. By the sands around Luskentyre, the Trust has thoughtfully created several glorious spots to pitch your tent or park your campervan. It's best to book in advance in the summer months. £

Self-catering

🏠 **Blue Reef Cottages** [158 C4] (2 properties, each sleeping 2) Scarista; ☎ 01859 550370; e info@stay-hebrides.com; w stay-hebrides.com. 2 separate properties that were among the first of the new generation of eye-catching luxury stays to crop up on South Harris. Stunning design replicates Neolithic housing, partly subterranean & with superb views over Scarista towards the Harris hills & Ceapabhal. Internal fittings & fixtures of equally high standard & including an observation deck. Wheelchair accessible. Low season £1,200/week, high season £2,100/week; shorter breaks available. **££££**

🏠 **The Broch** [158 C3] (sleeps 2) Borve; ☏ 01859 550358; e info@borvelodge.com; w borvelodge.com/room/the-broch. Claimed to be the 1st broch built in the UK since Roman times, you enter this 3-storey building via a slate drawbridge. High-end features include a 4-poster bed on the top floor underneath a circular skylight. £630 (3 days, low season) or £2,450 (1 week, high season). **££££**

🏠 **The Rock House** [158 C3] (sleeps 2) Borve; w borvelodge.com/room/the-rock-house. On the same estate & under the same management as The Broch, you will find The Rock House – an equally striking building, embedded in the ground. Interiors include driftwood furniture & shelves made from gneiss rock. £630 (3 days, low season) or £2,450 (1 week, high season). **££££**

✳ 🏠 **Fir Chlis** [158 D3] (sleeps 8) Seilebost; w fir-chlis.co.uk. A stunning addition to South Harris's coastal road, Fir Chlis is a contemporary property where a 1st-floor open-plan living room & covered balcony take in views across the bay to Taransay. Designed & furnished to an extremely high spec, this is the perfect getaway property in the perfect location. Low-season short breaks £495, to £1,500/week in summer. **£££**

✗ **Where to eat and drink** There are surprisingly few places to eat around Luskentyre, though those that do exist are extremely good. Otherwise, you will need to head for Tarbert, Scalpay, The Bays or Leverburgh.

✳ ✗ **Croft 36** [158 B5] Northton; ☏ 01859 520779; w croft36.com; ⏰ Mon–Sat until late, shorter hours in winter. This superb fine-dining take-away outlet is unlike anything you will have encountered before. Lift up the wooden lids of this self-service wooden roadside shack, overlooking the breathtaking waters of Scarista, & you can take your pick of crab ravioli, rabbit stew & dumplings, pasties & cakes. The food is of an extremely high standard & everything operates on an honesty system. 'The honesty box is very popular: people like to be trusted & we get many comments about it,' says Steve Olley, who runs the croft with his partner Julie & catches much of his fish off Borrisdale on the south coast of the island. 'I'm not sure we would sell diamonds there,' he jokes. 'It's worked very well & led us to "expand" from a kiosk to a shed & increase our range.' **££**

🍴 **Machair Kitchen** [158 C3] Nisabost; ☏ 01859 550333; e themachairkitchen@hotel-hebrides.com; w hotel-hebrides.com/the-machair-kitchen; ⏰ 10.00–16.00 & 18.00–20.30 Mon–Sat. Housed inside Talla na Mara. Superb views overlooking the Sound of Taransay & the hills of Harris. Good food ranges from seafood platters to excellent sandwiches. Only glitch is the rather formal nature of dining; if you've just finished a wind-battered walk, all you'll want to do is flop down, order a cup of hot chocolate & swallow a slice of cake whole. **££**

DONALD JOHN MACKAY: HOW LUSKENTYRE BECAME A HOTBED OF INTERNATIONAL SPORTSWEAR

There's a smattering of houses along the road through Luskentyre township, most of them holiday lets, but one of them is the home of weaver Donald John Mackay (w beath.net/luskentyre.htm) who works out of his green-washed studio just beyond the old cemetery. Donald John started up the Luskentyre Harris Tweed Company with his wife Maureen in 1991, initially just making and selling tartan tweeds. In 2003, he was contacted by Nike who were looking for some tweed samples to add to a series of women's basketball trainers. A 9,000m order of yarn later, the Harris Tweed industry had been rejuvenated and its image changed for ever. Originally Nike tucked the Harris Tweed emblem inside the shoe, leaving the outside world none the wiser of the origin of the attractive patterning: Maureen persuaded them to show it prominently on the tongue of the shoe. If Donald John is home, he will happily break off to talk about his work.

Temple Café [158 B5] Northton; **m** 07487 557626; **e** templecafeharris@gmail. com; ⏰ Apr–Sep 10.30–17.00 Tue–Sun & eves Sun, winter hours vary, enquire ahead. This Hobbit-like café, constructed from large stone bricks & with a domed roof, has a beautiful setting looking right across Northton sands. Light lunches, eg: spiced pea & coconut soup, salads & cakes, prevail during the day; the Sun evening menu (reservations mandatory) usually offers 3 choices, including sweet potato, garlic & machair thyme soup & roasted vegetables from the owner's croft with goat's cheese. Apart from hotels, this is the only place on Harris where you can get food & drink on Sun (despite perception to the contrary, only convention & not the law prevents small outlets opening on Sun). BYO. ££

What to see and do The first views of Luskentyre sands and the Sound of Taransay take your breath away. From the north, the spectacle opens up as you crest the A859 as it flicks west along a passage blasted out of otherwise impregnable Lewisian gneiss. Coming from the south the backdrop of the North Harris Hills is positively cinematic. Either way, it's no surprise that Luskentyre is regularly cited in pantheons of the world's great beaches. The route described here runs north–south from Tarbert to Leverburgh and Rodel, but can just as easily be explored in reverse.

Beginning some 8 miles southwest of Tarbert, the **Luskentyre Sands** ✳ [158 D2] herald an area of beaches and headlands that reaches 7 miles from east to west and 6 miles from north to south and is only curtailed by the rocky southern shores of Harris 3 miles north of Leverburgh. At low tide, the various beaches along the western shoreline seem to become conjoined and laced with rivulets of retreating and advancing water and ever-shifting dunes.

The eastern headwaters of Luskentyre are a brackish world of saltmarshes characterised by curious and extremely photogenic clumps of seaweed that resemble

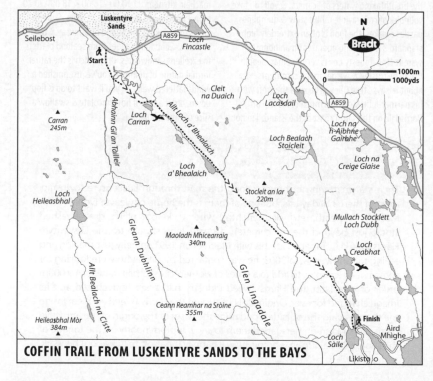

COFFIN TRAIL FROM LUSKENTYRE SANDS TO THE BAYS

5km (3 miles) one way; 1½–2hrs
OS Explorer 455 South Harris
Start: just east of Seilebost (⊕ NB081968)
Finish: Àird Mhìghe near Leacklea (⊕ NG116932)

Note that this is a linear walk, so unless you plan to retrace your steps you need to arrange transport or plan around the infrequent bus services. An atmospheric walkway cuts through the moors, linking the bays of Luskentyre with the rocky shores of the east coast. Known as the Bealach Eorabhat (the Coffin or Corpse Road), the path was used to carry those who had died on the east coast for burial on the deeper western shores. The irony was acute as many of the deceased would have previously been evicted from the west coast during the clearances.

The path is waymarked and clear from coast to coast. It offers an extraordinary geography lesson as you move, pace by pace, from one geological landscape to another. The gneiss on the moors and east coast is hard, acidic and impermeable, which means that the deep-seated U-shaped glens, rocky summits and boulder-strewn hillsides of this walk have changed little since the last Ice Age ended some 11,000 years ago. The path gently rises to disclose views east across the Minch, to Skye, the Cuillin and north towards Assynt. A pair of golden eagles nest in the cliff tops here. The route skirts around a house and an idyllic loch to meet the coastal C79 Bays Road by a bridge at Àird Mhìghe. You can retrace your steps or flag down the twice-daily bus here. Alternatively, follow the waymarkers east and north through the boulders for around 3km (almost 2 miles; about 40mins) to reach the A859 and the bus to Tarbert.

inflated lily pads. These are turf fucoids, small seaweeds that coagulate together to resemble mosses in extraordinary and mesmerising patterns. The whole of Luskentyre is a Site of Special Scientific Interest and the sand flats are rich in juicy foods such as ragworm, cockles and laver shells. At the head of this magnificent seascape is **Loch Fincastle** [159 E2], which is a good spot for dragonflies in summer. Right by the loch and close to the high-tide mark, a turning signposted for Luskentyre (Losgaintir) leads along an unclassified road to the township of the same name. This 8km (5-mile) track skirts along the northern shoreline with several places where you can stop and walk. There are excellent rockpools along here for children.

The road winds past a romantically positioned cemetery and descends to a car park with public toilets. A short walk over the dunes here deposits you on to **Tràigh Rosamol** [158 D2], an exquisite and almost perfect rectangle of white sand that gazes across to Taransay and, to the north, far along the Hushinish peninsula. Looking south, the beach appears to converge on a vanishing point; in reality, tides permitting, you can walk south and then west around the dunes for a mile or so, back past the cemetery and make your way up the rocks to the road at one of the points where the two meet. The Sound of Taransay at the mouth of the sands is one of the best places on the islands to see eider.

The turtle-shaped hump of **Taransay (Tarasaigh)** [158 C1] is visible just offshore for much of your journey along the west coast. The island was populated up until

TO THE MACLEOD STONE ABOVE IAR AND HORGABOST BEACHES

3¼km (2 miles); 1hr
OS Explorer 455 South Harris
Start/finish: lay-by above Iar beach (✪ NB039965)

An easy, short walk above Iar and Horgabost yields some wonderful coastal views. Begin at the small lay-by just south of Iar beach and walk back towards the beach, over a cattle grid and through the gate on the left to drop down on to the sands. Walk to the far end and clamber up the dunes on to the machair, making for the large singular standing stone ahead. Known as the Macleod stone, its origin is unknown. What has been established, however, is that on Midsummer's Day, the sun sets directly behind St Kilda on the horizon as viewed from this stone. Continue over the brow of the hill and drop down the other side, picking up a track by the metal gate towards the bottom of the descent. Go through the gate and turn right along the track to meet the A895 and walk for less than 1km (½ mile) back to the car-parking spaces.

1974, and bought from a local family for around £1 million in 2011. The new owners are the Borve Estate which was established in 1868 by Lord Dunmore, and owns 1,500ha on Taransay plus a similar amount on Harris. Taransay gained national fame in 2000 when BBC series *Castaway 2000* documented the year-long stay on the island by a disparate group of volunteers. Some 36 people, including eight children, were allowed to bring a few possessions and then reared their own animals, grew vegetables in polytunnels, lived in turfed pods and even built a school. All but a handful saw the year out.

The Borve Estate is one of the largest employers on Harris, and manages a herd of 220 red deer on Taransay, which competes for the rich grazing land with 400 sheep. The fertility of the island soil is enhanced by the laying down of seaweed. Native hardwood trees are being replanted on the island, which, given the rigours of the climate, are expected to take up to 20 years to gain a foothold. Borve also owns two eye-catching self-catering properties, The Broch and The Rock House (both page 161), and issues fishing licences. If you're staying at either of these, or Borve's other self-catering properties, the estate will take you over to Taransay. Open access applies to Taransay so the islands can also be visited independently by kayak/boat or on organised trips. The island is simply beautiful. With time to wander, you can yomp over open ground, crossing the isthmus that almost slices the island in two and visiting the cemeteries of St Keith (traditionally the burial place for men) and St Taran (after whom the island is named), which is said to have been a women-only graveyard. Folklore dictates that various ghoulish happenings occurred whenever the wrong gender was interred in either resting place. Finally, the island has long been a breeding site for a pair of golden eagles.

Back on the A859, heading south, the next beach you pass is **Seilebost** (pronounced '*SHELL-abost*') [158 D2], where the dunes push out at a right angle into Luskentyre sands, creating a beach within a beach. The dunes here can reach 11–14m (36–45ft) in height, but change their formation with every winter storm. This spot is internationally recognised for overwintering birds such as dunlin, bar-tailed godwit and knot. The former schoolhouse for the township is right by the beach and home to the Sparrowhouse Gallery [158 D2] (m 07521 702455; e fiona.

simes.art@gmail.com; ⊕ 10.00–17.00 Mon–Sat), the studio of Fiona Simes. Fiona produces many dramatic acrylic images of the birds of the adjacent machair and bay, and some particularly evocative linocuts.

Leaving Seilebost, the road then curves around a headland, and a turning on the right leads down below a campsite to **Tràigh Nisabost**, also known as **Horgabost beach** [158 D3]. Horgabost has a wonderful symmetry, with a gurgling stream and views across the bay of **Loch a' Siar** with a (photographer's dream) backdrop of the Harris hills. I was once beachcombing here with my children when we found what we thought was a beak of a tern; we sent a photograph to *BBC Countryfile* magazine for expert diagnosis, only to learn that it was in fact a squirrel jaw. How a squirrel bone came to be in a place nowhere near any suitable habitat for squirrels is a tale that only the tides can tell.

A half-mile on from Horgabost is **Tràigh Iar** [158 C3], another sandscape of striking symmetry, this time facing out towards Taransay. You can reach it by walking from the small car park at Horgabost back on to the road and turning right for 200m to a gate in a fence on the right.

Within walking distance of Tràigh Iar in the township of Nisabost [158 C3] is **Talla na Mara Community Enterprise Centre** (↖01859 503900; e admin@westharristrust. org; w tallanamara.co.uk; ⊕ 09.00–17.00 Mon–Sat), a futuristic building that serves as studios for artists and the home of the West Harris Trust (the name translates as 'the centre by the sea'). The excellent **Machair Kitchen** (page 161) is also here. Talla na Mara also stages live music performances. The artists working in the studio include Joceline Hildrey (m 07801 812261; e jocelinehildrey@yahoo.com), whose studio

THE HARRIS RIVIERA

Travel along the magnificent west coast of South Harris and it is hard to pull your gaze away from the drama of the sea and the shape-shifting rivulets and sands, from Luskentyre to Scarista and Northton. When you do, however, the local architecture can be almost as eye-popping. In a landscape where pebble-dash and long-deserted croft houses often prevail, the appearance of subterranean buildings and, just as conspicuously, modern properties with aesthetically pleasing sleek lines perched on skylines, can come as a surprise. Welcome to what some locals have coined 'the Harris Riviera'.

The 'riviera's' emergence has been a slow process. The game-changer was Scarista House (page 157), a former manse whose original owners, Alison and Andrew Johnson, showed how geography was not a barrier to lifestyle but could enhance it. They were followed by Rhoda and Neil Campbell, who constructed Blue Reef Cottages (page 160) with local architect Stuart Bagshaw. These distinctive turfed-roof properties blend into the hillside and are intended to mirror the design of Neolithic buildings. Others have followed suit, such as the part-subterranean creations The Broch and The Rock House at Borve (page 161).

A 'Hebrinavian' style is also emerging, with the Scandinavian sleek lines of Fir Chlis at Seilebost (page 161), arguably the supreme example, and others, such as Sound of Harris (page 169) at Strond. A stay at any of these properties does not come cheap, but, whether you rest your head there or not, the charm of all such properties is – typically of the Outer Hebrides – that they are the story of people rather than of the bricks and stone that make them; all the owners and architects involved are probably a bit non-conformist, many quite full of character, but are mostly quiet and understated folk.

CAUGHT ON CAMERA: PHOTOGRAPHING THE SANDS OF LUSKENTYRE

Amateur and professional photographers are drawn siren-like to Luskentyre, but doing justice to the breathtaking views and colours can be a daunting challenge. Photographer Steve Morgan explains how he went about his work while on a magazine assignment on Harris.

'The quality of the light is *the* most important factor in capturing the subtle beauty of such a wonderful landscape. An early start or indeed a late finish is essential to do photographic justice to somewhere as magnificent as Luskentyre.

'One evening, the weather forecast was encouraging and it seemed a dawn shoot would yield dividends. Sunrise was around 04.45. Rolling out of my warm bed at 4am with a cup of coffee to kick-start the day, a short walk took me to the dunes and beach.

'Having such a stunning beach all to myself was worth the early start. Knowing I was the first person that day to leave my footprints in the soft wet sands, the only person hearing the lap of waves in the still morning air was special and stays with me to this day.

'The subtle pre-sunrise light brought out the delicate colours of sea and sand dunes; the first shafts of low sunlight brought definition to the hills and contours of the ripples of sand stretching out along the shoreline. My first shots were of the sweeping beachscape, looking for form and composition in the juxtaposition of sand, sea and sky using a 20mm lens with a graduated grey filter to balance the light. This darkened the sky a little to make it appear more as our own senses would perceive the scene.

'As the sun gradually rose in the sky, shadows became more distinct and the contrast increased, allowing me to see images of patterns in the sand left by the retreating tide and the previous night's rain. The clouds were beginning to form and I was losing the light so I needed to work quickly. There comes a point about 2½ hours after sunrise when the quality of the light just "goes", when the sun is high enough in the sky to start being harsh. Then it's time for breakfast.

'The next best time of day for landscape photography is the last hour or so before sunset and I returned after a day photographing for my magazine assignment around the Isle of Harris. The sun had just set over the beach at Luskentyre revealing a different feel, a more monochrome look. Shooting with a 70–200mm f2.8 zoom lens, I was searching for patterns across the many curling rivulets and pools of water that reflected the remaining light of the darkening sky over the again deserted sands. A wonderful finish to a long but extremely satisfactory day.'

Equipment used: Canon EOS 5D mkIII, Canon 70–200mm L f2.8, Canon 24–70mm L f2.8, Canon 20mm f2.8.

Steve Morgan's work has included assignments for The Independent *and* Greenpeace. *See more at* w *stevemorganphoto.co.uk.*

window looks out across the Sound of Luskentyre. Birdlife features prominently among Joceline's pen-and-ink images and she also produces her own photographs on aluminium bases. Next door is a chocolatier, **Flavour** (m 07388 366361; e flavour. scot@gmail.com; w flavour.scot; ☉ 10.00–16.00 Mon–Sat, shorter hours in winter, enquire ahead), run by Chris and Nicola Loye. Chris is a chef by training. 'We moved up here with seasonal jobs three years ago. I'd been making chocolates in hotels for years,' he says. After selling out of their first batch of chocolates at a craft fair in two days, one thing has led to another. The Loyes' chocolates have a distinctive bite and taste less sugary than most, thanks to their decision to use panela, or unrefined dehydrated sugar. The couple temper the chocolate, which prevents the fats from separating, and avoid E numbers for colouring (their ruby-coloured chocolate is just that: sourced from the ruby chocolate bean). Keep an eye out for developments – the couple operate pop-up restaurants in places such as village halls and plan to set up a more permanent restaurant on Harris.

Continuing south of Iar, the next beaches, **Tràigh Bhuirgh** [158 C3] and **Tràigh Mhòr** [158 C4], push hard up against the rocks by the road at the township of Borve (Na Bhuirgh) and are thrilling places in bad weather as waves heave up against the shore and the road. A mile or so further south is the small township of **Scarista (Scarasta)** [158 C4], signified by the long-closed post office above the beach. The shell-beach here extends for 3 miles at low tide. Once again, sea currents change continually, creating a stunning effect with marooned outposts of sand surrounded by water. Like Seilebost, the dunes wobble out at right angles towards the sea, the grass on their ridges creating the appearance of a giant caterpillar. The views are very special indeed: the hill of Ceapabhal to the south, the North Harris Hills to the north and the Atlantic Ocean in between. From the ground up, the colour scheme is sensational: strips of greens, yellows, blues and the more metallic shades of the brooding hills. To get on to Scarista beach, look out for a post box just by a house across the road from Scarista House. There is a gate here that leads on to the dunes.

The A859 contours alongside the shoreline as it heads south for another mile or two from Scarista to the township of **Northton (Taobh Tuath)** [158 B5], a delightful one-lane hamlet that cuts across the southern fringe of the expansive sands of Tràigh an Taoibh Tuath. The beach on the south side of Northton, **Tràigh n-Uidhe**, is delectable, strewn with seashells, secluded and basks in lovely sunsets over the Sound of Harris. The perspectives across the northern sands are extraordinary, with the brackish shoreline pitted with sponge-like mosses and the substantial hill of Ceapabhal forming a backdrop. The machair at Northton is regarded by the RSPB and others as among the best that the Outer Hebrides has to offer: damp but not too dry and superb for birdwatching, even in winter. It's thought that Northton is one of the earliest sites where humans, and in particular hunter-gatherers, settled on Harris. Sites on the southwest shores of the township are believed to have been occupied since the Stone Age. Excavations have uncovered Neolithic, Beaker and Iron Age settlements. Archaeological digs have yielded carbonised hazelnut shells dated to 7000BC on the beaches. The shells are thought to represent remains of Mesolithic meals and are associated with debris from stone tool-making.

Just by the junction of the A859 and the turning for the township is a gem of an attraction, **Seallam! Visitor Centre** ✱ [158 B5] (☎ 01859 520258; e info@ hebridespeople.com; w hebridespeople.com; ⊕ Easter–Sep 10.00–17.00 Mon–Fri, Oct–Easter 10.00–17.00 Wed–Fri; £3/£2). A combination of a museum of island life and a genealogy centre ('seallam' means 'look', or 'let me look', in Gaelic). Seallam! offers an eye-opening lesson on the history of Harris and why it looks the way it does today. The excellent genealogy centre here, Co Leis Thu? ('To whom do you belong?'), unlocks the fates not only of many of Harris's sizeable diaspora, but also of those who emigrated from right across the Outer Hebrides. This is the place to learn about the culture of Scottish clans or to find help exploring your own Scottish roots. A map on the wall testifies to just how far the Harris population has dispersed over

4

6½km (4 miles) return; 3hrs
OS Explorer 455 South Harris
Start/finish: gate at western end of Northton (✪ NF987904)

It's well worth the slog from sea level to the 368m (1,207ft) summit of Ceapabhal, which looms high above the western edge of Northton sands.

If driving, park up with care on the lane through Northton, or on the track leading to Tràigh n-Uidhe.

Walk to the end of the lane that runs through Northton. Go through the gate and walk along the track for some 700m to a second one with a kissing gate. Go through this gate and keep on the track for another 350m. Where the track meets a fence coming in from the right, take the grassy left fork that cuts behind the dunes of Tràigh na Cleabhaig to reach a lonely ruined church, Rubh' an Teampaill, marooned on the headland. To continue to climb the hill, cut across open ground with the flanks of the hill on your left to rejoin the track then pass through a small gate. From here on, you're on open and sometimes boggy ground that begins to climb abruptly from sea level. The conspicuous white line across the hill is pegmatite rock, formed of granite with large crystals of pink feldspar.

There's no real path so the best way to reach the summit is to look up, pick out the obvious zigzag of grassy land near the top and make your way through increasingly stony ground towards it. Near the top, and once the worst of the steep climb is behind you, a path emerges and leads to the summit cairn. One of the joys of making this tough ascent is the mesmerising view of the currents flicking back and forward in the shallow lagoon-like waters off Northton. Return the same way: while it's less physically demanding, the rocky and often slippery ground combine with the sharp gradient to make it more treacherous than the ascent. Take care.

the past couple of centuries, and there are moving tales of the people who relocated out to the far-flung reaches of the earth. The exiles include James Harrison of HMS *Bounty* who, after the mutiny in 1789, settled on Pitcairn; James MacDonald of Barra, who was a guard keeping watch over Napoleon during his exile on St Helena; and Thomas Macleod from Stornoway, who accompanied Robert Scott on the ill-fated Antarctic Terra Nova expedition of 1910–13. Migrants from Harris may also have been the first Europeans to settle on Greenland. The stories make it abundantly clear that many of those who left Harris – and their descendants – would have moved back in a twinkling had economic conditions permitted. A useful word crops up time and again in Gaelic literature, and you'll see it at Seallam!: *cianalas*, which means the yearning for a place. The word has lent itself to a poetry genre, *bàrdachd cianalais*, usually written by those who have left their Hebridean homeland.

LEVERBURGH (AN T-OB) AND RODEL (ROGHADAL) South of Northton the scenery calms down and catches its breath as it descends to the port of Leverburgh. You will pass through here if you are headed for the southern isles, as the CalMac ferry links the port with Berneray across the Sound of Harris, while a couple of the St Kilda boats also depart from here. The A859 then tracks east to its conclusion at **Rodel** and the beautiful church of **St Clements**. From here, you have a choice of retracing your journey to **Leverburgh**, or picking up the C79 which winds its way up the east coast through **The Bays** back towards Tarbert.

Where to stay

Carminish House [158 C6] (3 rooms) Strond; 01859 520400; e info@carminish.com; w carminish.com; ⊕ Apr–Oct. Spacious 4-star guesthouse located just east of Leverburgh on the Borrisdale road. Wonderful views over Sound of Harris. 2 dbls & a twin, all en suite. **££**

Sorrel Cottage [158 C6] (3 rooms) 2 Glen Kyles, Leverburgh; 01859 520319; e paula@ sorrelcottage.co.uk; w accommodationisleofharris. co.uk; ⊕ Mar–Oct. Paula Williams has converted this croft house into a smart B&B with nice touches such as friezes of Buddha-like images. All rooms en suite. Small family room in loft sleeps 3. Bicycles for hire. **££**

Taylorhill Bed & Breakfast [158 C6] (2 rooms) Leverburgh; 01859 520266; e bookings@ taylorhill.co; w taylorhill.co. Located on the approach to Leverburgh. Both rooms snug & en suite. Guest lounge with TV. **££**

Am Bothan bunkhouse [158 C6] (18 beds) Ferry Rd, Leverburgh; 01859 520251; e info@ ambothan.com; w ambothan.com. 1 room with 6 beds, 3 with 4 beds. Wheelchair accessible. **£**

Self-catering

✳ **Sound of Harris** [158 D7] 8a Borrisdale; 01859 520208; e info@soundofharris.co.uk; w soundofharris.co.uk; see ad, 3rd colour section. 2 top-of-the-range self-catering properties in the slumbering & strung-out community of Strond (Sraanda) just east of Leverburgh. Straight out of the *Grand Designs* portfolio: the Big House & the slightly smaller Other House. Beautifully positioned with floor-to-ceiling windows providing unimpeded views over the sound. Loft-style design with high-end fixtures & furnishings, dramatic wall hangings by Donald John Mackay of Luskentyre (see box, page 161) & vintage mid 20th-century furnishings. The square Japanese soak tub – a truly indulgent square bath – is perfect after a day hiking the hills of Harris. Owners Rob English & Carol Graham live across the drive & are immensely helpful & knowledgeable. Rob may offer you pollock he's caught that morning for your supper, while Carol is striving to establish Leverburgh as a centre of weaving activity. Strongly recommended for special occasions. Both sleep 2: Big House £1,760/week, Other House £1,250/week. **£££/££££**

Grimisdale Guest House [158 C6] Leverburgh; 01471 820000; e farky@grimisdale. co.uk; w www.grimisdale.co.uk. Previously a well-regarded B&B now converted to self-catering. Superbly situated spacious house just behind Leverburgh, overlooking sea & moors. Don't be alarmed if you reach the owner's answerphone – he's a funeral director. Sleeps 13 in 5 en-suite rooms. £1,150/week. **£**

Where to eat and drink

✗ **The Anchorage** [158 C6] Leverburgh pier; 01859 520225; e theanchoragerestaurant@ gmail.com; w anchoragerestaurant.co.uk; ⊕ officially noon–21.00 (in reality the kitchen often closes much earlier) Mon–Sat. Some of the best fish & chips on the islands are served here by owner Sally Lessi & her team. Diners munch away while looking out of the window as the ferry trundles into view across the Sound of Harris. Cost of main meals can seem high but quality & size are good; take-away better value. Also gluten-free. Occasional short evening opening hours are a frustration – often stops serving food when the day's last ferry departs. **££**

✗ **Butty Bus** [158 C6] Leverburgh pier; ⊕ 07.30–15.00 Mon–Thu, 07.30–15.00 & 17.00–19.30 Fri–Sat. Fish & chips, calamari & filled rolls as you may not have had them served before, from a former 'butty bus' (canteen for actors & film crews). The bus is oriented for those taking or leaving the ferry across the Sound of Harris. Owner & cook is Chris Ross, who brought the bus all the way from Nottingham. 'We kept the name even though we don't call them butties on the islands – they're just bacon rolls,' he says. The pager you might notice dangling from the side of the bus is the call-out alert for Leverburgh lifeboat, moored just a few metres away. Chris is the lifeboat co-ordination manager, something that must come naturally after a life spent in the Merchant Navy before setting up this unusual meals-on-wheels. 'I'm the middleman between the coastguard &

After Lord Leverhulme – the Bodach an t-Saibuin, or the Soap Man – cut his losses on Lewis, giving up on crofters who would not be shifted from their refusal to buy into his vision of a fishing empire, he turned his attention to Harris. In 1919, he purchased the South Harris estate, including the small port of An t-Ob, colloquially known as Obbe, from the Earl of Dunmore. He immediately set about reviving the port's fortunes, investing £250,000 in a modern pier, processing plants, smokeries and a harbour that could accommodate a fleet of 50 deep-Atlantic fishing boats along with a school. Rather vaingloriously, the port was renamed Leverburgh. Such a scale of operations would rival major mainland ports such as Fraserburgh, Fleetwood and Grimsby, but the first trawlers, from Great Yarmouth, only rocked up in 1924. Whether, given time, the grand project could have been turned around we shall never know, as Leverhulme died in 1925. His estate and business partners had little appetite for the project, most of the jobs were lost and the port returned soon enough to its slumber. The estate, which had cost him £36,000, was auctioned off for just £900. As Roger Hutchinson says in Leverhulme's biography, *The Soap Man*, the industrialist was a schizophrenic character, neither entirely philanthropic nor wholly business-like and guilty of 'fanciful projections' that were soon incorporated into some vast strategy: a strategy 'that never really existed'.

the crew. I have to make the call as to whether we go out: 99% of the time we do.' I ask Chris if he lives nearby. 'I live in Finsbay now,' he says. 'Our family moved out after an argument with the neighbours.' I'm sorry to hear that, I reply. When was that? '400 years ago.' £

✕ **Sam's Seafood Shack** [158 D7] Roadside, Rodel; ⊕ Apr–Sep noon–19.00 Mon–Sat, Oct–Mar shorter hours, check 🟦. Rather like the adjacent Girnal (page 172), it's easy to drive past

this outstanding take-away seafood café without noticing. Mission control is a caravan converted into a kitchen. Run by Sam Barnes, former chef at Talla na Mara (page 165), the food is outstanding. The menu varies from day to day, depending on what Sam picks up from local fishermen, but can include seafood chowder, Hebridean crab with soda bread & island fish in lemon & seaweed beer batter. In summer months get there early as food often sells out quickly. £

Shopping The **Harris Community Shop** (an Clachan, Leverburgh; 📞01859 520370; w harriscommunityshop.co.uk; ⊕ 09.00–18.00 Mon–Sat) is usually well stocked with everything from flour to fishing nets for the rockpools. A chilled and frozen section has a huge range of good meats and fish. If you plan to self-cater, you can order provisions in advance. Upstairs is a good local souvenir shop and an exhibition on weaving. The area has three excellent shops that are experiences in themselves: The Hebridean Mustard Company, Borrisdale Tweed and GraNnie Annie's (see below).

What to see and do There's a slightly downbeat air to Leverburgh and, comprising little more than a couple of lanes half a mile from the quayside and a handful of industrial units, it will win no beauty contests. This may be the southernmost point of Lewis and Harris, but the Church here is as strong as anywhere; the Church of Scotland and the Free Church of Scotland (two services on Sunday) are barely 100m apart. The port does, however, have a well-stocked community shop and three good, if very different, eateries. Half a mile north of the village, look out for a small, neatly painted roadside shack at 10 Glen Kyles, which is home to **The Hebridean Mustard Company** ✳ [158 C6] 📞 01859 520346; e mustheb@hebrideanmustard.com;

w hebrideanmustard.com; ⊕ always; see ad, page 179), an artisan mustard stall. The homemade organic mustard is flavoured in varied ways, from honey to chilli, and is the work of Heike Winter, who lives in the adjacent house and is always happy to chat.

Leverburgh is also home to **Borrisdale Tweed** [158 C6] (✆01859 520788; e info@ borrisdale.co.uk; w borrisdale.co.uk; ⊕ 10.00–18.00 Mon–Sat). Housed in the former village post office, this gem of a shop displays the work of Carol Graham (who co-owns Sound of Harris self-catering in Strond). Goods are of an extremely high standard and range from cushion covers to bedspreads and throws.

Wandering around the quayside you may come across the industrial unit that is the workshop of **John Maher** (w johnmaher.co.uk), former punk and new wave drummer, notably with The Buzzcocks. Though John is happy to chat, this is not a studio or shop open to the public – instead he directs visitors to his website where you can order his highly regarded landscape and night photography online.

Far from spluttering to a conclusion, the A859 signs off with some brio as it heads to the harbour of **Rodel (Roghadal)**. Leaving Leverburgh the road shrivels to a narrow single track then becomes, a little unexpectedly, a moorland road that threads up and over a delectable glen. Just before it reaches Rodel, there is even a picturesque broad stream lined with alders to provide a rare sliver of Hebridean woodland.

A mile or so down the road, it's worth popping into **GraNnie Annie's** (sic) [158 D7] (✆ 01859 520712; e moorfieldannie@gmail.com; ⊕ 10.00–17.00 Mon–Sat,

---

🚶 FROM LEVERBURGH TO RODEL VIA BORRISDALE

5km (3 miles) one way; 1½hrs
OS Explorer 455 South Harris
Start: A859 Leverburgh by road sign for Borrisdale (⊕ NG024866)
Finish: St Clements Church, Rodel (⊕ NG047833)

A gorgeous and peaceful coastal walk links the port of Leverburgh with Rodel. From the A895, turn right in Leverburgh, signposted for Borrisdale, walk along the lane and then turn left above the port (where there is a footpath sign). Follow the lane for 3¼km (2 miles) through Strond (Srannda) and Borrisdale. The views out across the Sound of Harris to Pabbay, Berneray, North Uist and Skye are sublime while the foreground is an elemental-looking collage of raised turf and lochans. This little lane, however, is changing almost by the day, with new-build cottages and self-catering opening up in the hope of tapping into the burgeoning holiday market and the extraordinarily serendipitous views the road provides. As you walk along, you can't fail to be struck by the contrast between modern properties with their sleek floor-to-ceiling windows, crofting cottages and yet older houses that have already collapsed. That said, a good deal of the new build is tasteful and owners old and new appear to hold one another in respect.

At the end of the lane in Borrisdale, marker posts lead you gently across undulating open ground along a clear track with the tower of Rodel's church in clear view. To the southeast and visible as you reach higher ground is **Renish Point (Rubha Reinis)** [158 D7], the southern tip of Harris. The path brings you into Rodel just to the south of a small loch. You can return the same way, meet your prearranged pickup, or return along the A895, picking up a parallel track for part of the way past Loch Thorsageàrraidh and through Gleann Roghadail. Either return route adds around 5km (3 miles) to the walk.

often later in summer). Run by Annie Tempest, this engaging antique, curios and souvenirs shop sells a highly eclectic range of goods, from Harris Tweed to sea trunks, fireplace ornaments and gift cards.

The township of Rodel, centred upon its fine church, represents the southerly full stop of the A859. Just as the road dips down towards the church, you pass a derelict shell of a building on the seaward side of the road. This is the **Girnal**, a large iron-roofed storehouse with thick buttressed walls which dates to the 18th century. Sometimes charitably described as 'rendered in rubble', it made the top three when islanders were asked to name their favourite buildings in the Outer Hebrides (you are left with the suspicion that a sense of humour was responsible for its lofty rating). Plans to renovate and run it as a bakery, hostel or some such come and go.

An informal one-way system takes you anticlockwise around the diminutive headland at the road end, passing the former Rodel hotel and the tiny harbour where the ferry from Skye once berthed. Up until the mid 19th century, Rodel was a religious centre, a thriving crofting and fishing community, and the harbour, which dates to the 18th century and looks out to Skye, is easy on the eye.

The Macleods held Rodel until 1834, at which point the clan went bankrupt and sold up to the Dunmore family. Some of the derelict buildings here are testament to other failed dreams, this time those of Captain Alexander Macleod, who started building the harbour here in 1785 after buying Harris with money made during his time with the East India Company. Macleod imported fishermen from Lewis to teach the skills of the sea to relocated crofters and lent money at low rates of interest for investment in fishing boats.

The small loop road brings you almost full circle before passing the front door of **St Clements Church** ✳ [158 D7], maintained by Historic Scotland. This is a true delight and its clanking medievalism makes it well worth the effort to get here. The church dates from 1520, though it only had 40 years of service before the Protestant Reformation came along, at which point it fell into ruin, only to be revived 250 years later by Macleod.

Widely regarded as the finest pre-Reformation church in the Outer Hebrides, St Clements was influenced by the architecture of Iona Abbey off Mull, and its interior is decorated by wall tombs, local and religious scenes in relief and weathered effigies. The Macleods of Harris and Dunvegan are buried here and their tombs, simultaneously graceful and austere, dominate the interior. Three tombs are carved in black gneiss and depict knights. Centre stage is held by the grave of Alasdair 'Crotach' ('humpback') Macleod, the eighth chief of the Macleods who had the church built. The carvings behind his tomb are intricate and include a birlinn (a Highland galley) setting sail and an angel casting incense to the winds. A further five upright slabs are decorated with clan carvings. If the stepladder is in place, you can climb the tower. This can be an eerie experience since you will almost certainly have the place to yourself and the motion-sensitive lights are set on an extremely short timer.

The tower's exterior repays some scrutiny. You will pick out a carving of a 'Feileadh Mor', a garment that was the precursor of the kilt. Of much greater surprise is the explicit carving on the south tower of a semi-naked woman, her skirt lifted to leave little to the imagination. It's unclear if this was a fertility symbol or a device – recognised in parts of Ireland – to distract evil spirits that tried to slip into church on the coat-tails of pious worshippers.

Yet another unusual feature of the church is that it is the resting place of the late 17th-century bardess Mairi Nighean Alisdair Ruaidh, also known as Mary Macleod. She was the leader of a small band of female poets who performed the role of oral historians, or *seanchaidhs*, compendiums of Gaelic culture. Mary also served as a nurse at Dunvegan and it's thought she may have ended up at Rodel after being banished from Dunvegan for having strong allegiances to another branch of the Macleods. Mary's precise burial plot is uncertain but she is said to have requested to be buried face down to keep 'her lie-telling mouth to the underside'.

THE EAST COAST: THE BAYS (NA BÀIGH)

'The Bays Road' is the name given to the C79, a paved single-lane track that peels off the A859 just south of Tarbert and loops around Harris's rocky east coast, with its bays, inlets and precariously positioned erratic boulders. The track hugs the coastline for 20 miles before eventually reaching Finsbay (Fionnsabhagh) in the foothills of the hill of Roineabhal. Here the road forks, the eastern lane keeping to the coast for a further 3 miles to Rodel; the other route, an unclassified but perfectly passable road, circumnavigates the north and west of Roineabhal, reaching Leverburgh after 5 miles. The distance between Tarbert and Leverburgh along this route is around 25 miles; it will take a good hour or more to drive without any stops. A proper exploration of The Bays can easily turn into a day trip.

Most place names in The Bays have origins in 9th-century Viking settlements and include suffixes such as '-settr' (a grazing); and '-uagr' (a bay). Later, during the clearances, The Bays was one of the areas to which people were moved. Many crofters were forced to leave their homes on the more fertile machair along the west coast and were given the choice of either moving to The Bays and trying to eke out a living from land where the soil was thin and poor, or to Canada. Initially, many refused both but, at the point of a gun, many opted for the Bays. Even so, by the 1850s, large numbers had given up and 600 people from the Bays had taken a passage overseas.

The first thing that strikes you about The Bays is its elemental appearance, dominated by exposed sheets of Lewisian gneiss, scoured by glaciers during the last Ice Age, with ice-moulded boulders known as whalebacks breaking the surface of the unyielding ground. The contrast with the golden beaches and lush foreshore of the west coast could not be starker, but this part of Harris still possesses a magnificent, arguably violent, beauty that has much to offer.

This phenomenally tough landscape is sufficiently alien-like in appearance that it was used to depict Jupiter in the film *2001: A Space Odyssey*. Yet the gaps between these harsh features are filled with freshwater lochs that hold wild brown and sea trout. Here, white water lilies, along with bogbean and water violets, burst into flower over the summer.

WALKING THE BAYS

The Bays Road provides some fine options for walking. A number of short walks are signposted off the road along the way. Collectively they connect east-coast communities between Geocrab and Tarbert, a distance of some 26km (16 miles). To walk the lot in one go would be an endurance test; instead, the thinking behind the frequent walking posts you see is that you can park the car or hop off the bus, walk a circular route, following the waymarkers over open land for anything up to 5–6km (3–4 miles) then either retrace your steps or return to your starting point along the road or by walking on the ground close to it. You can take your pick of routes, depending on weather, light or just something that catches your eye. A particularly picturesque stretch of 2½km (1½ miles) links the township of Plocrapol with Scadabhagh, where the grace and shape of Loch Phlocrapoil would gain a podium place in any beauty pageant of Harris lochs.

The challenges of living here, however, remain obvious and you can be left with the feeling that the economy on the east coast is in the balance. Visit The Bays and you can, should you wish, eat a delicious slice of cake, buy some tasteful art and take in stirring views of Skye that serve as a backdrop to the monumental scenery. You will also see fishing boats hauled up too-small slipways, pass through villages such as Geocrab where, at the last count, there were nine empty, good-sized family houses, and pass abandoned coaches and rusting cars that have not been moved in 20 years. Then again, if you visit on a clear evening as dusk approaches, the rocks seem to change colour with every heartbeat; and you can feel a palpable darkness fall over the lower ground even as the setting sun flushes the higher land an intense shade of crimson. Pools even smaller than lochans, which you may not notice by day, catch a fleeting sliver of light and appear as lanterns or giant glow-worms among the heather. At such a time, the east coast of Harris is truly an enchanting place.

🏠 **Where to stay and eat** The area offers a small range of relatively inexpensive accommodation. Although there are no restaurants in The Bays, there is a handful of excellent cafés.

🏠 **Dunvegan View** [159 G4] (2 rooms) 9 Cluer (Cluther); ☎ 01859 530294; e anne. broadbent2@btinternet.com; w dunveganview. com. 1 dbl & a twin, both en suite, with views across to Skye. ££

🏠 **Flodabay Farm** [159 E5] (1 room) Flodabay; ☎ 01859 530353; e tonyandsharon@ flodabayfarm.co.uk; w flodabayfarm.co.uk. Just 1 light & airily decorated en-suite room at this beautifully positioned B&B overlooking a bay. Small patio at back with great views in good weather. Helpful owners also run the adjacent **⚑ motorhome park** (⊕ Mar–Nov; ££) with electricity but no showers or toilets. Good meals (£/££) for residents only sourced from the farm, including venison burgers & local seafood. ££

🏠 **The Old School House** [159 E6] (3 rooms) Finsbay; ☎ 01859 530420; w theoldschoolhousefinsbay.com; ⊕ year-round but requires advance notice in winter. All twins, renovated & decorated to a high finish by owners Alan & Panch Ross, 1 on ground floor, 2 on 1st floor; lounge & dining area. Offer a 3-course dinner for £35, much sourced from the owners' kitchen garden or from the fishermen's catch. ££

🏠 **Spinners Cottage** [159 F4] (1 room) Geocrab; ☎ 01859 530284; e kmairi28@yahoo. co.uk; w spinnerscottageharris.co.uk. An en-suite twin furnished with Harris Tweed trimmings. Rocky vantage point above The Bays provides lovely views from the sun porch. Guests have exclusive use of garden room which looks across to Skye. ££

🏠 **Tigh an Eilein** [159 E5] (2 rooms) 5a Flodabay; ☎ 01859 530270; e alleycatcj@yahoo. co.uk; w www.tighaneilein-harris.co.uk. En-suite dbl with views across the Minch; sgl with separate private bathroom. ££

⚑ **Lickisto Blackhouse Camping** [159 F4] Lickisto (Licesto); ☎ 01859 530485; e lickisto@live. co.uk; w lickistoblackhousecamping.co.uk. Enjoys a wonderful setting overlooking Loch Stocinis with 15 tent pitches & 4 campervan spaces separated by wild grasses & heather. Fresh bread available; blackhouse provides sheltered cooking facilities. Yurts (££) for hire. £

✕ **The Bays Community Centre** [159 F4] Leacklea (Leac a' Lì); ⊕ Jun–Oct 11.15–17.00 Mon–Fri. Something of a gem in a remote area, this friendly café serves bacon rolls, toasties, good cakes & proper coffee. Just to manage expectations, note that this lovely café is dependent on volunteers & so the decision on whether to open (& opening times) is taken on a year-by-year basis. £

✕ **Skoon Gallery** [159 F4] 4 Geocrab; ☎ 01859 530268; e info@skoon.com; w skoon. com; ⊕ Mar–Sep 10.00–16.30 Tue–Sat, winter times vary, check website. Run by artist Andrew John Craig & his wife, Emma. Andrew's work, including oil paintings of island landscapes, hangs on the walls & is for sale. The place to come for wonderful, towering scones, homemade by the owners, along with brownies & shortbread. £

What to see and do The Bays are a true moonscape that make for a beautiful journey through tiny hamlets by bike or on foot or bus. The route described here travels from north to south, though it can just as easily be made in the opposite direction. Two small roads, at Grosebay (Ghreosabhagh) and at Loch Stocinis, offer shortcuts back to the A859. The W13 bus runs twice daily (except Sunday) along the route in each direction between Tarbert pier and Leverburgh. The area is also home to a handful of art galleries and cafés that seem implausibly

HARRIS TWEED

The definition of Harris Tweed is taken extremely seriously, to the point that it is enshrined in law, with clear legal criteria laid down by the 1993 Harris Tweed Act. To meet the prescribed definition of Harris Tweed, tweed must adhere to strict specifications: a tweed must have been 'handwoven by the islanders at their home in the Outer Hebrides and made from pure virgin wool dyed and spun in the Outer Hebrides'. The certification trademark is the Dunmore coat of arms – an orb emblazoned with the Maltese Cross – granted in 1910 to prevent other manufacturers from claiming to produce Harris Tweed. The orb was chosen in recognition of Lady Dunmore, who brought Harris Tweed to a wider audience. She took an interest in the cloth after Lord Dunmore took over Harris in the 1840s. He commanded a private army and asked the local weavers to copy the Murray tartan for his soldiers' kilts. From this initial commission, word spread – and a successful industry emerged. Some observers say that the most important thing that ever happened to tweed was that Lady Dunmore put the price up. 'If you make something expensive, the rich will buy it,' says Ronnie Mackenzie of the Lewis Loom Centre (page 86).

Weaving was originally women's activity, but after the decline of the whaling industry and the arrival of mechanised looms, men took over the labour; at the turn of the 20th century there were some 1,000 male weavers across the islands. Following the outbreak of World War I, however, the weavers went to the trenches, and the women took up work at the looms. After the war, the looms provided suitable employment for returning soldiers, particularly those who were wounded. Today, unlike those pre-war days, weaving is a solitary occupation.

Harris Tweed offers reassuring proof that the Outer Hebrides comprises living, breathing communities that steadfastly hold on to skills and traditions. In 1976 weavers rejected plans to introduce power-driven factory looms, meaning that home-based weavers must continue to have mill-spun yarn delivered to their sheds. The industry, though extremely lucrative for Harris, is likely to remain essentially a cottage industry, albeit one with a global market.

Traditionally, wool was plucked by hand and woven to make clothing for the family and dyed with lichens, heather flowers, ragwort and other flowers, all of which introduce subtle colours: yellow from rocket and bog myrtle, a grey-black from iris, and gold from heather. Meanwhile, crotal, a flat grey lichen scraped off the rocks, provides the distinctive earth-red brown, and peat soot adds a burnished golden brown. Wool was even dipped in stale urine which worked well as a mordant, sticking the dyes to the fabrics. Extraordinarily, for a time these ingeniously sourced colours were banned by an Act of the Scottish Parliament, which made it compulsory for labourers to weave 'riochd-mallaichte', or the 'accursed grey'.

remote but appear to sustain themselves by dint of their usually extremely high-quality offerings.

The C79 Bays Road winds south of Tarbert to the minuscule village of Drinishader (Drinisiadar) [159 G3]. In the centre of the township, you come to Clò Mòr or Old School (✆ 01859 502505; e info@harristweedandknitwear.co.uk; w harristweedandknitwear.co.uk; ⊕ 09.00–17.30 Mon–Sat), a Harris Tweed exhibition offering weaving demonstrations.

You may occasionally hear or read the C79 described as the 'Golden Road'. The story goes that the moniker was coined to represent the phenomenal cost and Herculean labour required to blast a road through such an undentable landscape. The reality is a little more prosaic. The title was given to the stretch of road just south of Tarbert, running through Miabhaig, Ghreosabhagh and Stockinish (Stocinis), and was dismissively applied by a mainland newspaper critical of any funding of roads on the islands. According to Bill Lawson at Seallam!, the real cost was lower than expected, with the labour mainly met by local men. The stretch of road through **Plocrapol** ✳ [159 G3] is extremely scenic, with lochs and smaller lochans interspersed between a rolling rocky backdrop. A mile or two more down the road is the next township of Grosebay (Ghreosabhagh) [159 G4], home to the **Harris Tweed** showroom (✆ 01859 511108; e harrisknitwear@hotmail. com; w harristweedco.co.uk; ⊕ 09.30–17.30 Mon–Sat) and an adjacent shop. This represents the more traditional end of the tweed market and you will be greeted with a formality and civility that goes down well with a certain kind of clientele, evoking as it does an air of 19th-century lords, ladies and lairds.

The road flicks north along the shore of Loch Stocinis and just before a T-junction with a turn-off for Tarbert at Leacklea (Leac a' Li) is the Bays Community Centre tea shop (page 174). Close by, at the head of Loch Stocinis, look out for a remarkably poetic information board that eulogises about the millions of years required for the tide to carve the Lewisian gneiss into rockpools. The shoreline of this tidal loch is worth exploring; statuesque herons enjoy the camouflage of the rocks while blennies and crabs abound. The emerald and ochre seaweed here shines even more brightly among the barren landscape.

A picturesque stretch of the C79 sweeps down to **Geocrab** [159 F4], a township that sprawls over a wide area even as depopulation appears to threaten its existence. The unusual name means 'muddy inlet', and the community was established in the 1820s and 1830s by crofters evicted from the west side of Harris. Lord Leverhulme built spinning and carding mills here but, like his ventures elsewhere, it came to nought. The only turning in the village leads

WAULKING SONGS

Once woven, weavers would 'waulk' or shrink, beat and stretch the fabric to tighten the fabric and make it more felt-like, often working in time to traditional waulking songs, or *orain luaidh*. These were integral to the process of weaving, not least to relieve the monotony of the work, and specific rhythms accompanied different parts of the process. The songs were more about the lives, loves, births and deaths among the community rather than weaving; verses were sung by the leader and others joined in the chorus. No song was ever repeated, for this would bring bad luck to the workers, and offerings of milk were sometimes made to a fairy-woman or *loireag*, who was said to sit and observe the waulking.

SAVED FROM THE SUPERQUARRY

One of the UK's most extraordinary and outrageous planning proposals of recent times nearly came to reality above Leverburgh. In the 1990s, developer Ian Wilson put forward a plan to blow up and remove the mountain of Roineabhal in order to create a super quarry, with the resource – 600 million tonnes of rock over 60 years – to be used for hardcore for roads both on the islands and the mainland. Wilson maintained that the resulting landscape – possibly the world's largest manmade hole – would, over time, be flooded to create an artificial loch, boosting the fishing and sailing industries. Wilson went further and argued that the resulting dust and spoil would be mixed to create a fertile soil that would encourage forestry and crofting. The dynamite required to complete the job would have been the equivalent of six atomic bombs dropped on Hiroshima.

Even though Roineabhal is part of the South Harris National Scenic Area, the promise of long-term jobs initially suggested that the development would win the day and the Western Isles Council indicated it was inclined to support the project.

A public inquiry turned the tide, and a remarkable intervention may have swayed some wavering minds. One of the leading opponents, Alastair McIntosh, persuaded Sulian Herney – known as Stone Eagle and a native-rights campaigner in Canada – to testify about the impact of the quarry. Focussing not only on the physical but also the cultural and moral landscape of Harris, Herney declared: 'Your mountain, your shorelines, your rivers and your air are just as much mine and my grandchildren's as ours is yours.' After the inquiry, the council rejected the proposal, even though the head of the inquiry recommended its approval. The scheme was finally put to rest in 2000 when the Scottish government turned it down.

to the Skoon Gallery (page 174). The road continues south; by the junction for Quidinish (Cuidhtinis) you'll find the **Holmasaig Gallery** [159 E5] (✆ 01859 530401; w holmasaiggallery.com). This is home to artist Margarita Williams who has a wonderful collection of watercolour landscapes that capture the ever-shifting light of Harris. Her grandmother's cousin was schoolmaster on St Kilda. A mile further on is the community of Flodabay (Floeideabhagh).

The road then cuts inland briefly before returning to the shore at Ardvey (Àird Mhìghe), home to the **Finsbay Gallery** [158 E6] (1 Ardvey; ✆ 01859 530244; e info@ finsbaygallery.co.uk; w finsbaygallery.co.uk; ⊕ Easter–Oct 10.00–17.00 Mon–Sat, winter & Sun by appt). The first gallery to set up in The Bays showcases the work of mainland artists visiting the islands.

Ardvey merges into the equally tiny township of Finsbay, where another gallery, **The Mission House Studio** (✆ 01859 530227; w missionhousestudio. co.uk; ⊕ Mar–Sep 11.00–16.00 Mon–Sat; winter by appt), is worth pausing at. This is probably the most avant-garde of Harris's galleries and showcases the work of Beka and Nickolai Globe, fine artists and ceramicists. A visit is an experience in itself as background music reverberates gently off the exposed stone walls. Work includes stoneware bowls and more abstract ceramics, some of which are made from reclaimed material from the former church in which the gallery is housed. Beka's black-and-white photography is eye-catching and unconventional. 'I try to capture feelings in my photographs rather than pictures for tourists,' she says.

4

The journey between Leverburgh and Berneray is among the most dreamily beautiful in the UK, if not the world, something that is not lost on skipper John Docherty, master of the *Loch Portain* ferry that plies the route. John has lost count of the number of times he has safely navigated the ferry through the awkward waters of the sound – 'at least several thousand', he suggests – but the magic of his open-air 'office' never fades. 'We see gannets, seals, every time; if you're lucky we see a basking shark,' he says. Sea eagles often settle down on one of the low rocky skerries that creep above the tide, while otters are regularly spotted on the slipway at Berneray. 'You see an eagle at sunrise and it takes your breath away,' says John.

For passengers, the journey can be bewildering and some are alarmed when it appears that the ferry has turned around and is heading back to port. In fact, this is because John must navigate 24 switchbacks across the sound, squeezing through narrow channels, some of them just 60m wide. Red and green buoys mark the limits of the safe channels and are often positioned on skerries that pose a threat. 'Most of the rocks out here are named after someone who has bumped into them,' says John. All channels head north, with green buoys on the port side heading north. This explains why you sometimes see green buoys on the port side; and then on the starboard side; when the latter is the case, the ferry has negotiated one of its switchbacks.

At the lowest tide, there are some spots where the ferry all but skims the sea floor, which is just 0.3m below (although the ship's draft means this rises as the ship passes to 1½m, which will still strike the average landlubber as not providing much wriggle room). The ferry is powered by water-jet propulsion, so there are no propellers or rudders to scrape the sea bed. Occasionally, though, even this is not enough and the *Loch Portain* must sit in deep water for a few minutes while the tide rises. Particularly notorious are the skerries known as the Cabbage Group, which – John thinks – is named after a cargo of cabbages that foundered there.

The shallow nature of the waters means that the ferry cannot sail in darkness (though it has a dispensation in winter to leave an hour before sunrise, as nautical light soon illuminates the sound). Furthermore, the perilous nature of these rock-strewn, shallow waters means the ferry will rarely sail in winds of more than 50 knots. The ferry, incidentally, is moored at Berneray partly because the harbour there affords more shelter and partly because that is where the crew lives.

The circuitous nature of the route means that a distance of 5 miles as the gannet flies becomes 9½ miles at sea. CalMac has plied this route since 1996. Before that, travelling from the Uists to Harris would take 5 hours, and involve the 'Uist triangle', crossing the Minch from Lochmaddy to Uig in Skye and then back again to Tarbert.

Ask John about the intermittent plans for bridges or a tunnel between the islands and he raises an eyebrow. 'I think people come here for the fun that is involved in taking the ferry. Take that away and you miss the magic of these islands.'

The C79 forks at Finsbay, continuing south to Rodel, while an unclassified road loops back to Leverburgh. The latter road skirts the shores of Loch Langabhat and round Roineabhal before weaving west and south in the shadow of Beinn Tharsuinn to Leverburgh. The route's distance from Rodel to Leverburgh is 8 miles; as the road is very quiet it makes for enjoyable and easy terrain for walking as well, with scope for meandering in and out of the rockscape and inspecting the dramatic corries and gullies such as Srath Litean that indent the northern flanks of Roineabhal.

The southern end of the C79 constitutes a minor road that connects **Finsbay to Rodel**. The route takes you through perhaps the most barren landscapes of all, with rocks apparently either having been dropped from the sky or erupted from the earth. The geology changes here, and igneous rocks such as metagabbro, melatonalite and quarthosite take the place of the gneiss. Deposits of white anorthosite and red feldspar add a desolate tint to the spectacle. Around the base of the rocks you can pick out scrapes of determined tussocks of marram grass, whose russet colour echoes the faded pink tinge of the rocks.

SOUND OF HARRIS The 1-hour, 5-mile ferry sailing across the Sound of Harris links the northern islands of Lewis and Harris to the southern isles of North Uist, Benbecula and South Uist. The route is not only an economic driver but also one of the most beautiful sea journeys in the UK.

Departing from Leverburgh, the ship slaloms between countless islets, skerries and shallow water to maintain the navigation channel before slipping past the rocky reef near Berneray and making landfall there. The first admiralty charts of the waters were recorded in 1745, and the Sound has been recognised ever since as one of the most intricate sea routes in Scotland. Pirates had to hire local fishermen to ensure their safe passage through the waters, while smugglers of illegal whisky used their local knowledge to thwart any excisemen on their tail. At one time or another, several islands, such as Pabbay, Ensay (w friendsofensay.co.uk) and Killegray, were inhabited; today only Berneray is.

The ship performs so many twists and turns that you can be looking at the hills of Harris one moment and the deserted island of Pabbay, Skye or North Uist the next. You have the chance of seeing porpoises scuttling from the Atlantic to the Minch, gannets diving for fish and cormorants, razorbills, puffins, skuas and other charismatic birds dashing back and forth. A return foot passenger ticket is £7.60/£3.80 and many people make a day trip out of the journey. Serious thought has been given to harnessing the sound's tidal waters for renewable energy, though costs make this a probable slow burner. Every now and then plans are floated to traverse the sound with bridges and causeways from one island to another, though, again, a hefty price tag tends to dampen discussion. Accordingly, the ferry is likely to continue and enchant for decades to come.

5

St Kilda

> Whatever he studies, the future observer of St Kilda will be haunted the rest of his life by the place, and tantalised by the impossibility of describing it, to those who have not seen it.
>
> *James Fisher, naturalist, 1948 in*
> St Kilda: A Natural Experiment, New Naturalist Journal

The most remote archipelago in the British Isles, St Kilda resonates with images of epic travel, of an exotic island hard to reach but which rewards those who venture there with the experience of a lifetime. The islands are best known for the hardy community that lived on the main island of Hirta (Hiort) and which was evacuated in highly charged circumstances in 1930.

St Kilda comprises five islands plus attendant sea stacks and is positioned 45 nautical miles due west of Leverburgh on Harris. Soay is the most westerly, hidden for the most part behind the largest, Hirta, on which the islanders made their home on Main Street overlooking the natural harbour of Village Bay. Hirta's eastern ridges are all but conjoined with Dùn, while the stout lump of Levenish stands alone to the east. To the northeast lie Boreray and the two dramatic sea stacks of Stac Lee (meaning 'beautiful stack' in Gaelic) and Stac an Armin ('stack of the warrior').

The islands compete to outdo one another with their dramatic beauty: geometric sweeps akin to those of a South Pacific idyll pull the land up from sea level to high cliff ridges where they face the full rigours of the Atlantic Ocean. They include the highest sea cliffs in the British Isles, which at 376m (1,233ft) also dwarf the tallest building in the UK, The Shard in London, and the highest sea stack at 191m (626ft).

The stirring landscape is one of three reasons for the powerful magnetism with which St Kilda draws people from around the world, the others being its deeply moving social history and extraordinary seabird colonies.

The abundance of birdlife is unparalleled in the UK. At the height of the breeding season from May to August, St Kilda is home to a scarcely comprehendible 1 million seabirds, the largest colony in northwest Europe. This includes what was until 2015 the largest gannet colony in the world (now overtaken by Bass Rock in mainland Scotland) and the UK's largest puffin colony. For all these reasons, St Kilda is one of only 24 global locations to be awarded 'mixed' UNESCO World Heritage Status for its natural and cultural significance. Whether you are interested in one, all or none of these elements, a visit here is unforgettable. For a good number of those who make it here, doing so represents the achievement of a life-long dream.

HISTORY

The dramatic evacuation of the population in 1930 brought an end to continuous human habitation that lasted for at least 2,000 years. Consequently, St Kilda must

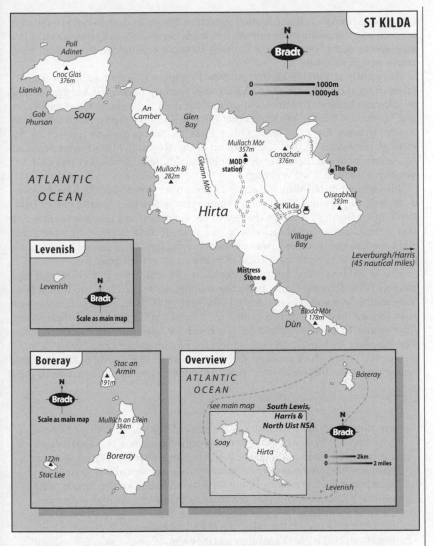

be one of the most comprehensively documented islands on the planet. The wealth of historical and anthropological research is all the more impressive since the evidence of family trees dies out if you go back more than a few hundred years and, beyond that, there is very little written evidence on human habitation of the islands.

The islands' origins are volcanic. Formed of gabbro, granite and dolerite and shaped by ice, rain and waves, they are unmatched anywhere in scale in the British Isles. They represent the remains of a large volcano active some 55 million years ago and whose remnant outline runs from Soay, around the southwest edges of Hirta, Dùn and Levenish and continues underwater to emerge at Boreray.

The islands' earlier history is hard to put together, relying on a couple of carved crosses and some poorly recorded 19th-century excavations on Hirta. Furthermore, because the working material for houses is presumed to have always been stone rather than wood, archaeologists have struggled to decipher any meaningful conclusions from evolving styles in architecture. The main clues to earlier habitation are prehistoric-looking stone implements made from Mullach Sgar dolerite, whose dark colour stands out from the oatmeal-coloured granophyre from which more recent structures are built.

As recently as 1997, researcher Andrew Fleming was documenting his primary research on the subject in the *St Kilda Mail*. Fleming uncovered hoe-blades used to cultivate the fields that are identical to those used in Neolithic times on Orkney and Shetland. Fleming speculated that early St Kildans relied on driftwood from North America for their hoes. Other finds include prehistoric pottery in the form of Hebridean Incised Ware, typical of the Neolithic of northwest Scotland. It's extremely likely, therefore, that a substantial human population was on Hirta between 4,000 and 5,500 years ago.

The earliest reliable historical accounts come from Martin Martin, who describes a capable and populous 17th-century community where the islanders spoke Gaelic. Crofting emerged, as it did in the rest of the Hebrides, and here the tenants paid rent to their landlord, the Macleods of Skye, in the form of feathers, oil, barley, milk and tweed. Farming, though, was secondary to the pursuit of seabird meat and the islanders scaled hair-raising vertical cliffs in pursuit of their quarry.

The St Kildans were famed as nerveless cliff climbers, retrieving eggs and gannets from dizzying ledges including the highest sea stack in the British Isles. They ate the flesh and eggs of razorbills, fulmars, guillemots, gannets, puffins, great auks (before they were driven extinct in the mid 19th century) and shearwaters. Eggs stored in peat ash could be preserved for eating in the winter months. Records show that in the 1830s islanders took 4,000 gannets and 20,000 fulmars; at the start of the 20th century, the islanders were still taking 5,000 guillemot eggs every year. These exertions made islanders physically different from their

SOAY SHEEP

Everywhere on Hirta you will see the native Soay sheep. Thought to have been introduced by Vikings or even during the Bronze Age, these animals are the only wild sheep colony in the British Isles and since the 1930 evacuation have had no interference from humans. They are remarkably goat-like in appearance and have none of the fat of lambs raised for the Sunday table on the mainland. Almost as common as the sheep are the researchers studying them: Soay sheep are subject to one of the longest-running animal studies on the planet. The sheep are not only wild but are believed to have bloodlines that go back centuries and they remain genetically close to their wild ancestors. All this offers the unprecedented chance to observe at close hand how the animals have evolved, and how they continue to do so. Studies focus on which genetic traits tend to get selected when the animals breed and why their populations crash every so often. Recent research – added to with every year that passes – suggests that climate change in the form of milder winters and wetter summers is making the population stronger as the grass grows longer and more abundant. Though wild (strictly speaking, 'feral'), Hirta's sheep are habituated to humans and visitors can find them semi-tame. In contrast, the sheep on the plateau of Boreray are said to be much more wary: when you cruise around Boreray's waters you will pick out the sheep on improbable ledges, where they seem certain at any moment to tumble into the sea but – so the researchers say – rarely do.

mainland counterparts: due to the climbing of cliffs after seabirds, their ankles were unusually thick and strong.

Stories of marooned St Kildans abound, and none is more dramatic than that of the fowlers (three men and eight boys) who were dropped on to Boreray in 1726 for a routine gannet catch but ended up staying for nine months after smallpox devastated the population of Hirta and no-one came to collect them. The remnant population was fewer than 30; and it is thought many of those left soon after. A St Kilda census has recently come to light, dated to 1764, which records that the population quickly recovered and rose to 90 people. 'It shows that in many senses St Kilda was just another island of the Hebrides,' says Bill Lawson of Seallam! (page 167). 'It had plenty of food – eggs, birds, fish – why wouldn't people want to live there?' The same census also recorded – to Bill's surprise – several McVicars, which historically has been a Uist name. This discovery has prompted new thinking about the varied ways in which St Kilda was populated, as by and large most inhabitants hailed from Harris.

Religion emerged around this time as an important influence, and missionaries and ministers became the islanders' main point of contact with the outside world. History, it's fair to say, has not judged the impact of religion on St Kilda favourably. The St Kildans proved vulnerable to the strictures of zealous visiting clergy, who inspired devotion and, in turn, dismantled a good deal of the island's rich diversity, customs and tradition. Dancing and music were seen as frivolous and few poems and songs survive; precious farming time was lost to the requirement to regularly attend church.

The emigrations of the 19th century that characterised the highlands and islands did not pass St Kilda by. In one desperate episode, 36 St Kildans emigrated to Australia in 1852, only for half of them to die on the voyage or shortly after arrival, whether from the effects of dysentery, diarrhoea or measles.

Most accounts infer that the arrival of tourism shook up island culture almost as much as religion. The islanders had until this time seemed able to survive on their hard-to-reach but abundant natural resources, and achieve long-term if precarious sustainability in a cashless economy.

The first tourists arrived in 1834 by steamship in search of what had been billed as a 'primitive society' and soon the structure of St Kilda's economy began to change. With money received from landing fees and the sale of trinkets, the St Kildans were able to purchase flour, fresh meat, fish, sugar, tea, coal and paraffin from the mainland. But an increasing dependence on this trade made matters harder in winter when months would pass without contact with the outside world. In 1886, a visitor, Robert Connell, recorded how 'You can't be long on the islands without discovering the great moral injury that tourists and sentimentalists and yachtsmen with pocketfuls of money are working upon a kindly and simple people.'

Yet it would be deeply simplistic to imply that the St Kildans lived in a golden world of prelapsarian innocence until the arrival of tourists whereupon they fell prey to unforgiving capitalism. They were intensely practical people, observing a St Kilda Parliament, whereby the men met each morning to discuss the day's tasks.

Other factors later came into play that combined to make life yet harder. The Navy pulled out after World War I, triggering a short wave of emigration from the islands. Fewer birds were caught by those who remained and the community became increasingly reliant for winter supplies on the chance passing of trawlers.

It can be easy to romanticise the decision to abandon St Kilda. While there is little doubt that many of those leaving would have found the process emotionally demanding, there is a strong case for saying the depopulation was in fact a rational and practical process. Dr Kevin Grant, an archaeologist who lived on St Kilda for

The provenance of the collective name for the islands is as unclear as much else about them. Since there was never a saint called St Kilda, various theories have been put forward. These include the suggestion that the name is a corruption of an Old Norse word for the spring on Hirta, 'childa', or the Norse 'sunt kelda' (meaning 'sweet wellwater'). Others propose that Kilda is merely a corruption of the Gaelic name for the main island, Hirta, or that Kilda arose from a series of cartographic errors by early seamen. Several origins of the name Hirta, meanwhile, have their merits, including 'stag', 'gloom', 'shepherd' and 'land of the west'.

three years, made this point forcefully in *The Silent Islands*, Alex Boyd's photographic record of the archipelago (page 296). To sentimentalise the evacuation, says Grant, is to portray the islanders as 'a backward people incapable of embracing change'. Instead, he argues, the real reason 'was not the failure of the St Kildan way of life in the 20th century but the improvement of living conditions elsewhere'. After World War I, living standards were rising, and the government was increasingly providing services such as health care and education, which were difficult to deliver on St Kilda. 'Several families clearly felt,' says Grant, 'perhaps for the first time, they were likely to be better off elsewhere.'

By 1928, just 37 St Kildans were left, of whom only seven were able-bodied men. With the departure of so many young people, life became unsustainable and the remaining islanders applied to be evacuated. Their departure on 29 August 1930 brought to an end an extraordinary period of human habitation. For the most part, they headed for the mainland, where the men were provided with forestry work. The last surviving former resident of St Kilda, Rachel Johnson, died in 2016 at the age of 93. She had been eight years old when she left.

The islands were given to the National Trust for Scotland (NTS) in 1957 and the Trust has maintained a hands-off approach to conservation and intervention, with minimal infrastructure and allowing its own and other experts to study how an island's ecology develops with the lightest of human footprints. The NTS leases some land on Hirta to the Ministry of Defence which operates a radar-tracking station. This is linked to the rocket range on South Uist (see box, page 245) and sits atop Mullach Mòr at the head of Village Bay.

GETTING THERE AND AWAY

Although not administered by Comhairle nan Eilean Siar, the council for the Outer Hebrides, St Kilda is included in this book because of its great historical links to the islands and because, with very few exceptions, it can only be reached from Harris and Lewis. A boat is the only way for the public to get to St Kilda and several operators make the run across the Atlantic from the west coasts of Harris and Lewis in around 2½ hours.

The journey is undeniably part of the experience. On a clear day, the islands of Hirta and Boreray become visible soon after clearing anchorage and thereafter the distinctive sea stacks emerge on the horizon. As you travel, your skipper will keep an eye out for dolphins and whales, including minke whales, and slow down to enable you to watch and photograph them. Some 5 miles out to sea you pass across the Hebridean Deep Water route, a water highway for heavy shipping vessels.

St Kilda really is seabird city. The world's second-largest gannet colony is home to 60,000 pairs of the birds, along with the UK's largest fulmar colony (67,000 pairs) and its largest puffin colony (140,000 pairs). You will also see storm petrels and Manx shearwaters in the orders of hundreds, if not thousands: these birds tend to forage even further out into the Atlantic Ocean, roaming over large distances off the continental shelf, before returning at or after dusk. St Kilda was also the last place in the UK where the now-extinct great auk was seen: the final one to be caught on Stac an Armin in 1840 was one of the last known to be in existence. All is not well, however, with these seabird colonies. A succession of surveys on Hirta since 2000 (Soay and Boreray were surveyed in 2019) has revealed declines for species including fulmars, kittiwakes, common guillemots and razorbills, amid rising sea temperatures and fish-depleted seas.

It can be easy to overlook some of the other curiosities of the islands. Prime among these is the St Kilda wren, formally *Troglodytes troglodytes hirtensis*, which has evolved into a much larger subspecies of the mainland wren and which you will almost certainly see and hear. While the house mouse became extinct shortly after the 1930 evacuation, the St Kilda field mouse, a subspecies of wood mouse, has moved on to bigger things, almost doubling in size. Some 58 species of moth and butterfly have been recorded.

Flora thrives doughtily in cliff-ledge communities, wet heath and grasslands. In all, 180 flowering plants and ferns have been identified on the islands, compared with around 2,000 on the mainland. Hardy species include heath spotted orchid, milkwort, sundew and cottongrass. Tree cover, self-evidently, is at a premium, and scrub species are limited to creeping and dwarf willows. More than 120 types of wild flower have been identified on Boreray, despite its steepness and even more severe exposure to the elements.

You will be accompanied for much of the journey by gannets returning to St Kilda; they often fly in breathtaking lines, almost beak to tail, lifting up and down in rhythm with the waves. Puffins scuttle away from the wake of the boat, their paths criss-crossing with those of loping storm petrels. As you approach the islands, the birds converge on a scale that is simply extraordinary, funnelling magnetically towards St Kilda in a way that can bring to mind the stampede for Boxing Day sales.

The trip is not for everyone: while the boat operators will not usually sail in winds any stronger than a Force 4, this can still seem choppy in a small vessel, and swells can persist even in light winds. Consult a pharmacist before travelling if you have concerns about seasickness. The return journey is often smoother as you are sailing with the prevailing currents and winds, rather than into them. All skippers are experienced sailors and trips have a safety record second to none. They will not sail if they think there is any risk of adverse weather. This can be frustrating if you wake up to a beautiful sunlit morning with calm seas, but the conditions out in the Atlantic might be very different. It's also worth noting that good sailing weather does not always equate with clear skies. Low mist or fog can make St Kilda hugely atmospheric but will not deliver the picture-postcard impressions that may have inspired your visit. It can be helpful to manage your own expectations ahead of the trip.

TOUR OPERATORS Typically, you are asked to book for a two-day window to allow for bad weather. If the trip doesn't run on day one, it will hopefully run on day two. If the trip does run on day one, an additional second trip at short notice is sometimes put on the next day, weather and demand permitting. So if trips are booked up during your stay, it is worth asking to be put on standby. Operators start trips in May and keep going if there is demand into September. Some slots get booked up a year in advance, though you should be able to book with some confidence around three months ahead. Looking to book at the last minute because the short-term weather forecast is good can sometimes work but risks disappointment.

Return fares cost £170–250 for adults and £120–195 for children. That said, because of the potentially rough boat trip and the rugged terrain on the islands, it is recommended that only children aged 11 years or older travel. Operators have different policies on refunds if bad weather prevents sailings: some refund in full, others refund minus an administration fee and others will offer alternative trips.

Kilda Cruises 01859 502060; m 07760 281804; e angus@kildacruises.co.uk; w kildacruises.co.uk. Sends 2 boats to St Kilda: *Orca III* & *Hirta*. Their shop in Tarbert has a small but uplifting display with some interpretation of the islands.

Sea Harris 01859 502007; m 07760 216555; w seaharris.com; see ad, 3rd colour section. Run by the friendly Seumas Morrison, trips depart from Leverburgh. The *Enchanted Isles* is a custom-built 12-seater that is designed to take the sting out of the sometimes choppy waters. A good aft deck is the perfect place to watch St Kilda recede to the horizon at the end of the trip. Seumas is genial & good company &, space permitting, may invite you to sit in the co-pilot's seat & chat about life on the high seas.

Seatrek 01851 672469; e bookings@ seatrek.co.uk; w seatrek.co.uk. Operates out of Miabhaig in Uig on the west coast of Lewis.

Uist Sea Tours m 07833 690693; e uistseatours@gmail.com; w uistseatours.co.uk. Fast boat trips depart from Benbecula (Mon, also Wed in summer), arriving on St Kilda in just 2¼hrs.

A TYPICAL DAY TRIP TO ST KILDA

Boats leave Uig and Harris around 08.00. Generally, your boat docks in Village Bay off Hirta around 10.30. Hirta is the only island on which visitors can make landfall and you get to spend 5 hours here. On arrival, you are given a safety briefing and a useful map.

Typically, you might explore Main Street with its mixture of collapsed and restored houses and the museum. Between April and September, rangers, archaeologists and wardens from the NTS are on hand and happy to chat. Most people walk up The Gap, a valley behind the village that leads to views across to Boreray and the sea stacks of Stac Lee and Stac an Armin. The more energetic will climb further to Conachair and the highest cliffs in the British Isles. You then have time to buy a souvenir before the skipper asks you to return to the quayside.

Boats then usually spend another hour or so trundling alongside the island of Dùn, to view the large puffin colonies, and cruising around Boreray and the stacks. This also enables you to catch glimpses of the island of Soay, which, for the most part, is hidden behind Hirta. Before heading back to Harris or Lewis, your crew may serve tea and ginger cake, the latter said to help counter seasickness (for most visits, unless operators specify otherwise, this is the only food served; you should bring your own lunch). You usually arrive back in Harris or Uig around 19.00.

WHERE TO STAY

A single day trip is nowhere near enough to see all of what St Kilda has to offer. By staying longer, you not only have the place to yourself to explore at leisure but can catch some of nature's magical sights, such as the Leach's storm petrel returning at dusk from far-flung fishing grounds to its nest burrows.

There are two ways to stay. You can sign up as a volunteer for a National Trust for Scotland (NTS) working holiday. Typically, these are for fortnight slots in May or June. In return for your fee (around £855), you get board and lodging and spend your days helping with restoration work around Village Bay, such as rebuilding drystone walls or cleits. Spaces on these work parties get snapped up quickly: if you're interested, keep an eye on the NTS website (w nts.org.uk) from October the year before you wish to visit.

Alternatively, you can camp in the fields behind the old military buildings for £20 per night (max 5 nights). Bookings must be made through the NTS (📞 01463 232034; e stkildainfo@nts.org.uk). You must bring all your food and equipment with you, though you may use the toilet and washing facilities in the main NTS buildings. Spaces are usually limited to no more than ten (sometimes fewer). Remember that camping will double the cost of your boat trip out to the islands and back as the operators must keep one place free for you on the return. Further information on the islands and staying there can be found at w kilda.org.uk and w nts.org.uk. The island's NTS rangers, incidentally, keep an entertaining twitter feed at 🐦 @StKildaNTS which can give you an inkling of what may lie in store.

SHOPPING

A small souvenir shop sells everything from St Kilda-themed T-shirts to body warmers, books and cuddly toys; it will even send postcards for you. The shop also sells copies of the *St Kilda Mail*, an occasional booklet that updates you on recent archaeological findings and anecdotes about island life.

WHAT TO SEE AND DO

The first sight of **Village Bay** on **Hirta** is breathtaking: a vast, green amphitheatre of land encircles the bay, rising abruptly from sea level to the highest cliffs in the British Isles. The village that was evacuated in 1930 runs just back from the shoreline and comprises 16 houses along **Main Street**, which curves around the northern half of the bay, just behind some incongruous quayside military infrastructure. Today, they are a mixture of restored and collapsed blackhouses. All have – or had – thick and sturdy stone walls. A number serve as temporary homes to NTS staff, volunteers and researchers.

What you are looking at today is the last phase of crofting settlements, from 1830 to 1869, comprising croft houses, strips of land and a share of common grazing for cattle. Walking around the village, the silence broken by the sloshing of waves and the cawing of seabirds, the ghosts of the recent past can seem palpable.

Working your way along the bay from the quay, you pass an anti-ship gun put in place in 1918 after a German U-boat shelled the village to destroy a radio mast. The first building you come to is the **church**, or **kirk**, built in the mid 19th century with a simple and plain interior that reflects the austere view of the Free Church of Scotland. This also houses the schoolroom, built in 1884. A row of desks remains, along with an attendance register and a schoolmaster's desk that

5

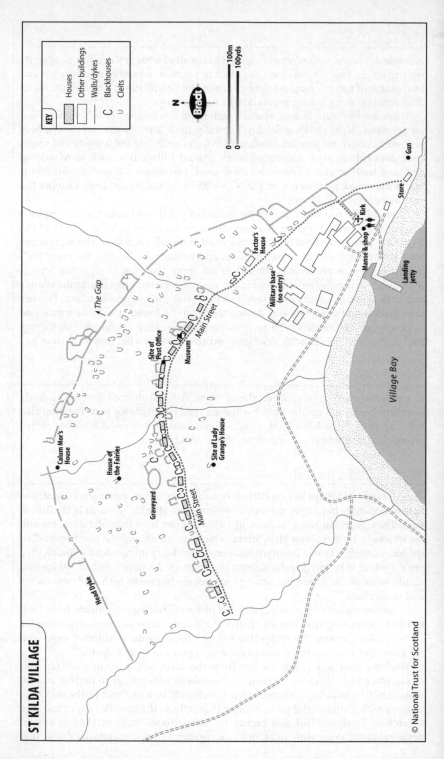

© National Trust for Scotland

During his visit to St Kilda in 1697, Martin Martin described the extraordinary ritual by which men would flaunt their masculinity and prowess to women by perching on what was known as the **Mistress Stone**, located southwest of Village Bay. The behaviour has echoes of strutting peacocks or other means by which the animal kingdom and nature determines who gets to breed: the Mistress Stone 'resembles a door exactly,' said Martin. 'Upon the lintel of the door, every Bachelor-Wooer is by an Ancient Custom obliged in honour to give a Specimen of his Affection for the Love of his Mistress.' This involved standing on his left foot and adopting a bowing posture with his hands clenched. 'After he has performed this, he has acquired no small Reputation, being always accounted worthy of the Finest Mistress in the World; they firmly believe that this Achievement is always attended with desired success.'

looks more like a pulpit. The adjacent **manse** is home to NTS offices, a small shop and has a public toilet.

At the eastern edge of Main Street you first come to the Factor's House. Originally home to the laird's representative on the island, it now houses researchers and National Trust for Scotland staff. Heading along the village, **house number 3** has been converted into a thoughtful museum. This is the former home of William and Mary Ann MacDonald, who had 11 children. There are good accounts of the history of the island, the wildlife and a modest collection of seabird eggs and trinkets. Other buildings nearby include the old post office.

To the west of the village is the enclosed **graveyard**. Most of the tombstones are plain, or have weathered away. The more recent ones are of St Kildans who left the islands but who requested to be buried in the earth of their island home. Up behind the graveyard is a substantial pile of rubble known as **Calum Mor's house**. More than 1,000 years old, this semi-subterranean house is a corbelled beehive shape of monumental proportions yet is said to have been built in a day by the eponymous Calum to prove his worth after he was overlooked for fowling on Boreray. Also just behind the graveyard is the **House of Fairies**, an earth house with a turf-covered, subterranean entrance. First excavated in 1844, it was found to house Iron Age potsherds (broken ceramic material), a Viking-age spearhead, and animal bones. To the south of the graveyard, on the slopes below Main Street, is the site of **Lady Grange's House**. The original house was timber-roofed, and when it fell in, it was rebuilt as a cleit – though some archaeologists have also detected remnants of a blackhouse in the structure. The doorway is believed to be original; the wooden lock (of a design peculiar to St Kilda) can be found at Dunvegan Castle on Skye. The house was where Lady Grange was imprisoned between 1734 and 1742. Her story was extraordinary: her husband, James Erskine, Lord Grange, had her kidnapped and sent to St Kilda because he feared she would betray his support for the Jacobite rebellion. Erskine went as far as claiming she had died, and staged a funeral for her. Eventually freed, Lady Grange lived out her life on Skye.

Main Street is backed and fronted by drystone walls, restored enclosures and a large number of **cleits** (pronounced 'cleets') or storehouses. These squat round structures are all but embedded in the ground and were used to keep eggs, fish and meat. Some are thought to date back more than 2,500 years and many were built with great precision; they run up behind the village in lines of striking symmetry.

Just north of the graveyard lies a subterranean croft thought to date to a similar age as the hoe-blades mentioned above; such discoveries still leave unanswered the question of just how peoples could have sailed here, presumably in the dugout canoes they used to move around the coastlines and inland waterways of the Hebrides.

Your time on land allows you to explore further afield. The most popular walk is up to **The Gap**, behind the village. This steep climb takes around 20 minutes and leads through a minefield of cleits to an opening on the skyline from where you have uninterrupted views of Boreray and its stacks. Be mindful though that the hill here has no back to it and that the sheer cliffs can spring themselves on you in a way that might startle even the most nerveless of tightrope walkers.

From The Gap, many walkers push on west towards **Conachair**, where the cliffs, at 376m (1,233ft) are the highest in the British Isles (Conachair's summit itself is 430m (1,410ft) high). This is a dizzyingly steep climb, for the most part over open ground; where a path is visible it runs thrillingly close to the exposed cliff edge. You should allow an hour to get from The Gap to Conachair and its summit cairn. The birdlife here is simply spectacular with fulmars, kittiwakes and great skuas (also known as bonxies), the last of which will skim your head should you get too near their nests. The cliffs of Conachair are staggering in scale, and their mixture of intense green flanks and granite edges make for an extremely severe spectacle. From the summit cairn, you can continue west along and down the ridge to the radar station and pick up the military road that zigzags back down to the village. You should allow 2–3 hours to complete this horseshoe. The walk is arduous, and it can be difficult at times to see tracks above and below you, or to determine whether the routes have been chosen by sheep or humans. It is in fact much easier to do the entire horseshoe walk in reverse, heading up the military road from the village first. By first walking up the military road, you achieve much of the height over easier ground, and it is far easier to navigate your way to Conachair from the radar station and then descend to The Gap.

Your 5 hours will pass quickly, and you cannot hope to see all that St Kilda has to offer on a single visit. Other places worth exploring include the headland to the southwest of Village Bay, where much of Hirta's birdlife resides and you may see seals playing among the natural arches. A stroll here and back will take an hour or so. **An Camber**, located to the northwest of the bay and reached first by the military road and then by yomping over open ground, is remote, extremely beautiful and gives the best views of Soay. A hike up here and back to sea level will take a good 2½ hours. Another good hike is to walk east from The Gap up the steep and pleasingly geometric sweep of **Oiseabhal**, with its height of 293m (961ft). You should reckon on 45–60 minutes to climb from The Gap to the top and back.

A day visit to St Kilda is rounded off in the most spectacular way. Back on your vessel you sail up to the rocky base of **Dùn**, a spiny tapering island separated by a chink of Atlantic from Hirta. Puffins nest here in such vast numbers that their stuttering flight makes the air seem full of soot. Your boat will then usually head east to **Boreray** and its attendant sea stacks, **Stac Lee** and **Stac an Armin**, the latter of which, at 191m (626ft), is the highest such structure in the British Isles. Stac Lee is home to a colony of 14,000 northern gannets, while Stac an Armin was once home to the now extinct great auk and retains remnants of a bothy used for shelter by St Kildans while fowling. Boreray, despite its daunting appearance of inaccessibility, may have had an Iron Age wheelhouse on its plateau, where there is also possible evidence of ancient field systems and, more certainly, the remains of a small village.

Dwarfed beneath these vast vertical rocks and bobbing in the relentless rollers, your boat can feel like a toy tub in a bath. From May to August, their sheer faces are crammed with gannets, and their absurdly fattened chicks squeezed along every semblance of a ledge. These are the precipitous cliffs – with sloping, slippery traverses and step-wide fissures – up which St Kildan fowlers, barefoot and rope bound, would pull their way to harvest the young *gugas*, a desperately perilous task undertaken by men, women and children. Your boat skipper will point out the unlikely 'piers' – near-vertical slabs of rock – where the fowlers would jump ashore. Martin Martin thought it 'next to impossible' to climb these rocks but was disabused of this notion when he was shown a stone-built house that provided shelter for the men in between climbs.

6

Berneray (Beàrnaraigh) and North Uist (Uibhist a Tuath)

BERNERAY (BEÀRNARAIGH)

Not to be confused with Great Bernera (on Lewis) or the uninhabited island of Berneray south of Barra, this is a sleepy island of vast shell-sand beaches, hills and a tight-knit if dispersed community. If for some reason you don't feel other islands in the Outer Hebrides offer sufficient solitude, then Berneray – little more than 2 miles from both north to south and east to west – is the place to come. Most visitors discover Berneray on a day trip but often get hooked on the place and return to base themselves here for longer.

Berneray is connected by a causeway to North Uist and the island's small slipway also serves the Sound of Harris ferry and is thus the only link between the northern islands of Lewis/Harris and the Uists. Accommodation, the shop and most places of interest are scattered along the edge of Bays Loch. Berneray is working hard to maintain its cultural identity: Gaelic is widely spoken and the island has the highest percentage of people in the Outer Hebrides stating their religious denomination as Church of Scotland (60%).

In the third week of July each year, the island celebrates **Berneray Week** (page 194), a festival that, as Berneray's native Gaelic population grows older, is becoming ever more important as a means of retaining a local culture.

HISTORY As with other islands across the Outer Hebrides, Berneray's pre-history is assembled from the numerous points of archaeological interest including a standing stone and remnants of cairns. Evidence of a Norse presence is apparent in the name of the island itself, which comes from *jarnar-øy* and means either 'Bjorn's island' or, perhaps less likely, 'bear island'.

The Isle of Berneray lies at the northern end of the Uists, but its strategic position in the north of the Sound of Harris made it highly attractive to the dominant clans of the region. Historically Berneray was owned by South Harris and for centuries it was known as Beàrnaraigh na Hearadh and owned by the Macleods of Harris. Its fertility – there is little peat to be found on the island – meant that it attracted settled populations, and, during the Macleod era, potatoes were grown here specifically to feed Harris. In the late 18th and early 19th centuries, Berneray's population was more than 700, almost five times what it is today. The relatively high numbers were sustained by the kelp trade (kelp was used in the manufacture of soap and glass), but when the industry collapsed the island's fortunes took a dramatic turn for the worse. A succession of poor harvests and the potato famine of 1846–51 saw emigration on a large scale, mainly to

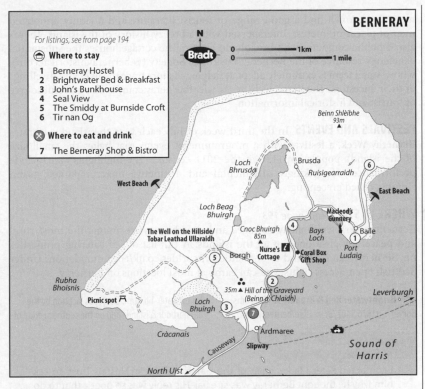

For listings, see from page 194

Where to stay

1 Berneray Hostel
2 Brightwater Bed & Breakfast
3 John's Bunkhouse
4 Seal View
5 The Smiddy at Burnside Croft
6 Tir nan Og

Where to eat and drink

7 The Berneray Shop & Bistro

Nova Scotia (Canada). The same challenges faced many neighbouring islands, and today Berneray is the only inhabited island in the Sound of Harris.

GETTING THERE AND AWAY At its southern end, Berneray is joined to North Uist by a causeway. A small car and passenger ferry, the *Port Lochatin*, plies the Sound of Harris from Leverburgh on Harris (CalMac: 0800 066 5000, from outside the UK +44 1475 650397; w calmac.co.uk) and docks at **Ardmaree (Àird Ma-Ruibhe)** on the southeast tip of Berneray. There are usually three or four sailings a day; one-way fares are £14.35 (car) and £3.80/£1.90 (passengers). Be aware that the shallow waters of the sound mean that in bad weather the service is often the first on the islands to be cancelled. On a sunlit, still morning, this is an enchanting place. If you have an early crossing, keep an eye out for turnstones pecking along the shoreline or otters slithering over the green kelp. The slipway is 10 miles from Lochmaddy on North Uist, most of it a single-track road with passing places, and a good 25-minute drive.

GETTING AROUND Berneray may be small but sights of interest are widely scattered so to some extent you need to plan your time here. The youth hostel is more than 2 miles from the Berneray Shop and Bistro, while the Nurses' Cottage lies halfway between the two. A reliable bus service connects with ferries, and stops at both Ardmaree terminal and the hostel. For up-to-date timetables, visit w cne-siar.gov. uk and use the menu to find 'bus services'.

TOURIST INFORMATION The excellent **Nurses' Cottage Visitor Centre** (⊕ May–Aug 11.00–15.00 Mon–Sat) is a community-owned venture halfway along the island's main road. You'll find a good range of tourist literature and a jaunty annotated map of places of interest, interspersed with a breezy history of the island. There's also a public computer with broadband access. The cottage houses the substantial genealogy resource of the Berneray Historical Society (w bernerayhistorical.com), whose small team is extremely adept at helping visitors trace the lives and dwellings of their ancestors. The island website (w isleofberneray.com) is also a useful source of tourist and historical information.

FESTIVALS AND EVENTS In the third week of July each year, the island celebrates **Berneray Week**, a festival with a programme of events that belies the small size of the island's population (138 at the 2011 census). The highlights can include performances of strikingly ornamental and distinctive unaccompanied psalm singing, called precenting.

 WHERE TO STAY *Map, page 193*
Berneray's very few holiday cottages and guesthouses are among the most rural and peacefully positioned of all the islands. A full list of self-catering properties on Berneray can be found at w visitouterhebrides.co.uk/accommodation. Under Scottish open access rights, you can camp at most locations on Berneray.

Brightwater Bed & Breakfast (3 rooms) Borve; \01876 540273; w isleofberneray.com/   brightwater-bb.html. Gorgeous location by the old harbour & island shop on the southern edge of

---

SMALL BUT SPECIAL

I contacted Peter Clarke, chair of the Gatliff Hebridean Hostels Trust, to ask him why he thought Berneray was special. His reply was so poetic that to do it justice it is recorded here in full.

'What makes Berneray special? Berneray is a home from home, a refuge from the wind and rain, the club which would admit Groucho Marx as a member, a place where a few friends old and new can gather over a bite to eat and enjoy each other's company around the warm stove, share tales of the hill and the road.

'The door is never closed; our hostel is open all year round. You may have the place to yourself, or you could walk in on a party! The hostel is on the edge of the sea, so hostellers can sit outside and watch the majesty of the rising tides, or wonder at the power of nature, the ever-changing scene over the Sound of Harris. Some days northern Skye and the mainland are visible. On other days, it is as if the curtains were closed. The shore of North Uist is to the south; South Harris to the north. With a keen eye or lens it is possible to see the tower of Rodel Church standing tiny beneath the hill of Roineabhal on Harris.

'Perhaps for the first time you will sleep under a thatched roof in a traditional thatched cottage, or if you prefer, in a tent under the stars. The Northern Lights are seen at the hostel in spring and autumn.

'Winters are dark. In summer, the islands are bathed in brilliant light. The sun merely dips below the horizon for a couple of hours. There is always the breeze and the possibility of rain but in the summer this all soon passes over to the mainland. If you want to be alone, you are 2 minutes' walk from Berneray's East Beach. There you can be lost in your own thoughts with the only sounds the chorus of nature: the lapping of the sea and the breeze.'

the island. 1 dbl & 2 twins. Run by the welcoming Jackie Macleod, offers traditionally furnished but spotless & cosy rooms. When the weather's behaving, Jackie's patio is a rather life-enhancing place from which to take in the sea views. Evening meals by arrangement. **££**

🏠 **Seal View** (2 rooms) 16 Backhill; 🕿 01876 540209; e andrew@sealview.com; w sealview. com. Well-run B&B with spacious rooms. Centrally positioned with every chance of seeing seals close by in Bays Loch. 1 dbl & 1 family room sleeping up to 4 (5 at a squeeze). **££**

🏠 **Tir nan Og** (2 rooms) East Beach; 🕿 01876 540333; e tirnanogberneray@btinternet.com. This restored farmhouse is situated by a sandy bay right at the far end of East Beach. 2 dbls with sea view, 1 en suite, with an extra cabin bed for children. Owners also run a seasonal café (£) serving crab rolls & homebaked goods. **££**

🏠 **Berneray Hostel** (21 beds) Baile; e ghht@ gatliff.org.uk; w gatliff.org.uk. Superbly located, perched on a headland on the east coast, overlooking East Beach (Tràigh Bheadaire). The hostel, which has something of a cult following, is based in 2 restored blackhouses with thatched roofs. The 3 dormitories are unsegregated. The sgl bed in the room known as Shady Corner, looking out through a window over the Sound of Harris,

has to be one of the best & cheapest places to wake up across the entire island chain.Modern kitchen with a Smeg cooker. The only obvious drawback is that there are just 2 toilets & 1 shower. Campers who pitch nearby can also use the washing & cooking facilities for a small fee. The hostel is part of the Gatliff Hostel chain that also operates on Harris and South Uist. Note that, as with all Gatliff hostels, you cannot book in advance but the trust promises that, even at the busiest of times, you will not be turned away. **£**

🏠 **John's Bunkhouse** (8 beds) 23 Borve; 🕿 01876 540229; e johnsbunkouse@gmail.com; w johnsbunkhouse.com. 3 rooms (2 sgl bunk rooms with shared facilities, 1 dbl bunk room en suite), suitable for guests with limited mobility. Well equipped with kitchen & guest room with peat-burning stove. Bike room. Located near ferry & ideal for cyclists tackling the Hebridean Way. **£**

Self-catering

🏠 **The Smiddy at Burnside Croft** (sleeps 2) Borve; 🕿 01876 540235; w burnsidecroft.com. Renovated to a high specification, the Smiddy is all on 1 level with category 2 (assisted) wheelchair access throughout. Prince Charles stayed here during his discreet visits as a working crofter (see box, page 196). £615–820/week. **££**

✗ **WHERE TO EAT AND DRINK** *Map, page 193*
The only place for substantial meals on the island is the **Berneray Shop and Bistro** (🕿 01876 540288; e bernerayshopandbistro@gmail.com; w bernerayshopandbistro. co.uk; ⏱ 10.00–15.00 Mon–Fri, 10.00–16.00 Sat year-round, Apr–Sep also 17.30–20.30 Mon–Sat; **££**). Recently renovated and run by North Uist couple Abigail and Ruairidh Nicholson, the building has a nautical theme which reflects the leaning towards seafood on the menus. Good food is prepared by a full-time chef including langoustines from Lochmaddy Bay, grilled lobster and spinach crêpes with ratatouille.

SHOPPING The **Berneray Shop and Bistro** (see above) for contact details; shop ⏱ 09.00–17.30) is well stocked with groceries and souvenirs. The **Coral Box Gift Shop** (w ecwid.com/store/coralbox; ⏱ Apr–Sep 10.30–17.00 Mon–Sat), located on the jetty by the harbour, is a quirky and creative seasonal mobile souvenir store run by locally born Eilidh Carr. It's an excellent place to pick up souvenirs, which include Eilidh's own photographs (she studied photography at Aberdeen University before returning to Berneray) and presents for the folks back home.

Berneray artist Sharon MacPherson (w sharonmacphersonart.com) often exhibits in the bistro and its shop. Her singular depictions of island topography and wildlife exude a good deal of grace. Sharon hopes to have a studio space on Berneray (or North Uist) within the lifetime of this edition of the guide. Raised on the island from the age of six, Sharon works not only in watercolour but in oil,

Berneray's £6.6 million causeway linking the island to North Uist was opened by Prince Charles in 1999. As the current Lord of the Isles – a title that has origins in the 12th century – he was an obvious choice for the ceremony. Since 1493 the title has been held by the eldest son and heir apparent of the King of Scotland – and, since the creation of the Kingdom of Great Britain, of the reigning monarch. The Prince famously spent time on Berneray living incognito as a crofter. He first visited in 1987, staying with Donald Alex 'Splash' MacKillop and his wife Gloria who introduced him to the daily routine and chores of crofting. He planted and lifted potatoes, cut peat, dipped sheep and planted trees. The islanders maintained a code of silence so that the visits escaped the radar of the world's media. He returned in 1991 to make a BBC documentary *A Prince Among Islands*.

Charles told islanders that he found crofting inspirational and in tune with his own philosophical outlook on farming. He is reported to have put his experience to use on his organic farm at Highgrove in Gloucestershire.

Returning for the opening of the causeway, the Prince – by that time well known for his strong views on design – praised the way the structure blended into its setting and the provision of facilities such as otter culverts near the shore and another larger culvert for fish, cetaceans and seals. He also approved of the efforts, including fencing, to keep rabbits off Berneray and from nibbling away at its precious ecology.

and graphite and charcoal. Her work, she says, is rooted in this remote landscape. 'Wanderings along the coastlines, machair and moorland on the Isle of Berneray and neighbouring islands provide limitless subjects for my work.'

OTHER PRACTICALITIES There is no bank on Berneray, though the bistro and shop take cards. Your nearest **ATM** is the Bank of Scotland in Lochmaddy. For non-urgent **medical** matters, you should contact the North Uist Medical Practice in Lochamaddy (page 204); for urgent problems you'll need the Uist and Barra Hospital in Balivanich (page 204) on Benbecula. Both are reached by causeways – no need for ferries. You'll find the **post office** (Failte, Backhill; ⊕ 09.30–13.00 Mon–Tue, Thu–Fri) just north of the Nurses' Cottage.

WHAT TO SEE AND DO Berneray's **West Beach** is hailed by many as the best across the whole of the islands. That is some claim, given the competition, but you might just agree. The whole of the west coast is effectively one unbroken strip of glistening shell sand. Oddly enough, while the beach is the island's dominant feature, it can take some getting to: it is located more than a mile away from Berneray's modest population centre, can be reached by just the one road, and the back of the beach is fenced off to prevent livestock from straying, with only a few intermittent gates to allow access. Don't be deterred though; the best way from the main east-shore road is to follow the lane inland to **Borgh**, which winds its way through the machair for 1½ miles to a picnic spot. From here, it is a short walk through a gate and across dunes to the beach.

Just back from this shoreline, Berneray's western flanks are dominated by the machair. As elsewhere, this billiard-table-smooth grassland is transformed in summer into a rainbow of wild flowers. Orchids abound, as do corn marigolds, poppies, buttercups, red clover and field gentians. Butterflies and bees are also drawn to the grass.

Back along the main road, the colonies of harbour and Atlantic grey seals in **Bays Loch,** just to the north of the harbour, are a popular attraction and they often haul out for a breather at low tide. Heading east along the road, the oldest-surviving building on Berneray is the 16th-century **Macleod's Gunnery**, situated close to the hostel. This was once the home of – and is named after – a 17th-century knight. Close by is a cluster of traditional blackhouses, some of which have now been restored.

The conspicuous building a few hundred metres north of the hostel and overlooking **East Beach** is a private home constructed from the ruins of a 19th-century church designed by Thomas Telford. The church provided one entrance for islanders and another for those who rowed over from the neighbouring island of Pabbay. The church fell into disrepair in the 1930s and suffered the indignity of having its roof stripped and shipped off to Scalpay. The process of rebuilding it in 2012–13 was documented by Channel 4 series *Restoration Man*.

Berneray also boasts a couple of decent hills to climb. In the southwest of the island, between oval-shaped Loch Bhuirgh and the Borgh road, lies **The Hill of the Graveyard** (Beinn a' Chlaidh). A 10-minute walk up this modest rise leads to **Clach Mhòr**, a standing stone nearly 2½m above ground and the same dimensions below. Also on the flanks of the hill lies **Tobar Leathad Ullaraidh** (The Well on the Hillside). The water taken from this well was always considered the most pure and fresh on the island and was used for both christenings and distilling whisky.

While whisky distilling was brought to an abrupt halt on Berneray in 1820, it continued illicitly on Pabbay. The islanders were astute enough to establish an understanding with the Sound of Harris ferryman Iain Paterson: whenever he ferried excisemen from Harris to Pabbay he would lower his sails, giving the islanders time to hide their stills. All was well until the excisemen grew suspicious and took a different boat to Pabbay and caught the islanders red-handed. The tale goes that the banning of whisky was a driver for the emigration from Pabbay that soon followed; in truth, greater forces – harvest failures, famine and premeditated clearances – were at play than whether you could get hold of a dram or two.

Another attractive and easy place to walk to is the headland at **Cràcanais** beyond the western edge of West Beach and above Loch Buirgh. There is an old graveyard here and striking views across to North Uist. Finally, open-access laws mean that you can walk around the entire coastline of Berneray (sometimes on grassy tracks, at other times on open ground), a distance of around 14½km (9 miles). This will take 3–4 hours but can make for a wonderful day's exploration, perhaps picnicking along the way on West Beach.

THE GIANT OF BERNERAY

Of all those who migrated from Berneray, none stood taller, in the most literal sense, than Angus MacAskill. Born in Siabaidh in 1825, Angus was taken by his parents to Cape Breton in Canada at the age of four. He grew to a height of 2.36m (7ft 9in) and for a while earned a living touring with the promoter Phineas T Barnum, forming a little and large act with Major Tom Thumb, who was just 90cm (3ft) tall. Angus toured Europe and met Queen Victoria, though he never returned to Berneray, and died at the age of 38 in Canada.

5½km (3½ miles); 2hrs
OS Explorer 454 North Uist & Berneray
Start/finish: Brusda (⊕ NF922826)

This short walk along the north and west edges of Berneray gives a good flavour of the lie of the land, a climb up the highest hill (Beinn Shleibhe) and a taste of the magnificent West Beach. Begin from Bays Loch by taking the road signposted for Brusda and follow it as it climbs then swoops down to a vast expanse of pancake-flat land. If driving this section, park with care so that farm vehicles can pass and turn (walking from Bays Loch to Brusda will add 1½km (1 mile) to your total walking distance). Follow the track towards the coast; it soon becomes grassy and forks as it bends to the left. Keep straight ahead on the right-hand track and aim for the small gap in the distant dunes. To your left is Loch Bhrusda, where otters often come to drink and clean their fur. Between May and September keep to the path as the machair and marshy land support ground-nesting birds. Go through the gate, up the back of the dunes and on to the beach. Turn right and walk for 800m (½ mile) along the sands. Where the beach bumps into a rocky foreshore look out for the yellow waymarker posts. These will direct you behind the beach and briefly back the way you came. After a few metres, at a fence, a clear track emerges. Turn left to follow this and the waymarkers all the way uphill to the summit and trig point of Beinn Shleibhe (pronounced 'leva'). Although just 93m (305ft), this is Berneray's highest hill and on a clear day, the views are exceptional. Much of the north coast of Uist is visible, as is Skye; perhaps the most delectable view is due north, across the Sound of Harris to the dunes and sands of Northton on South Harris, and beyond, deep into the Harris hills. With binoculars you should just be able to pick out Rodel church on the eastern edge of Harris. Countless islets and skerries break the water's surface of the Sound of Harris. Berneray is unusual in that it has no workable peatbeds, so the men of the island traditionally rowed through the Sound to cut peat where they could find it. To return, retrace your steps downhill: sometimes there is a small wooden stile in place so that you can hop over the fence and head back to Brusda; if not, you must retrace your whole route.

NORTH UIST (UIBHIST A TUATH)

On a map, North Uist looks like a half-completed island, a waterworld whose coast and hinterland has been punctuated by vast white-sand beaches, hundreds of small lochs, a few large hills and infilled with empty peat moorland. The largest loch, Loch Euphort, almost cuts the island in half.

Romantically known as Tir an Eòrna ('the land of barley'), North Uist is in many ways the easiest island to explore and nose around: not too big that you miss out on key sights, but not too small that you can zip through it.

While today's population is just 1,619, the island can feel much busier in season, when visitors congregate at the main places of interest. The islanders are strongly Protestant and, although Sunday observance is not quite as universal as on Lewis and Harris, the island is, in religious terms, more of a natural partner to its northern neighbours than to its southern ones. You still need to plan ahead: you will not be able to buy petrol or groceries on the Sabbath here (instead, head over the causeways to Benbecula).

Many people's first encounter with North Uist is the port of **Lochmaddy (Loch nam Madadh)**, which offers a pleasant if rather sleepy introduction. Its one sight as such is the excellent **Taigh Chearsabhagh Museum and Arts Centre**, though the port's rocky shoreline lends itself to some pleasant walking.

Among the island's many archaeological features, the Neolithic cairn of **Barpa Langass** is the most visually arresting; close by is the stone circle of **Pobull Fhinn**. Near the township of Solas (Sollas) on the north coast you will find the remains of the Udal wheelhouses and traces of many other settlements half-buried where the dunes meet the machair. Wildlife lovers are well rewarded. To the northwest is the **RSPB reserve of Balranald**, a true heaven for birdwatchers if ever there was one, while the single-track **Committee Road**, which cuts across the interior, is also fantastic for birdwatching. The North Uist machair sees corncrakes successfully breed most years and the recent arrival of a pair of white-tailed eagles, which nest in the plantation near Vallay on the north coast, has brought further good news: in 2019 the pair successfully reared a chick.

Along its north coast, North Uist has some of the finest **beaches** in the Outer Hebrides. These gems are usually off the beaten track, located down grassy lanes or reached only through mountainous dunes.

North Uist also has a handful of islands of its own – it's easy not even to notice when you move from one to the other along often subtle causeways – that repay exploration. **Baleshare (Baile Sear)** to the southwest is an extensive prairie-like flatland irrigated with sea lochs and channels. To the southeast, the haunting beauty of the intertidal currents of **Loch Shornaraigh** on the island of **Grimsay (Griomasaigh)** can stop visitors in their tracks. On the north coast, a tidal walk out to **Vallay (Bhalaigh)** is a mesmerising experience. Further offshore, the Monach Islands are a wonderful collection of skerries, islets and larger lumps that offer memorable wildlife watching.

While there is much to see and do, some North Uist charms reveal themselves when you are idling. This might include watching boats bring the catch of the day into **Kallin harbour** or just taking in the backdrop of the east coast, dominated by Eavel (Eabhal), North Uist's highest hill at 347m (1,138ft), whose distinctive cone shape all but collapses into the surrounding lochs, and the delightfully named twin hills Lì a Tuath (Beautiful North) and Lì a Deas (Beautiful South). Unsurprisingly, this delightful landscape has exerted a siren-like magnetism on artists; and one of the joys of visiting North Uist is the opportunity to drop in and see what the island's creatives are up to. A handy place to start is the website w uistarts.org, which lists more than 30 studios and outlets to visit.

HISTORY North Uist provides some of the earliest evidence for the presence of humans in the Outer Hebrides and has the highest density of tombs – 20 or so – on the islands. This has given rise to speculation that the island historically enjoyed an elevated religious or political status.

Among the most important settlements are those found at Udal (see box, page 217), where the imprint of a timeline running from the Neolithic all the way through to the late 19th century confirms that North Uist has consistently been considered a favourable site for human habitation.

Vikings most certainly had a presence on the island, evidence for which comes from the numerous Norse place names found here – 'Uist' itself comes from *i-vist*, a Norse word for house. Che, son of King Cruthnie who is credited with founding the Pictish kingdom, is said to be buried in a tomb on the island.

6

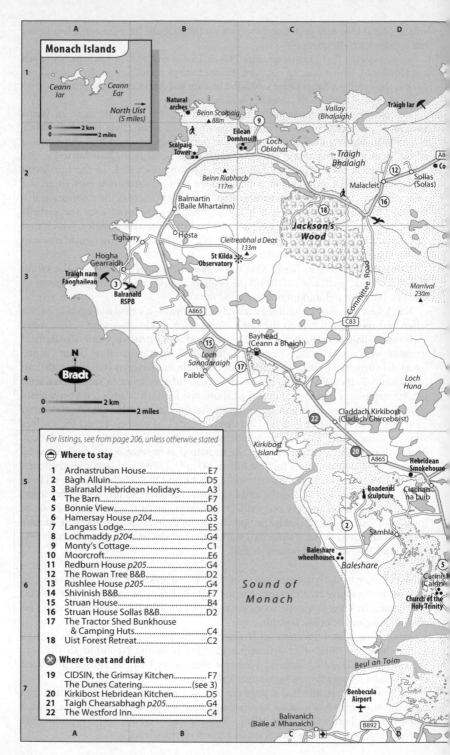

For listings, see from page 206, unless otherwise stated

Where to stay

1	Ardnastruban House	E7
2	Bàgh Alluin	D5
3	Balranald Hebridean Holidays	A3
4	The Barn	F7
5	Bonnie View	D6
6	Hamersay House *p204*	G3
7	Langass Lodge	E5
8	Lochmaddy *p204*	G4
9	Monty's Cottage	C1
10	Moorcroft	E6
11	Redburn House *p205*	G4
12	The Rowan Tree B&B	D2
13	Rushlee House *p205*	G4
14	Shivinish B&B	F7
15	Struan House	B4
16	Struan House Sollas B&B	D2
17	The Tractor Shed Bunkhouse & Camping Huts	C4
18	Uist Forest Retreat	C2

Where to eat and drink

19	CIDSIN, the Grimsay Kitchen	F7
	The Dunes Catering	(see 3)
20	Kirkibost Hebridean Kitchen	D5
21	Taigh Chearsabhagh *p205*	G4
22	The Westford Inn	C4

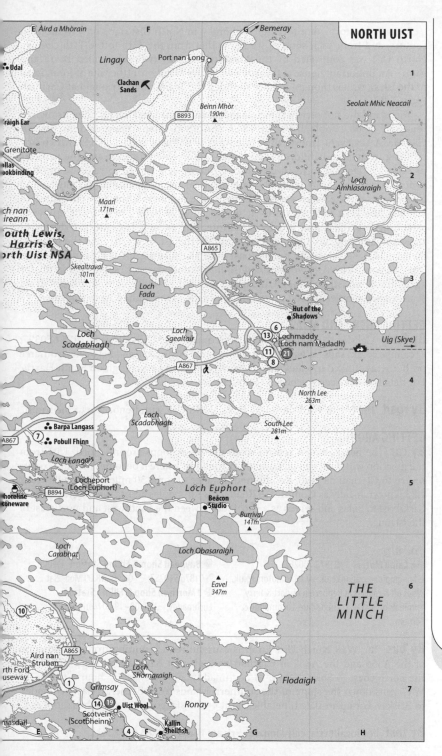

E Àird a Mhòrain

F

G ↗ Berneray

•• Udal

Lingay

Port nan Long

ràigh Ear

Clachan
Sands

Grenitote

B893

Beinn Mhòr
190m ▲

Seolait Mhic Neacail

llas
okbinding

ch nan
ireann

Loch
Amhlasaraigh

outh Lewis,
Harris &
rth Uist NSA

Maarl
171m ▲

A865

Skealtraval
101m ▲

Loch
Fada

Loch
Scadabhagh

Loch
Sgealtair

Hut of the
Shadows

A867

6

13

Lochmaddy
(Loch nam Madadh)

11

21

Uig (Skye) →

8

North Lee
263m ▲

Loch
Scadabhagh

South Lee
281m ▲

•• **Barpa Langass**

7 •• **Pobull Fhinn**

A867

Loch Langais

Locheport
(Loch Euphort)

Lóch Euphort

Beácon
Studio

B894

horeline
toneware

Burrival
141m ▲

Loch
Carabhat

Loch Obasaraigh

Eavel
347m ▲

THE
LITTLE
MINCH

10

Àird nan
Struban

A865

rth Ford
useway

1

Grimsay

Loch
Shornaraigh

Flodaigh

asdall

14 19 Uist Wool

Scotvein
(Scotbheinn)

Kallin
Shellfish

Ronay

4 F

E

G

H

Recorded history – both written and oral – in North Uist starts only in the 16th century, and from such sources we know that from the 13th to the 14th century North Uist was controlled by the MacRuairi family (who also ruled Barra and Rum). An important figure at this time was Amy MacRuairi (the wife of John, Lord of the Isles), who is thought to have founded the Teampall na Trionaid at Carinish (page 220).

The island did not escape the clearances, and Lord MacDonald, then its owner, removed 2,500 people between 1849 and 1856. Many emigrated to eastern Canada. A key event around this time was the Battle of Sollas in 1849, which saw crofters, women and children take on law enforcement officers and the workers of Lord MacDonald to resist eviction. Crofters were forced to relocate in often brutal circumstances to accommodate sheep farms; many moved to Langass and Locheport on the eastern shores, though large numbers ultimately emigrated to Canada, the USA and Australia. It would be 1899 before new townships were established at Sollas and nearby Grenitote. The ancient Hebridean industry of seaweed gathering has a modern twist on North Uist. You can't miss the seaweed factory, Uist Asco, on the north coast near the turning for the Berneray ferry. The company dries *Ascophyllum nodosum* (or knotted wrack) seaweed, mainly for agricultural industries; though, in 2017 it shipped a 3 tonne consignment of dried seaweed 3,800 miles to feed prize racing camels in the United Arab Emirates.

GETTING THERE AND AWAY

By ferry CalMac (☎0800 066 5000; from outside the UK call ☎+44 1475 650397; w calmac.co.uk) sails between Lochmaddy and Uig on Skye and between Ardmaree on Berneray (linked by causeway to North Uist) and Leverburgh on South Harris. For details of services, see pages 41 and 50.

By road The North Ford causeway links North Uist with Benbecula to the south.

GETTING AROUND

By car The heart-shaped coastal road, the A865, loops around North Uist from the junction with Clachan na Luib to Lochmaddy, where it becomes the A867 on its return to Clachan na Luib, a combined distance of some 30 miles. The single-track C83, known locally as Committee Road, cuts for 4 miles across the moors north of Kirkibost to Solas and serves as a shortcut between the southwest and northeast of the island.

Car hire
🚗 **Laing Motors** ☎01878 700267; e laingmotors@yahoo.co.uk; w laingmotors.co.uk. Drops off & collects at Benbecula Airport & ferry terminals of Eriskay, Lochboisdale, Lochmaddy & Berneray.

Petrol
⛽ **Bayhead Shop & Filling Station** Paible; ☎01876 510257; ⏱ 08.00–18.00 Mon–Sat
⛽ **J Morrison Shop & Filling Station** Lochmaddy; ⏱ 09.00–19.00 Mon–Sat

By bus The W18 North Uist Loop is a useful route, running from the junction of the A856 and the A867 at Clachan na Luib past Bayhead, to Balranald, along the north coast to Solas and on to Lochmaddy, a journey of 1½ hours. The W16/W17 runs down the spine of the southern islands from Berneray via Lochmaddy to Eriskay. For up-to-date timetables, visit w cne-siar.gov.uk (search 'bus services').

By taxi For local taxis, call **Menzies Private Hire** (m 07833 357241).

TOURIST INFORMATION The useful Visit Scotland visitor centre in Lochmaddy closed in 2018 for reasons understood only by those who made the decision. Tourist information for North Uist can be found at the village's Taigh Chearsabhagh centre (page 206). Online information can be found at w isle-of-north-uist.co.uk.

FESTIVALS AND EVENTS Events to look out for include the North Uist Highland Games and the North Uist Agricultural Show (w northuistshow.btck.co.uk), both held in July.

TOUR OPERATORS

Lady Anne Boat Trips ☎01870 602403; e ningledew@aol.com; w uistboattrips.com. Based at Kallin harbour, offers a wildlife circuit of Ronay island & exploration of bays at foot of Eaval (£30/£20). Day trips to Monach Islands (see box, page 213) & runs Bonnie Prince Charlie-themed trips, which land ashore at sites associated with the prince. Even if you tire of the omnipresent royal, this is a good trip as you see some attractive places such as Prince's cave at Glen Choradail on South Uist or Rossinish beach on Benbecula.

Western Isles Wildlife ☎01876 705665; e steveduffield70@gmail.com; w western-isles-wildlife.com. A trained biologist, Steve Duffield runs a number of timetabled themed tours & bespoke day trips (£55 pp, min 2 people) tailored to your interest, covering birds, mammals including otters, & flora. Day trips focus on the Uists & Benbecula; week-long tours go further north, taking in Lewis, Harris & the Shiant Isles, as well as Mingulay. These include accommodation & meals. Spring tours feature corncrakes, in summer the machair.

SHOPPING Run by islanders Jonny Ingledew and Kate MacDonald, **North Uist Distillery Co** (Knockline, near Bayhead; m 07763 854022; e hello@northuistdistillery.com; w northuistdistillery.com) does not yet have a shop front; instead you can order online or by phone and pick up the same day at island shops across the Uists and Benbecula. Jonny comes from a fishing background, while Kate is a native Gaelic speaker. Given their deep North Uist roots, they are committed to the island's resources and are producing their whisky from bere, a local and ancient strain of barley grown on North Uist, Orkney and few other places. 'It's a romantic notion, bere is a heritage grain that has always been grown on North Uist,' says Jonny, 'and it has a viscosity from flavoursome oils that the usual barley used for whisky lacks.' Plans for a fully fledged distillery depend on fundraising but include a shop based in a traditional blackhouse near Clachan na Luib. The couple hopes to produce whisky by 2022 or thereabouts. In the meantime, they have produced a gin, Downpour, to get things ticking. Check their website for updates.

Bayhead Shop & Filling Station Paible; ⊕ 08.00–18.00 Mon–Sat. A well-stocked local shop run by MacLean's Bakery. It has everything you need for self-catering including good frozen meals, such as roast pork in gravy for just £4.50 that can feed 2 people, & frozen desserts such as rhubarb crumble or jam & coconut sponge. Also operates a useful post office.

Co-op Solas; ⊕ 07.00–22.00 Mon–Sat. A decent supermarket with a wide range of produce, always reliably stocked.
J Morrison's Shop & Filling Station Lochmaddy; ⊕ 09.00–19.00 Mon–Sat. Stocks the basics, but its range is less diverse & more traditional than other island stores.

ACTIVITIES Ron Wyvill (☎ 01876 500296) is a local ghillie who offers inshore **fishing trips**. North Uist Angling Club at Cladach Kyles (☎01876 580341) is also a helpful source of information for anglers. The RSPB (w rspb.org, search 'Balranald') runs regular guided walks from May to September, including otter trips at Langass

Arts and crafts are a strong feature of North Uist. By following roadside signs and even looking round your accommodation, you will encounter high-quality and innovative paintings, glasswork and ceramics in cafés. Much of the enjoyment of this art is gained by stumbling upon it unexpectedly. If, however, you want to seek out a particular artist the helpful Uist Sculpture Trail (w isle-of-north-uist.co.uk/attractions/uist-sculpture-trail) provides the definitive listings.

plus tours around its Balranald reserve and the nearby Loch Sanndaraigh at Paible (RSPB members £2/non-members £5/children free).

OTHER PRACTICALITIES

Bank
$ **Bank of Scotland** Lochmaddy; \01876 500824; ⊕ 09.30–16.30 Tue–Thu. ATM.

Medical
✚ **North Uist Medical Practice** Lochmaddy; \01876 500463; w north-uist-medical.co.uk; ⊕ 08.30–17.30 Mon–Fri

✚ **Uist & Barra Hospital** Balivanich; \01870 603600; w wihb.scot.nhs.uk/ospadal-uibhist-agus-bharraigh. Also has a drop-in GP surgery.

Post offices
✉ **Bayhead Shop & Filling Station** Paible; ⊕ 10.00–13.00 Mon & Thu

✉ **Taigh Chearsabhagh** Lochmaddy; ⊕ 10.00–16.00 Mon–Fri

LOCHMADDY (LOCH NAM MADADH) Lochmaddy's diminutive size can take you by surprise, and arriving by oversized ferry at the modest waterfront can feel a little like Gulliver making landfall in Lilliput. The addition of a pontoon in 2014 has attracted launches and yachts but has yet to inject any sense of reinvigoration into what is – apart from the 30 minutes either side of the Uig ferry arrival and departure – a decidedly somnolent village. Lochmaddy does, however, have a good collection of places to stay, and North Uist is small enough that you can comfortably use it as a base for exploring the island.

⌂ **Where to stay, eat and drink** Lochmaddy has several accommodation possibilities, and a full list of self-catering options can be found at w visitouterhebrides.co.uk/accommodation.

⌂ **Hamersay House** [201 G3] (8 rooms) \01876 500700; e info@hamersayhouse.co.uk; w hamersayhouse.co.uk. A small hotel, located a couple of minutes' walk north of the village centre, strikingly painted in bright blue panels with a tasteful marine décor. Ask for a room with a view across the moors or towards the sea, not the car park. 1 room downstairs suitable for wheelchair users. There's a snug bar & a larger dining room open to non-residents. A decent & creative menu (approx £35 for 3 courses; ££) includes starters of pigeon with black pudding crumbs & mains such as poached halibut with braised octopus. £££

⌂ **Lochmaddy Hotel** [201 G4] (15 rooms) \01876 500331; e info@lochmaddyhotel.co. uk; w lochmaddyhotel.co.uk. Despite its rather domineering presence in the heart of the village overlooking the waterfront, this hotel just about warrants its 3 stars. Ask for a room with a view over the harbour – number 15 is probably the best bet. A convivial bar offers decent food (£/££): specials includes North Uist lamb casserole with chorizo mash. The slightly more formal restaurant offers scallop starters, pizzas, local steaks & seafood linguine (££). B/fast open to non-residents; pancakes a good bet for anyone arriving or departing on the morning ferry to Uig. **££**

🏠 **Rushlee House** [201 G4] (3 rooms) 📞 01876 500274; **w** rushleehouse.co.uk. Tucked away off the main road, 300m to the north of the village near Hamersay House. All dbls with en-suite showers; lounge with a homely snug feel. Drying facilities for cyclists & walkers. **££**

🏠 **Redburn House** [201 G4] (4 rooms) 📞 01876 500301; **e** info@redburnhouse.com; **w** www.redburnhouse.com. On the waterfront, next to the shop, Redburn House is an extraordinary warren of a place with something to suit everyone, from B&B to self-catering. B&B has full wheelchair access including shower. On request, owners hand over full use of kitchen, effectively turning the property into a self-catering rental. In addition, a self-contained apt sleeps 12 in 5 bedrooms across the top 2 floors. A recently built split-level 1-bedroom annex sleeps 3 adults or a young family. Separate from the house but still in the grounds is the Boat House, a self-catering property (sleeps 5). Self-catering £420–720/week **£**, B&B **££**

✖ **Taigh Chearsabhagh** [201 G4] 📞 01870 603970; **w** taigh-chearsabhagh.org; ⏰ 10.00–16.00 Mon–Sat. Housed in the arts centre on the waterside north of the ferry terminal, the café serves excellent cakes, rolls, local salmon & coffee. In good weather, ask for the outside seating area, which can be easy to miss. **£**

🚶 **AROUND LOCHMADDY AND THE HUT OF THE SHADOWS**

6½km (4 miles) if bridge is open, 9½km (6 miles) if closed; 1½–2½hrs
OS Explorer 454 North Uist & Berneray
Start/finish: Lochmaddy quayside

This engaging walk explores the creeks around Lochmaddy and an unusual camera obscura. From the quayside, walk past Lochmaddy Hotel and turn right by the petrol pumps, signposted to the Uist Outdoor Centre. Bear first right to follow a small shoreline loop road past a tiny harbour; despite the abandoned boats and boarded-up houses, the woodland along the shore makes for a picturesque setting. Walk up the lane to the crossroads and turn right past Hamersay House hotel. Keep going along the road as it becomes a track and veers to the right. Go through a kissing gate and follow the narrow path to the slim suspension bridge ahead. You will often see red deer fording the strong currents of water here. The tall and austere, three-storey building ahead is the Sponish House, once home to the island sheriff and subsequently part of a seaweed-processing factory.

Once across the bridge, turn right following the sign for the Hut of the Shadows, which is just a few metres along the shore. The hut's turfed roof gives it a Neolithic appearance. The reason for its name (Both nam Faileas in Gaelic) becomes evident once you enter and your eyes adjust: this is actually a camera obscura and a live moving picture of Lochmaddy is projected on to the back wall.

When you leave, close the rickety gate to keep sheep out. Continue along the shore, following waymarkers that soon lead you uphill, with a large shed down to your right. Make your way across to the obvious cattle grid and gate then walk up the track, with a house on the right, along the shores of Loch Houram. At the main road, turn left to return to Lochmaddy.

Note: At the time of publication the suspension bridge was closed for safety reasons. Plans to reopen it have been delayed while ownership and responsibilities for the required work are established. If the bridge is still closed, you can get to the camera obscura by doing this walk in reverse to reach the hut and then retracing your steps.

What to see and do The main sight – the *only* manmade attraction – in Lochmaddy is the arts centre, **Taigh Chearsabhagh** ✳ [201 G4] (✆ 01870 603970; w taigh-chearsabhagh.org; ⊕ 10.00–17.00 Mon–Sat; museum £3/£1.50), which houses an excellent small museum, a good bookshop, a temporary exhibition space and a fine café (page 205). Originally built as an inn in 1741, the centre is an important cultural focus for the local community. The museum often showcases displays from St Kilda, such as the messages islanders squeezed into bottles and cast into the sea, in the hope that they would reach the mainland. The centre is also home to an important genealogy database.

Although small, Lochmaddy has an incredibly indented coastline. Author Mairi Hedderwick (of *Katie Morag* fame) has observed that, should you walk in and out of every indentation of the village's shoreline and be prepared to get your feet wet, you will clock up 70km (43 miles) and 'still be in hailing distance of the tourist office'.

Autumn brings livestock from across the Uists to Lochmaddy for auction. It can be fascinating to watch the selling of cattle and sheep before they are transported off the islands in large trucks to the mainland and onwards to market.

AROUND NORTH UIST For the most part the circular A865 keeps close to the coast and gives easy access to the key sites on North Uist. The route described from page 209 heads in a clockwise direction from Lochmaddy.

🏠 **Where to stay** In addition to accommodation options highlighted below, many self-catering properties are available to rent on North Uist. A good selection is listed at w visitouterhebrides.co.uk/accommodation.

🏠 **Langass Lodge** [201 E5] (11 rooms) Locheport; ✆ 01876 580285; e langasslodge@ btconnect.com; w langasslodge.co.uk; ⊕ Easter– Oct. One of surprisingly few places on the islands that conveys the ambience of a historical Highland hotel, this former hunting lodge has tastefully decorated rooms with fine tweed curtains, swish soaps, & cups & teapots from Anta pottery near Inverness. There are 5 rooms in the atmospheric main lodge & 6 in a modern but thoughtfully decorated, light annex, where there is a good-sized family room that can sleep 5. Some of the annex rooms have French windows on to the garden; all have good views across to Eavel & Grimsay. Although the grassy play area is small, the surrounding flanks of Beinn Langass & the loch shore are a wonderful natural playground. The lodge is perfectly positioned for the walk to Barpa Langass & Pobull Fhinn. The hotel restaurant (£££) can hit high spots, especially with local venison & fish dishes such as halibut with quinoa or turbot with mushroom risotto, but is sufficiently expensive to be something of a special-occasion experience. There is a snug traditional bar & a lighter, more open, bar that looks out over the island. £££

🏠 **Ardnastruban House** [201 E7] (2 rooms) Grimsay; ✆ 01870 602452; w ardnastruban-house.co.uk. 1 dbl & 1 twin, both en suite. Guests' lounge & dining room. Close to Shivinish & just off the main road, on the southern shores of the Grimsay circular road. Friendly hosts Margaret & Stewart Wiseman welcome you with a hot drink & homemade cake. Sitting down with an OS map, they will highlight local places of interest. The communal dining table offers views over the channel that separates Grimsay from Benbecula. It's unusual to find much more than a lawn around most properties in the islands but Ardnastruban is an exception. 'I'm a keen gardener but have found during the 13 years we have lived here that gardening in the Hebrides – although often rewarding – is a constant challenge, being dependent on the weather, particularly the wind,' says Margaret candidly. 'It's possible to grow a wide range of plants here because we seldom get frost & have plenty of long summer days. Escallonia, hebe, senecio & fuchsia do extremely well, as does hawthorn, but climbers are a disaster.' ££

✳ 🏠 **Bàgh Alluin** [200 D5] (2 rooms) Baleshare; ✆ 01876 580370; w jacvolbeda. co.uk. This strikingly designed house, with large windows giving views right across North Uist, has an isolated location on Baleshare. The house is the home of expressionistic Dutch artist Jac Volbeda & is to a large extent a homage to the owner's personality & his work: quirky & a little unconventional. Jac's often large-scale, evocative, slightly abstract landscape acrylic paintings decorate much of the property. Both bedrooms are light, airy & stylishly fitted with matching pine beds & window frames & leather chairs. The dbl is upstairs while the downstairs twin is suitable for travellers with limited mobility (there is a ramp to the property). Jac is good company & happy to talk about the islands. 'I came here for the first time in winter & stayed for 6 months. When I first arrived on the ferry in Tarbert, I felt like I was coming home. I'm not like the Pope kissing the ground, but every time I come back from a trip I'm so happy.' He will also discuss his work: 'My pictures are not of specific places; they are just my feelings, how I felt on the day I went for a walk, or when I painted it,' he says. 'I've always been inspired by coastal scenery. You get vibrant colours in summer, while in winter my pictures are completely different. I start on a blank canvas & never know quite what I will paint. Sometimes it's quite easy, sometimes it's a struggle but people seem to like them.' B/fast is continental but generous. **££**

🏠 **Bonnie View** [200 D6] (2 rooms) 19 Carinish; 📞 01876 580211; e bonnnieview19@ yahoo.co.uk. The view certainly is bonnie here – as is the welcome from owner Heather Morrison – looking out across the bays around Benbecula & Baleshare with St Kilda visible on a clear day. Traditional décor in snug, spotless rooms, both en suite. Set back from main road, just south of Clachan junction. **££**

🏠 **The Rowan Tree B&B** [200 D2] (3 rooms) 4b Middlequarter, Solas; 📞 01876 560445; e enquiries@therowantree.co.uk; w therowantree. co.uk. Decent-sized, comfortable rooms at this friendly north-coast B&B, run by Alistair & Linda Hopper. Disabled access with ramp to front door & specially adapted ground-floor room. This & 1 upstairs room overlook hills where golden eagles are often sighted; the upstairs back bedroom overlooks the machair, coast & silhouette of St Kilda. As Linda says: 'When we were thinking of moving here, we just thought that was a nice view to look at while we were washing up the dishes.' A small reading area on the 1st floor has a selection of

DVDs, including *Whisky Galore!* (perfect for a rainy day). Eggs for b/fast come from the hosts' chickens. DBB options for residents only (£14 pp) include homemade fish pie, spaghetti bolognese & Alistair's speciality, cranachan, the traditional Scottish dish of oats, cream, whisky & raspberries. **££**

🏠 **Shivinish B&B** [201 F7] (2 rooms) Grimsay; 📞 01870 602481; w shivinish.net. Modern B&B on the southern side of the circular road around Grimsay. Friendly welcome from Anne MacKinnon, who will offer her home-baked cakes on arrival. Both rooms (1 dbl, 1 twin) en suite. Min stay 2 nights. **££**

✳ 🏠 **Struan House** [200 B4] (1 room) Knockintorran; 📞 01876 510787; e enquiries@northuistbedandbreakfast.com; w northuistbedandbreakfast.com; ⏰ Apr–Sep. Just 1 dbl at this peaceful B&B in the northwest of the island, thoughtfully decorated in cream & pastel colours. Level access makes it suitable for travellers with reduced mobility. Floor-to-ceiling windows in b/fast room & a telescope allow you to watch wildlife as you eat. Award-winning garden brims with flowers tended by owners Anne & Graeme Robertson, who use a low stone perimeter wall to protect shrubs from gales. Graeme used to work for the RSPB, knows his birds & describes his garden, which overlooks Loch Sanndaraigh, as 'corncrake central'. A hefty 106 bird species have been sighted from the house; these include a hen harrier that feasts on the starlings roosting in the stunted garden trees & a white-tailed eagle that picks off wigeon from the loch, which is also home to a family of otters. A lovely place to stay, where the company of your hosts makes it that extra bit special. **££**

🏠 **Struan House Sollas B&B** [200 D2] (3 rooms) Solas; 📞 01876 560385; e shonnieshep@ hotmail.com; w struanhousesollas.co.uk. Beautifully & lovingly furnished house enjoying pole position overlooking the Strand towards Vallay & Tràigh Ear. 1 dbl, 1 twin & 1 family room with either en-suite or private facilities. Warm welcome guaranteed from hosts Peggy & John MacPhee. Evening meals available (£22 for 3 courses) including seafood platters, chicken & bacon with leek & crêpes with chocolate sauce. **££**

Camping
⛺ **The Tractor Shed Bunkhouse & Camping Huts** [200 C4] Paible; m 07952 163080;

w northuistbunkhouse.co.uk; ⊕ Apr–Oct.
Innovative turf-roof huts & bunkhouses with
showers/cooking facilities. **£/££**

⚲ Balranald Hebridean Holidays [200
A3] Hougharry; ☎ 01876 510304; e info@
balranaldhebrideanholidays.com;
w balranaldhebrideanholidays.com. 14 camping
pitches & 15 caravan sites with electric hook-ups.
Ideally positioned, as name suggests, for RSPB
reserve. **£**

⚲ Moorcroft [201 E6] Carinish; ☎ 01876
580305; e morrisons17@hotmail.com;
w moorcroftholidays.co.uk. Just off A865, 1 mile
south of Carinish. Beautifully positioned for views
of the southern islands. Hot showers, kitchen &
dining table. Also offers camping pods (**£**), branded
as Hobbit Homes, complete with futons, & there's a
bunkhouse on site with 3 twin bedrooms (**£**). **£**

Self-catering

✳ **🏠 Uist Forest Retreat** [200 C2] Claddach
Vallay; ☎ 01876 560894; m 07799 066277;
e hello@uistforestretreat.co.uk; w uistforestretreat.
co.uk ; see ad, 3rd colour section. Stunning collection
of 3 self-catering treehouses, each sleeping 2, in the
forest overlooking the tidal sands of Vallay. Owners

Kathryn & Angus Johnson are passionate about their
island & its natural environment & this is reflected in
the design of the lodges. Think freestanding baths,
gorgeous furnishings, turfed roof, with stunning
views across the strand towards Pabbay, wood-
burning stoves. Prices range from £130/night (low
season, min stay 3 nights) to £1,225/week (high
season). Water comes from a borehole 52m below
ground. The couple have a licence to place a camera
overlooking the white-tailed eagle nest in the
woods. **£££**

🏠 Monty's Cottage [200 C1] (sleeps
2) Griminish, near Hosta; ☎ 01835 822277;
w unique-cottages.co.uk, search 'Monty's Cottage'.
This exquisitely restored crofthouse served as
home for Monty Hall during his TV series *Monty
Hall's Great Hebridean Escape*. Atmospheric fittings
including multi-fuel stove amid open-plan design
& wood-shuttered windows. £675/week. **££**

🏠 The Barn [201 F7] (sleeps 3) Grimsay;
☎ 01870 602074; w thebarngrimsay.co.uk. Floor-
to-ceiling windows & decking area allow visitors to
make the most of the cottage's beautiful position,
overlooking sea lochs that cut between Benbecula,
Grimsay & North Uist. £600/week. **£**

✕ Where to eat and drink

✕ The Westford Inn [200 C4] West Ford;
☎ 01876 580653; w westfordinn.com; ⊕ noon–
23.00 Mon–Thu, noon–midnight Fri, noon–01.00
Sat, 12.30–23.00 Sun, food service ⊕ noon–
14.00 & 17.30–21.00 Tue–Sat, noon–15.00 &
17.30–21.00 Sun. After the dramatic takeover of
the Carinish Inn at Clachan na Luib by the Free
Church of Scotland in 2008 (which prompted
inevitable tabloid headlines of 'pews not booze';
don't turn up at the church looking for Sun lunch),
North Uist has got a pub back. Located just a
few paces up the road from Claddach Kirkibost,
this venture is run by Eilidh & Colin Murray,
who manage to keep regulars & visitors happy
while bringing up a young family. Starters cover
all bases, ranging from haggis & cheese melt
to smoked salmon; mains include homemade
monkfish scampi, highly regarded steaks, Cajun-
spiced chicken & fried local haddock. Try the
crofters board, a selection of meat, local smoked
fish, cheeses, bread, salad & red onion marmalade
(£21.90). The bar is one of very few on the islands
not attached to a hotel & opens on to what is an

equally rare beer garden. Extensive wine list &
ales from across the Minch on Skye, plus a peat-
burning stove makes this a cosy place. Frequent
music nights have quickly transformed the inn
into a popular destination. **££**

✕ CIDSIN, the Grimsay Kitchen [201 F7]
Caenn na h-Àirigh; ☎ 01870 603359; e info@
grimsay.org; w grimsay.org/cafe; ⊕ Apr–Sep
11.00–16.00 Tue–Fri, Feb–Mar & Oct–Dec 11.00–
16.00 Wed–Fri. This small café is very much what
the Outer Hebrides are all about: the unexpected
gem set back from the main tourist routes.
Established by the tireless Dana MacPhee (who
also runs Uist Wool; page 221) the café is housed
in Grimsay's community centre & sells cakes & hot
food using ingredients grown in the centre's own
greenhouse. Occasionally opens for Sat lunches in
the high season – check website. **£**

✕ The Dunes Catering [200 A3] Balranald
Hebridean Holidays campsite; ⊕ May–Sep
11.00–15.00 Mon–Fri, 11.00–16.00 Sat–Sun. A
decent seasonal mobile food kitchen serving cakes,
soup & rolls. **£**

✳ ✕ **Kirkibost Hebridean Kitchen** [200 D5]
Claddach Kirkibost Community Centre; ☎ 01876
580390; w claddach-kirkibost.org/our-cafe;
🕑 10.00–16.00 Mon–Sat, shorter hours in winter.
A truly fantastic café overlooking the waters that
separate North Uist from Baleshare & Kirkibost
Island. Doorstep sandwiches filled with flaky
salmon, delicious leek & potato soup (wee bowl
£4.50, big bowl £5.95) & excellent oatcakes with
Uist crab or peat-smoked sea trout (£10.50).
Cakes are good & come in substantial portions.
Strike lucky & cream-filled profiteroles won't have
sold out by the time you arrive. Food served in a
cosy setting surrounded by ever-changing local
artwork. A small but good collection of homemade
chutneys & books for sale. The centre also serves
as a cultural & social enterprise hub for the local
community. £

What to see and do The A867 from Lochmaddy to Clachan na Luib is probably
the best-maintained stretch of road in the Outer Hebrides and cuts a canyon-like
route through the gneiss and moorlands. Some 4 miles west of Lochmaddy is the
signposted turning for **Barpa Langass** [201 E4], a Neolithic tomb dramatically
perched below the summit of Beinn Langass. The chambered cairn is a large
circular structure 25m in diameter; on its east side, a small concave forecourt leads
to the entrance passage. This leads to an internal burial chamber, the walls of which
comprise six huge slabs of stone that support a corbelled roof. You used to be able
to enter the cairn and nose around, but the 2011 collapse of a passageway means
that – at the time of writing – this is closed and it is dangerous to try and access it.
Things may change as the local archaeological group is working on reopening it.

The site is one of the oldest standing buildings in northern Europe. Thought
to have been used continually for more than 1,000 years, it may have served a
communal purpose rather than been designated for an important leader. Tombs
such as Barpa Langass were built across the Outer Hebrides. Excavations close to
the cairn have revealed evidence for a settlement site. Prevailing thinking suggests
that local Neolithic peoples regarded their ancestors as integral to their world view,
so such tombs acted as social or territorial signifiers and perhaps offered links
between the living and the dead. Unusually, the tomb is not aligned with either the
winter or summer solstice.

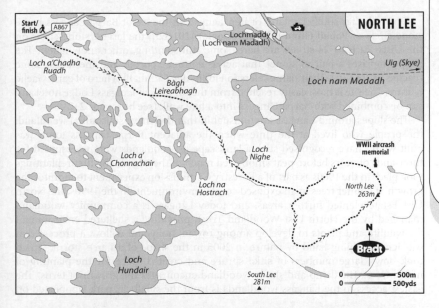

16km (10 miles); 5hrs
OS Explorer 454 North Uist & Berneray
Start/finish: roadside, 1½km (1 mile) southwest of Lochmaddy (✤ NF894679)

This fine walk is a good deal easier than tackling North Uist's landmark hill, Eavel, and has the bonus of rewarding views of the island's watery landscape from the summit of North Lee (Lì a Tuath). The name is appropriate, as it means 'Beautiful North' in Gaelic and overlooks the second largest area of sealoch in Europe. The walk also passes under the shadow of South Lee (Lì a Deas), or the 'Beautiful South'.

If driving, there is space either side of the start point to park; alternatively, you can walk from Lochmaddy, which will add a total of 3km (2 miles) to the walk.

The area around North Lee is designated a Special Area of Conservation on account of its inlets, bays, bog plants, red deer, raptors and wading birds, so look out for bulbous and meadow buttercups, sheep's sorrel, short-eared owl and, with luck, golden and white-tailed eagles.

This route is well signposted and, after passing through a roadside gate, you follow a track southeast directly towards the hill. The route passes north of Loch a'Chadha Ruadh, crosses a stile to open moorland and weaves north of Loch na Hostrach and to the south of Loch Nighe. At the foot of the hill, cross a fence and bear right (south) to begin the ascent of the hill from the southwest. The route is clear all the way to the summit.

Continue northeast for a further 350m to the trig point and then start to descend. You will pass a memorial to a World War II aircrash in which all ten crew members died. Continue to descend, following a gentle anticlockwise direction to return to the path that leads back to the A867.

Down the far southern flank of Ben Langas, in the lee of Barpa Langass is the stone circle of **Pobull Fhinn** (**Fingal's People**) [201 E5], the largest stone circle on the Uists. At least 24 stones are here, some still standing, others now fallen. The ring comprises a pair of stones that act as entrance portals and the tallest stone reaches to 2m (7ft). Their name refers to Fionn Mac Cumhaill, a hero of early Gaelic culture. The site is most easily reached from the car park at Langass Lodge hotel and can be combined with Barpa Langass into a fine walk (see box, page 212).

The slopes around Langass are unusual in that they have substantial **woodland**: the people who lived at the time when the adjacent Barpa Langass tomb was built would have recognised such a landscape as woodlands were widespread for thousands of years before peat smothered much of the island. The first replantings took place in the 1960s as part of a Forestry Commission experiment to monitor the growth of conifer trees in an exposed coastal environment. In the 1990s, the North Uist Estate planted further areas, and today Langass is a community woodland managed by the North Uist Woodland Trust, providing a sheltered environment for wildlife and plants to develop among rowan, holly and willow, a process that was lent a helping hand by nature in 2005 in the shape of a fierce storm, which took down large numbers of sitka spruce and created space for the planting of native trees. The damp and shady woodland encourages the growth of ferns. The easiest access to the Langass woodlands is from the small car park signposted off the A867 (this is a few hundred metres north of the turning for Barpa Langass car park). From here a network of footpaths twists and turns through the woods and is particularly suitable for children. Small songbirds that you will not commonly encounter elsewhere on the islands can be seen here, including chaffinch, siskin, willow warbler (in summer), pied wagtail, robin, wren and goldcrest. Sooner or later, the paths lead to the grave of Hercules the bear (see box, below). If in doubt, just follow the waymarked bear paw prints.

Just west of Langass, the 6-mile dead-end B894 along the shores of **Loch Euphort** is worth exploring. Several artists have studios along here. Near the A867 is **Shoreline Stoneware Gallery** ✳ [201 E5] (↘01876 580697; e louise.shoreline@gmail.com; w shoreline-stoneware.co.uk; ⊕ Easter–Oct 10.00–17.00 Mon–Sat, 14.00–17.00 Sun, other times, whenever the sign is out; see ad, page 222). This is the studio and home of Louise Cook, a sculptor who draws heavily on the resources of the shores. Her pottery is beautifully and unusually shaped, sometimes echoing clay wicker baskets or resembling abstract shallow bowls. It's the colours that are most eye-catching, embellished by materials Louise finds on the beach. 'I'm a prolific scavenger on the shore,' she laughs. 'I use a lot of natural material that I find on the beach to provide me with the right texture to incorporate into the surface design of different pieces.' These include shells, rocks, seaweed, fishing nets and plastic bottles. Louise uses recycled glass to give a watery rockpool effect to her bowls; and the fine glacial till of the beach as a glaze to give her work a golden-chestnut tone. 'You can feel some of the texture coming through, so it still retains some of the honesty of the material,' she adds. As I leave her studio, Louise laughs again and

WHEN A BEAR ROAMED NORTH UIST

One unlikely animal you'll find in the Langass woods is Hercules the bear, who is buried here, close to a 2m (7ft) tall statue commemorating him and his improbable – but true – adventures in the Outer Hebrides.

Bought as a cub from a wildlife park in Aviemore, Hercules featured in Disney movies and the James Bond film *Octopussy*. He came to worldwide notice in 1980 when he went on the run around Benbecula and North Uist. Hercules had been 'resting' in between scenes for a toilet-paper advert: his owner took him for a swim along the coast of Benbecula when the rope snapped, and off Hercules went. He evaded capture for 23 days, giving the slip to the army, police and hundreds of volunteer searchers. At one point, the search was called off, and it was assumed he had either drowned or starved to death. Then he was spotted by a crofter on North Uist, some 20 miles from where he escaped, shot with a tranquilliser gun and airlifted back to his owners at Lochmaddy. He had lost 127kg (20 stone) in weight, because, being domesticated, he was clueless as to how to forage for berries and other food. Yet this inability may have saved his life: since he was habituated to humans, he had no concept of attacking anyone. The saga provided the inspiration for a rather moving novel, *The Summer of the Bear*, by Bella Pollen. The Londoner was 19 and on holiday on Benbecula with her two younger siblings while the drama unfolded. Pollen's story is not centred on Hercules but tells of a mother and her three children who retreat to the Outer Hebrides to try to make sense of the sudden death of the children's father. Jamie, the youngest child, struggles to understand where his father is and comes to believe that the escaped bear is his father.

says: 'What I do is a lot of fun. I probably smile too much when I'm working.' Louise is the kind of person who can inspire you to do the same.

At road's end, Fiona Pearson produces her watercolours at the **Beacon Studio** [201 G5] (✆ 01876 580274; ⊕ 10.00–17.00 daily). Fiona is the driving force behind the Uist Studio Trail and her paintings specialise in landscapes in oil and watercolours that capture the dreamy interplay of colour to be found on the island. Fiona's studio is not a formal gallery as such but she is always happy to talk about her art and its relationship with North Uist.

The A867 continues to a T-junction with the A865 at Clachan na Luib. Turning right (north), the **Hebridean Smokehouse** [200 D5] (✆ 01876 580209; w hebrideansmokehouse.com; ⊕ 08.00–17.30 Mon–Fri, 09.00–17.00 Sat) is located 300m on the left. As with many food outlets on the islands, you should not be deterred by an unpromising exterior that resembles a corrugated air-raid shelter, for inside the tiny shop sells native strains of peat-smoked salmon, along with gravlax, trout, scallops and pâté. They also offer a mail-order service.

The viewing gallery is worth a few minutes of your time. Here you can see fish being gutted, filleted and cured before being placed in the smoking kilns. The effect is rather like that of *The Lion, the Witch and the Wardrobe* as you follow the process through the kiln and out the other side where tweezers are used to remove the pinbone from the smoked fish (these are deliberately left in during the smoking process to prevent the meat collapsing) before the product is packaged.

All fish here is farmed – wild salmon populations across the Outer Hebrides could not remotely begin to sustain demand – but the fish used are Hebridean, descended

🚶 AROUND LANGASS

4km (2½ miles); 2hrs
OS Explorer 454 North Uist & Berneray
Start/finish: car park on A867 by Barpa Langass (⊕ NF835658)

The chambered cairn and Pobull Fhinn stone circle can be visited on a reasonably easy circular walk. This is a beautiful short hike with every chance of seeing red deer, especially early morning, birds such as stonechat and between May and August, cuckoos. The surrounding slopes are also something of a nursery ground for fledgling golden and white-tailed eagles. From the car park for Barpa Langass on the A867, turn left and walk down the road for 200m to the turning for Langass Lodge. Walk along the track past the hotel to the high deer gate. Go through this and follow the track towards the loch then uphill along the recently laid track (part of the Hebridean Way; see box, page 50). This climbs away from the jetty up the slopes of Ben Langass. Pobull Fhinn is a short distance off to the right, the stones rising out of the heather. Continue up the track towards the brow of the hill and then turn sharp left off the main path up a grassy track following wooden waymarkers. There's a short spell of open ground where you must thread your way around the soggier parts until you reach a trig point. There are fine 360° views here, with much of Benbecula laid out to the south, the mountains of South Uist behind and Eaval dominating the foreground. Barpa Langass is clearly visible downhill and the route is waymarked by posts; there are boards to help with most boggy stretches. From the cairn, a gravel path leads back to the car park.

MONACH ISLANDS

Also known as Heisker, there was once a low-tide land connection between the Monach Islands and North Uist, but the former were marooned by an extraordinary storm in medieval times. They now lie 5 miles northwest of North Uist. The islands have the world's second-largest colony of grey seals, with around 8,000 pups born here every autumn. The islands are also an important overwintering area for several hundred barnacle geese, while hundreds of greylag geese and fulmars breed here. The islands have been uninhabited since 1949 but are still grazed by sheep, and fishermen use the old schoolhouse for shelter in summer. A handful of boat operators (page 76) offer trips out here.

from local wild stocks and raised in freshwater hatcheries on the rocky east coast before being reared for two years in low-density seawater lochs. The smokehouse claims to be unique in using Scottish native strains – other Scottish-farmed salmon is of Norwegian genetic origin. You will notice the difference between the end product here and what you generally find in supermarkets back home: there is none of those telltale big white lines of fat or grease; instead the fish is firm and moist.

The excellent café at the **Claddach Kirkibost Community Centre** (page 209) is just a mile or so north up the A865.

Just north of Kirkibost is the community of **Paible**, which skirts around the Atlantic shoreline. At its heart is the freshwater **Loch Sanndaraigh** [200 B4] and, just to the north, the salty **Loch Paible**. These watery worlds make for wonderful birdwatching territory and the area is home to 30 breeding pairs of corncrake: visit late evening in late spring or summer and you will be treated to a haunting, rasping chorus of these birds, though they generally remain hidden amid the iris leaves or among nettle patches on croft land. In 2016, a gyrfalcon caused a stir when it flew in, almost certainly from Greenland, promptly caught a goose and ate it on the croft land at Balemore adjacent to Loch Sanndaraigh. You can find some remarkable video and images online of the sated bird looking as if it knows it has over-eaten, but that the meal was just too good to give up.

Towards the northwest edge of the A865, follow the brown sign for **Raon Gleidhteachas Bhaile Raghnail (Balranald Nature Reserve RSPB)** [200 A3] (✆01463 715000; w rspb.org.uk, search 'Balranald'; ⊕ always; visitor centre at Goular Cottage ⊕ Apr–Aug 09.00–18.00 daily). Turn left on to this road and follow it until it splits near the township of Hogha Gearraidh. Take the left fork, signposted (accurately if prosaically) 'toilets', to reach the car park and the whitewashed visitor centre.

This is the premier and most accessible nature reserve on the southern islands with 650ha of sandy beaches, rocky foreshore, machair, marshes and dunes. Many wading and farmland birds nest on the flower-rich machair, and this is the best place to hear and even see rasping corncrakes and corn buntings with their more rattling song. An information centre explains the importance of traditional crofting for these birds and other wildlife. Spring in particular is sensational here: skuas and divers out at sea and huge flocks of turnstone, purple sandpiper, dunlin and sanderling along the shoreline. In summer, there's a perpetual stand-off between nesting lapwings and predators seeking their chicks: the protective parents regularly give chase to crows and do not stop their 'mobbing' attacks until danger has passed. Autumn heralds the arrival of large numbers of the Greenland population of barnacle geese which graze in densely packed flocks. Winter brings

Berneray (Beàrnaraigh) and North Uist (Uibhist a Tuath)   NORTH UIST (UIBHIST A TUATH)

6

213

crowds of starlings feeding on the fields and high-tide line, whooper swans and hunting merlins attracted by mixed flocks of skylark, twite and snow bunting.

The machair here has other gems too, including the northern colletes, a solitary mining bee that has rebounded after the colony here was all but wiped out by a storm in 2005. The great yellow bumblebee also thrives here, thanks to the flower-rich machair, late cutting, and ungrazed land that provides the continuous supply of nectar the creature requires.

Wildlife aside, the landscape of Balranald is sublime; the sand here is formed of shells rather than rock, has a pale Caribbean colour to it and is dispersed by the winds far inland. A signposted **nature trail** guides you for 3 miles around the reserve, following tracks to Tràigh Iar, around the headland and back along the edge of Tràigh nam Faoghailean. It's a beautiful, astonishing landscape where you can feel as though you are walking through a blizzard of green and white.

Back on the A865 and a short way beyond Balranald is a waymarked turning inland for the St Kilda observatory. A winding road leads up the hill of **Cleitreabhal a Deas** [200 C3] to a telescope where you can get good views of St Kilda, though it is visible to the naked eye in good weather. Keep an eye on developments a couple of miles due north of the viewpoint: outline planning approval has been granted for a St Kilda visitor centre and viewing point to be developed on the summit of Beinn Riabhach. In addition to providing displays about the island – with less emphasis on its evacuation in 1930 – the community behind the project hopes to provide information on other deserted and depopulated islands, including Boreray, the Monach Islands and Vallay. As with similar plans in Uig on Lewis (page 129), securing the funding remains the issue.

The north of North Uist is an empty place indeed, with few townships but often striking stone walls that climb the steepest of hills then finally peter out. These divide farming land into historical runrigs, such as those around Baile Mhàrtainn, where farmers would each take an annual turn of a strip of land, ensuring no-one gained a long-term advantage over their neighbour. The few 'sights' in the conventional sense include **Scolpaig Tower** [200 B2], which enjoys a watery location overlooked by Beinn Scolpaig. This striking hexagonal tower, planted firmly in Loch Scolpaig, looks from a distance as dramatic as any broch but is in fact a folly dating to the 1830s. Look closer, however, and you may see some remnants of the original *dùn* on which it was constructed, together with long-crumbled blackhouses on the south side of the loch. To reach the tower walk west, around the south of the loch, from a track off the A865.

If you're looking for a little natural drama, head for the sea arches that lie tucked behind Beinn Scolpaig. To reach them, continue along the track for 350m past the tower and farm until it peters out. Then contour clockwise around Beinn Scolpaig for about ¾ mile and you will find yourself pretty much on top of the arches. Take care as this is one of those Outer Hebrides innocuous coastal strips that suddenly transforms into a cliff edge abrupt enough to shake you out of any reverie.

A little further on, Loch Olabhat is home to a small, artificial islet, **Eilean Domhnuill** [200 C2], one of the Uists' most important sites of Neolithic activity. The collection of stones, marooned in this freshwater loch, once formed a small settlement. The upper layers of the site still keep just above the water surface, something that says much about its history: it's thought that gradually rising water levels forced the inhabitants to repeatedly dump rubbish and rubble to enable them to keep living on the islet. To reach the loch, turn left off the A865 on to the small track towards Griminis. Turn left again and walk around the south side of the loch. The promontory can be accessed on foot, but Eilean Domhnuill is fenced off and you must settle for the view from the loch's peaty edges.

The A865 then veers to the southeast around vast Vallay Bay. The island of Vallay itself is separated from North Uist at high tide but can be reached across the sandy strands of Tràigh Bhalaigh at low tide. The island is uninhabited and is the site of the ruined mansion of Erskine Beveridge, a textile manufacturer and archaeologist who conducted important fieldwork in the Outer Hebrides in the late 19th and early 20th centuries.

The northeast of North Uist is designated a Special Protection Area for divers, and the area supports 40 pairs of red-throated divers and five pairs of black-throated divers. A turning here marks the start of the **C83 Committee Road** [200 D3], a single-track thoroughfare that passes no site of human habitation and heads southwest across the island back to Kirkibost. The road is a good place to simply park up and wait for birds such as short-eared owl. Several hen harriers nest in the plantation (known locally as Jackson's Wood) that overlooks Vallay on the north of the island. 'All the birds of prey display in spring but the hen harriers show such commitment,' says wildlife guide Steve Duffield. 'They really throw themselves into it. You can easily see them from the side of the road without disturbing them.'

The woodlands also host both the white-tailed eagle (the UK's largest bird) and the goldcrest (the smallest), the eagles nesting deep in the woods. An RSPB hide halfway along the road is the obvious place to hover in search of flutterings great and small; but another excellent place is the informal layby by the quarry towards the northern end of the road (⊕ NF792715). At this location you are not only unobtrusive but can enjoy fine sightlines of white-tailed eagles and harriers as they leave and return to the woods. (For startling images of a white-tailed eagle sitting on top of a dead red stag, 📺 watch?v=WTnjYl5U2j0.) The woodlands look mature but the trees were only planted in the 1990s to provide timber for the biomass boiler at the island's seaweed factory.

The A865 continues east, skirting around the community of **Malacleit** before passing through **Solas (Sollas)**. A mile further along the road you come to the studio of **Sollas Bookbinding** ✳ [201 E2] (12A Grenitote; 📞 01876 560338; e ask@ sollasbooks.com; w sollasbooks.com; ⊕ 09.00–15.00 Mon–Fri, call ahead), run by the extremely talented Corinna Krause. Drop by and you will discover there is more to the enterprise than repairing books; Corinna produces patterned and skilfully

🚶 TO THE ISLAND OF VALLAY   Map, page 216

6½km (4 miles) return; 3hrs (inc time on Vallay);
Explorer 454 North Uist & Berneray
Start/finish: By a minor road (⊕ NF781737) to the left of the A865 as it passes the plantation west of Malacleit

Getting to Vallay (pronounced 'VAR-lay') involves a straightforward and glorious walk but it is time-consuming and you must set off just as the tide begins to fall. Park thoughtfully on the minor road and continue on foot across the strand for just under 3km (2 miles). Keep the smaller island ahead, Torogaigh, to your left and then head northwest towards Vallay. Once on the island, you can explore the remains of the deserted Vallay House, its predecessor the 16th-century Old Vallay House and a 19th-century farmstead, plus, on the northern side of the island, the church Teampull Orain. The later Vallay House – built for Erskine Beveridge – still retains the husk of its baronial-style mansion heyday.

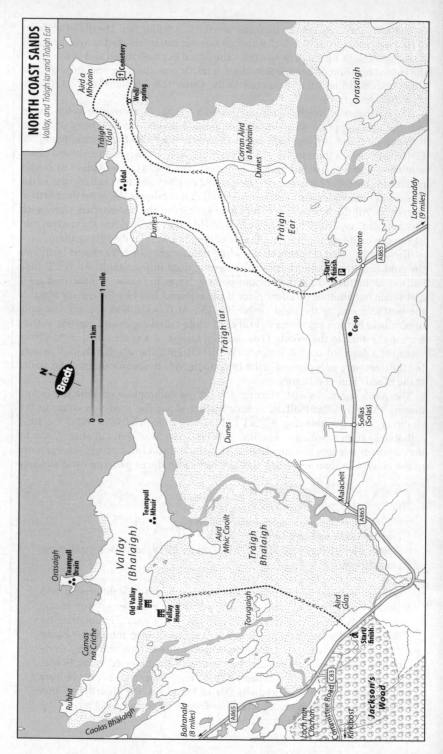

NORTH COAST SANDS
Vallay, and Tràigh Iar and Tràigh Ear

Cemetery
Aird a Mhòrain
Well/
spring
Tràigh
Udal
Udal
Corran Aird
a Mhòrain
Dunes
Dunes
Tràigh
Ear
Orasaigh
Start/
finish
Grenitote
Lochmaddy
(9 miles)
A865
Co-op
Sollas
(Solas)
Malacleit
A865
Tràigh Iar
Dunes
Orasaigh
Teampull
Òrain
Teampull
Mhuir
Valley
(Bhalaigh)
Old Valley
House
Valley House
Camas
na Crìche
Rubha
Caolas Bhalaigh
Balranald
(8 miles)
A865
Aird
Mhic Caoilt
Tràigh Bhalaigh
Torugaigh
Aird
Glas
Start/
finish
Loch nan
Clachan
Committee Road
(C83)
Kirkibost
Jackson's
Wood
A865

N
Bràgh

0   1km
0   1 mile

JOIN SEA HARRIS ON A DAY TRIP TO ST KILDA – THE ISLANDS ON THE EDGE OF THE WORLD

SEA HARRIS

This volcanic archipelago with its spectacular landscapes is situated 50 miles west from Leverburgh on the Isle of Harris. St Kilda was home to an island community, who, until 1930, survived the inhospitable conditions here for thousands of years. The cliffs of Boreray and its stacs are the highest in the UK, and are home to one of the world's largest colonies of northern gannets.

St Kilda is one of only 39 locations in the world, and the ONLY one in the UK, to be awarded dual World Heritage Status for natural and cultural heritage by UNESCO.

Departing from Leverburgh, experience this incredible place for yourself on the trip of your life. Upon arrival at St Kilda, passengers can explore the island and its haunting remains of the village at their leisure, or the more adventurous can head for the hills for spectacular views and gaze down at the sea below from the highest sea cliffs in Europe.

No visit to St Kilda is complete without the breathtaking tour of Boreray and its stacs. This is the highlight of the St Kilda trip and Sea Harris excels at ensuring this is a once-in-a-lifetime passenger experience.

Book online now to reserve your place on the Enchanted Isle, which was custom built for the St Kilda day trip, is the fastest and most comfortable of all the local day-trip vessels and offers the shortest crossing. We look forward to welcoming you aboard.

We also excel in shorter 3- and 5-hour trips to the Shiant islands, and other shorter boat trips around Harris's islands and coastline on our 'Canopy RIB' Pabbay. Please visit our website or call for further details.

Please visit our website for further details of this once-in-a-lifetime trip

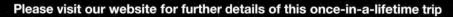

BOOK ONLINE AT www.seaharris.com

Tel: **01859 502007**   Mob: **07760 216555**   Email: **seumas@seaharris.com**

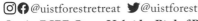

A HISTORY OF UDAL

The Udal headland you walk across today represents the bare remnants of a spectacularly rich and important archaeological site. The majority of this sandy and grassy peninsula was excavated over a period of 30 years dating from the 1960s, primarily by archaeologist Ian Crawford. The long-term dig, which continued until 1994, yielded more than 32,000 finds.

Finds at Udal include Neolithic layers of stones, among them a large upright stone nicknamed the great auk owing to its resemblance to the extinct seabird; a Bronze Age skeleton; 'jelly baby' houses from the Iron Age (named for their squat, figure-of-eight outline and wide, splayed entrances); and remains of a Viking longhouse.

Some of the stones still visible form rough outlines of Neolithic dwellings and pre-date the machair; others are remnants of what are known as the Udal wheelhouses, ritual buildings dating to around AD100–200.

While the grassy imprints and some walls remain, everything important – including the skeleton – appears to be gathering dust in storage in Stornoway, awaiting funding to support its display. Nevertheless, while frustratingly understated and under-interpreted, Udal is as important an archaeological site as you'll come across in the Outer Hebrides, including Callanish.

intricate writing books of the kind that might make for a travel journal. Her books are popular with artists and writers and, delicately composed, often using wax and paste paper, are works of art in themselves. Corinna's Coptic books, bound and sewn with delicate chain stitches and paying homage to ancient Egyptian tomes, are particularly striking. Corinna learnt her trade from a master bookbinder in her home town near Berlin. 'As a teenager I wrote poetry, as you do,' she explains. 'And I did one Christmas inflict my teenage angst poetry on my mum and dad in a handmade book. And that really triggered the desire to learn how book blocks are sewn and book covers are made properly.'

It's tempting to assume Corinna's work is inspired by the delicate lights of North Uist, which can be said to resemble the translucent pages of finely produced books. Corinna says this may now play a part in what she does, but more important, she asserts, is the space and time she has to be creative and to do so on an island not short of other like-minded artists. 'My passion for the craft came first but the geological and coastline patterns and colours of Uist have found their way into my work, no doubt.' If you want to learn more, Corinna offers bookbinding courses.

The beautiful and huge sands of Tràigh Iar lie just north of Solas. Getting to them can require as much effort as reaching Vallay: park with care along the road opposite the Co-op in Solas and simply keep walking north, towards the sea. As elsewhere, this is a good place to see birds. I once saw a snowy owl huddled down by a fencepost here, unable to fly up without being mobbed by lapwings and oystercatchers; undeterred, it (or another snowy owl) seems to reappear here every couple of years. The dunes feel as though they are sky-high here; they're great fun, but, if you're with children, be mindful of sheer drops to the beach.

Just before the A865 finally loops back into Lochmaddy, North Uist has another beach worth visiting at **Clachan Sands** ✳ [201 F1]. Reached down the B893 Berneray road, the beach lies at the end of the second signposted lane for Clachan sands and cemetery (ignore the first sign). There are two cemeteries, the older a stirring jumble of tombstones on a hill, and from this point the road deteriorates

11¼km (7 miles) return; 3hrs
OS Explorer 454 North Uist & Berneray
Start/finish: small car park at end of narrow spur road north of Grenitote (⊕ NF817754)

If a wander out to Tràigh Iar has whetted your appetite for North Uist's beaches, you can embark on a longer walk that takes in not only Tràigh Iar but the parallel (and equally stunning) Tràigh Ear, as well as a clutch of seemingly endless hidden bays, magical spits and headlands that draw away to the horizon. In summer the machair bursts into colour, but this is a stunning walk at any time of year, with huge skies and far-reaching vistas. From April to August be sure to keep to farm tracks to avoid disturbing breeding birds. Note that, although this walk takes in Tràigh Iar, it is best started around 1½km (a mile or so) further east, at the Grenitote car park just off the island ring road.

From the car park walk north along the sands of Tràigh Ear with farmland and the dunes to your left (after 200m there is a burn to cross by stepping stones; alternatively dip inland and use the adjacent bridge). The township name, Grenitote (Greinetobht), comes from two Norse words, *grein* meaning 'arm' or 'bifurcation' of a stream, and *toft*, an abandoned site of a house. Follow the curve of the sands for 1½km (1 mile) or so until they peter out by the shingle spit of Corran Àird a Mhòrain. The light on this bay, particularly at low tide, or just before the ebb is complete, can often be remarkable, resembling a collage of varying contrails of yellow, white and green.

Walk through the dunes of the spit and another bay opens up in front of you. Bear left and once again follow the curve of the dunes as they sweep in a crescent towards a grassy headland. Towards the end of the bay a cemetery becomes visible. To reach it follow any of the many tracks that cut up into the grassy bank. Go through a farm gate and drop down to the cemetery. This is the resting place of the Macleans of Boreray, the island clearly visible to the

dramatically. The machair just behind the beach where the lane finally gives up has become an unofficial car park, but is rarely busy; outside the summer months you may well have it to yourselves. The beach of Tràigh Lingeigh is a glorious half-crescent, with sparkling white sand rising to dunes and marram grass. To the west, just over the grassy brow is another beach, Tràigh Hornais, which is a little narrower but just as graceful.

SOUTH, TOWARDS BENBECULA Heading south at the junction of the A865 and A867 at Clachan na Luib, you quickly reach the turning for **Baleshare** [200 D6]. Strictly speaking, though you may not notice it among all the watery lochs, Baleshare is a tidal island connected to North Uist by a jagged stone causeway that looks as though it was chiselled and put into place by hand. The name tells a tale: in Gaelic Baleshare means 'east village'; its twin island, the west village, was washed away by the same ferocious storm that marooned the Monach Islands from North Uist. Baleshare enjoys the European nature designation of a Special Area of Conservation, a status that elevates its importance above even that of UK national parks (though how Brexit will affect such designations remains unclear) and provides a formidable shield of environmental protection. This is also another of North Uist's birdwatching hotspots: there is a colony of northwest. The last laird there was buried here in 1821 and boasts the most conspicuous headstone.

If you have time, there is a small freshwater spring down to the right of the cemetery as you look out to sea. To find it, retrace your steps through the gate and turn immediately left following a faint grassy track downhill. Where this track turns sharp left, continue down the slope and on to the beach. Turn left, go over the first large rocks, and, as you clamber over the second set of rocks, look for an incised cross on a rock face to your left. The spring of fresh water is right next to it.

To continue the walk return up the short slope, go through the gate and bear half-left uphill, following farm tracks through the machair. You're headed for the trig point at Àird a Mhòrain, which, although only 40m above sea level, will not be immediately visible. As soon as you see it, contour along the most convenient grassy ridge. The views from the trig point are magnificent. Both Tràigh Iar and Tràigh Ear are far below, the former indented with smaller bays; whichever way you look lie headlands and sweeping dunes. Further west are the Monach Islands, to the north Pabbay, Berneray and the North Harris Hills. You may even pick out the inter-island ferry weaving back and forth from Leverburgh.

Turning south, drop down to the gate and on to the exquisite small beach of Tràigh Udal. Just behind here you will come across several mounds indented with stonework. Concentrated here are 5,000 years of continual human occupation, from the Neolithic all the way along the timeline to the present day (see box, page 217).

Leaving the Udal mounds behind, follow tracks up through the grass to emerge above a small, unnamed but delightful west-facing bay. At the far side of this bay go over the grassy banks, and the vast dunes of Tràigh Iar lie before you. To complete the walk, wander halfway around the bay and go up and over the obvious break in the dunes. You'll see a broad farm track running left to right in front of you. Turn right along this and follow it back to the car park.

ever-feisty Arctic terns and you may see the occasional merlin scooting through on the hunt for prey.

The best access to Baleshare's 3 miles of shoreline is achieved by following the brown picnic-table-and-tree road signs, though it's over-egging things to describe the stony clearing they lead to as a picnicking idyll. The location though, above a slender but huge strand of beach, is magnificent. The southern part of this beach makes for lovely walking, with views towards Benbecula, and you can pick out the dunes of Ceann Ear, one of the Monach Islands, in the distance.

Located near the road end here at A' Ceardach Ruadh (The Red Smiddy) are the **Baleshare wheelhouses** [200 C6]. The elements are slowly in the process of blowing away the sand that has covered them for centuries, meaning that to visit this place is to see archaeology unfold in front of your eyes. The wheelhouses (⊕ NF776617) take time to find and are on the west side of Baleshare, where the machair ends in a low sandy ledge above the beach.

One other spot on Baleshare is worth seeking out. Look for the signposts directing you to the **Roadends sculpture** [200 D5], a sweeping ceramic tiled seat designed by artist Colin Mackenzie and local schoolchildren and deliberately placed at a vantage point to encourage you to linger over the surrounding views. Several such sculptures are dotted around the Uists – there's another at the end of the B894 along Loch Euphort.

South of the turn-off for Baleshare is the township of **Carinish (Cairinis)**. Two ruined churches here are signposted from the A865. You are directed to a small car park by a closed church from where it is a short walk to the **Church of the Holy Trinity (Teampall na Trionaid)** [200 D6]. The land here was once held by the abbot

🚶 ✳ AROUND LOCH SHORNARAIGH, GRIMSAY

2½km (1½ miles); 1–1½hrs
OS Explorer 453 Benbecula & South Uist
Start/finish: on northern loop of road around Grimsay (✪ NF863574)

The north shores of Grimsay are extremely picturesque, with freshwater and seawater lochs cheek by jowl, all fringed by gently rolling moorland. A short walk around the shores of Loch Shornaraigh (Loch Hornaraigh) gives a flavour of this landscape. In sunshine and at low tide, this is an idyllic spot. Moreover, you can also, should you wish, bag a couple of important archaeological sites along the way.

The best place to start is at the western end of the loch – if driving you need to park on the roadside – at ✪ NF863574. Walk up behind the house by the shore and bear slightly to the right to drop down to a tiny stream separating Loch Shornaraigh from the sea loch of Bàgh Tràigh; at its narrowest point the stream is barely the width of a hiker's boot. Even so, there are stepping stones here to tell you that you're in the right place. Clamber up the other side and keep ahead (headed southeast) with the fence on the right to a gate. Go through the gate and walk ahead, keeping close to the shore on your right. There are occasional sheep tracks through the heather but for the most part this is open ground.

Up to the left and easy to miss – since you are likely to initially pass below it – is an Iron Age wheelhouse. Antlers and whalebones were uncovered when it was excavated in the 1990s. Viewing the structure from its eastern side, you can pick out the outline of an even earlier roundhouse that underlies the wheelhouse. Continuing east, still with the loch on your right, a fence stands in the way. At its midpoint, this is low enough that most people will be able to straddle it without touching; otherwise you need to take a short diversion to the gate to the north of the wheelhouse and work your way back up the other side of the fence. This will only add 5 minutes to the walk.

Follow the shoreline as close as you wish and follow it around the southeastern head of the loch and back the other side, where the ground is more undulating. In the loch, you'll see the remains of Dùn Bàn on a rocky islet. The latter is smothered with stumpy trees and looks rather like a hedgehog having a bad hair day. The *dùn* holds four beehive cells within the walls of a circular tower that is barely visible through the foliage. Look closely and you will notice a submerged causeway connecting the islet to the shore.

Return along the southern shore to your starting point. Ahead, the North Ford causeway is visible and at low tide the waters retreat to reveal a mesmerising spectacle of submerged fields across Bàgh Tràigh. There are few places in the Outer Hebrides that so magically capture the interplay of tides as this spot.

of Iona (an island off Mull) but Erskine Beveridge (of Vallay fame) maintained that beehive cells pre-date the church on this site. Oral tradition maintains that the church was an important place of learning in the early medieval period. Trinity Temple's origins as a monastery and possibly a college of some sort have led to it being put forward as Scotland's oldest university. More certain is the claim that the sons of various medieval chieftains received their education here. To reach the church, you walk alongside the 'ditch of blood' (Feith na Fala), which commemorates a battle at Carinish between the MacDonalds and marauding Macleods from Harris.

Grimsay

Grimsay You can clip the western tip of **Grimsay (Griomasaigh)** without realising you have even left North Uist. The island is well worth pausing at. On the southern side of the circular road around Grimsay is **Uist Wool** [201 F7] (5 Scotvein; \01870 602597; e info@uistwool.co.uk; w uistwool.com; ◷ Dec–Apr 11.00–16.30 Mon–Wed, May–Sep 11.00–16.30 Tue–Fri, tours ◷ Jun–Jul 14.00 Fri; £3), a community venture launched by Dana MacPhee in 2016. Should you tire of Harris Tweed, then Uist Wool will give you a different perspective. There's a viewing panel where you can peer inside the mill and see wool being spun on refurbished 19th-century machinery. This is complemented by a shop where you can see the end product such as ripple hats and gloves, generally made by local weavers. Dana runs open days when you can enter the woolshed and feel the textures of different fleeces: Hebridean wool can feel like butter and seems to retain the shape of the animal. 'The wool is like wine, it can depend on the year the animal has had, the weather,' she explains. 'A good-quality animal produces a good-quality wool.'

The venture is a good example of just how dogged you need to be to get an enterprise off the ground in this part of the world. Dana secured funding from 24 different sources that gave her the necessary £900,000 to achieve lift-off. 'I had an interest in bringing benefit to the area I live in. There are so many talented people here, weavers who are just creating things for themselves. They are very creative, very innovative and contemporary. I just hope this can inspire people locally to see what can be done.'

Just before the Grimsay circular road begins to loop back towards North Uist, a short walk leads to the remains of St Michael's Chapel, located on a promontory at the southeast corner of the island. To reach it, park in the large turning space (✪ NF877552) just above the Kallin shellfish operations. The ruins are clearly visible in the distance. Follow the track off to the right for 200m and then turn right towards a house along another track. Just behind the hillock on the left, look for the very faint, almost indecipherable track that leads to the temple. This involves 10 minutes of plodding over open ground, so, although this is a very short walk, you should probably wear boots. The chapel lies within a small disused graveyard and only the west gable survives. Although small and ruined, the chapel is significant in the history of the Outer Hebrides as it is attributed to Anne MhicRuairidh, wife of John, the first Lord of the Isles, and as such would have been built before 1390.

Back on the Grimsay circular road, a service road leads down to **Kallin Shellfish** [201 F7] (✆ 01870 603258; e office@namaraseafoods.co.uk; w namaraseafoods. co.uk; ◷ 09.00–16.00 Mon–Fri, Apr–Sep also 10.00–15.00 Sat), a small fish company that catches lobster and crabs, generally from the Atlantic west coast, and langoustine and scallops from creels dropped in the deeper reaches of the east-coast Minch waters. A small shop is attached to the production buildings where you can pick up a cooked lobster ready to eat for around £15, along with scallops, crab-claw meat and smoked scallops. The quayside makes for a striking photograph with piles of discarded scallop shells heaped up in unintended homage to a Neolithic midden mound.

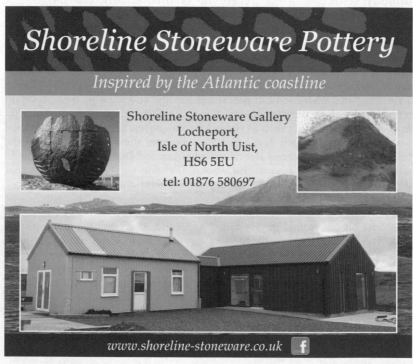

7

Benbecula (Beinn na Faoghla)

Benbecula is one of those resonant place names that epitomises the edge of the UK. A tiny island, squeezed between North and South Uist and with a population of just 1,283, Benbecula is some 8 miles long by 8 miles wide and can be traversed in less than 10 minutes. Many visitors make the mistake of dismissing it as merely a transit zone on the way to Barra, yet this is an island with plenty to detain those with the time and inclination: it's fringed on three sides by glorious beaches and dunes, the wildlife punches above its weight for such a small parcel of land, and there is a fascinating sense of transition from the Presbyterian north to the Catholic south of the islands.

Benbecula (the stress is on the second syllable, '*ben-BECK-you-luh*') is also often portrayed as a land of almost unrelenting flatness, though this depiction can be a little overplayed. The clue lies in the island's Gaelic name, Beinn Na Faoghla, which translates as 'the mountain of the fords'. The single 'mountain' in question is Rueval (Ruabhal), which rises to the less-than-mighty heights of 124m (406ft) above sea level, from the surrounding low-lying lands. That apart, Benbecula is a true waterworld, a place aptly described as more loch than rock. Many people who pause here find the island staggeringly mournfully beautiful.

The island has three townships that you are likely to visit or pass through: Balivanich (Baile a Mhanaich) on the north coast of the island, Nunton (Baile nan Cailleach) on the west coast, and Liniclate (Lionacleit) to the south. Balivanich is the main administrative centre for the southern islands and has council offices, the airport, a bank, post office, the excellent Uist and Barra Hospital along with other services, such as fuel and supermarkets.

The island has two distinctive landmarks that can be seen from miles around: Rueval, and the coned-shaped water tower attached to the army base in Balivanich.

HIGHLIGHTS

The main thing to do on Benbecula is walk up **Rueval** (see box, page 232). The summit is modest but rising among these flatlands it's high enough to give superlative views. The west-coast beaches, such as **Culla Bay**, are backed by machair and are exceedingly beautiful. The main township of **Balivanich** need not detain you on account of its sightseeing but it too is fringed by lovely beaches and sea lochs. On the southern side of Benbecula is the township of **Liniclate** with a modest museum. Between the two is **Nunton** and the island's main historical site, the **Temple of Mary (Teampall Mhoire)**. Nearby stands **Borve Castle**, a ruined 14th-century tower.

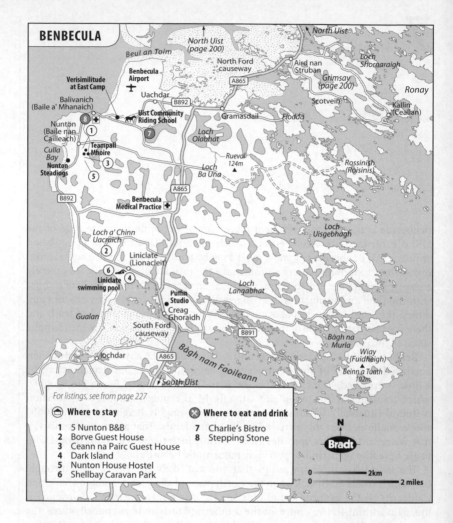

For listings, see from page 227

Where to stay

1 5 Nunton B&B
2 Borve Guest House
3 Ceann na Pairc Guest House
4 Dark Island
5 Nunton House Hostel
6 Shellbay Caravan Park

Where to eat and drink

7 Charlie's Bistro
8 Stepping Stone

HISTORY

Knowledge of Benbecula's prehistory record is relatively scant compared with that of other Hebridean islands. Finds include a Beaker (early Bronze Age) site identified at Rossinish (Ròisinis) on Benbecula, as well as a Pictish stone of granite carved with symbols, and Iron Age pottery on a settlement mound near Benbecula Airport. The island's recorded history only dates to the 6th-century establishment of a monastery. It was not until the 13th century that the monks of Iona acquired land here and a separate parcel was given to nuns from Benbecula. After the Norse occupation concluded in the 13th century, Benbecula was held by the MacDonalds of Clanranald, a powerful family on South Uist. They were descendants of the first Lord of the Isles, who was also a MacDonald. They dominated affairs for 500 years but were ultimately forced to sell Benbecula to pay off bad debts.

Central to Benbecula's history are the escapades of Bonnie Prince Charlie. After his defeat at Culloden in 1746, Bonnie Prince Charlie fled from the loyalist forces and made for the Hebrides. Blown off course in a severe storm, he was driven up the Minch and made landfall on Benbecula at Rossinish on 26 April. The prince hid around Rueval, then returned to Rossinish to escape from the Uists disguised as an Irish spinning maid, Betty Burke, and accompanied by Flora MacDonald. The event was recorded in the folk song 'Over the sea to Skye'.

Colonel John Gordon of Cluny purchased South Uist and Benbecula from the Clanranald in 1838. Cluny proved one of the most ruthless landlords of all, with a policy of clearances forcing many residents to emigrate to Canada. He used the land he acquired to expand Nunton Farm into a sizeable sheep farm. By 1850, his clearance policies had caused a national outcry.

In more recent times, changes in military presence have had a considerable impact on Benbecula's population. The army presence has waxed and waned over the years since the military first arrived as World War II began, and the island saw its population almost double until the early 2000s.

RAF Benbecula still operates long-range radar tracking over the North Atlantic but the days of masses of soldiers marching down the main street of Balivanich, and of the 200 families who sustained two local schools, are long gone. Today, much of the barracks stands empty. The site is operated by Qiniteq, and foreign troops are as likely to come for training as British ones. Benbecula was used heavily during the 1982 Falklands conflict for final training as the landscape of dunes, coast and moorland was considered similar to the terrain that awaited in the South Atlantic.

GETTING THERE AND AWAY

BY AIR Benbecula is home to the airport (Port-adhair Behinn na Faoghla) of the Uists and was established as a military base at the outbreak of World War II. Some

CROSSING THE NORTH FORD

Before the causeway was built, the crossing from North Uist to Benbecula was regarded as among the most treacherous in the Outer Hebrides. The causeway replaced the North Ford which could only be crossed when the tide was out and – even then – only with the help of expert guides, who were often faced with tracing new routes after winter storms moved the sandbanks. At high tide, a boat plied between Carinish and Gramisdale. The ford was marked by a series of cairns and was navigable on foot for those who knew the way in fine weather and during spring tides. Contemporary accounts suggest you had to be nimble to make the 4-hour traverse as the ford was open for just 1 hour either side of low tide. A traveller in the early 1900s – quoted in Ray Burnett's book *Benbecula* – described the North Ford as follows: 'Before us lay miles of mud and water, interspersed with islets and black rock and dark tangles of seaweed clinging to them.' His guide told him that losing the path was dangerous: 'A yard or two to either side of it means that you are in quicksands which immediately swallow any man, horse, cart or trap that deviates from the path.'

A Benbecula priest of the same era, a Father Macdougall, told of a night when he lost his bearings during an evening crossing in bad weather: 'I lost my horse and trap in the quicksands. The tide overtook me and washed me away; but in the end I reached an islet out west there, and so remained until two men in a boat found me the next evening.' High winds and tidal surges occasionally see waves overtop the present structure, and calls continue among the local population for a larger and more resilient causeway.

of the original buildings still survive from this period. The airport has two flights a day to Glasgow (1hr) and Stornoway (20mins) with Loganair (page 42). It's a pity that short-notice, discounted fares are not available for the Stornoway–Benbecula route as it offers stunning views over the North Harris Hills and the lochs of North Uist and Benbecula. Perhaps because of its proximity to the army base, the airport has more of the paraphernalia of airports the world over: high fences, barbed wire and a formality that is lacking at Stornoway and Barra airports. A small café here (⏲ hours vary, but normally 07.00–18.00 or until last flight) is run by the Island Kitchen chain which manages the Stornoway Airport café.

BY ROAD The North Ford causeway is the longest in the Outer Hebrides and runs for 5 miles between Gramasdal on Benbecula and Carinish on North Uist. This dramatic structure was opened by the Queen Mother in 1960 and 355,600 tonnes of rock were required for its construction. There are three bridges along its length; two to allow boats to reach the main channels and one for drainage. A single-track road runs along the top of the causeway with nine passing places to each mile. The South Ford causeway runs for half a mile to connect Benbecula to South Uist, via the tiny island of Creagorry.

GETTING AROUND

The A865 dog-legs its way through the island whereas the B892 skirts around the western perimeter. The latter is by far the most part scenic and cuts through large areas of machair with several stopping-off places where you can easily access the striking dunes. The B891 incises the watery remoteness of the island's southeast. Note that many place names are signposted in Gaelic only. In particular, you may search in vain for anywhere called Nunton as road signs call the township by its Gaelic name, Baile nan Cailleach.

The W16 **bus** links Balivanich with Lochmaddy on North Uist and Berneray. The W17 connects Balivanich with South Uist, running all the way to Lochboisdale and Eriskay. The service travels along the west coast of Benbecula from Balivanich via Nunton, Liniclate and Creagorry to Carnan stores on the northern tip of South Uist. The journey from Balivanich to Eriskay takes 2 hours. For up-to-date timetables, visit **w** cne-siar.gov.uk (search 'bus services').

Petrol stations are closed on Sundays but there are automatic petrol stations that take cards and cash 24 hours a day, every day, at both Seaview filling station in Balivanich, and at Creagorry (Creag Ghoraidh), towards the southern end of the island, just north of the B892 Liniclate turning with the A865.

HEN HARRIERS

Benbecula is one of the best places in the UK to see hen harriers. Several pairs nest on the island and although you can never guarantee a sighting of wildlife, this is one species, in this particular place, where the odds really are stacked in your favour. You will struggle to spot this creature back on the mainland, where it has been subject to decades of illegal persecution. You may well see them as you drive, cycle or walk along any of the roads; the flanks of Rueval are another excellent place. The male hen harrier is easy to identify as its grey wings appear to be tipped in black ink (the female is brown so looks more like the more common buzzard); in spring and summer you may observe the male pass a prey item it has caught to its mate in mid-air.

CAR HIRE
🚗 **Ask Car Hire** 🖊01870 602818
🚗 **Car Hire Hebrides** 🖊01870 603228;
w carhire-hebrides.co.uk; see ad, page 131
🚗 **Laing Motors** 🖊01878 700267;
e laingmotors@yahoo.co.uk; w laingmotors.co.uk.
Drops off at & collects from Benbecula Airport.

🚗 **MacLennans Garage** 🖊01870 602191

TAXIS
🚕 **A1 Taxis** m 07769 637755
🚕 **Buchanan's Taxis** 🖊01870 602277
🚕 **MacVicar's Taxis** 🖊01870 603197

TOURIST INFORMATION

Benbecula has no Visit Scotland centre. Tourist information can instead be found at the Taigh Chearsabhagh arts centre in Lochmaddy (page 206). MacGillivrays (page 228) also stocks leaflets and offers advice. B&Bs here are helpful, too, as are shops. Information is also available at w isle-of-benbecula.co.uk.

FESTIVALS AND EVENTS

Open to both locals and tourists, **Eilean Dorcha** (w edf.scot) is an annual summer music festival held in late July. A key part of the festival is to identify local talent and give them a wider audience, but bands with a broader reach such as the Vatersay Boys (page 276) and other cèilidh groups are often featured.

WHERE TO STAY *Map, page 224*

🏠 **Dark Island Hotel** (42 rooms) Liniclate; 🖊01870 603030; e reservations@darkislandhotel. co.uk; w darkislandhotel.co.uk. This 2-storey hotel caters mainly for coach parties. Prices, like many hotels on the islands, are higher than they ought to be (£150 for a family room is likely to send most visitors with children off to the hostel, or those on South Uist or Berneray). Some rooms have a contemporary feel, with minimalist art on the walls; others are more traditional with counterpanes of a certain vintage & wallpaper to match. Standards vary hugely, so ask to see your room before you agree to stay. Although there are steps down to the rooms, the hotel is supportive of travellers with mobility problems: call ahead to let them know what you might require. The bar is convivial & shares a decent pub-grub-style menu with the slightly more formal restaurant (**££**); there's also a public bar with pool table & TV. Borve sands are just behind the hotel. The hotel's name comes from an evocative air, a slow, piping song that accompanied a 1960s BBC TV series, *The Dark Island*, which was filmed locally. **£££**

🏠 **5 Nunton B&B** (3 rooms) Nunton; 🖊01870 603463; e lindamacdonald5@aol.com. Friendly B&B, run by super-helpful Linda MacDonald, with a light & breezy feel typified by the motto posted on the wall in one of the bathrooms: 'Bathroom rules: wash, brush, floss, flush.' Located just to the north of the old graveyard. **££**

🏠 **Borve Guest House** (4 rooms) 5 Torlum; 🖊01870 602685; e info@borve.scot; w borve. scot. Has 3 en-suite rooms, while a twin room has a private bathroom. Guest lounge with TV, books & board games. The guesthouse overlooks a vast stretch of marram grass & machair & has the ruins of Borve Castle just to the rear. **££**

🏠 **Ceann na Pairc Guest House** (4 rooms) Nunton; 🖊01870 602017; e ceann-na-pairc@ hotmail.co.uk; w ceann-na-pairc.com. Located on a working croft down a long drive just the other side of the graveyard from 5 Nunton, though the B&Bs are unrelated. Its 3 dbl rooms & a twin are spick & span; all are en suite & there is also a comfortable guest lounge. Culla beach is just a short walk away & there's a decking area to take in views of the island flatlands. The helpful owners will store bicycles & lend you fishing gear. Between May & Sep they ask guests to stay for min 2 nights. **££**

🏠 **Nunton House Hostel** (4 rooms, each with 4 beds) Nunton; 🖊01870 602017; e nuntonhousehostel@hotmail.co.uk; w nuntonhousehostel.com. Inside this rather grey, dour & forbidding building is a rather good hostel (it gets a 5-star rating from the Scottish Tourist

Board). Each of the dormitory rooms has an en-suite shower, there's a peat-burning stove standing in the original Inglenook fireplace, a modern kitchen with many basics provided free of charge, & a TV & laundry. **£**

⚑ Shellbay Caravan Park Liniclate; ☎01870 602447. Just along from Dark Island Hotel, this caravan site has wonderful views south towards South Uist & easy access to the dunes. **£**

✖ WHERE TO EAT AND DRINK *Map, page 224*

The rigid Presbyterianism of the north has been left behind and you will be able to eat most things you want on a Sunday, though opening hours are usually shorter. For a small island, Benbecula has some good – and good-value – places to eat.

✱ ✖ **Charlie's Bistro** ☎01870 603242; w charlies-hebridean-bistro.business.site/ Dunganachy; ⏰ 09.00–23.00 Mon–Thu, 09.00–01.00 Fri, 10.00–01.00 Sat. Located on the C85 road from Balivanich to the A865, this seafood bar & restaurant has swiftly established a reputation for modern dining on the island. Run by the folk from the Salar Smokehouse salmon company on South Uist. Also does excellent b/ fasts (it's a mystery why so few cafés across the Outer Hebrides offer this) before easing into its lunchtime & evening repertoire of local mussels & langoustines, grills & curries. Everything is sourced – if not always originated – from the island. The name of the bistro, incidentally, has nothing to do with the Bonnie Prince; rather it's a nod in the direction of Charlie, the corner-shop owner

from the 1970s who sold haberdashery & crofting machinery from the original building. **£/££**
✖ **Stepping Stone Restaurant** Balivanich; ☎01870 603377; e ewen@sinpeag.net; ⏰ 11.00–20.00 Mon–Sat (Jul & Aug until 21.00), noon–18.00 Sun. The restaurant has a well-run feel to it. Come hungry as portions are often extremely generous. There's a good range of specials such as fillet of sole & Barra scampi along with standard & filling fare of burgers & the like. The décor is thoughtful too & makes the best it can of the restaurant's absence of views, with frosted glass with motifs of the Gaelic alphabet & local art. They also know how to make a good coffee. This is a good-value choice, run by Ewen MacLean, 1 of the founders of the MacLeans bakers & butchers business (see box, below). **£**

SHOPPING

MacGillivrays (☎ 01870 602525; w macgil.co.uk; ⏰ 09.30–17.30 Mon–Fri, 09.30–16.00 Sat, May–Jul noon–16.00 Sun) is something of a regional institution. Selling everything from souvenirs to wellington boots, boxes of jelly babies and carpets, this

---

RUNNING A SMALL RURAL BAKERY IN A WORLD OF MULTI-NATIONALS

Owners Allan and Ewen MacLean started their business in 1987. 'There was no baking whatsoever on the island, so we thought we had a good chance,' says Allan. 'We were both chefs by training, we had a passion for food. The intention was to sell day-to-day items and try new things now and then and see if they catch on.' A perennial popular buy is goose pie, which has enjoyed a successful three-year trial run. Like other local traders, Allan sighs when the conversation comes to supermarket home deliveries from the mainland. 'It makes it difficult but it also makes you more determined. We provide a service that supermarkets can't and we have a face behind the product.' The brothers are clearly doing something right as they have also made a success of the Bayhead store on North Uist after taking it over (page 203).

small department store caters – as it must do to survive – to both a local clientele and tourists. It also has what are probably the best-stocked bookshelves in the Outer Hebrides with a good range of historical books relating to the islands, as well as fiction.

For food on the go, picnics or if you are self-catering, then **MacLeans Bakery** ✳ (☏ 01870 602696; e enquiries@macleansbakery.co.uk; ⏲ 09.30–17.30 Mon–Sat; see box, opposite) in Uachdar, on the airport road is an excellent choice. You can buy everything from pancakes, butterscotch doughnuts and oatcake canapés to take-away slices of steak and even gooseburgers. They also do home deliveries of a wide range of ready meals on the Uists, Benbecula and Barra and will shortly expand to deliver to Harris and Lewis. This service includes dishes such as chicken casserole and rhubarb crumble – enough to feed two people – all for less than £8.

Another good choice for stocking up is **MacLennans** supermarket (Balivanich; w maclennanssupermarket.co.uk; ⏲ 08.00–20.00 Mon–Sat, 11.00–16.00 Sun), a locally and family-owned retailer that shows many other regional supermarkets around the UK a thing or two when it comes to sourcing fresh fruit and fresh bread. There is also a good-sized **Co-op** (⏲ 07.00–22.00 Mon–Sat, 12.30–22.00 Sun) at Creagorry, just by the ford to cross to South Uist.

Just north of this ford stands the **Puffin Studio** crafts shop (☏ 01870 603885; ⏲ 10.30–17.00 Mon–Sat) run by Austen and Susan Dancey in what used to be a post office. Austen was a former operations manager at the Hebrides Rangehead on South Uist (see box, page 245) and now specialises in picture framing. He is keen to support local artists and has sourced goods and souvenirs from across the islands to stock the shop.

ACTIVITIES

Despite its name, the friendly **Uist Community Riding School** (☏ 01870 602808; e info@ridehebrides.org; w ridehebrides.org) is based at East Camp on the eastern outskirts of Balivanich. Riding a horse across the sands of Benbecula and the Uists makes for a magical experience. Tourists and novice riders are welcome, and staff are happy to accompany first-time riders and children. They also have ponies that children can look after for a day. East Camp is also home to the studio of Madeleine Ostling (w verisimilitude.co.uk; ⏲ check website), who produces strikingly stylish and contemporary knitwear. Benbecula's waters are clear and full of wildlife. Explore them by snorkelling and free-diving with Tom Ross of **Benbecula Freedive and Fitness** (☏ 01870 603324; e rossi941@googlemail.com; w freedive-uk.com), who offers equipment, advice and company. The adventurous may be drawn to Tom's night dives on the South Uist lochs. **Cycling** Benbecula's flat, quiet lanes is a joy, and on two wheels is the most dramatic way to traverse the causeways.

OTHER PRACTICALITIES

BANK
$ Bank of Scotland Balivanich; ☏ 01870 602096; ⏲ 10.00–15.00 Mon–Fri. Has an ATM.

MEDICAL
✚ Balivanich Community Clinic Balivanich; ☏ 01870 602266
✚ Benbecula Medical Practice Griminish; ☏ 01870 602215

✚ Uist & Barra Hospital Balivanich; ☏ 01870 603600

POST OFFICE
✉ Balivanich post office ⏲ 09.00–17.00 Mon–Tue & Thu–Fri, 09.00–14.00 Wed, 09.00–12.30 Sat

Balivanich sprawls along the north coast and, dominated with ugly military barracks designed in the most brutalist concrete style, it wins no beauty contests. However, the township is useful for the chores associated with travelling and has a couple of places worth seeking out for food and to visit. You can't miss MacGillivrays (page 228), as it stands directly opposite the army water tower and is well worth visiting for its eclectic offerings.

Heading anticlockwise on the B892 from Balivanich, turning right half a mile south of the township for Àird leads to a parking spot where you can climb up to the tumbling dunes above **Culla Bay**. The west-facing beach is safe for swimming and the gorgeous sweep of sand and shingle, with seabirds flying overhead, is a pleasant place to wander.

The machair behind Culla Bay has been the subject of an environmental project over the past few years, the Scottish Machair LIFE+ project (**w** machairlife.org.uk), in which the RSPB, Scottish Natural Heritage, Comhairle nan Eilean Siar (Western Isles Council) and the Scottish Crofting Federation all play key roles. This has sought to enrich the machair by measures such as laying down seaweed as fertiliser, spring cultivation and sowing, and late harvesting as well as letting some land lie fallow. This approach is intended to help corncrake, lapwing and the great yellow bumblebee; the area's international importance as a breeding site for corncrake has seen it designated a Special Protection Area.

A magnificent, nameless beach runs for more than a mile down the west coast of Benbecula. You can access it most easily from the grassy layby off the B892 just north of the turning for **Griminis**. The beach is also regularly and dramatically altered by storms that can transform it into a shingle bay overnight, and then

🚶 TO FLODDA (FLODAIGH)

2 km (1¼ miles); 30mins
OS Explorer 453 Benbecula & South Uist
Start/finish: layby/turning area at Flodda (⊕ NF843554)

Just south of the North Ford causeway, a turning to the east leads to the scattered township of Flodda. A short walk from the end of the road leads to an excellent vantage point for watching harbour seals. If driving, park at the road end, but avoid doing so between 08.00 and 08.45 and 15.30 and 16.30 when buses turn around here. If coming by bus, it's 2km (1.2 miles) from the turning to the road end. Follow the main track ahead that goes slightly uphill. You'll soon pass an abandoned car that has been here for as long as anyone can remember: each time I walk past another part of it has fallen off. There used to be a light-hearted pamphlet entitled the 'Seal News' posted in the front window screen, which provided some surprisingly insightful information about the seals but this has disintegrated since the sun-roof was blown in. A print-out of walking instructions remains on the dashboard and is just about legible. To reach the seal viewing point, keep straight ahead as the main track bends to the left, following a clear grassy track and keeping the fence to your right. After some 350m, you will find yourself about the shoreline. Seals are often hauled out on the many islets here, and you may also see grey herons stealthily prancing around the shallows.

re-cover it with sand just as quickly. While the beach is gorgeous, in summer the rocky bay at its head is notorious for accumulating seaweed, which can produce a stench strong enough to drive you off the sands.

Further south is the tiny but scattered community of **Nunton**. Keep an eye out for the small signs for Baile nan Cailleach which tell you that you have arrived here – though the church remnants and cemetery are an obvious enough landmark. The origins of the ruined **chapel of Teampall Mhoire** lie across the waters of the Little Minch on Iona. A Benedictine community of monks was established on Iona in 1203, and over time they acquired land on the Uists (Benbecula was at that time included in this region), known as Baile a' Mhanaich, 'the monks township' (today's Balivanich). Another portion of the land was given to the Iona convent Baile nan Chilleach, or 'township belonging to the nuns'. Teampall Mhoire is therefore dedicated to the Virgin Mary to underline the link and is a good example of a typical medieval church. In the 16th century, the chapel fell into disrepair, though the graveyard remained in use. The chapel roof has long gone but the gables and the lower walls hang on, surrounded by tombstones entirely mantled in lichens.

Just across the road from the chapel is **Nunton Steadings**, an 18th-century farmstead with slate roofs and casement windows. The bell in the front gable was rung to bring workers in from the field during the 18th century. (The local community hopes to raise funds to restore this attractively ruined pile.) Back across the east side of the road, **Nunton House** is one of the oldest buildings on Benbecula. Though it has been substantially altered over the centuries, it was once – as the name suggests – part of the nunnery. In the early 18th century, the house became the principal residence on the Uists of the MacDonalds of Clanranald and was implicated in sheltering Bonnie Prince Charlie: Clanranald's wife dressed the Prince as Betty Burke, Flora's maid in Nunton House to aid his escape. It later became the residence of the notorious Colonel John Gordon of Cluny (page 225).

The next township along from Nunton is **Liniclate**, where you'll find the **Island Museum** housed in Liniclate School (✆ 01870 603692; e museumU&B@cne-siar. gov.uk; w cne-siar.gov.uk (click on 'museum nan eilean' and follow links); ☉ Mon– Sat but times vary, call ahead). The museum is extremely modest in size – really more of an exhibition space – and will not take up more than a few minutes of your time. Pop in if you are passing through, but don't build your day around the place. The school **swimming pool** (✆ 01870 603693; e LionacleitSportsCentre@cne-siar. gov.uk; w cne-siar.gov.uk/lsc/swimmingpool.asp; ☉ daily, times vary, call ahead) is open to the public and is extremely handy if you are anywhere on Benbecula or the Uists and looking for something to do in bad weather, particularly on a Sunday.

A good way to appreciate the beauty of Benbecula's coastline and machair is to follow the modest trail behind the Dark Island Hotel in Liniclate (page 227). Walk through the hotel car park across a cattle grid to the giant wind turbine and turn right along the sandy track. The path runs behind the dunes almost as far as the ruins of **Borve Castle** (☉ 24hrs; free). You can reach this 14th-century castle ruin by either of the tracks from the main road. The ruins are testament to the shifting landscape of Benbecula as it was almost certainly built on a small islet in a tidal loch that has long been infilled with sand and soil. The substantial remains are of a ruined tower house built for Amy MacRuairi, the first wife of John, Lord of the Isles, around 1350. The Clanranalds then occupied the house until abandoning it during the 1715 Jacobite Rising. You can return by the same route, or follow the road to make this into a circular walk. The loch just north along the road from the castle, **Loch a' Chinn Uacraich**, is a locally recognised spot to see otter.

8km (5 miles); 2hrs
OS Explorer 453 Benbecula & South Uist
Start/finish: car park by municipal waste tip (⊕ NF813534) just east of the A865 & 3km (1.8 miles) south of Uachdar

If you climb just one hill in the Outer Hebrides, this should be the one. This walk explores the boggy moors of eastern Benbecula from the safety of an access track and leads up to the summit of Rueval. There's a mixture of open ground and paths near the summit but its modest height of 124m (406ft) means there is much less effort than required to scale the heights elsewhere. The walk is not signposted but the route is easy to follow and in good weather the summit is always in clear view.

The walk starts from the car park by the recycling centre and municipal waste tip. Don't be deterred by the high metal fence that rears up along the lane, and the ugly bank of rubble. Things get better and this walk dismisses the waste tip at a stroke by simply striking out east, towards Rueval along a track (in effect, this is a continuation of the access road from the A865) into open, unoccupied moorland.

The route follows the northern shore of **Loch Ba Una**, with wheatears striding around (the male distinguished by its 'robber-mask' eye-stripe) and stonechats often hovering around the gorse. The grainy dots on distant ledges may well be white-tailed or golden eagles, while more easily identifiable buzzards float on the breezes above. Along with hen harriers and short-eared owls (which frequently fly over the moors, hunting in broad daylight), this makes for an astonishing number of charismatic species for such a short walk. You can often spot a hen harrier floating just below the summit of Rueval, occasionally settling and disappearing down in the bracken. Please don't investigate too closely, just in case they are nesting nearby.

Here and there you pass large squared-off chunks of excavated peat, taken from huge gullies that cut deep and far into the moors, ending in a blur

The **east side** of Benbecula is largely left to its own devices. There is no great farming activity, and it's particularly hard – even by the standards of the Outer Hebrides – to pick your way through the bogs and open moorland. In some respects, this makes the area a de facto nature reserve. However, if you explore any of the tracks here, either towards Flodda or towards Rossinish, you have a chance of seeing hen harrier, short-eared owl, otter and golden and white-tailed eagles.

Near the southern end of Benbecula, it's definitely worth turning off the A865 and heading east along the B891 (locally called the Peter's Port road) for 4 miles to the pier at the road's end where you come face to face with the island of Wiay (Fuidheigh). Access to Wiay is by sea only; there is no pier there. Ask locally – Linda MacDonald at 5 Nunton B&B (page 227) is helpful – about a boat to take you across.

Visitors may be dropped off at a bay, Bàgh na Murla, on the west side of Wiay. There follows a precarious scramble along seaweed-covered rocks to reach a sheep path that takes you to an old cottage overlooking the bay. The building dates back to the early 19th century and, although the roof has disappeared, the thick stone walls remain.

of inky-black, soggy bleakness. Peat cutting has been practised here for centuries and, as fuel prices have increased over recent years, it has seen something of a resurgence.

After around 450m, or about two-thirds of the way along the loch, look out for the narrow but distinct path on the left by a small quarry and marked with a small cairn and a wooden post. Take this path, which heads northeast, to ascend the southern flank of Rueval. As you ascend, one or two smaller paths break off and make their own way uphill, although they all later converge near the summit. From the loch shore, it should take about 15 minutes to get to the top where the low-lying surrounding land gives Rueval a disproportionately elevated view of the fretwork of innumerable inlets and lochs that speckle the landscape. The causeways that link Benbecula to North and South Uist and to Grimsay are clearly visible; to the south the Beinn Mhòr range on South Uist looms large, and these in turn give way to Barra at the southern end of the island chain.

Everywhere, houses look like pieces of Lego dropped from the sky. Looking north, Benbecula's tiny airport nudges against the sands. To the east, across the Minch, the Cuillin peaks on Skye bare their jagged teeth on the skyline.

Retrace your steps to the loch shore where you have a choice: you can return to the start; or you can continue eastwards for another 3km (2 miles) where the path seemingly falls into the water, but in reality peters out at Rossinish.

The RSPB runs regular evening walks from spring to autumn around Rueval (w rspb.org.uk, search 'Balranald'; members £2/non-members £5/children free), with the chance of seeing the birds mentioned above, plus divers.

The summit also has significance for long-distance hikers. The Hebridean Way (see box, page 50), Scotland's newest long-distance footpath, links the causeway-accessed islands that make up the Outer Hebrides, from Vatersay to Lewis. Walking up from the south – the recommended route – Rueval is the first sizeable bump you will encounter and need to clamber over. From the summit you can see more than half of its 252km (156-mile) length, and gaze deep into the North Harris Hills.

A short walk leads to the top of Beinn a Tuath and affords spectacular views across the Minch to Skye and also North and South Uist. You can also gaze down at Wiay's three lochs shimmering in the sunlight.

The island has abundant wildlife, including lapwings, oystercatchers, geese, eider ducks, herons and birds of prey such as buzzards, sea eagles and golden eagles. You may also see red deer swimming from island to island, and seals make regular visits to the bay in front of the old house. Otters are resident on Wiay and pods of dolphins and porpoises swim in the surrounding waters.

If Wiay is known to the outside world at all, it is for a cave, known as Prince Charlie's Rest, which is found to the east of the island at the foot of Beinn a Tuath. Bonnie Prince Charlie is said to have skulked here after the Battle of Culloden. Benbecula people were sympathetic to the Jacobite cause. Boat tours from Kallin (page 38) will take you here as part of tours along the eastern sea lochs of Benbecula and the Uists.

Wiay has been deserted since 1901 but islander Iain Monk, whose family had a croft on the island for generations, recalls – from stories told to him by relatives – how potatoes and fish were staples of the daily diet, herring and mackerel salted and stored in barrels to provide sustenance over the harsh winter months. There was a smallholding of cattle, sheep and hens, hay and corn were cut manually with a scythe and the potato 'lazy beds' were fertilised with rotten seaweed lifted from the shore. Peat for the home fire was cut, dried and stored in a peat stack beside the house. As with so many other islands, depopulation came soon enough: the Monks relocated to the Benbecula township of Haclait while other families emigrated.

Even if you don't make it on to Wiay, the B891 is a delightfully secluded road to explore, on foot, bicycle or by car. You have a good chance of seeing otters at the numerous small causeways, as well as a great deal of birdlife.

8

South Uist (Uibhist a Deas) and Eriskay (Eirisgeidh)

A glance at a map of South Uist immediately suggests a striking resemblance to the outline of Chile, if on a more modest scale: a long, thin land with ocean to the west and mountains to the east. Eriskay manages to shoehorn beautiful beaches, a surprisingly rugged interior – grazed by photogenic ponies – and a good deal of remarkable history into its dimensions.

SOUTH UIST (UIBHIST A DEAS)

Ó mo dhùthaich, 's tu th'air m'aire,
Uibhist chùmhraidh ùr nan gallan…

O my country, of thee I am thinking,
Fragrant fresh Uist of the handsome youths…

…Tir a'mhurain, tir an eòrna,
Tir 's am pailt a h-uile seòrsa,
Far am bi na gillean òga
Gabhail òran 's 'g òl an leanna…

…Land of bent grass, land of barley,
Land of all things in plenty,
Where there are young men and youths,
A place of songs and drinking ale…

…Nam biodh agam fhin do stòras,
Dà dheis aodaich, paidhir bhrògan,
Agus m'fharadh bhith 'nam phòca,
'S ann air Uibhist dheanainn seòladh.

…If I was in possession of the wealth,
Of two suits of clothes and a pair of shoes,
And if the fare was in my pocket,
Then for Uist I would be sailing.

'Ó mo dhùthaich', traditional song and South Uist anthem, composer unknown. An emigrant lament for South Uist, translated by Margaret Fay Shaw and John Lorne Campbell and published in her book *Folksongs and Folklore of South Uist* (Birlinn, 1999), reproduced with kind permission of the National Trust for Scotland – Canna House.

South Uist is one of those places that looks the part: an island on the edge of the British Isles. There's a stirring Atlantic coastline and wildflower-filled cornfields plus isolated glens and hills laced with lochs. It's also empty – just 1,897 people live here – and the meagre population is widely scattered, creating a vast, open landscape where isolated homesteads appear to have been dropped like pieces of Lego from the skies. Photographer Margaret Fay Shaw depicted the atmosphere of the islands beautifully in the 1930s when she wrote of a land with 'thatched houses standing like haystacks on the rim of the world'.

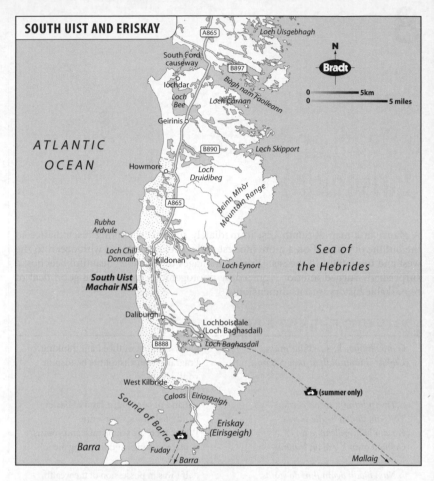

SOUTH UIST AND ERISKAY

ATLANTIC OCEAN

Sea of the Hebrides

A865
Loch Uisgebhagh
South Ford causeway
B897
Iochdar
Bàgh nam Faoileann
Loch Bee
Loch Carnan
Geirinis
B890
Loch Skipport
Howmore
Loch Druidibeg
A865
Beinn Mhòr Mountain Range
Rubha Ardvule
Loch Chill Donnain
Kildonan
Loch Eynort
South Uist Machair NSA
Daliburgh
Lochboisdale (Loch Baghasdail)
B888
Loch Baghasdail
West Kilbride
Caloas Eiriosgaigh
Sound of Barra
Eriskay (Eirisgeigh)
(summer only)
Barra
Fuday
Barra
Mallaig

0 — 5km
0 — 5 miles

From north to south, the island stretches for 25 miles and, at the widest point on its east–west axis, runs for 9 miles. Fjord-like sea lochs eat deep into this rocky, peaty landscape with its bleakly beautiful moors that offer wonderful sunrises and sunsets. In high summer, a half-light prevails at night that all but fends off the darkness before dawn returns. The abundant freshwater lochs, shallow seas and an absence of light pollution contribute to a liquid light and a crystalline air that seem to bounce up to the sky and back again, magnifying the folds and creases of the overlooking mountains.

Mountains run down the length of the east coast, broken up by a quartet of four major lochs. This is also, though, a land of undulating flatness, as if unseen but gentle eddies were rolling along just under the machair, causing fields to rise up like the crest of waves, hiding the Atlantic Ocean until you are almost upon it. When you do reach the coast, you are standing on a more or less continuous shoreline of 20 miles of brilliant-white beaches.

South Uist can feel remote, a sentiment that local people often express: to them not just Edinburgh and London, but Stornoway too, can feel a long way away. This can translate into the view that South Uist is the Cinderella of the islands, with as much to offer the visitor as any other but overlooked by mainstream tour operators with their eye on the rich and more immediately accessible pickings of Harris and Lewis.

As is the case with the northern isles, the underlying geology of South Uist is Lewisian gneiss. The Uists and Benbecula represent its weathered southwesterly reaches. After the last Ice Age some 10,000 years ago, the islands were colonised by grasses and a light scrub of hazel and birch, later followed by oak, elm and pine. Land clearing for grazing animals meant that most of this cover had disappeared by 2500BC while the melting ice sheets submerged a vast area of the west coast. Over time, the gradual accretion of millions of seashells pounded by the Atlantic, followed by colonisation by plants, created the Uist machair. The interior is characterised by peat bogs and, almost imperceptible to the naked eye from ground level, a canal system known as the *ligidhean*, which has drained the land for many generations. These may also have served as waterways for islanders to navigate along (they would certainly have been safer and quicker than walking across boggy land). This under-researched system is highly complex, spanning the length of the island – and parts of Benbecula – and oral tradition says that sections were built in the 18th century by Dutch engineers. They – and whoever built the original *ligidhean* – were clearly highly skilled for they left a landscape spirit-level flat: look at an Ordnance Survey map of South Uist and the near total absence of contour lines to the west of the spinal north–south road is remarkable. The *ligidhean* are hard to pick out from sea level but a particularly important one is known to drain water off Loch Kildonan in the south of the island.

The sand of the Uists is striking too: it comprises broken stones and the shells of small crustaceans and minuscule vertebrates that truly sparkle in sunshine. Where there is more surviving granite rock, the sand tends to be a paler white or a muted yellow; in other areas, you find a coarser red sand made up of eroded granite.

Beach shingle on Uist is particularly sought after for making concrete, tracks, road base and in foundations, but it is a non-sustainable resource. Little shingle is replenished from offshore, and its removal, coupled by an increase in severe gales and high tides, is exacerbating coastal erosion on South Uist, where the low-lying machair is protected behind a belt of vulnerable sand dunes.

Crofting plays an important part in sustaining the biodiversity of the machair. Most crofters on South Uist keep sheep and one or two cattle. As recently as the 1970s, crofters ploughed the machair with horses and a single furrow plough. The shoreline, too, has always been a rich source of material for the business of everyday island life. Right up until the 1960s, mattresses were made from seaweed, beds from driftwood. Along the coast, tradition has also seen islanders gather dulse (a seaweed, good with butter or as a broth) and carrageen, a delicate seaweed used for milk pudding.

In 2006, South Uist, along with the adjacent islands of Eriskay and Benbecula, pulled off Scotland's biggest community buyout when they purchased 37,230ha of sporting estate for £4.6 million. It's now run by a community company called **Stòras Uibhist** (w storasuibhist.com), who have responsibility for almost all of the three islands and a number of small outliers. The estate is home to more than 850 tenant crofters, and the economy is based on the staples of aquaculture, agriculture, fishing, food processing, construction and increasingly tourism.

HIGHLIGHTS Tourist maps can give the impression that everything of interest on South Uist is within a stone's throw of the main road, the A865. Yet this is far from true: more than any other island in the Outer Hebrides, the key on South Uist is to get off the spinal route. You will find the island's true beauty by exploring the lanes and tracks – some signposted, others not – that filter west into the machair or east alongside the sea lochs that have removed vast geological chunks of the island.

The north of the island is flatter and in many ways resembles the landscape of North Uist and Benbecula. Here **Loch Bee (Loch Bì)** provides dramatic views and wildlife-watching opportunities, the shoreline of **Loch Càrnan** is worth exploring, and you can visit the workshop of **Hebridean Jewellery**.

Further south are two more large lochs: **Loch Druidibeg (Loch Druidibeag)** and **Loch Skipport (Loch Sgiopoirt)**. Along much of the west coast, the flowering machair is as spectacular as anything found further north. The air is full of birds, and all year you can see high drama between predators and prey. A good place to see flowers and birds is the open land around **Rubha Ardvule (Rubha Àird a'Mhuile)**, while nearby you will also find the early Christian remains of **Howmore (Tobha Mòr)**. The excellent **Kildonan Museum** provides some fascinating insights into island life and culture. The major mountains are worth exploring, particularly **Hecla (Thacla), Beinn Choradail, Beinn Mhòr** and, further south, **Beinn Ruigh Choinnich**, though their summits are for experienced walkers and climbers only (page 260). **Loch Eynort (Loch Aineort)**, arguably the most beautiful of South Uist's

FAUNA AND FLORA OF SOUTH UIST

For many visitors, one of South Uist's major attractions is its wildlife. Much of the island has been designated as a National Scenic Area, a Scottish government classification that recognises its 'outstanding scenic value in a national context' and which strives to safeguard it against development. In addition, the island's EU nature sites include a Special Protection Area at Kilpheder and a Special Area of Conservation that covers the majority of the South Uist machair.

'It's the abundance and diversity that really gets you,' says Steve Duffield, who runs Western Isles Wildlife, which offers guiding services (page 203). 'You have a real diversity of landscapes: the acidic moorlands and the machair plains. Each provides very different habitats; they are almost marginal and very harsh.'

In addition, the waters of the west coast of South Uist are unusually shallow, a legacy of vast sand deposits laid down thousands of years ago. This encourages the growth of kelp beds and seaweeds; high tides and storms throw large amounts of these plants on to the shore, attracting birds all year round. The cultivation of the land also attracts wildlife, and both fallow and cultivated machair appeal to different flower species. The former encourages clovers and kidney vetch while those in crop attract corn marigold. This mix attracts lots of insects, already drawn to a soil enriched with seaweed, and the rich profusion of wild flowers makes a dramatic backdrop for skylark and lapwing, which are still common on South Uist, along with corncrake, corn bunting, belted beauty (a moth) and great yellow bumblebee. Lochs adjacent to the machair are rich in nutrients and support wildfowl.

The juxtaposition of coast and mountains is mainly responsible for the dramatic interaction of prey and avian predators. 'The close proximity of these landscapes – the moors, mountains and the machair – creates such a preponderance of birds,' explains Steve, who likens the fate of the waders to that of living next door to unwelcome neighbours. 'The raptors tend to nest in the east, in the moors, but they depend on the machair for their food.' They go for small birds and larger waders, but golden eagles have even been known to attempt to catch a hen harrier and have taken short-eared owls. White-tailed eagles can also turn up almost anywhere; the machair is a good place to see them. 'It can sound gruesome but it's nature red in tooth and claw,' says Steve.

great lochs, carves its way east under a mountain shadow. Finally, South Uist tapers to a southerly tail around a huddle of communities that include the rather desultory port of **Lochboisdale (Loch Baghasdail)**, **Daliburgh (Dalabrog)** and **Kilbride (Cille Bhrighde)**. South Uist has several important archaeological remains, of which the most spectacular were the composite mummies found at **Cladh Hallan** in 2001. Just before the causeway to Eriskay, the **Big Garden** at East Kilbride, with its food and tweed offerings, should also be high on your list.

HISTORY Until recently, South Uist was thought to have no stone circles: then a moorland fire revealed stones in the heather hills east of Askernish (Aesgernis) in the south of the island. During the Iron Age, there was a change to the way settlement was distributed across South Uist, with people moving inland from the coastal machair, establishing houses every half mile or so, as they began to cultivate the peat soils of the interior.

There is no evidence of churches on South Uist before AD1000. However, after the Norse occupation of the wider Hebrides, the powerful Clanranald emerged as the dominant family. Descended from the first Lord of the Isles, they ruled South Uist for more than 450 years from the late 14th century. The island's connection with Clanranald only came to an end – and a sorry one it was – in 1837, when it was sold to pay off bad debts.

Living here, though, has always been hard: emigration began in the 1770s, but by the early 19th century many more families had given up in the face of a series of storms and sandblows (where windswept sand becomes grainy and denuded of any vegetation) that devastated crops. Worse was yet to come with the clearances that saw families evicted and the land turned over to sheep farming. On South Uist, these clearances were for the most part enforced by Colonel Gordon of Cluny, who bought the island from the Clanralds as a package with Barra, Eriskay and Benbecula. At that time, the island population was more than 7,000, four times its current number. Subsequent emigration on a colossal scale eviscerated the population. The potato blight in the 1840s proved the final straw for many, leading to five years of famine. While religious faith burns strongly here, as it does further north, these are Catholic lands far removed from the 'wee-frees' of Lewis, Harris and North Uist.

GETTING THERE AND AWAY
By ferry CalMac (☎ 0800 066 5000; from outside the UK ☎ +44 1475 650397; w calmac.co.uk). The island benefits from a direct summer route from Mallaig to Lochboisdale (which replaced the circuitous route via Barra in 2016). The sailing takes 3½ hours. Locals point out that the present timetable is not ideal: the ferry arrives in Lochboisdale at 20.50 Monday to Saturday and at 18.30 on Sunday, which means you should have made accommodation plans in advance; cyclists in particular have been found late at night still scrambling around for accommodation. The return to the mainland departs from the port at 07.00 Monday to Thursday and at 06.20 Friday to Sunday, which means an early start to meet the 45-minute check-in deadline. One-way fares (return fares are double) are: car £60.85, adult £11 and child £5.50. Note that when the winter timetable operates (Oct–Mar), many services from Lochboisdale sail to and from Oban, rather than Mallaig.

By road The South Ford causeway connects the northern end of South Uist to Benbecula via the tiny islet of Creagorry, while another causeway links the southern tip of the island to Eriskay. Triangular warning signs to watch out for 'otters crossing' greet you at both ends of the island and make for a popular photo opportunity.

GETTING AROUND

By car The A865 runs north–south the length of the island from Càrnan to Lochboisdale. The majority of the road now has a lane in each direction but still narrows to a single track with passing places at unexpected moments. Allow plenty of time if you are at the wrong end of the island from the ferries at Lochmaddy or Lochboisdale. The B888 runs south at Daliburgh to the Eriskay causeway.

One thing you may notice is that driving is noticeably faster than on the islands further north, and motorists coming in the other direction are less likely to yield. Perhaps it's just that the southern islands get fewer tourists, that people have long journeys to and from work or the prevailing flatness of the island's main artery that makes this the case.

Despite this, the road can throw up unexpected delights such as stags standing on rocks just metres away, or birds of prey flying alongside your vehicle. The beauty, though, of South Uist's road network is the small lanes that break away at right angles from the A865 and make a dart through flatlands to the Atlantic coast or carve their way painstakingly through the nuggety, harsher landscape of lochs and mountains to the east.

The only automated 24-hour petrol station that takes cards is in Lochboisdale, although the card machine can be erratic. There's no petrol at the northern end of the island, so it is best to make sure you have petrol for the 25 miles north to Creagorry on Benbecula (page 226).

Car hire
🚗 **Laing Motors** Lochboisdale; 📞 01878 700267; e laingmotors@yahoo.co.uk; w laingmotors.co.uk. Drops off & collects at Benbecula Airport & at the ferry terminals at Eriskay, Lochboisdale, Lochmaddy & Berneray.

Petrol
⛽ **Burnside filling station** On the Daliburgh–Eriskay road; ⏱ 07.00–22.00 daily

By bus The W17 bus connects most communities on the island and services are dependable if infrequent, making it a sometimes frustrating exercise to visit places by public transport. The route runs down the spine of the southern islands from Bernerary via Lochmaddy to Eriskay, and some services explore the small villages off the main road too, although these can require advance booking. For up-to-date timetables, visit w cne-siar.gov.uk (search 'bus services').

By taxi A useful service for hillwalkers without transport is **AM/PM Taxi** (m 07957 798374). Reckon on a fare of £15 from somewhere in the middle of the island, such as Loch Eynort to either the top or the bottom of the island.

🚗 **MacVicars taxis** 📞 01870 603197

TOURIST INFORMATION
Uist Gifts & Information Centre (Lochboisdale; 📞 01878 700777; e uistgifts@gmail.com; w uist-gifts.myshopify.com; ⏱ 10.00–17.00 Mon–Sat, 16.00–19.00 Sun) is the go-to place on South Uist. Visit Scotland pulled out of Lochboisdale in 2016 but have now been superseded by the initiative of islander Donnie Steele. Located right by the ferry port, the shop provides information, as well as an impressively eclectic range of Uist-themed souvenirs and clothing, including beanie hats, cufflinks and fridge magnets. That this shop, which operates as a community interest company, exists at all says a good deal about how passionately islanders feel about South Uist. 'The decision to close the old visitor centre stunned

The Ceòlas music festival and school takes place every summer in Daliburgh and has been a catalyst for Gaelic song and dance on the Uists. The first festival was held in 1996 to explore the intriguing similarities between fiddle tunes played in Cape Breton – to where many people from South Uist emigrated – and piping tunes in Scotland. Tellingly, the performers that year all came from abroad and prompted islanders to become involved.

The programme is organised by Ceòlas (w ceolas.co.uk). This local organisation celebrates and promotes local Gaelic culture and heritage and has been a key driver in the island's social and cultural resurgence, collaborating with the local community through schools and other means. The festival involves singing, music and step dance. 'The culture was alive in the community anyway,' says Mary Schmoller of Ceòlas, 'But we now have groups of young people with degrees in Gaelic music. That never used to happen.'

Mary also thinks the festival says something more about Gaelic culture on South Uist. 'We were the victims of the clearances but we can't live our lives as victims. The impact of that was tangible until very modern times. Gaelic is our first language and that matters for how we think about the world and our values.'

The artist Margaret Joan MacIsaac, who has attended Ceòlas, described the festival's importance thus: 'It is exciting to know like seeds taken by the wind how our culture is taken worldwide to grow and flourish. It takes the negative of forced exodus and turns it into the positive of the sharing of rich experiences, language, laughter, skills and love.'

Poetry too still thrives on the island. In 2014, Niall Campbell, a poet who spent his childhood on South Uist, won one of the UK's richest poetry prizes, the Edwin Morgan Poetry prize, with *Moontide*, a debut collection that evoked the island where he grew up.

Gaelic music CDs are worth seeking out in South Uist shops and tourist sites. In particular, an anthology of songs sung by local people *Gaoth an Iar* (*The Wind from the West*) says much about the important role music plays. The lyrics of the title song give a good flavour:

Gaoth na seige gaoth an eisg	Wind for hunting, wind for fishing,
Gaoth na seilge mun mhainnear	Wind of the cattle by the house
Gaoth na feamann anns a chroic	Wind of the seaweed by the rocks
Gaoth an eòirn air gach machair	Wind of barley on every machair

me and made islanders furious,' says Donnie. 'There was a real want and need for such a facility – we had 1,500 people in here in the first eight weeks we opened.'

SHOPPING Located near Loch Càrnan on the A865, **Lovats supermarket** (☉ 08.00–18.00 Mon–Sat, 14.00–16.00 Sun) stocks the usual groceries plus ready meals from the Orasay Inn and curries from Café Kisimul on Barra. Just as handy is the **Co-op** at Creagorry on the southern tip of Benbecula (page 229).

The **Co-op** at Daliburgh (☉ 07.00–22.00 Mon–Sat, 12.30–22.00 Sun) is the only place to buy groceries in the southern half of South Uist. Souvenirs can be picked up at the inventive Uist Gifts & Information Centre in Lochboisdale (see opposite).

South Uist (Uibhist a Deas) and Eriskay (Eirisgeidh) SOUTH UIST (UIBHIST A DEAS)

8

ACTIVITIES Uist Archaeology (✆ 01878 700053; e walks@uistarchaeology.com; w uistarchaeology.com/walks) offers a range of excellent guided **archaeological tours** for both specialists and the curious. Dr Kate MacDonald and Dr Rebecca Rennell will take you to Norse farmsteads, Iron Age brochs and Neolithic tombs. As Kate puts it: 'You see the sites in the wild, without the polished interpretation centres and car parks that can detract from them. People get a real sense of discovery.'

Cycling is a good way to see South Uist. Though far from the flatlands they are sometimes portrayed to be, the terrain is easy to get around by bicycle (and gives those cycling the Hebridean Way northwards a chance to bank some relatively easy miles before they hit the North Harris Hills. Tommy MacDonald (✆ 01870 620283; m 07740 364093; e macdhomhnaill@gmail.com), just by the main road at Howmore, hires bikes by the day or longer for those cycling from the Butt of Lewis to Eriskay. He can arrange for bikes to be collected from either end of the route so you don't have to cycle all the way back.

Fishing is a great way to spend time outdoors on South Uist. Boats, ghillies and the like are easily available, as are permits (£25–60/day, based on 2 rods per boat). The key point of information is South Uist Fishing (✆ 01878 700101; e info@ storasuibhist.com; w southuistfishing.com), a helpful organisation that will give advice on where to fish and what permits you need.

With some 190 freshwater lochs, South Uist makes for some of the finest wild game trout and salmon fishing in Europe. The lack of fish farms in the western watershed of the islands has kept the gene pool pure and, according to local rumour, stocks can be traced back to the Ice Age. Brown and sea trout have thrived on the rare combination of shell sand and alkaline machair lochs on the west side. The peaty and acidic moorland hill lochs, lower in nutrients, cultivate a smaller but sportier fish, and, according to local fishermen, the hard-won fish in the hills of South Uist are a challenge for even the experienced angler. The sea-trout lochs of South Uist also offer an excellent opportunity to catch salmon.

A good option for **boat tours** is Lochboisdale-based Uist Sea Tours (m 07833 690693; e info@uistseatours.com; w uistseatours.com). Friendly David Steele runs various tours: looking for bottlenose dolphins in the Sound of Barra (£40/£25), to the Monachs (£70/£50) and sailing around Mingulay, south of Barra (£70/£50). Also available are evening tours around Uist coastal waters with seafood and drinks included. David has recently added St Kilda to his destinations. Check the website for details.

Askernish Golf Course (✆ 01878 700101; e info@askernishgolfclub.com; w askernishgolfclub.com) lays claim to being the oldest **links golf course** in the world and has something of a reputation among the global golfing community. Accordingly, it features on most golfing bucket lists of courses to play at; devotees are known to fly in, play a round of golf and depart the same day. The original nine-hole course on Askernish machair was laid out by one of the game's most revered golf course architects, 'Old' Tom Morris, on a visit to Uist in the 1880s. Morris and a companion travelled to South Uist by cart, train and steamer to lay out a course which he described as 'second to none in the various elements which go to make up a really good golf course'. A few years ago, Askernish was completely redesigned as an 18-hole course. The course is open year-round, and a daytime round costs £45 (less in winter); the rate for a twilight round, popular in summer, is £35. The clubhouse is open to non-members, is licensed and has comfy sofas from which to enjoy the views, whether you are a golfer or not.

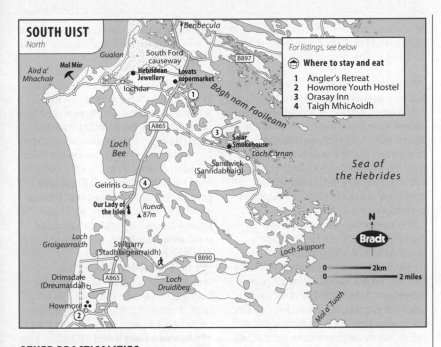

For listings, see below

⊛ **Where to stay and eat**

1 Angler's Retreat
2 Howmore Youth Hostel
3 Orasay Inn
4 Taigh MhicAoidh

OTHER PRACTICALITIES
Bank
$ Bank of Scotland Lochboisdale; ✆01878 700399; ⏰ 10.00–16.00 Mon & Fri. Has an ATM.

Medical
✚ **Balivanich Community Clinic** Balivanich, Benbecula; ✆01870 602266
✚ **South Uist Medical Practice** Daliburgh, South Uist; ✆01878 700302

✚ **Uist & Barra Hospital** Balivanich, Benbecula; ✆01870 603600

Post office
✉ **Daliburgh** ⏰ 08.30–17.30 Mon–Tue & Thu–Fri, 08.30–13.30 Wed, 09.30–13.00 Sat
✉ **Lochboisdale** ⏰ 09.00–17.30 Mon-Fri (closed lunch 13.00–14.00), 10.00–14.00 Sat

NORTHERN PART OF SOUTH UIST: FROM LOCH CÀRNAN TO LOCH BEE (LOCH BÌ) AND HOWMORE (TOBHA MÒR)
Exploring the northern part of South Uist requires you to turn off the A865. To the west are the dunes and strands of **Iochdar** and the **Hebridean Jewellery** gallery, to the east are the lonely shores of **Loch Càrnan**. Further south along the coast are the pre-Christian ruins of **Howmore**. Interspersed along the way are a series of sea and freshwater lochs that are dramatically traversed by causeways.

⬆ Where to stay and eat *Map, above*
One thing worth noting is that, while there is a handful of good places to stay at the northern end of South Uist, most accommodation is centred in and around Lochboisdale in the south. While the distance between the causeways at either end of the island is not great, this can become a tiring and repetitive drive, and time-consuming if using the infrequent though dependable buses. For that reason, if you want to explore the northern end of the island and struggle to find accommodation there, you might consider basing yourself on Benbecula or North Uist. A list of self-catering places to stay on South Uist and Eriskay can be found

at w visitouterhebrides.co.uk/accommodation. As for eating, apart from the café at Hebridean Jewellery (page 246), there is nowhere in the top half of the island where you can simply pop in for a sandwich and a cuppa.

Orasay Inn (9 rooms) Loch Càrnan; 01870 610298; e info@orasayinn.co.uk; w orasayinn.com. A small hotel standing in supreme isolation among the stark moors around Loch Càrnan, run by Alan & Isobel Graham. A cosy place, rooms decorated with local photography. The best choices are the deluxe rooms 3 & 4, furbished in chocolate tones, with walk-in shower, sofa & decking area with views across the moors. All accommodation is at ground level with a ramp at the front of the property; both deluxe rooms are wheelchair accessible. Its excellent restaurant (**£££**) – airy & light, & smartly furbished in scarlet tones, with views to Rum & the Cuillin on Skye – has a reputation as the Uists' best, thanks to Isobel's cooking. It is open to non-residents (booking advisable) & has a decking area for alfresco dining in good weather. The couple have good contacts with local fishermen, so starters include mussels, crab cakes & clams; mains include Hebridean paella & monkfish scampi. If you're not in a fishy mood, try Isobel's excellent chicken curry or beef from the owners' herd of Highland cattle. Most other meats, including game, come from the islands, as do most vegetables. If you've room afterwards, cheesecake & apple crumble vie for pudding. **£££**

Angler's Retreat (3 rooms) 1 Ardmore, lochdar; 01870 610325; e info@anglersretreat.

net; w anglersretreat.net. Warm en-suite rooms include a ground-floor dbl accessible to travellers with mobility problems. Property boasts a midge-free area, kept bite-free thanks to a midge trap. Despite the name, this is not exclusively an angler's haunt – the owners have an extensive knowledge of fish but also of wildlife & local walks. They will freeze any catch you bring home & offer use of a private boat on the loch. Evening meals (residents only) £20 for 3 courses. Owners Gary & Fiona Bateman have recently installed a comfortable self-catering pod (sleeps 4) in their grounds – good value at £75/night. **££**

Taigh MhicAoidh (3 rooms) West Gerinish; 01870 620379; e taighmhicaoidh@hotmail.co.uk. 3 en-suite dbls with TV, tea & coffee. Wonderful location overlooking Loch Bee. Comfortable, light guest lounge at the back. **££**

Howmore Youth Hostel (16 beds) e howmore@gatliff.org.uk; w gatliff.org.uk/howmore-hostel. 1 of the 3 Gatliff hostels in the Outer Hebrides, Howmore is housed in a restored thatched blackhouse with the 13th-century ruins of Howmore right next door. 2 dorms of 6 beds & 1 of 4. Good kitchen with microwave, gas rings, crockery & drying towels. Separate toilet & hot showers. No advance bookings. **£**

What to see and do It's all too easy after crossing the causeway from Benbecula to drive past the turning east to **Loch Càrnan**, about 1½ miles further south. Yet this quiet road gives a classic introduction to South Uist's beauty: a long, winding single track into a land of striking emptiness. Loch Càrnan is undisturbed at its headwaters, and the road passes a community wind farm as it edges its way east and south. The drive to the road end is pretty – once you have passed the power station – and generally hugs the shores of the loch before dribbling to its conclusion at a small promontory on the island's eastern shoreline. Here you can pull over and walk down through the gate to the small headland and take in a fetching landscape of tranquil lochs.

Some 2 miles down the Loch Càrnan turning and just past the wind turbine is the **Salar Smokehouse** ✳ (01870 610324; w salarsmokehouse.co.uk; ⏰ 09.00–16.30 Mon–Fri). The smokehouse was taken over and rejuvenated by local resident Iain MacRury in 2015, and the excellent shop sells various cuts of fish, including a whole side of salmon for around £35. The speciality is the flaky Salar smoked salmon, whose thick texture is achieved by curing, drying and cooking the fish at high heat before smoking it. This is done to a secret recipe that Iain fiercely protects.

Unexpectedly, this salmon-oriented business has one of the most thoughtful gift shops you'll find in the Outer Hebrides. Iain is evangelical in his ambition to promote local crafts and foods, so just about everything here is sourced locally and tailor-made for the shop. This includes soaps made by Samantha Johnson on Benbecula plus walking sticks and Tartan barrel bags made by local couple Donald and Helen MacAuley. 'Some of these people would never find an outlet for selling things that they just do at home,' says Iain. Perhaps the most eye-catching items are the bespoke products from Hebridean Jewellery, which include necklaces in the shape of a wave (the Salar Smokehouse motif). 'The more people can find out what these islands do, what they make, the better. The islands can feel very fragile at times. You have to support the local community, otherwise it's gone,' Iain says.

Back on the A865, the hill of Rueval (not the one on Benbecula) looms up to the east of the road, home to the paraphernalia of the **Hebrides Rangehead** (see box, below). Just as conspicuous is the statue of **Our Lady of the Isles**, carved by Hew Lorimer from white granite. At 9m (30ft) tall, it is the largest religious statue in Britain. The work is unusual in that it features the infant Christ held up to the shoulder of Mary, rather than cradled in her arms. You get a good view from the statue along the coast of the Uists. The statue is an emphatic reminder that you have left the Protestant north behind, and it is no coincidence that the Madonna and the military stand in such close proximity to one another. 'It was a political statement,' explains Mary Schmoller of Ceòlas, which promotes Gaelic culture and heritage on the island, 'in the sense that the islanders wanted to show the army that, while

MOD FIRING RANGE

The Ministry of Defence (MOD) established the Hebrides Rangehead on top of Rueval in 1957 and over the years has used its resources to test tactical nuclear missiles, air-to-air and ground-to-air missiles. The site is currently managed by Qinetiq, a defence contractor. The construction of the rocket range prompted a huge and rather hurried programme of rescue archaeology, which uncovered a Viking house at Driomòr and wheelhouses at Gerinish and Solas. Testing involves missiles fired out over the Atlantic and tracked by a base on St Kilda. For this reason – and to some local environmental scepticism – the MOD has consistently objected to proposals for local wind farms, arguing that they interfere with radar.

Talk comes and goes that the site faces closure, but for now it is still used for some high-level testing. In the autumn of 2015, NATO forces conducted a 'maritime theatre missile defence' exercise offshore, during which South Uist became the first place in Europe to launch a space rocket, when an 'exo-atmospheric intercept' missile was fired.

Terrestrial exercises are infrequent, but firing times are posted on the Grogarry lodge track (✛ NF755398) and on information boards in all harbours across the Uists. When the range is in operation, red flags are raised and red lights are shown on access roads. The key imposition on travellers at these times is that you will not be able to walk along the beach at Staoinebrig, Bornais or Drimsdale (close to Howmore) or in the machair northwest of Loch Bee around Àird a' Mhachair. More rarely, the army hosts larger international exercises offshore and when these occur the military has a habit of block-booking accommodation across the Uists, so it's always worth calling well in advance to secure a bed.

Coming from the north, the causeway crossing to South Uist can be exhilarating, cutting across the sea for more than half a mile. But this belies the problematic and sometimes tragic challenges that have been associated with traversing the sea here. The causeway in use today replaced an eight-span single-lane bridge constructed during World War II which humped its way from bank to bank to facilitate access to the military airport on Benbecula. The new causeway was completed in 1982 at a price tag of £2.2 million; the opening ceremony took place in a howling gale.

In January 2005, a storm claimed the lives of five members of the same family in Iochdar: two young children, their parents and a grandfather. The family were believed to have got into trouble as they left their home to escape the flooding in two cars. The bereaved families believe the causeway was a significant factor in the deaths of their loved ones, and say that it acted as a dam. This meant that the wind-driven Atlantic was unable to pass through the blocked channel and instead spilled out on to the surrounding land like an overflowing bath and submerged the coastal roads to a high watermark of more than 1.8m (6ft). For several years, relatives and other campaigners have called for openings to be cut in the causeway, so that sea water can escape. The island council has said such a move would not be cost effective, but the campaign continues with significant local support and feeling.

there is a militaristic world, a material world, there is also a spiritual world.' Smaller statues of the Madonna guard other access tracks to the range, ensuring that no personnel can enter the rangehead without receiving such a reminder.

On the northwest edge of South Uist is **Hebridean Jewellery** (✎ 01870 610288; w hebrideanjewellery.co.uk; ⊕ 09.00–17.30 Mon–Sat), a hugely successful artistic outlet. Their engaging and distinctive work, produced in the studio next to the shop, has Celtic and Pictish features, such as rings engraved with Gaelic motifs. There are also fetching earrings in the shape of seabird feathers and seahorses plus bloodstone, aventurine and topaz set in intricately patterned brooches. Expect to pay anything from £40 to £400. Nowadays, the company is a workers' co-operative, which took over when founder John Hart retired in 2011. Jewellers are trained in-house. 'John was keen that the company stayed in the Hebrides,' says the shop's manager Billy MacPhee. 'He wanted to keep the tradition going.' The company also has an outlet in Stornoway (page 84). The café (⊕ same hours as shop) serves salmon bagels along with toasties, wraps and an impressive range of metropolitan barista coffee (£). The location is stunning and, if the tide is out, a delightful walk across the sands leads to the dunes at Gualan. Keep an eye on tide times, however, as the sea rushes in.

The headland at **Àird a' Mhachair**, west of Iochdar, is an elemental place in high winds – wonderful for watching seabirds – and has fine views right down the coastline. Large colonies of black-headed gulls are often seen on the machair here. The beach here at **Mol Mòr** makes for a short but pleasant walk; the best place to park is above the western end of the beach, from where you can walk northeast along the shoreline.

Heading south, the A865 slices straight across **Loch Bee (Loch Bì)**. This wonderful loch is home to one of the largest swan colonies in Britain as well as other wildfowl, among them hundreds of greylag geese. A highlight is a resident population of 700 mute swans, which you can tell apart by their bills, which are largely more orange compared with the yellow bills of other swan species. The sight of these birds determinedly paddling and slicing through a headwind is quite a spectacle. Whooper swans overwinter here in smaller numbers.

The loch is brackish and actually – just – bisects South Uist from west to east via a couple of floodgates at pinch points north of Beinn Tairbert. At its eastern end, the loch squeezes between the lowest-lying contours of the rugged moors and bursts into life again as **Loch Skipport (Loch Sgiopoirt),** a huge sea loch with narrow entrances, controlled by tidal valves, that empties into the sea on the east coast. The road link across Loch Bee is thought to be the oldest causeway in what is known as the Western Isles spinal route.

Three miles south of Loch Bee, **Loch Druidibeg,** with its dark peaty waters, could not be more different in character. Many seabirds congregate at the water's edge, including great black-backed gull and sanderling, while in spring and summer you are likely to see many nesting oystercatcher, lapwing and black-throated diver. Geese and golden plover see out the winter here. Accordingly, this is a good place to see birds of prey from the nearby mountains on the hunt for a meal.

The loch's status as a National Nature Reserve (NNR) was withdrawn a few years back; the decision was uncontroversial and was seen to reflect the comparative difficulty of public access to the loch rather than any poor environmental management. Given the loss of NNR designation, it is ironic that access has improved tremendously in the past couple of years thanks to a stretch of the Hebridean Way (see box, page 50) that now cuts across the loch. This provides a welcome, much-needed route for visitors to explore the loch's austere beauty. Park your car or bike by Loch Druidibeg in the lay-by on the B890 (✪ NF790382). From here, the track is clear and goes through a kissing gate before winding across the moors. You can walk as far as you want: a short stretch of the route is on open ground with obvious waymarkers, but for the most part there is a gravel track, stretches of boardwalk and even a bridge. You've every chance of watching a swan skim down on to the loch and paddle away silently, unruffled, its neck long and stiff, its body still, as if dragged along by an unseen underwater pulley, or of passing a sheep's skull that has been picked clean by scavengers. It can all *feel* wonderfully remote without actually being so. To the south, the Beinn Mhòr range looms up, while the MOD rangehead and its companion Madonna gaze down on you from the north. The route meets the A865 at the junction with Drimsdale (Dreumasdal), and it will take you about 45 minutes to reach here. Return by retracing your steps.

Follow the B890 east to its conclusion and you spring yourself upon **Loch Skipport**. The winding road is a picturesque affair: along the way look out for the unexpected sight of monkey puzzles and rhododendron planted by a landowner who planned to build a house in the grounds but, losing patience at the slow growth that followed, built on the machair instead. I was directed to make the journey to the end of the road by Anne MacLennan, who runs the Lochboisdale post office and remembers playing on the jetty as a child. The village at Àird Horragaigh across the pier here was inhabited until the 1970s. When electricity came to the Uists, for reasons of cost this community was not connected to the grid and was subsequently abandoned. You can just see the roofs and gables of a couple of the buildings. The view across to the mainland from here is sensational: Skye looks close enough to reach out and touch. Once upon a time, the pier, now on the point of collapse, was where the Royal Yacht *Britannia* would dock. Loch Skipport is also a good place to look out for hen harrier, golden eagle and short-eared owl; you have a good chance of seeing them if you follow the waymarked track from the small car park south around the headland to Caolas Mòr, a lovely rocky bay and a walk of no more than 10–15 minutes or half a mile.

⚊ ✳ FROM THE MOOR TO THE MACHAIR *Map, opposite*

9½km (6 miles); 3hrs
OS Explorer 453 Benbecula & South Uist
Start/finish: lay-by on the B890 (✪ NF790382)

As described on page 247, you can explore Loch Druidibeg and retrace your steps. If you have the inclination, you can extend that walk considerably by taking in a glorious stretch of machair the other side of the main road. Follow the Hebridean Way across Loch Druidibeg from the lay-by to the A865. Cross with care and go straight ahead along the track to Drimsdale House. The contrast of colour between the dark green of the loch shore and the bright green of the machair and the step-by-step transition between the two is striking and fascinating to trace. The birdlife changes too: on the loch you may see swans and golden plover; on the machair the sky in spring and summer is full of lapwing and skylark.

As you approach Drimsdale House at Dreumasdal, look out on the left for the small loch with the squat, stone ruins of a castle in the middle, linked to the shoreline by a submerged walkway. This is Caisteal Bheagram, a ruined 15th/16th-century oblong tower, far diminished from its once-mighty status as a Clanranald stronghold. Keep walking to the end of the paved lane and then keep ahead along the track, keeping Drimsdale House and farm buildings to your right. At the end, turn right through the gate following a purple waymarker post. Keep on this path with the coast away to your left. Pass one lane on your right; when you reach a second lane (✪ NF758398) turn right, walk down the lane past Groigearraidh and across the A865 past Hopewell Cottage.

Walk down the B890 – it's a very quiet road – for 1½ miles back to the small lay-by. In an ideal world, you would time your walk to complete this stretch on a fine summer evening to the accompaniment of a bronzed sun bouncing off the burnished peaty-brown of the lochs as it sets over the Atlantic.

A couple of miles south along the A865 is the signposted turning for **Howmore** (**Tobha Mòr**). Travel along the narrow lane, which is lined by some enterprisingly restored blackhouses and you reach the fractured remains of walls, gables and a still-consecrated churchyard. These make up the ruins of Howmore, which are regarded by archaeologists as the most important Christian site in the Outer Hebrides. Howmore is believed to have been an important ecclesiastical centre from early medieval times, dating to the 8th century when the area was effectively an island, cut off from South Uist by a narrow, marshy waterway. Today's visible remains are thought to date from AD1200 and to resemble early Irish–Celtic monastic sites. 'Tobha' comes from an old Norse word for 'mound', and the four ruined churches and chapels sit on a mound surrounded by low-lying lumpy and uneven land.

The graveyard is the largest feature and within it are four Celtic crosses. Other elements of ruined, roofless chapels are scattered within and outside the graveyard. There are two carefully maintained graves from World War I. The ruins were also home to the 16th-century Clanranald stone, which bears the coat of arms of the clan. In 1990, the stone was stolen (though no-one noticed for three months) and discovered in a London flat five years later. The stone was found during a house clearance after the occupant died, prompting media and local talk of a curse that struck anyone who desecrated the site. You can walk down to the coast from here –

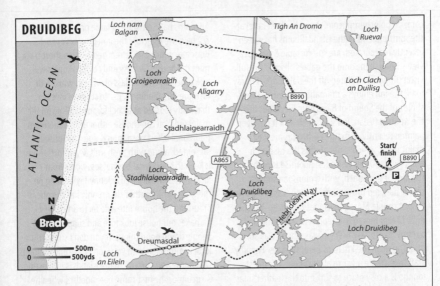

just head to the left of the large Church of Scotland. When you reach the T-junction with the grassy track, turn left and head to the small bridge under which runs the outflow of two lochs. Turn right here to follow the Howmore River to the sea where the high dunes are backed by marram grass.

SOUTHERN PART OF SOUTH UIST: FROM LOCH EYNORT (LOCH AINEORT) TO KILDONAN AND ON TO LOCHBOISDALE

The further south you go, the emptier South Uist seems to get, with houses few and far between and little for company except a Patagonia-style landscape and the increasingly towering presence of the Beinn Mhòr mountain range. Turning off the main road will reward you with some of the most picturesque parts of the island along the shores of **Loch Eynort**.

On the opposite coast, **Bornais** and its prehistoric remains jut out into the Atlantic, while a few miles south the charming **Kildonan Museum** should not be missed. A small number of scattered and rather stark communities huddle together at the bottom of the island, where you can satisfy any longings you may have for a pub meal. There are few sights to 'do' as such here, so instead the key is to get off the main road and explore one of the most unpopulated – and depopulated – parts of the UK.

⌂ Where to stay *Map, page 251*

⌂ **Borrodale Hotel** (12 rooms) Daliburgh; 🕿 01878 700444; e reservations@borrodalehotel. co.uk; w isleshotelgroup.co.uk. 9 en-suite rooms, 3 with private bathroom. All rooms have been redecorated in recent years, although the same can't yet always be said for the bathrooms & furnishings. 1 recently installed room downstairs for travellers with limited mobility, though the door opens directly on to the lounge. The Borrodale's white-&-green chequered façade is visible from miles around. Its Hebridean ensemble of fixtures & fittings has a certain charm & includes

a snug lounge with exposed stone walls, heavy doors & fireplace. Family room sleeps 4 & has benefited most from the latest lick of paint. The bar can be a convivial place to eat & drink, offering a good list of malts. The same menu (**££**) is served in both bar & restaurant & ranges from standard fare (pies, fish & chips) to local salmon carbonara & – perhaps tongue in cheek – a 'gateau of haggis & neeps'. Prices can feel rather high for what you get. **£££**

⌂ **Polochar Inn** (11 rooms) Polochar, near Daliburgh; 🕿 01878 700215; e polocharinn@aol.

249

com; w polocharinn.com. By far the best hotel at the southern end of the island. Rooms have been recently redecorated, are comfortable & have sea views, though in some the gables obscure the full vista. Gloriously isolated off the Daliburgh–Eriskay road, the inn enjoys a dramatic position on the shores of the Sound of Barra with views out to the Atlantic Ocean. It always feels as if it has been painted recently, & fixtures & fittings are well maintained, which is not always the case with hotels in the Outer Hebrides. Room 34 is probably the pick of the bunch, with a monsoon shower, sofa & dark red furnishings. The inn was taken over by Uist couple Morag Macinnes & Duncan Aitkens in 2018. For Morag this represents something of a return home. 'My first job was when I was 16, washing up in the kitchens here,' she says. Friendly staff help create a warm atmosphere. The guest lounge is a cosy place to sink into the leather sofas while a public bar at the back has more of a pub feel, with a dartboard & snooker table. The same menu (££) is served in both the lounge bar (with exposed stone walls & recesses decorated with local art) & the restaurant (a pleasant grey-blue tone to the furnishings). Seafood tends to be very good (including Barra scampi) & steaks are huge. Children's meals available. The name 'Polochar' comes from the Gaelic poll a'charra (meaning 'inlet of the stone') & refers to the lichen-encrusted standing stone outside the front door. Its provenance is uncertain but its position suggests it may have been a waymarker for prehistoric seafarers (the origins of the pub itself are thought to be as a staging house for passengers at a time when the ferry to Barra left from the adjacent shore; the solid stones inside the entrance are believed to hark from these – as yet – unspecified times). £££

⌂ **Ard Na Mara** (5 rooms) Kilpheder; ☎ 01878 700452; e info@ardnamara.co.uk; w ardnamara. co.uk. All rooms en suite & luxuriously furnished. A couple of the upper dormer rooms are spacious enough to verge on the status of suite. The name means 'high above the sea' & reflects the position of the B&B, 6 miles north of Lochboisdale. ££

✳ ⌂ **Heron Point** (4 rooms) 452 Lochboisdale; ☎ 01878 700073; e info@heronpoint. co.uk; w heronpoint.co.uk. This is an excellently run & convivial B&B, one of the very best in the Outer Hebrides & really worth seeking out. A twin & a dbl are downstairs, with another twin & dbl upstairs.

All rooms have en-suite or large private bathrooms & 2 have views across the inner waters of Loch Boisdale, which can be reached along a short track from the house. Owners Andy & Jan Biddles will welcome you with a glass of wine or whisky. B/fasts are outstanding & it's no surprise to learn that Andy worked as a chef for many years on the mainland. You can choose either from a succulent traditional b/fast or salmon & eggs, beautifully presented, along with fresh fruit & yoghurts. Andy is keen to boost local businesses; works from local artists William Neil & Jenny Taylor hang on the walls, which rather charmingly has the effect of turning the house into a de facto art gallery. 'It makes our house look nice and supports local people doing good things. If you don't support the local community, then you won't have one for long,' says Andy. Andy's route to the islands is interesting & circuitous: he first came here aged 13 when he hitch-hiked his way from Leicester. There is a TV in the cosy lounge, which is always open & can be a good place to put the world to rights with fellow guests. 'My hope is that people arrive as strangers & leave as friends,' says Andy. Pet friendly – this is a rare example of a B&B that has had a positive online review from a dog. ££

⌂ **Kilvale Bed & Breakfast** (3 rooms) 240 Garryhellie, near Daliburgh; ☎ 01878 700394; e maggie_steele@hotmail.com; w kilvale.com. A charming B&B just north of Daliburgh, run by friendly Margaret Steele. Comfortable en-suite rooms have thoughtful colour schemes – painted & furnished in seascape-blue, violet or coffee cream & overlook either the high hills or the coast. This is an appealing place: many of the pictures reflect Margaret's childhood on South Uist; there's a picture of the red telephone box that she had to walk a mile from her house to use & another of hay being gathered in sheaves – like mini wigwams – which was one of her childhood duties. 2 rooms are suitable for travellers with reduced mobility. ££.

⌂ **Lochboisdale Hotel** (15 rooms) Lochboisdale; ☎ 01878 700322; e karen@ lochboisdale.com; w lochboisdale.com. All rooms en suite, including that rare thing in the Outer Hebrides, a 5-bed family room. The hotel struggles on manfully, against both time & the elements: a handful of rooms are quite good – room 7 has a standalone bath – but many could do with a lick of paint & you always hear any wind that

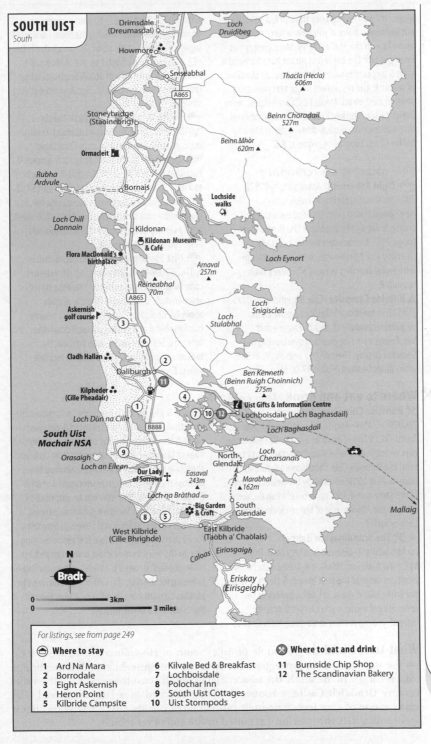

SOUTH UIST
South

Drimsdale
(Dreumasdal)

Loch Druidibeg

Howmore

Sniseabhal

A865

Thacla (Hecla) 606m

Stoneybridge
(Staoinebrig)

Beinn Choradail 527m

Ormacleit

Beinn Mhòr 620m

Rubha Ardvule

Bornais

Loch Chill Donnain

Kildonan

Kildonan Museum & Café

Loch Eynort

Flora MacDonald's birthplace

Arnaval 257m

Reineabhal 70m

A865

Lochside walks

Askernish golf course

Loch Snigiscleit

Loch Stulabhal

Cladh Hallan

Daliburgh

11

Ben Kenneth (Beinn Ruigh Choinnich) 275m

Kilpheder (Cille Pheadair)

4

7 10 12

Uist Gifts & Information Centre
Lochboisdale (Loch Baghasdail)

Loch Dùn na Cille

B888

Loch Baghasdail

South Uist Machair NSA

9

Orasaigh
Loch an Eilean

North Glendale

Loch Chearsanais

Our Lady of Sorrows ✝

Easaval 243m

Marabhal 162m

Mallaig

Loch na Bràthad

Big Garden & Croft

South Glendale

8 5

West Kilbride
(Cille Bhrighde)

East Kilbride
(Taòbh a' Chaòlais)

Caolas Eiriosgaigh

N

Bradt

0 _____ 3km
0 _____ 3 miles

Eriskay (Eirisgeigh)

251

For listings, see from page 249

🛏 Where to stay

1 Ard Na Mara
2 Borrodale
3 Eight Askernish
4 Heron Point
5 Kilbride Campsite
6 Kilvale Bed & Breakfast
7 Lochboisdale
8 Polochar Inn
9 South Uist Cottages
10 Uist Stormpods

✖ Where to eat and drink

11 Burnside Chip Shop
12 The Scandinavian Bakery

blows. It's well enough run though & a solid, if not uplifting, choice if you have a ferry to catch or arrive late on the Mallaig ferry. More energy has been put into the bar & restaurant based around a light & airy conservatory dining area. At the time of research, the restaurant décor was poised for another freshen up. Meals (££) are eclectic, from basics such as chicken Kiev to more adventurous Uist scallops *à la crème* & skate wing in black butter sauce. Lobster on request. ££

Self-catering and camping

🏠 **Eight Askernish** Askernish; 📞01878 700828; e mail@eightaskernish.scot; w eightaskernish.scot. Located near the golf course & run by the couple at the Big Garden (page 258). A converted crofter's cottage sleeping 4 in 2 bedrooms, with a cosy lounge with wood-burning stove. £575/week high season. £

⚠ **Kilbride Campsite** Cille Bhrighde; m 07751 251522; e mailbox@kilbridecampsite.co.uk; w kilbridecampsite.co.uk; ⏰ Easter–end Sep. Enjoys a stirring position overlooking the Sound of Eriskay. The café (⏰ seasonally in line with campsite, then 09.00–17.00 Mon–Sat,

noon–16.00 Sun) is open to non-campers, enjoys an enviable view overlooking the Sound of Barra & serves toasties & cakes alongside an all-day b/fast (£). Also run a new hostel on site (6 rooms; £), rooms all en suite, mix of dbls & rooms for larger groups & with open-plan lounge & wood-burning stove. £

🏠 **South Uist Cottages** North Boisdale; 📞01878 700371; e roderick@southuist-cottages. com; w southuist-cottages.com. 3 cottages managed under the brand: Canach is a converted barn that sleeps 4 at North Boisdale & is attached to a near-identical property, Kelp. Both cost £450–600/week. The nearby Corncrake, meanwhile, is a stone house that sleeps 6 & costs £580–800/week. Lovely setting, tucked away in the bottom left-hand corner of the island. £

🏠 **Uist Stormpods** (2 pods) Lochboisdale; 📞01878 700845; e uiststormpods@btinternet. com; w uiststormpods.co.uk. 2 striking turfed wooden pods shoehorned into the hillside above Lochboisdale. They each sleep 2 people comfortably, 4 at a push if you pull down the sofabeds. Self-contained, with kitchenette, microwave, outdoor tables & superb lochside views. £

✕ Where to eat and drink *Map, page 251*

✕ **Burnside Chip Shop** Daliburgh; 📞01878 700029; ⏰ May–Aug 16.00–21.00 daily, Sep–Apr 16.00–21.00 Thu–Sat. After a stop-start existence over recent years (more stop than start, truth be told) the Burnside Chip Shop was up & running once more in 2019. Located by the petrol station of the same name. Pick up excellent fish & chips & drive up the A865 to one of the sea lochs, such as Loch Eynort. £

✳ ✕ **The Scandinavian Bakery** Lochboisdale; w uistscandibakery.com. Run by Emma Axelsson, this home-based bakery produces some of the best breads & treats across the entire island chain. It's not a bakery in the conventional sense – you can't just drop by. Instead, you must order in advance from Emma's

website & pick up from her home in Lochboisdale. Everything is beautifully presented & options range from cinnamon buns to fresh sourdough, bags of brownies & Swedish specialities such as chocolate oat truffles & *biskvi*, an almond base of Swiss meringue buttercream covered in dark Belgian chocolate. You may not be surprised to learn that Emma is Swedish & born to parents who have been professional bakers in Sweden for 20 years. Emma is flexible & if you're arriving late on the ferry from Mallaig & want to pick up some goodies, or need brownies to take cycling or hiking for the day, she will oblige. You need to purchase a minimum number of items, though this is usually a small amount.

What to see and do A couple of miles south of Howmore, an attractive loop on the west coast circumnavigates the townships of Sniseabhal and Stoneybridge (Staoinebrig). To the south, the adjacent lane trundles past the remains of the 18th-century **Ormacleit Castle**, a roofless building attached to a later farmstead. The castle is one of very few stone-built castles on the islands. Just a few years after it was constructed, the interior was gutted by fire and never rebuilt.

The turning for **Bornais** leads to the lonely headland of **Rubha Ardvule (Rubha Àird a'Mhuile)**. If you drive or cycle, continue down the lane and keep left where the road bends right and keep going to park by the large church that stands in splendid isolation. From here, a lovely walk (2½ miles return) along a farm track leads through the machair to the headland. After passing a cattle track, a small interpretation board sheds some light on the seemingly flat landscape close by: look hard and you might be able to pick out a handful of mounds that are traces of one of the largest and most important Norse settlements in Scotland. The biggest mound was excavated and identified as the large house or hall of an important Viking chief and his family.

To get to the loch, continue on the winding track. Tempting as it is to walk on the machair, try to keep to the track during the breeding season to avoid disturbing the many ground-nesting birds. You may well be accompanied by peeping oystercatchers and the upward fluttering of skylarks.

Rubha Ardvule is one of few substantial rocky headlands along the west coast of South Uist and is an excellent place to spot passing birds such as shearwaters, gannets, petrels and skuas, along with nesting eiders and Arctic terns. There are fine views south to Barra, while northwards you can pick out the omnipresent water tower on Benbecula. Sunset on the flanks of Beinn Mhòr brings a sensational collage of colours, while its neighbour Beinn Choradail has a distinctive castellated summit that from this vantage point resembles a rakish top-knot. It's worth noting that this headland is within the Hebrides Rangehead danger area, but closures are infrequent.

On the other side of the A865, the turning for **Loch Eynort** ✳ cuts deep into the eastern half of South Uist and is one of the most delectable roads to explore. After half a mile, the narrow lane splits in two and the southern arm nudges southeast to a small jetty and panoramic views of the loch with a mountain backdrop. The northern track is by far the better option, though, and threads its way between hills and the loch to a dead-end beneath the hill of Beinn Bheag Dheas. This is good walking territory in the glowering shadow of Beinn Mhòr, with several paths leading from the car park.

A large part of the hillside by the car park is subject to a programme of woodland restoration – the vision of one man, Archie MacDonald, who lives nearby. This is a habitat you will find in few other places on the Uists. So far, Archie has planted more than 100,000 trees, from conifers to birch and holly. His efforts are bearing fruit as the trees begin to mature and the woodland becomes full of birdsong you will rarely hear elsewhere on these islands. There are several gravel paths to explore too: while none is waymarked, they thread through the gorse and either loop back on themselves or coil upwards to vantage points on Beinn Bheag Dheas, where Archie has managed to hump a bench to just below the summit.

A separate track from the car park follows the loch shore further east: after a stile and a small footbridge, the path carries on as a grassy track (look out for the gneiss picnic tables along the way), and you can meander below the foothills of Beinn Mhòr, which looks temptingly adjacent. Don't be seduced into an impromptu hike up the flanks, however, as the ascent is a serious undertaking in any weather, and there is no clear or consistent waymarked track to follow. If you want to walk up this hill (page 260), then seek out a specialist hiking book (page 298).

The loch shore by the car park is a great place to see white-tailed and golden eagles, which nest nearby within glaring distance of one another; with patience and luck, you may see all eight of the Outer Hebrides' birds of prey from this spot in a single day, along with otters. The advice of wildlife expert and tour guide Steve Duffield is simple: 'If you slow down and take your time, things come to you.'

8

Just south of Loch Eynort on the A865 is the **Kildonan Museum** ✳ (\01878 710343; w kildonanmuseum.co.uk; ⊕ Easter–Oct 10.00–17.00 daily; £3), one of those great little museums that make travel far from home so rewarding. The museum has benefited from recent redevelopment and highlights include an excellent display of how life on South Uist was lived until quite recently, including beds made from driftwood and mattresses from seaweed. Storytelling, crofting life and the unfolding of the clearances are all covered in thoughtful ways.

The revamp has, above all, enabled 'Kilpheder Kate' finally to be given a public airing. Kate is the name given to a skeleton dating to AD790 of a woman from **Kilpheder (Cille Pheadair)** some 6 miles further south. The woman was about 40 years old when she died, and remarkably precise tests have shown that she suffered from arthritis in her spine, jaw and right thumb. Her skeleton is laid out impressively within an air-controlled cabinet. Just inside the gate to the museum is a reconstruction of the Pictish square cairn in which she was found. The tomb's shape is unusual for the Hebrides and has been compared to those in Shetland.

The museum does a fine job in conveying to the visitor the cultural impact of the clearances on both those who left and those who stayed. Many emigrants eulogised the landscape and way of life; the museum collection includes artefacts, stories and visual recollections. The museum also houses the 16th-century Clanranald stone stolen from Howmore, which is thought to have been carved to commemorate John of Moidart, a 16th-century chieftain of the Clanranald (page 248). The fascinating and historically important photographic archive of Margaret Fay Shaw (see box, opposite), a folklorist and photographer, is also housed here.

The museum and facilities are accessible to people with limited mobility. An excellent shop (⊕ Easter–Sep 11.00–16.30 Mon–Sat, 13.00–16.00 Sun) across the courtyard from the museum showcases the innovative Uist Craft Producers (w uist-craft-producers.org.uk), a group of 40 local artists. Only work produced on Eriskay, South Uist, Benbecula and North Uist can be displayed. Artists on exhibit include stoneware specialist Miranda Forrest of Hebridean Glazes (\ 01878 710360; e miranda.forrest@tesco.net). Miranda's ceramic work uses only material that she can find on South Uist, such as the ash from her hearth and copper, which, though not naturally found on the island, can be located if Miranda rummages hard enough on the machair and beaches where it may have been discarded or washed up during the refurbishment of lighthouses. She uses these materials to striking effect, creating mesmerising patterns through the medium of the raku firing method: super-fast heating of (usually) stoneware followed by plunging it into cold water.

The museum's café (⊕ Easter–Oct same hours as museum, winter usually 10.00–16.00 Thu–Sun, check website; £) goes about its business with some gusto. As well as good coffee and cakes, it serves DIY paninis (including a black pudding option), fish finger butties and homemade milkshakes.

More or less opposite the museum, a small lane heads west to the promontory of Trolaisgeir. The 220m causeway that traverses Loch Kildonan here is one of the earliest such crossings, having been constructed for cart traffic many decades ago. It is still seen as a vital village link.

Flora MacDonald's birthplace is marked by a cairn and signposted off the main road to the west at Milton (Gearraidh Bhailteas), just south of Kildonan. Born in 1722, Flora's moment of fame came in 1746, when she agreed to help keep Bonnie Prince Charlie out of the hands of government forces after his botched rebellion had led to a crushing defeat at Culloden. Charlie was sent to Flora's brother's shieling, and she agreed to help him slip away to Skye, dressed as Betty Burke.

Few outsiders have depicted the landscapes, culture and people of South Uist as knowledgeably or with such love as Margaret Fay Shaw (1903–2004). Born and brought up near Pittsburgh and Philadelphia, USA, Shaw first visited Scotland in 1921 and settled in South Uist in 1928. There she lived, and became close friends with sisters Pèigi and Mairi MacRae of North Glendale. She learned Gaelic, became increasingly interested in the songs of the island and embarked on a career in photography.

Not only was Shaw a pioneering female photographer but she worked with tools and resources that were, in every sense, a lifetime away from our world of digital, Instagrammable images. She had to heave an ungainly 4½kg Graflex camera up hillsides, across peat moors or along cliff edges and then laboriously load the camera with metal sheaths and cut film. She once noted how 'I would liked to have developed the film myself but the water was from a stream that was filled with peat particles that I had no way to filter.'

Shaw married folklorist John Lorne Campbell and they moved to Barra before relocating to Canna in the Inner Hebrides. Their former home, Canna House, is now owned by the National Trust for Scotland and is home to the bulk of her vast archive of some 9,000 photographs and prints, along with moving images and transcriptions of folk songs. A good selection of these is always on view at the Kildonan Museum (see opposite).

Shaw retained an extraordinarily modest approach to her work and was never sentimental, nor did she seek to eulogise her subjects. 'It was a life that I loved,' she wrote. 'I never looked at it from an anthropological point of view… it was just for the pure enjoyment.'

That said, her love of South Uist comes across more clearly than that of any other island she came to know. 'Of all the islands I'd visited, there was something about South Uist that just won me; it was like falling in love. Of course, I was not looking for *islands*: I was looking for a way to live my life.' Her thoughts may chime with many visitors: although this is a purely anecdotal observation, if one asks long-term, regular travellers to the Outer Hebrides which island prompts the most intense emotion, South Uist comes out on top, time and time again. Shaw's grave is in the Cladh Hallan cemetery, near Daliburgh, along with those of the MacRae sisters.

It's a dramatic and true story, with the exception that this is almost certainly not where Flora was born. According to Anna Badcock and other archaeologists who co-authored *Ancient Uists*, there is evidence that Flora lived here for a time, but the houses are believed to have been occupied by kelp labourers and their families between the 1790s and 1820s, and not at the time of Flora's birth in 1722. Her real birthplace remains unknown, but it's fair to say it may well have been in the vicinity of the farm that stands here today. The remains of several blackhouses are visible among the pasture.

Reading about Flora's life on the weather-battered information board here, it's striking that subsequent events in Flora's life were just as remarkable. She was predictably jailed for aiding the prince; upon release she returned to Skye, married and migrated to North Carolina, where her husband fought for the British in the American War of Independence. Ultimately, she returned to Skye, all of which could be said to say something about where her true loyalties lay.

The tourist board has put together a **Bonnie Prince Charlie Trail** (w visitouterhebrides.co.uk, search 'Bonnie Prince Charlie Trail'). You should be able to pick up the leaflet at any tourist information centre and at the Kildonan Museum. It's loosely tied together by the main locations where the prince hid. Few of the sites are worth seeking out in their own right, but the trail provides a useful crash course in the travails of the prince and his escape by the thickness of his petticoat (see box, page 155).

Just the other side of the A865 from Milton lies the hill of **Reineabhal**, where an excellent example of a Neolithic chambered cairn is located on the lower northern slope. The cairn is 3½m (12ft) high and surrounded by a more or less circular group of larger stones. The chamber cannot be accessed, but to visit the cairn turn east off the A865 at the Mingearraidh crossroads. After 350m, take the track where the road forks to the right. The cairn is visible at the end of the track, about half a mile from the fork.

The A865 splits at Daliburgh (Dalabrog), forking east to Lochboisdale, while the B888 heads south towards Eriskay. Apart from the Borrodale Hotel, the sizeable

SOUTH UIST STORYTELLING

South Uist was one of the last places in western Europe where oral histories and tales continued to be handed down from one generation to another, and the oral culture of the Uist islands is said to have been among the strongest in the world. Islanders had little reliance on written texts, which meant that history was recorded – and places, names and traditional values kept alive – through storytelling.

At the Kildonan Museum, you can learn how tales were best performed, as the displays inform the visitor, by 'men with clear heads and wonderful memories, generally very poor and old, living in remote corners of remote islands and speaking only Gaelic. In short, the greatest tradition bearers are those who have lived most at home, furthest from the world and who have no source of mental relaxation beyond themselves and their neighbours.'

Stories were generally told around the open fire of the blackhouses. The prospects of this culture continuing beyond the early 20th century looked bleak with the outbreak of World War I. The Outer Hebrides contributed 6,200 men to the cause, more than 1,000 of whom were killed or went missing in action, which some say was the highest per capita casualty rate across the British Empire. Soon after those surviving men returned – those who might pick up the baton of storytelling from their elders – the blackhouse open fire was replaced by stoves which physically changed how people might sit and socialise.

The museum's case is that to eulogise the blackhouses for their role in oral culture is misleading and dangerous, and that wallowing in nostalgia achieves nothing and can lead to misrepresenting the past. 'You have to remember the diseases in the blackhouses,' says Ronald MacKinnon, a volunteer at the museum. 'The stoves were a step in the right direction.' Ronald says the culture of storytelling endured because modern communications did not arrive until much later. He maintains that the cultural strength of South Uist emerged despite poverty, persecution and the injustices of the clearances, not as a consequence of them: 'If you were in a township, only one or two people would have a radio; you still met and talked at church, at weddings, funerals. The tales stayed on.'

Church of St Peter's and a useful Co-op, there is little else to the township. The post office (page 243), however, is proof of the adage that you should not judge a book by its cover: in this case, the unprepossessing uPVC and weather-pummelled exterior conceals a shop well stocked with souvenirs and gifts, a hot-drinks machine and excellent island photography by postmaster Jeff Martin.

The archaeological remains of **Cladh Hallan** are signposted from the B888 in Daliburgh and reached along the road to the burial ground. Park by the graveyard, walk back along the track past the transmitter mast and turn right along the sandy track at the fingerpost sign for the site. What's on view is small but striking: three roundhouses, one of which is in the process of becoming a lochan, as water slowly accrues in its hollows.

The most remarkable discovery at Cladh Hallan is a truly bizarre collection of human bones, or 'bog bodies', as they have become known. Analysis of these has shown that, despite being so close to the sea, the Bronze Age peoples of South Uist ate predominantly meat and relied on fish for just 10% of their protein. The Bronze and Iron Age site was first inhabited around 2200BC, and a small U-shaped house was replaced around 1250BC by a roundhouse with low stone walls and a timber roof. It's thought that up to seven such buildings were constructed at Cladh Hallan and then rebuilt and reoccupied over the following 600 years. The remains of the better preserved of the two double roundhouses (dating to 500BC) can be visited on the north side of the track, some 200m nearer the sea.

The most startling discoveries were the human skeletons buried beneath the floors. One was of a young child, the others were a possible young female adult, an adult male and an adult female. Even more striking, though, was not just the fact that Bronze Age people of South Uist were able to mummify their dead, nor that these were the first prehistoric mummies to have been found anywhere in Britain; it was that both adult bodies comprised bones from three different people. The head came from one body, the jaw from another and the torso from a third. Radiocarbon dating has placed the torso at around 1500BC (early Bronze Age), but the other body parts belonged to humans who expired 100 years later. The mummification of these composite skeletons was probably achieved by encasing the body in the acidic peat bogs. Whether these were important ancestors or an example of a common practice is a tale that has yet to be told. When the analysis of the remains is complete, the Kildonan Museum, the Museum nan Eilean in Stornoway and the National Museum of Scotland in Edinburgh will each display one 'body'. It's a short walk from the site to the shore, where there are views of Barra, Vatersay and Mingulay ahead.

With its grid-like layout of lanes and tracks, the bottom left-hand corner of South Uist (west and southwest of Daliburgh) lends itself to easy exploration on foot or two wheels. As it is pancake flat you can cover a lot of ground in the course of a half or full day. You can walk south along the beach from Cille Pheadair all the way to the tidal island of Orosay (Orosaigh), a distance of 3.2km (2 miles). The walk across beach and rocky outcrops to Orosay is no more than 300m at low tide; the wild flowers are a delight in spring through to July and you can enjoy fine views up and down the coast and across to Barra. A Neolithic site, An Doirlinn, has been identified between the shore and the island. Exploring this area can also take in the remote, crumbling cemetery just inland from the island and the small lanes that skirt Loch Dùn na Cille and Loch an Eilean (there are still people in nearby townships who will not walk past these lochs at night, for fear that kelpies may snatch them and tug them under the water). Looking south as you near the main road you'll pick out the striking concrete slabs that join together to form Our Lady of Sorrows, a building straight from the textbook of Brutalist architecture.

The tiny township of **Lochboisdale** has something of an end-of-the-world feel. Perhaps it's the windswept flatlands that lead to it, but you wouldn't be surprised to see tumbleweed blowing down the main street on a Saturday afternoon. The hotel, which must once have been a stirring landmark to welcome ships to a safe berth, has seen better days. The village's fortunes may be changing for the better though, thanks to the opening of the friendly and super-enthusiastic Uist Gifts & Information Centre (page 240) at the quayside. Meanwhile, a new marina was completed in 2015, allowing yachts to moor here, and the new direct (summer-only) ferry route from Mallaig on the mainland should inject further life into the place. The village and surrounding townships are also good bases for exploring the countryside, the archaeological remains that are so abundant here, and walking the beaches or among the mountains. The play park here also has to be one of the most beautifully positioned in the UK, overlooking a loch where, in between hurtling along the zip wire, children can keep their eyes peeled for otters and eagles.

On a clear day, you can see Ardnamurchan Point on the mainland (the most westerly point of Britain as geographical pedants like to point out, rather than Land's End). The village's other saving grace is a clutch of good B&Bs. The village livens up each year for the run up Beinn Ruigh Choinnich (everyone calls it Ben Kenneth). The walk up the hill will take most people 2–3 hours there and back; the record for the run is 29 minutes.

At Kilbride on the southern tip of South Uist is **The Big Garden and Croft (An Gàrradh Mòr)**, an eye-catching, walled, permaculture garden (☏01878 700828; e mail@hebrideanwoolshed.co.uk; w biggarden.scot; ⊕ Apr–Sep 10.00–17.00 daily). The garden is also home to the **Hebridean Woolshed** (e mail@hebrideanwoolshed. scot; w hebrideanwoolshed.scot; see ad, 3rd colour section) and both establishments are run by enterprising couple Denise and Jonathan Bridge.

The Bridges moved to South Uist in 2002 and bought the croft with its walled garden. The land had historically been the laird's kitchen garden, the walls made from shell and rock from the shore. Having cleared the brambles and transformed the rough lawn of coarse grass, they saw their work all but undone by a hurricane-force storm that tore through in 2005. Undaunted, they persevered, benefiting from soil 1m deep (unusual on the islands and a striking contrast to the inch-thin machair soil just a stone's throw away) and fertile from centuries of mixing of seaweed and manure. Today, they rear hens within the garden before relocating them to their croft on Eriskay, where they also rear Hebridean sheep and geese. Vegetables are grown by a mixture of crop rotation, companion planting and bloody-mindedness, and with no pesticides. 'Things are always emerging and developing,' says Denise. 'It's fair to say that gardening here is not for the faint-hearted.'

The Bridges sell frozen cuts of two-year-old, or Hogget, lamb ('everything grows slowly here and takes time to mature,' explains Denise), including legs for £25–45 and shoulder shanks from £6. You can also pick up jams and chutneys, including a delicious lemon curd that gets its striking colour from the free-range eggs.

🚶 THROUGH GLENDALE

14½km (9 miles); 3–4hrs
OS Explorer 453 Benbecula & South Uist
Start/finish: road's-end North Glendale (⊕ NF790177)

Just about everyone heading south from Lochboisdale is bound for Eriskay and/or the Barra ferry. But if the idea of a walk through a remote, gloomy glen appeals, then the craggy, rather foreboding hills on the inland, east side of the B888 hides a magical walk linking the small communities of North and South Glendale. The moorland valley element of this walk lasts for just 2 miles but you find it feels disproportionately remote.

This walk assumes you have either a bicycle or a car. If there is no space at road's-end at North Glendale, park further back up the road, though always with consideration for others. You'll also need good boots; trainers will be inadequate. The first three-quarters of the walk is simple: walk due west along the road to the B888 and turn left. After 2½ miles, turn left again and continue past the Kilbride campsite with striking views across the bay to both Eriskay and Barra. Where the road turns right for the Eriskay causeway, keep ahead on the narrow lane, signposted for South Glendale. Continue to road's end (pass a bus turning space), which is where the rugged drama of this walk kicks in.

Go through the gate by the house and follow the track uphill. The path is always clear but gets ever squelchier as it climbs towards the brow. The hill of Easabhal, to the west, and Marabhal, to the east, glower down at you as you skirt to the east of lonely Loch na Bràthad. Golden eagles frequent this valley and a sighting adds a frisson to what just feels an isolated spot of the world. After half a mile Loch Chearsanais comes into view. The small clefts between the hills seem inviting and promise elevated views of this bleak landscape but do so with caution as they can be extremely soft underfoot.

Just north of Loch Chearsanais the track meets another grassy track that joins from the east. While this second track looks intriguing on the map, it is a serious undertaking and should be discounted on this occasion, for it winds its way over ever-deeper peat bogs, fording burns where bridges have collapsed, on its way to the coast and the very periphery of South Uist at Thairteabhagh. Instead, bear left and follow the path to return to North Glendale.

While the walled garden itself is not open to the public, the woolshed, in a corner of the garden, is where Denise produces high-quality wool products, such as cushions and little bags, as well as wool kits for hats, cowls and fingerless mittens. Denise does her own dyeing, taking crotal from the rocks, which gives a tan colour to the wool, and using nettles for shades of yellow and green. She also offers short weaving courses to visitors. A visit makes for a final, joyous surprise for those leaving the isles, or a delightful welcome to those coming up from Barra.

Hillwalking on South Uist South Uist is often considered to consist of flatlands, but that rather ignores the fact that it has the best of the southern hills, including a trio of impressive peaks: **Hecla**, also known as **Thacla** (606m/1,988ft), **Beinn Choradail** (527m/1,729ft) and **Beinn Mhòr** (620m/2,034ft), which dominate the skyline and can even be seen from the mainland.

Beinn Mhòr is the Uists' highest peak, and the Outer Hebrides' only 'Graham' (the term used for hills in Scotland of 610–762m (2,000–2,499ft). Despite their modest height, these three peaks are demanding of stamina, nerve and, in places, climbing technique. They eyeball the Cuillin range across the Minch on Skye and have razor-sharp edges almost as demanding as you would find there; they can narrow to points as thin as a gymnast's bar in places with 300m (1,000ft) sea drops.

The pay-off, however, for reaching their summits is some of the most wonderful and far-reaching views you will get anywhere in the UK and an outstanding wilderness experience. All three hills involve walking over open ground, through an often boggy landscape, where paths are frequently little more than goat tracks, unreliable or non-existent. There are even instances of walkers ending up waist deep in bog. For all three, remoteness is an important consideration, and sound judgement is probably even more essential than a map and compass. Before attempting any of these summits, you should obtain a specialist book on hillwalking in the area (page 298), and for that reason the routes are not described in detail here.

Each mountain presents its own challenges. The ascent of Beinn Mhòr can be begun from the end of the road in north Loch Eynort and is a 6-hour, 9½km (6-mile) round hike; alternatively, you can start from Sniseabhal just off the main road north of Loch Eynort for an ascent from the west. Beinn Mhòr has ditches and, closer to the summit, loose scree to contend with.

The route to Hecla begins either from the parking space a mile down the B888 from the A865, or from the road end at Loch Skipport. Again, these routes can be boggy and perhaps startling in places with steep corries, gullies and cliffs to watch out for. Hecla's summit is for the nerveless with a head for heights. Beinn Choradail, meanwhile, is usually hiked in combination with Hecla and can involve some genuine rock climbing, dispiriting cul-de-sacs and negotiation of a steep 'chimney'-style stack.

The adventurous but exhilarating loop of all three hills is usually walked from the Loch Skipport road south to Loch Eynort. This walk can easily take 7–8 hours and on the southern side is likely to traverse seriously boggy ground. The author's personal experience is that these hills are in a different league from the hills of Harris. If you attempt any of these walks, then tell your accommodation and leave them a sketch of the route you plan to take. The walks should of course only be undertaken in fine weather.

ERISKAY (EIRISGEIDH)

People often intend to scurry through Eriskay on the way to or from Barra only to find themselves halted in their tracks by the island's charm and beauty. Just 3 miles from north to south and 2 miles from east to west, Eriskay is probably best known for the tale of *Whisky Galore* and the subsequent Ealing Comedy based on the true travails of opportunistic islanders who endeavoured to stash away the booty of a shipwreck. The island also has a resonance for those with an interest in the journey of Bonnie Prince Charlie. The population of fewer than 200 is scattered around the north and west of the island, with no real focal point other than a good shop and pub. Despite these modest dimensions and demographics, Eriskay does not feel like a fragile community on the verge of depopulation, and there's an evident prosperity here, more so than you find on much of South Uist.

HISTORY Named after the Old Norse for 'Eric's Isle', the history of the island overlaps to a great extent with that of South Uist, Barra and Benbecula. All four islands were bought by General Gordon of Cluny in 1838, with a view to turning them into sheep farms. Eriskay, though, was not suited to grazing, and, ironically, many crofters on the other islands, when forced off their own lands, opted, at least initially, to relocate to Eriskay's meagre marginal land (unwanted by Cluny) rather than emigrate.

The ponies that are so associated with the island are entirely habituated to people and will delight visiting children. The ponies are thought to be pure-bred descendants of the island's original animals – unlike the cross-bred Highland pony on the mainland. Their historical presence was far from ornamental: they

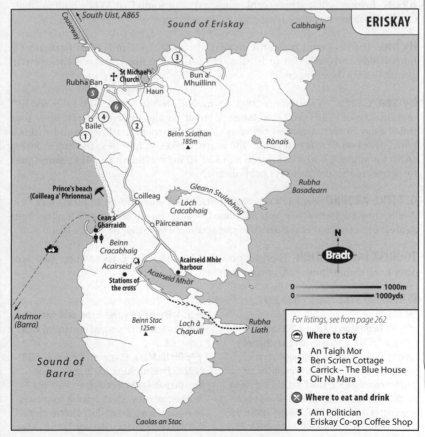

ERISKAY

- South Uist, A865
- Causeway
- Sound of Eriskay
- Calbhaigh
- St Michael's Church
- Rubha Ban
- Haun
- Bun a' Mhuillinn
- Baile
- Beinn Sciathan 185m
- Rònais
- Rubha Basadearn
- Prince's beach (Coilleag a' Phrionnsa)
- Coilleag
- Gleann Stulabhaig
- Loch Cracabhaig
- Cean a' Gharraidh
- Pàirceanan
- Beinn Cracabhaig
- Acairseid
- Acairseid Mhòr harbour
- Stations of the cross
- Acairseid Mhòr
- Ardmor (Barra)
- Beinn Stac 125m
- Loch à Chapuill
- Rubha Liath
- Sound of Barra
- Caolas an Stac

N

Bradt

| 0 | 1000m |
| 0 | 1000yds |

For listings, see from page 262

Where to stay
1 An Taigh Mor
2 Ben Scrien Cottage
3 Carrick – The Blue House
4 Oir Na Mara

Where to eat and drink
5 Am Politician
6 Eriskay Co-op Coffee Shop

were used for carrying peat, seaweed and harrowing. As farm vehicles developed in the 20th century, their numbers declined steeply and intervention only came in the 1970s with the establishment of The Society for the Preservation and Development of the Eriskay Pony, which has successfully reared a rising population from a low base of just 20 females and one stallion. From May to September, they are confined to the hills in order to allow the machair flowers to flaunt their beauty.

The causeway joining Eriskay to South Uist is a relatively recent development and the link gives fishermen from the South Uist area – who operate about 45 boats – important access to the excellent anchorage at Acarsaid in southern Eriskay. The island football pitch has also had its place in the sun, as FIFA has designated it one of the world's eight most remarkable places to play football; the pitch enjoys a scenic location on the west coast of the island, overlooking the Sound of Barra, and perhaps just as remarkably, occupies one of the few areas of level ground on the island. Music has also been something of a feature and the 'Eriskay Lilt', a love song from the island, became popular in the early 20th century from a Gaelic song collection by Marjory Kennedy-Fraser. At the last census, Eriskay had the highest percentage of any island in the Outer Hebrides stating their religion as Roman Catholicism, at 82%.

GETTING THERE AND AWAY

By car Eriskay is linked by a scenic causeway with South Uist. When built in 2000–01, the causeway was the largest civil-engineering project of its type in the UK.

By bus The W17 runs down the spine of the southern islands from Berneray via Lochmaddy on North Uist to Eriskay. For up-to-date timetables, visit w cne-siar. gov.uk (search 'bus services').

By sea CalMac (✆ 0800 066 5000, from outside the UK ✆ +44 1475 650397; w calmac.co.uk) runs the *Loch Àlainn*, a small car and passenger ferry, up to four times a day in each direction between Cean a' Gharraidh on Eriskay and Ardmor (Àirdmhòr) on Barra's east coast. The journey takes 40 minutes. The return fare is £6.50 for adults, £3.30 for children and £22.40 for a standard car. The nearest port for ferries to the mainland is Lochboisdale.

GETTING AROUND Eriskay's roads are hilly, twisty and amount to little more than 2 miles in total. In practice, you only need a car if you are arriving or leaving. Your nearest petrol station is at Burnside, just south of Daliburgh on South Uist.

TOURIST INFORMATION There is no official outlet. The Eriskay Shop (see box, opposite), with helpful staff, is your best bet.

 WHERE TO STAY *Map, page 261*
B&Bs

🏠 **An Taigh Mor** (3 rooms) 15b Balla; ✆ 01878 720717; e antaighmorbandb@gmail. com; w antaighmor.com. Contemporary & spacious rooms, mix of dbls & twins, all en suite, 2 with views of the Sound of Barra, the 3rd facing South Uist. Lovely mezzanine guest lounge with views out to sea. Run by Bill & Maggie Justice, who have relocated here after living in London for 20 years. This represents a return home of sorts for Maggie whose parents moved from Eriskay in the 1950s. **££**

🏠 **Oir Na Mara** (3 rooms) 5B Baile; ✆ 01878 720216. Excellent choice, just across the road from the pub. Run by friendly Mary MacInnes, who welcomes guests with delicious homebakes. All en-suite rooms, thoughtfully decorated with different colour schemes. The large dbl with a bay

COMMUNITY SHOPS

One feature of the Outer Hebrides is the number of community-run local shops which can put those rural chain stores you see on the UK mainland to shame. The Eriskay Co-op (page 264) was the first to go down the route of a community-owned food store on the islands. In 1979, the only shop and post office on the island was threatened with closure, when the owner retired and no-one came forward to take his place. In response, the local community started a co-operative and raised finance by buying £50 shares in the business. A total of £7,500 was raised, and matching government funding enabled the community to build a new shop and start trading.

As a co-operative, the Eriskay Shop became a corporate member of the Co-operative Group and has been able to order a regular supply of goods, fresh fruit and vegetables directly through the group. This has enabled the shop to overcome the sizeable logistics challenges of this part of the world and make a real difference to the quality of produce and the shop's viability. The shop fulfils a vital role on the island, enabling people to meet and carry out all of their weekly shopping locally. A bus service is provided twice weekly to the shop for Eriskay residents who have no transport, and there's a delivery service for those who are housebound. With eight staff, the shop is the largest single employer on the island and offers flexible working hours to parents. All profits are reinvested in the business. Community shops that have since opened up on Scalpay (now sadly closed) and in the South Lochs on Lewis turned to the Eriskay model for their template. 'The shop contributes to the viability of our community in a very marked and direct way,' says Catriona Walker, the shop manager. 'It's the hub of the community, the major source of news and information, and it contributes to decreasing social isolation particularly among our elderly Gaelic-speaking population.'

view is probably the pick. There is a guest lounge with a small collection of books. **££**

Self-catering

🏠 **Carrick – The Blue House** Bun a' Mhuillin; ☏ 01878 700828; e denise@ uistselfcateringcottages.scot; w carrickeriskay. scot. Another cottage owned by Denise & Jonathan Bridge (who run The Big Garden, page 258, &

manage the Eight Askernish property on South Uist). Modern & stylish. Guests are welcome – but not expected – to help on the croft, mucking out the hen coop or feeding newborn lambs. Sleeps 5. £930/week high season. **££**

🏠 **Ben Scrien Cottage** m 07855 931131; w eriskayholidaycottage.co.uk. Stands above the road to the ferry & has tremendous views across the Sound of Barra. Sleeps 7. £575/week. **£**

✖ WHERE TO EAT AND DRINK   *Map, page 261*

✖ **Am Politician** 3 Baile; ☏ 01878 720246; e ampolitician@hotmail.com; ⓕ ampolitician1; ⌚ Easter–late Sep 11.00–late Mon–Sat (food served noon–20.30), 12.30–late Sun (food 12.30–20.30), Oct–late Mar noon–21.30 Mon–Thu, noon–late Fri–Sat (food noon–20.00), 12.30–20.00 Sun (food 12.30–20.00). Named after the SS *Politician* (see box, page 266), this friendly & rightly well-regarded pub has benefited from a recent takeover by a local couple. Creative menu includes

Barra scallops for starters (these typically arrive the same day, on the morning ferry) & good fish mains, as well as halloumi burgers & vegetable curry. Homemade meringue is the pick of the filling puddings. The Politician has 2 original whisky bottles from the ill-fated steamer positioned on the bar (1 from the boat, the other recovered from the peat bog), though the whisky inside is not palatable (the original lead caps have long made any surviving whisky undrinkable). The bottles can be unexpectedly fascinating to behold, with imprints reading 'King's Ransom Scotch Whisky'. Keeping the bottles company are a cutlass destined for cutting sugarcane in Jamaica & a US World War I flare gun, both recovered from the ship. To their credit, the pub staff never tire of talking about the whole saga & happily bring out photographs & memorabilia for inspection, including original photographs of the booty being taken off the ship & an original Jamaican banknote. There is good disabled access for travellers with limited mobility. ££

✖ **Eriskay Co-op Coffee Shop (Co Chomun Eirisgeidh)** Rubha Ban; 📞 01878 720236;

e eriskayshop@gmail.com; ⊕ 09.00–18.00 Mon–Sat, Jun–Aug also 10.00–13.00 Sun; see ad, page 234. This tiny coffee shop inside the Eriskay Shop is a gem. The small space is imaginatively furnished with tables, chairs & counters fashioned from whisky barrels (sadly, not from the SS *Politician*). Along with good coffee & tea, the coffee shop sells island souvenirs & craftwork . This small outlet & the adjoining Co-op shop are run by Catriona Walker, whose phenomenal energy has seen both garner a huge following & flourish on the widespread goodwill of visitors. Both are community owned by shareholders. £

OTHER PRACTICALITIES
Medical
✚ **South Uist Medical Practice** Daliburgh; 📞 01878 700302
✚ **Uist & Barra Hospital** Balivanich, Benbecula; 📞 01870 603600

Post office
✉ **Eriskay Shop** Rubha Ban; ⊕ 09.00–14.00 Mon–Tue & Fri, 09.00–noon Wed, 09.00–13.00 Thu; see ad, page 234

WHAT TO SEE AND DO Eriskay is overlooked by St Michael's church at Haun in the heart of the island. If you don't fancy yomping over open ground to a high vantage point, this is the place to come and survey the lie of the land. The church altar is shaped like the prow of a ship and outside stands a ship's bell, rescued from the *Derflinger*, a German ship sunk some way north in Scapa Flow in 1919. Otherwise, Eriskay is an island on which to meander, perhaps climb a modest hill and stroll along beaches such as Coilleag a' Phrionnsa by the ferry slipway for Barra.

The best-quality gift to take home from Eriskay, if a pricey one, is an Eriskay jersey, one of the rarest pieces of craftwork in Scotland. Traditionally, these intricately patterned jerseys were woven by local women for their fishermen husbands. Today, just two ladies on the island make them, and each has their specific pattern, though they adhere strictly to the custom of using fine needles, ensuring the jersey is seamless. So far, no-one from younger generations has chosen to learn the craft, raising the possibility that this tradition may one day be lost. In keeping with tradition, the colours available are cream or navy blue, though the knitters will enquire if another colour of wool can be sourced. The jerseys are designed to be a tight fit and come with either a crew neckline or a stand-up with two buttons at the side. This skilled and time-consuming labour does not come cheap, and jerseys typically cost £250. The Eriskay Shop (see box, page 263) occasionally has one in stock; usually, though, you will need to order one. The shop can put you in touch with the knitters and they will post the sweater to you. The waiting time is six to nine months.

Whether you are on two feet or two or four wheels, the southeast corner of this interest-packed island is also worth exploring. Where the island road swings right towards the Barra ferry quay, instead go straight ahead downhill, signposted for **Acairseid**. You'll pass a red post box and after 350m the road turns right, while a grassy track goes straight ahead. Turning right leads shortly to the small harbour of Acairseid where the island's smaller boats go to and fro to gather their inshore lobster and crab pots. If you head straight along the grassy track, a short walk of 500m or so leads to a particularly picturesque corner of Eriskay. Ignore the small footbridge that leads to the deserted house on the right. Instead, keep ahead and

6½km (4 miles); 1½–2hrs
OS Explorer 452 Barra & Vatersay
Start/finish: Eriskay Shop, Rubha Ban

This short hike has all the ingredients of a perfect walk: great views, a wonderful beach, a pub and a café – in short, Eriskay in a nutshell. You can start this walk at any point along the route, but if you have a car it's probably courteous to park down by the slipway for the Sound of Barra ferry terminal. Cross the cattle grid and take the path to the sandy beach, Coilleag a' Phrionnsa, where Bonnie Prince Charlie landed on his return from France in July 1745. He landed with just seven supporters, a handful of weapons and little money. One local figure of authority, Alasdair MacDonald of Boisdale, told him to go home. Undeterred, the Prince only half-heeded his advice, heading instead for the mainland, raising an army of sorts but bumping – decisively and fatefully – into loyalist forces at Culloden a year later. Among the machair here is one flower, the pink convolvulus (or field bindweed), known locally as Prince Charlie's rose. Those with romantic imaginations claim the first flower sprouted from a seed that slipped from the prince's shoe.

The beach is a gorgeous crescent of sand, and out to sea you may well spot gannets crashing into the water. At the north end of the beach, follow the grassy track up on to the machair and around the headland to reach a couple of smaller but equally delectable bays where Eriskay seems to simply crumble into the sea. Just offshore is (Calvey Island) Calbhaig, where the SS *Politician* foundered, though the wreck is scarcely visible even at low tide.

If the tide is out, you can continue on the seaward side of the cemetery; if not head for the road and turn left. Either way you soon reach the Am Politician; you can break your walk for a drink here or continue up the lane, turn right and then first right again to reach the Eriskay Shop. Continue uphill and pass a statue of the Madonna protected by a white picket fence. Keep going uphill and just beyond a transmitter mast take the path off to the left that continues uphill. Down below you can see the football pitch: the local team plays in an inter-island competition with teams from the Uists and Barra and has sent players for trial with Scottish Championship teams on the mainland.

As you walk away from the road, a few paths seem to cross one another here. Look out for the waymarkers and if you don't always see them, just keep the slopes of Beinn Sciathan well to your left and stick to the path where you see it. Ahead you will see Loch Cracabhaig: keep this well to your left. Soon you will see another waymarker on a small brow. Head for this post and you will soon see the top of a water-treatment plant that leads to a track that you follow down to the road. Turn right uphill along the road and then first left to return to the slipway.

follow the narrowing track as it winds its way towards the shore where it terminates by the sea amid a serene gathering of miniature peaty pools.

A second, longer but rewarding, walk explores the west and south sides of Acairseid harbour. Return to the post box, turn left and walk for 200m up the track over the hill. After you descend you soon come to a small copse. Look up along the rock face to your right and you'll notice images representing **Stations of the Cross**. These were

THE SS *POLITICIAN* AND *WHISKY GALORE* (!)

In 1941, the 8,230-tonne cargo ship the SS *Politician*, bound for Jamaica and New Orleans, foundered on rocks just off the coast of Eriskay. Islanders rushed to assist the crew and passengers, and once all were safe they turned their attention to the cargo. Their enthusiasm for doing so should be put in the context of wartime privations and food shortages: the cargo included nearly 300,000 Jamaican 10-shilling notes, but of greater interest were the 260,000 bottles of whisky. It is said that the island men, knowing that recovering the bottles was legally dubious, wore their wives' dresses so as to avoid getting incriminating ship oil on their clothes.

The government view was that since the duty on the whisky was to have been paid in the United States, laws of salvage did not apply: it wanted the whisky back. The tale of how the islanders unloaded the booty and then hid it when the customs men came knocking has passed into lore.

Inspectors tracked down most of the bottles, and a few people served short jail sentences for theft. Meanwhile, the Jamaican banknotes began turning up all over the world, from Benbecula to Liverpool, Switzerland and the United States. The whisky saga was retold – with some panache and embellishment by Barra resident Compton Mackenzie – in his novel *Whisky Galore* ('galore', incidentally, is a corruption of the Gaelic 'gu leòr', meaning 'plenty'). Soon after, Ealing Studios realised the saga had rich material for a film, and Barra was chosen as the location for the (now classic) comedy *Whisky Galore!* starring Basil Radford, Joan Greenwood, James Robertson Justice and a young Gordon Jackson. Even Compton Mackenzie had a bit part as Captain Buncher. *Whisky Galore!* was a huge hit and was retitled *Tight Little Island* for the US audience. In 1987, a professional diver, Donald MacPhee from South Uist, found eight bottles of whisky in the wreck. He sold them at auction and walked away with £4,000. A remake of the film, starring Eddie Izzard and Gregor Fisher (best known for his TV comedy character Rab C Nesbitt), was released in 2016 to some sympathetic but mixed reviews – given the superlative nature of the original, this was perhaps unsurprising.

painted on slates taken from the old parish church in 1970 by Father Calum Macneill, then the parish priest. The old stone cottage by the wooden cross further up is now in a state of utter disrepair but is still used intermittently for services; the service for the Stations of the Cross is still held up here during Lent every year. The determined walker can keep climbing further, though you will be either stepping in peat-squelch or yomping on heather. While you do see Barra from the brow (a 5-minute walk from the cross), the best views are still from the slopes of Beinn Sciathan.

Returning downhill to the track, you now have the option of a further delightful 3km (1.8-mile; return) walk. Turn right, with the harbour of Acairseid Mhòr to your left and follow the track as it winds around the bay. Look out for an impressive sculpture of a stag above the bay and then, after the last house, cross the stile to your left. Again, keep to the thin but clear track as it winds its way above the shore. This soon swings gently uphill, over another stile and away from the bay. The bracken here is tenacious but the path is clear and delivers you above the isolated and peaty waters of Loch à Chapuill. The path, remarkably for somewhere so little walked, is good and winds its way all the way down to the sea, where a rocky inlet opens up with views across the Sea of the Hebrides towards Skye and Rum.

9

Barra (Bharraigh) and Vatersay (Bhatarsaigh)

There's plenty of truth in the tourist-literature claims that Barra is the Outer Hebrides in miniature. Barely 7 miles wide and 8 miles long, the island has a castle, many beaches, a decent hill to climb and a picturesque 'toytown' port to frame the view. As is the case on islands further north, the east coast is rocky and dominated by peat, while the west is characterised by a narrow strip of fertile machair soil.

Between them, **Barra** and **Vatersay**, the two most southerly inhabited islands of the Outer Hebrides, boast more than 10 miles of sandy beaches, many of which you can be confident of having entirely to yourself. Even by the standards of the Outer Hebrides, these are quiet islands. The largest community is found in the village of Castlebay in the southwest of the island; elsewhere you'll find a series of straggling isolated townships and houses strung out around the coast. The north of the island is dominated by the vast sands of Tràigh Mhòr and the township of Eoligarry, where Compton Mackenzie, author of *Whisky Galore*, once lived and is now buried. Although small, Barra is stout and hilly, the highest point being Heaval (Heabhal) at 383m (1,256ft), and the rolling topography has created some small but unexpectedly lush nooks and crannies of woodland, particularly around North Bay on the east coast.

The journey to Barra by sea can be stirringly beautiful. In particular, the 45-minute trip from Eriskay crosses the Sound of Barra, where there's every chance of spotting golden eagles on the updrafts, seals hauled out on skerries, gannets diving for fish and pods of bottlenose dolphins.

Vatersay is linked by a causeway to Barra and has three dramatically beautiful beaches and a surprisingly rugged interior. A tiny township clings on to its southern shores, but you will see far more cattle there than people.

BARRA (BHARRAIGH)

HISTORY The first settlers on Barra arrived during the Neolithic period, or New Stone Age, some 6,000 years ago, and were based at Allt Easdal on the south of the island, close to the modern-day causeway to Vatersay. They were clearly an enterprising lot, for Barra has no flint, so they instead manufactured tools from flints washed up along the shoreline from neighbouring islands. A characteristic of Barra from this time is the number of megalithic tombs, known as passage graves, which endured for several centuries. The Bronze Age on Barra, however, remains a mystery to be unpicked; the leading expert on the island's archaeology, Professor Keith Branigan of the University of Sheffield, has reported that the entire compendium of bronze

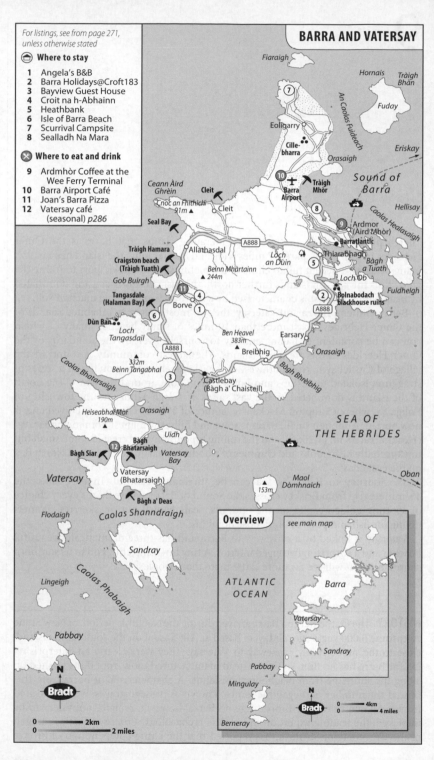

For listings, see from page 271,
unless otherwise stated

Where to stay

1 Angela's B&B
2 Barra Holidays@Croft183
3 Bayview Guest House
4 Croit na h-Abhainn
5 Heathbank
6 Isle of Barra Beach
7 Scurrival Campsite
8 Sealladh Na Mara

Where to eat and drink

9   Ardmhòr Coffee at the
    Wee Ferry Terminal
10 Barra Airport Café
11 Joan's Barra Pizza
12 Vatersay café
    (seasonal) p286

Fiaraigh

Hornais

Tràigh
Bhàn

An Caolas Fuideach

Fuday

Eoligarry

Cille-
bharra

Orasaigh

Eriskay

Barra
Airport

Tràigh
Mhòr

Sound of
Barra

Ceann Àird
Ghrèin

Cleit

Caolas Healasaigh

Hellisay

Cnoc an Fhithich
91m

Cleit

Ardmor
(Aird Mhòr)

Seal Bay

Barratlantic

A888

Loch
an Dùin

Thiarabhagh

Bàgh
a Tuath

Tràigh Hamara

Allathasdal

Craigston beach
(Tràigh Tuath)

Beinn Mhàrtainn
244m

Loch Ob

Fuldhelgh

Gob Buirgh

Borve

Bolnabodach
blackhouse ruins

Tangasdale
(Halaman Bay)

Dùn Bàn

Loch
Tangasdail

Ben Heaval
383m

Earsary

Orasaigh

A888

Breibhig

Bàgh Bhrèibhig

332m
Beinn Tangabhal

Castlebay
(Bàgh a' Chaisteil)

**SEA OF
THE HEBRIDES**

Heiseabhal Mòr
190m

Orasaigh

Uidh

Maol
Dòmhnaich

153m

Oban

Bàgh
Bhatarsaigh

Bàgh Siar

Caolas Bhatarsaigh

Vatersay
Bay

Vatersay

Vatersay
(Bhatarsaigh)

Bàgh a' Deas

Flodaigh

Caolas Shanndraigh

Sandray

Overview

see main map

Lingeigh

Caolas Phabaigh

**ATLANTIC
OCEAN**

Barra

Pabbay

Vatersay

Sandray

Pabbay

Mingulay

Berneray

N

Bradt

0   2km
0   2 miles

N

Bradt

0   4km
0   4 miles

work found on the island amounts to half of a small cloak fastener. The Iron Age too has revealed scant evidence of any significant change in lifestyles, tools or pottery. However, during this time, the islanders became adept at exploiting the sea, hunting seals and catching seabirds, including shags. The subsequent Viking presence on Barra is thought to have been more temporary than further north.

It was during the Lords of the Isles period in the mid 14th century that the Macneil chiefs of Barra emerged as the dominant presence (having reportedly first appeared on the scene in the 11th century). As Branigan puts it, the Macneils adopted the well-established model of rule that involved 'feasting and feuding, marriage and political alliances, and raiding at land and sea'. To the outsider, one of the most eye-catching features of the Macneils is the colourful monikers they gave to their rulers. The 35th chief was Roderick the Turbulent, a later one was known as Roderick the Gentle.

In 1839, the 41st chief of the Macneils – Roderick the General – was declared bankrupt. Barra, Vatersay and neighbouring small islands were put up for sale and bought by the Aberdeenshire landowner Colonel Gordon of Cluny for £38,000. People were soon cleared off their land and either relocated to even more barren areas of the island or dispatched across the Atlantic. Between 1841 and 1851, the population of Barra fell from 2,363 to 1,871 (today Barra and Vatersay combined are home to just 1,264 inhabitants). In 1851 alone, Cluny evicted 450 tenants who were taken against their will to Lochboisdale on South Uist and shipped to Quebec. This particular incident remains one of the most notorious in the history of the Outer Hebrides. Those who refused to leave were hunted down and physically bundled aboard the ship, children were seized and boarded, irrespective of whether their parents were taken as well, and a milkmaid was pulled away while milking a cow.

The potato blight, which arrived on Barra in 1846, had a catastrophic impact on an already benighted people, who were now reduced to collecting cockles from the beach at Tràigh Mhòr for survival. The blight only accelerated Cluny's clearances: the entire north end of the island was divided into farms, where tenant farmers enjoyed a fearsome reputation for harsh treatment of their workers. In the second half of the 19th century, Barra's fortunes turned for the better, as the fishing industry, particularly the herring catch, expanded. Conditions on land, however, were little better, and there was no improvement when Cluny's son took over, despite the Crofters Holdings Acts of 1886, which established legal definitions of crofting and granted security of land tenure to crofters. By 1900, the simmering resentment boiled over into a series of raids and seizing of farms by desperate and furious families. In 1906 and 1907, farmers from Barra and Mingulay seized land on Vatersay and became known as the Vatersay Raiders. The men trusted in the custom by which, if you built a home and lit a fire in it from dawn to dusk, you were entitled to tenure. The land was held by Cluny's daughter-in-law, who had no hesitation in pursuing the raiders in court: ten were jailed, but the national outcry forced the government to buy Vatersay from the Cluny family through the Congested Districts Board and partition it into crofts.

A regular ferry from Eriskay to Barra was only established in 2003; before then, you had an awkward and time-consuming journey to reach South Uist. An intermittent ferry linked Castlebay and Lochboisdale as part of the Oban service and barely did so at all during winter. Events and organisations on Barra were cut off from a major source of potential participants to the north, and tourists were unable to travel easily to all the main islands. When the ferry service at Ardmor was launched, it was finally possible to travel from Ness in northern Lewis to Barra in a single, if long, day by car – actually only about 145 miles sat behind the wheel of your vehicle – but hitherto an impossible dream.

GETTING THERE AND AWAY

By ferry CalMac (📞0800 066 5000; from outside the UK call 📞+44 1475 650397; w calmac.co.uk) operates a daily service from Glasgow via Oban (where almost everyone embarks) to Castlebay. This crosses the Sea of the Hebrides, as the more southerly reaches of the Minch are known. Journey time is 4¾ hours. An additional service runs on Wednesdays from Oban to Castlebay via Coll and Tiree (page 42). For the latest timetables, visit the CalMac website.

CalMac runs a small car and passenger ferry up to four times a day in each direction between Eriskay and Ardmor (Àird Mhòr) on Barra's east coast. The journey takes 45 minutes. The return fare is £6.50 for adults, £3.30 for children and £22.40 for a standard car.

The port at Ardmor has a waiting room with useful information about current activities such as walking and kayaking. Outside is an eye-catching sculpture of three otters in pursuit of a salmon – keep your own eyes peeled as this is a good spot to see the real deal.

By air Barra Airport is unconventional to say the least, positioned on a vast beach on the northeast edge of the island, the hard sand providing the runway (see box, page 272). The airport is connected to Glasgow Airport by flights with Loganair (page 42). A taxi from the airport to Castlebay or the Eriskay ferry slipway at Ardmor costs approximately £12; the airport bus meets incoming flights and costs £2. You may find taxi drivers politely reluctant to make the journey from the airport to Ardmor, as it requires them to come from Castlebay on the other side of the island. They may go as far as telling you it is merely a 15-minute walk between the two points: it's actually closer to an hour. That said, if the weather is good, you are travelling light and have time before the Eriskay ferry crossing, then it is a lovely walk along the quiet roads – you can't get lost, just turn left at the signpost for the ferry.

Despite its unconventional location, the airport caters well for travellers with limited mobility. If you require assistance, contact the information desk at the airport (📞01871 890212). Facilities include a disabled toilet, wheelchairs, ramp facilities, a stair climber and disabled parking bays. At the time of writing, the airport café was excellent but the tender for running it was due to be renewed in early 2020 (page 275).

GETTING AROUND

By car The main road on Barra, the A888, runs for 14 miles; it is circular and mainly coastal. In the northeast of the island near North Bay (Bàgh a Deas), it connects with the road to the airport, which in turn peels off east to the Eriskay ferry at Ardmor.

Car hire
Hire cars are in short supply & you should reserve well ahead of your visit.

🚗 **Barra Car Hire** 📞01871 890313
🚗 **Isle of Barra Beach Hotel** (Page 273) Also hires out cars for £60/day.

Petrol
🅿 **MacLean grocers** Main St, Castlebay; ⏰ 08.00–17.30 Mon–Sat, 11.00–13.30 Sun. The only fuel on Barra. Pay in store.

By bus The W32 circular serves Barra and all townships, including North Bay, Tràigh Mhòr airport, Ardmor slipway (for the Eriskay crossing) and Eoligarry. The W33 runs across the causeway to Vatersay three times a day (but less frequently during school holidays). Services are reliable, but the W32 timetable changes frequently as it serves the airport and times its journeys to coincide with flights. Buses do not run on Sundays. For up-to-date timetables, visit w cne-siar.gov.uk (search 'bus services'). The popularity of Barra's bus services means that it's useful to book in advance (m 07506 072309), particularly if you have luggage.

By taxi For local taxis, try **Barra Taxis** (☎ 01871 810012), **J Campbell** (☎ 01871 810216) and **Brevig Taxi** (m 07807 279954).

By bicycle Cyclists will find that, despite its small size, Barra is a defiantly undulating island. The main road climbs steeply east out of Castlebay, while for anyone cycling all the way up to the Butt of Lewis, the two hairpin climbs that take you over to Vatersay will be a good gauge of your fitness.

🚲 **Barra Bike Hire** ☎ 01871 810950; m 07876 402842; w barrabikehire.co.uk. Rents out well-maintained bikes, all with helmets, pumps & repair kits. Based in Bùth Bharraigh but will deliver & pick up bikes from your accommodation. Adult bikes £16/day, kids' bikes £8/day, discounts for successive days.

TOURIST INFORMATION Although the Visit Scotland visitor information centre closed in 2017, its role has been taken on – augmented even – by the excellent **Bùth Bharraigh shop** ✳ (☎ 01871 817948; e info@buthbharraigh.co.uk; w barrashop. co.uk; ⏲ Apr–Sep 10.00–19.15 Mon–Sat, noon–16.00 & 18.00–19.15 Sun, Oct–Mar 10.00–18.00 Mon–Sat, noon–16.00 Sun), located just below the Castlebay Hotel. The shop provides good advice, books, accommodation and hires out bikes (page 276). At the time of writing, the location of the shop was under threat, thanks to a decision by the island's council to close it and rebuild on the Barra Industrial Estate, on the western edge of Castlebay. The proposal was universally opposed by the community and a lengthy process of appeals is underway (follow the shop website for developments). Another good source of information is w isleofbarra.com.

FESTIVALS AND EVENTS The Barra and Vatersay Island produce show (for details, check with the **Bùth Bharraigh shop**) is held every September in Castlebay. This exhibition of cakes, crafts and local life is well worth visiting.

TOUR OPERATORS Rob Daly runs small group trips around Barra and Vatersay through **Barra Island Tours** (☎ 01871 810225; m 07972 375494; e robwdaly@yahoo. co.uk; w barraislandtours.co.uk). Tours visit both the main sites of interest and harder-to-reach places, including the abandoned village of Bolnabodach. Rob charges £27.50–30 per hour (not person), and trips tend to last 3–5 hours and take up to six people. Another option is **Dan's Island Tours** (☎ 01871 810497; m 07807 526134).

🏠 **WHERE TO STAY** *Map, page 268, unless otherwise stated*
Accommodation on Barra is a mixed bag. There are certainly some shining lights – particularly among the B&Bs – but a few places may well seem expensive. While you should feel free to give constructive criticism where it is due, bear in mind that the logistics involved in modernising properties can be substantial, with materials available only on the mainland and builders at a premium. And, while you may not agree with it, the business model that keeps some places afloat and open for the local community in the dark winter months is one that depends on lucrative summer trade. The same shortcomings used to be levelled at food,

Tràigh Mhòr (Big Beach) airport is well named, and a landing here is high on the bucket list of aviation enthusiasts. Barra Airport describes itself as 'the world's only commercial airport that has runways washed twice daily by the tide' (a phrase that distinguishes it from other beach landings around the world). Three runways are marked in the hard sand of the beach, and since these are under water at high tide, the flight timetables vary significantly.

The flights are something of a social occasion, attracting tourists and locals who sit on the grassy banks of the dunes behind the vast cockle strand. Although procedures are refreshingly relaxed, it is easy to forget that this is not Trumpton: regulations about trespass apply when the aircraft approaches, lands, idles and then takes off, something that takes as little as 15 minutes.

The Glasgow–Barra route is served by a 19-seater Twin Otter light aircraft. These can only fly in crosswinds lower than 25 knots; if you've not flown in such an aircraft before, it can be an exhilarating experience for some, disconcerting for others, as the vibrations, noise and movement can take you by surprise. The safety demonstration is given by the co-pilot, and in even moderate winds, the aircraft can slosh around, leaving you feeling like the marble in one of those handheld games where the aim is to ease the ball into a hole in the centre. The journey is stunning in cloudless weather, with views of Mull, Staffa, Col and Tiree. The landing on the ridged beach is bumpy and the aircraft small enough that you can look out of your window and pick out individual cockles on the sand and onlooking oystercatchers. It's easy to over-egg things, though, and it is worth bearing in mind the excellent safety record of the runway – the last time an aircraft was written off at the airport was 1951. Furthermore, the Twin Otter's record in the UK is first class; the pilots who ply this route are vastly experienced and have flown in similar and tougher conditions the world over.

Captain Fabio Giovacchini gives an insight into the special role the flight plays in island life, and the challenges it can throw up for pilots. 'You might look at the beach and think it is a wide landing area, but actually we treat it like a proper runway,' he explains. Having landed seaplanes in Alaska and more locally on Loch Lomond, Fabio is attuned to the unique demands of the flight and landing. 'Every flight involves a lot of investigation. We can know the times of the tide, but sometimes the tide doesn't quite do what we expect it to do; perhaps there's a storm surge, nature just decides to do something else. This is much more interesting for me.

'But flying this route is a real privilege. We are more than just another airline – this is more than just another flight. Yes, we bring tourists here, but we also take islanders to the mainland to meet relatives, to have medical treatment. We have a social role to play, and it seems right that we do that.'

though this has improved considerably in recent years. Quite why Barra has had to play catch up with its neighbours is perhaps explained by the fact that the island has enjoyed direct links to both the mainland and the Uists for only the past few years, and by the lack of a substantial population.

🏠 **Castlebay Hotel** [map, page 279] (15 rooms) The Square, Castlebay; 📞 01871 810223; e stay@castlebay.com; w castlebay-hotel.co.uk; ⏱ closed Christmas–New Year. The hotel has a mix of dbls, twins, sgls & a family room. There must have been a time when the Castlebay Hotel, commanding the best position above the harbour, was a landmark, welcoming sight for those arriving by boat. Today it is a tired, over-priced affair, only mentioned here because it is so conspicuous & of use if you really struggle to find a bed elsewhere. The best room, the Macneil suite, overlooks the bay but comes with an eye-watering & unjustified £215 price tag. The restaurant (££) used to be better value, but when you ask for the catch of the day & end up with battered cod & chips for £19, the current state of affairs becomes all too apparent. £££

🏠 **Craigard Hotel** [map, page 279] (9 rooms) The Square, Castlebay; ☎01871 810200; e craigardh@aol.com; w craigardhotel.co.uk. The hotel has benefited from a recent facelift thanks to a new owner, who, true to his word, took the building back to the studwork. Rooms 2 & 7 enjoy bay views, but the pick are the 2 annex rooms at the front (both dbls), which have wide windows opening out on to decking with views of the bay. The residents' lounge has a wood-burning stove & is a cosy place in which to curl up on a rainy day. The small bar is lively, especially at w/ends when a never-ending list of music gigs is shoehorned into a corner; the Vatersay Boys regularly play here (this does mean the downside to staying here is the late-night music). The restaurant (⏰ 12.30–14.00 & 17.30–21.00 daily; ££) enjoys a fine view over the bay & is consistently good. Starters can include a ½ lobster for less than £10 (compare that with what you would pay in Devon or London!). Fish/shellfish dominate the mains & are refreshingly free of smothering sauces; you get the feeling you are – rightly – paying for the taste of the catch, such as lemon sole (£16.50) and Barra scallops (£22). £££

🏠 **Isle of Barra Beach Hotel** (39 rooms) Tangasdale Beach, Tangasdale; ☎01871 810383; e barrahotel@aol.com; w isleofbarrahotel.co.uk; ⏰ May–Sep. The hotel has pride of place on the west coast, north of Castlebay. It overlooks & has access to Tangasdale beach. It just about pulls off a quirky architectural design intended to resemble an upside-down ship that has crashed on to the rocks. Continuing this theme, the en-suite rooms are designed as cabins; all are bright & breezily decorated in blue & white nautical style with wicker furniture & portholes on the doors. Make sure you ask for a sea-view room; those on the 2nd 'deck' have the best views. The lounge, eyeballing the waves that crash on to the beach, is one of the best places across the Outer Hebrides to enjoy a

sundowner; the 2nd bar, aptly named the Blue Bar for its furnishings, is particularly snug. Also has a small cinema room (popcorn available) when weather is bad. The hotel hires out electric bikes. There's a hammock & shower outside for guests returning from the beach. The restaurant (££), with the emphasis on seafood, is very good if a bit expensive: scallops with garlic (£27), haddock fillet (£17.50). Good cheese board. £££

🏠 **Angela's B&B** (4 rooms) 108 Upper Borve; ☎01871 810287; e angela-108@live.co.uk. An excellent, modernised B&B with layout that differs from the traditional crofthouse you tend to encounter on Barra (most crofthouses tend to run across just the 1 ground floor; Angela's is 2-storey & includes a modern wing with large windows opening out to the sea). All 4 rooms (2 trpls, 2 sgls) are on the 1st floor & open on to a lounge area that creates the feel of a loft apt. Trpls are en suite, sgls share a bathroom. An airy b/fast room & lounge downstairs have views through large windows in 3 directions. A good choice for families or a small group. ££

🏠 **Bayview Guest House** (3 rooms & 1 log cabin) Nask; ☎01871 817981; e info@barra-bayview.co.uk; w barra-bayview.co.uk. Located ½ mile west of Castlebay, on the road to Vatersay, this thoughtfully run B&B enjoys – as the name suggests – pole position when it comes to views. Enjoy the spectacle of the bay with the island of Maol Domhnaich filling the skyline. Sunrises here are superb but sunsets throw a glowing red light across the island. All rooms (1 twin, 1 dbl & 1 family sleeping 4) are en suite, with 2 facing the bay). Martin & Barbara Macneil-Smyth recently took over the property, have redecorated & have sourced captivating yesteryear pictures of the island. The adjacent log cabin (en suite, sleeps 2; ££) has a veranda on which to enjoy a sundowner. ££

🏠 **Croit na h-Abhainn** (3 rooms) Borve; ☎01871 810624. Spacious rooms with pine flooring, smartly & unpretentiously furnished with beds, chairs & drawers, in a large house beautifully situated on the crest of a small hill. A bright, roomy guest lounge has views across the machair to the sea. ££

✳ 🏠 **Heathbank Hotel** (5 rooms) Northbay; ☎01871 890266; e info@barrahotel.co.uk; w barrahotel.co.uk; ⏰ Nov–Sep. This small, well-run & peaceful hotel on the north side of the island bulges at the seams of its official 3-star rating. Has

1 dbl, 2 twins, 1 sgl, & a trpl that can squeeze in a family of 4. All rooms are en suite & similarly but immaculately furnished with a vaguely seascape theme. A recent addition is a 'log pod' (en-suite wood cabin; sleeps 2) in the garden. The restaurant (££) has a short but good menu & owner Marion Macneil is nudging the restaurant towards becoming wholly seafood based: 'I focus on what we have around us – Barra on a platter,' she says. All dishes are homemade & draw heavily on local food, particularly fish landed in the bays just a few metres away. Look out for scallops with bacon, black pudding & pea purée or local haddock. Look out for Marion's homebaking on the cake stand, & carrageen – her seaweed pudding. 3 bottles salvaged from the SS *Politician* stand proud in a glass cabinet in view of diners. In good weather, you can dine in the front garden. This hotel typifies the best of the Outer Hebrides – an owner who puts her heart & soul into the business. **££**

🏠 **Hillside B&B** [map, page 279] (3 rooms) 25 Glen, Castlebay; ☎ 01871 810293; e dndmacneil@btinternet.com; w isleofbarra. com/hillsidenew.htm; ⏱ Apr–Oct. The 2 dbls are en suite (1 overlooks the bay, the other faces a hill) & the sgl has private bath & shower. An airy residents' lounge offers partial sea views. Friendly welcome with homebaking left daily in bedrooms. Owner also runs an adjacent 2-bed self-catering cottage (£475/week; £). **££**

🏠 **Sealladh Na Mara** (2 rooms) 11a Ardmor; ☎ 01871 890743; e lornareckord@aol.com; w bedinbarra.com. 1 dbl, 1 twin, both en suite with fine views over Sound of Barra. Among the more unusual offerings to guests is a rake with which you can collect cockles from Tràigh Mhòr. The owner will cook them for you. **££**

🏠 **Barra Holidays@Croft183** 183 Bolnabodach; m 07534 085505; e barraholidays@ gmail.com; w croft183.com. A well-run multi-purpose campsite located on the east side of the island. Beautiful setting with views across to both South Uist & the Inner Hebrides. Options include pitches for tents & motorhomes, 5-room hostel (inc good en-suite family rooms), static caravan (sleeps 5) & self-catering cottage (sleeps 5). Centre stage is taken by the yurt (sleeps 5) made from yak hair & including TV, private toilet & cooking facilities. **£/££**

🏠 **Dunard Hostel** [map, page 279] (5 rooms) The Square, Castlebay; ☎ 01871 810443; e info@ dunardhostel.co.uk; w dunardhostel.co.uk. An excellent hostel with a good-sized lounge & cooking area. Great sea views. 2 rooms with bunk beds, 2 twins & family room sleeping 4. Extremely reasonable prices, eg: £70 for family room. Shared shower & toilet. Property was used as a base for filming the original 1940s Ealing Comedy version of *Whisky Galore!*. **£**

⚟ **Scurrival Campsite** Eoligarry; ☎ 01871 890292. A blissfully isolated location 3 miles beyond the airport. Toilets & showers & a good-sized kitchen. **£**

✕ WHERE TO EAT AND DRINK *Map, page 268, unless otherwise stated*

Barra enjoys an abundance of food resources with sheep, cattle and chicken on land. A dozen or so trawlers fish out of Barra, along with creel boats that collect lobsters and edible, shore and velvet swimming crabs. Much of the produce is exported immediately to markets in Spain and France, though local cafés and restaurants are increasingly shifting to sourcing their food from their doorstep. Look out for the local producer mark, a green circle with a white cross slightly left of centre that signifies what you are eating or buying has been made on Barra – an idea that deserves to catch on elsewhere in the island chain. Most places also serve children's portions.

❋ ✕ **Café Kisimul** [map, page 279] Main St, Castlebay; ☎ 01871 810645; e harris@cafekisimul. co.uk; w cafekisimul.co.uk; ⏱ noon–16.00 Mon–Sat, evening sittings 18.00 & 20.00 Mon–Sat, 17.30 & 19.30 Sun; see ad, 3rd colour section. This delightful restaurant & café is one of those places that really makes travel worthwhile. Food is excellent, staff charming & the décor, dotted with the owner's own artwork, creates an ambience that so many places find difficult to achieve. The food wonderfully combines Indian flavours with Barra resources. Starters include scallop pakora; Indian mains include chicken or lamb with a choice of half a dozen different sauces with specials such

Many visitors are surprised to find a high-quality café selling curries in the remote backwaters of Barra, but Café Kisimul's reputation is such that it even gets take-away orders from Tiree and Coll, which are delivered by ferry. The eaterie was established by Rohail and Pauline Bari, who moved to Barra from Glasgow in 2002. 'We didn't have any particular plans when we came here,' says Pauline. Asked to host curry nights for local events, the response was so positive that they decided to set up the café. 'We just decided to do home cooking,' she says. 'It was Punjabi cooking, we learnt it from Rohail's mother and sisters. It just worked and it grew bigger than we expected. If you eat it yourself and you're not happy, then you shouldn't be selling it. I hate it when I go to a restaurant and see chefs and staff that just don't care.' And the Italian side of the business? 'We took the view that not everyone in a family or party would want curry and kids in particular like pasta.'

The key, according to Pauline, is to use fresh rather than powdered ingredients. 'We had staff peeling garlic for days on end. People are amazed at how we source everything but it's just a case of slick logistics and people you can trust.'

The claim made by many patrons that Kisimul is Scotland's best curry house is based on solid ground. In 2010, the café reached the final of the Tiffin Cup, a UK national competition where Members of Parliament nominated their favourite curry house. Kisimul won the Scottish division and made it through to the final, which saw them serve their food to chefs and celebrities at the Houses of Parliament. Getting the monkfish, scallops and sauces from Barra to Westminster involved several journeys by road, two flights and a good deal of ice. They just missed out on first place, but the tale of a small café on a tiny Hebridean island taking on the UK's finest made national news. Kisimul's story took a sad turn in 2015 when Rohail died, but with huge support from the local community the couple's son Harris picked up the torch and took over the kitchen. 'He used to pester us when he was small, asking us how to make the dishes,' says Pauline. 'I'm just glad he did.' In addition to dining at Café Kisimul, you can pick up their pre-cooked and frozen meals at Bùth Bharraigh, the Eriskay community shop & supermarkets in Benbecula.

as monkfish & cod in a tuna masala. There's an unexpected Italian menu of equally high standard that includes Barra salmon spaghetti. Pudding menu features mango strips with cream. Recent innovations include braised squid curries with paprika. There's a good wine list – late author Iain Banks loved the Lebanese wine that is still on sale – along with Cobra beer & local ales. Music nights (some Thu) involve local musicians playing while you eat. ££

✕ Barra Airport Café Airport; barraairportcafe; ⏱ Apr–Sep 10.00–16.00 daily, Oct–Mar 10.00–15.00 daily. At the time of writing, the tender for this excellent café was up for bids. The hope is that it will remain in the hands of islanders rather than be outsourced to an international chain. Either way, the café is expected to continue in a similar vein, offering hot drinks, cakes & savouries. Just as popular with locals as with passengers. £/££

✕ Ardmhor Coffee at the Wee Ferry Terminal Ardmor ferry terminal; ⏱ Apr–Sep 06.30–18.00 daily, Oct–Mar 08.30–16.00 daily. Superb little café serving hot drinks & cakes, located in the waiting room by the Barra–Eriskay ferry slipway. Run by the tireless Sharon Cox (formerly of the airport café). Having brought 1 espresso machine from Birmingham for airport brews, Sharon now has a 2nd with which to welcome ferry passengers. One of the official pit stops for hikers & cyclists on the Hebridean Way. If you need warming up, try the hot chocolate with chilli & cream. £

Blasda Café [map, page 279] Barra Development Estate; ⊕ May–Sep 09.00–15.30 Mon–Thu, 09.00–19.00 Fri, 10.30–17.00 Sat, winter slightly shorter hours. Small café offering soup, scones & hot meals to sit down or take away. Specials on Fri evenings include crab salads. £

✗ **Joan's Barra Pizza** [map, page 279] 3 Borve, Castlebay; ☎ 01871 810570; ⊕ 17.00–20.00 Fri–Sat, possibly also Wed & Thu in Jul–Aug – call ahead. Look out for this excellent take-away pizzeria where food is made in an Italian stone oven by Joan MacPhee & her daughter Maria Howat. 12in pizzas £9 including choice of toppings, ranging from mushroom, pineapple & chorizo to black pudding. Also excellent homemade ice cream using eggs from Joan's croft. 'My hens are good layers,' says Joan. 'The sauce recipe is my own, we make the dough in the morning, we just want to make everything from scratch, as homemade as we possibly can.' £

✗ **Macroons Tea Room & Castlebay Post Office** [map, page 279] Main St; ☎ 01871 810312; ⊕ 09.00–16.00 Mon–Fri, 09.00–12.30 Sat; post office ⊕ same hours. Another of the Outer Hebrides' clutch of enterprising post offices, this fine tearoom enables you to drink & eat after sending your postcards homeward. Serves homemade sultana scones & cakes with various teas & coffees. Both tearoom & post office are run by Chris & Diane Dillerstone, who relocated here from Yorkshire after Chris was made redundant. While Chris acknowledges the need to make a profit, he is keenly aware of the social element attached to the enterprise. 'This is a meeting place, a lifeline for the community,' he says. The couple chose Barra simply because Diane was a fan of *Whisky Galore!* & wanted to see where it was filmed (Macroon was the name of the postmaster in the film). 'Barra is a majestic place,' says Chris. 'Apart from cricket & Yorkshire beer, this place has everything.' For self-evident reasons, order tea & it will be the Yorkshire variety that you get. £

ENTERTAINMENT These are the islands that gave Scotland, and indeed the UK, the Vatersay Boys (w thevatersayboys.com), a five-piece band with accordions, pipes, whistles and guitar, who offer a different take on Highland and Gaelic dance music. They regularly play on the islands. The Craigard Hotel (page 273) has regular gigs with local and mainland bands.

SHOPPING For **groceries**, the eclectic offerings at MacLean grocers (Main St, Castlebay; ⊕ 08.00–17.30 Mon–Sat, 11.00–13.30 Sun) range from a butcher's counter to dairy, fresh fruits, newspapers and cakes. The Co-op (⊕ 07.00–22.00 Mon–Sat, 12.30–22.00 Sun) lies 350m west of Castlebay centre on the Castlebay Development Estate. An intriguing, engaging community enterprise shop, **Bùth Bharraigh** ✱ (page 271; ☎ 01871 817948; e info@buthbharraigh.co.uk; w barrashop. co.uk; ⊕ Mar–Oct 10.00–19.15 Mon–Sat, noon–16.00 & 18.00–19.15 Sun, winter 10.00–16.00 Mon–Sat, noon–16.00 Sun; free Wi-Fi) sells hot drinks, homemade traybakes and biscuits (try the ones flavoured with seaweed), as well as more substantial meals to take away including ready-to-eat curries from Café Kisimul, such as Hebridean lamb sag. Bùth Bharraigh also sells local tomatoes and spices, flour and other ingredients if you are camping or self-catering. It is a good place to pick up a souvenir such as locally made shampoo bars and bobble hats made from bamboo. All profits are reinvested in the shop and community projects. The shop is also a useful pit stop for cyclists embarking on (or finishing) the Hebridean Way, offering free water refills, a laundrette, and cycle repairs and bike hire.

While **Bùth Bharraigh** is a good place for souvenirs, you may be invited to reciprocate by leaving something behind in the form of a bunting flag, which will add to the Barra Bunting project. So far, more than 300 visitors have decorated small flags that are hung up in the shop and used to dress island events such as the annual produce show. If you don't have time during your visit, you can take a flag away, decorate it at home and post it back.

Tucked away down a small service road immediately beneath Bùth Bharraigh is **Hebridean Toffee** (Unit B, Castlebay; ❧ 01871 810898; e hebtoffee@aol.com; w hebrideantoffeecompany.com; ⏲ 09.00–17.00 Mon–Thu, 09.00–19.00 Fri–Sat, noon–16.00 Sun, shorter hours in winter, enquire in advance, usually Thu–Sat), which sells gift-wrapped toffee made on the premises 'by the pouch' (or bag) for £3.25. The shop also sells cakes and ice-cream sodas for consumption on its outdoor decking area, known as 'The Deck', which overlooks the bay. Hot food (£), ranging from burgers to toasties, is served daily. On Fridays and Saturdays they cook fish specials, such as hake fillet and chips, as well as homemade curries.

On the western edge of town, on the Barra Industrial Estate, you'll find **Padula's Barra Island Stores** (❧ 01871 810846; ⏲ 09.00–17.30 daily), another really good local shop, stocking fresh fruit, homemade ice cream made from Jersey cream by owner Helen McLymont. This also serves as the island hardware store, so you can pick up some gardening tools should you feel the need.

Next door is **Isle of Barra Distillers** (❧01871 810582; e info@isleofbarradistillers. com; w isleofbarradistillers.com), home to the UK's most westerly gin producers. The gin is distilled on site by local couple Michael and Katie Morrison, who use carrageen seaweed from the island shores to give the gin its USP. Future plans involve relocating to Eoligarry, where they hope to lay down their first whisky.

ACTIVITIES Kayaking is a great way to see the coast. Chris Denehy is the owner of Dunard Hostel (page 274), and operates **Barra Surf Adventures** (❧ 01871 810443; w barrasurfadventures.co.uk), offering kayak day trips, surfing (including beginners' lessons), snorkelling with seals, and coasteering (£45/£25, discounts for groups). Chris also runs longer trips through **Clearwater Paddling** (❧ same; w clearwaterpaddling.com). Week-long trips around the coast of Barra and Vatersay cost £775 per person, including all food, wild camping and some nights in a small lodge attached to the hostel. Half-day escorted kayaking trips are also available for £35/£20. 'Barra is just perfect for kayaking,' says Chris. 'There are so many little islands that you can come off the sea and know there will be nobody else on the beach. This area is as good as anywhere in the world for kayaking.'

OTHER PRACTICALITIES
Bank
$ Royal Bank of Scotland Main St, Castlebay; ❧01871 810281; ⏲ 10.00–16.00 Mon–Tue & Thu–Fri. Has ATM.

Medical
✚ **Clach Mhile surgery** Castlebay; ❧01871 810282

✚ **St Brendan's Hospital** Castlebay; ❧01871 812021

Post office
✉ **Castlebay** ⏲ 09.00–17.30 Mon–Fri, 09.00–12.30 Sat

WHAT TO SEE AND DO It's with good reason that the village of **Castlebay** features in most tourist literature of the Outer Hebrides. The harbour curls picturesquely around the bay and ancient **Kisimul Castle** that stands in splendid isolation just offshore. **Tràigh Mhòr** beach should not be missed. In 2011, the beach topped a worldwide poll as the most spectacular place to land an aircraft, beating off the rival claims of the Nepalese runway of Lukla. Less well advertised is the fact that Tràigh Mhòr is one half of a spectacular tombolo, a rare example in the UK of back-to-back beaches that connect one island to another. Barra also has a wealth of birdlife, from gannet to the nationally embattled corncrake. The island is firmly on the migratory flightpath, and spring and autumn see Amercian waders blown off course – sometimes chimney swifts wind up here too – along with ospreys making a pit stop. Other raptors include resident white-tailed and golden eagles and hen harriers. Curiously, the island has no short-eared owls (which are common on South Uist). It does, however, have good numbers of pipistrelle bats. The many narrow glens and folds of the island hills are infilled with woodland where you will commonly see goldcrests and occasionally firecrests. Otherwise, Barra is an island simply to explore at leisure, turn off the circular road to stroll across beaches, dawdle by silent lochs, explore the small pockets of woodland, or sip a coffee and stare at the beauty of Castlebay harbour.

Castlebay (Bàgh A' Chaisteil)
Everything is within walking distance in Castlebay. The main street, lined by cafés, petrol pumps, the bank and grocery store, runs downhill to the port. Standing high above the bay is the village **church of Our Lady Star of the Sea**, which opened at Christmas in 1888 with, reports say, all of its 800 seats occupied. Either side of the church stand two stately hotels with more than a hint of faded grandeur (page 272).

Medieval **Kisimul Castle** (✆ 01871 810313; w historicenvironment.scot, search 'Kisimul'; ⊕ Apr–Sep 09.30–17.30 daily; £4.80/£3.60) is the major attraction in Castlebay. Steeped in history, it is well worth a visit. Marooned on a rocky islet in the middle of the bay, this is the ancient seat of the Clan Macneil. The origins of the castle are lost deep in time but could, depending on the source you read, date between 1030 and 1450.

At high tides, the castle seems almost afloat, its three-storey tower house accompanied by a curtain wall shaped to fit snugly upon the rock on which it stands. The boat from the jetty – included in the admission charge – leaves every half-hour, and the journey takes a couple of minutes. Once inside, there are several places to explore via low-ceilinged tunnels and uneven staircases. The great hall was undergoing restoration at the time of writing but there is much else to explore. The Macneil bedroom upstairs includes a 20th-century bath, a reminder that this has remained a residence into the modern era, and the dining hall walls are adorned by some unnervingly pointy-looking Brown Bessies and halberds retrieved from the battlefields of Culloden.

You can also walk along the castle's crenulated walls. It was from such a lofty position that, so the legend goes, a steward would proclaim every evening that 'the great Macneil having finished his meal, the princes of the earth may dine'. The castle was all but destroyed by fire in 1795, and further misfortune came when heavy debts eventually forced the Macneil chiefs to sell Barra in 1838. However, a descendant, Robert Lister Macneil, the 45th chief, purchased the estate 100 years later and went about restoring his ancestral seat with the help of the clan diaspora. Today, the site is leased by the Macneils to Historic Environment Scotland for a rent of £1 and a bottle of whisky per year.

A short walk from the pier is **Dualchas** or **The Heritage Centre** (The Square; ✆ 01871 810413; w in development at time of writing; ⊕ end Apr–end-Sep 10.30–15.00 Mon–Fri; £4/free). Dualchas is a Gaelic word for heritage or tradition, and you may find that this rather spartan centre has an engaging quality that makes you linger over its black-and-white photographs of Barra, a schoolmaster's desk from Mingulay and other memorabilia. The centre's account of the clearances and their impact on Barra is one of the angriest and most scathing you will encounter. Dualchas also offers a genealogy service and can trace ancestral records back to 1805. A small café here keeps the same hours.

CASTLEBAY

For listings, see from page 271

Where to stay
1 Castlebay
2 Craigard
3 Hillside B&B

Off map
Dunard Hostel

Where to eat and drink
4 Café Kisimul
5 Macroons Tea Room &
  Castlebay Post Office

Off map
Blasda Café

N

0 ____ 50m
0 ____ 50yds

Dunard Hostel (200m), Dualchas,
St Brendan's Hospital, Co-op (350m),
Blasda Café, Isle of Barra Distillers &
Padula's Barra Island Stores (450m),
Vatersay (2 miles)

Clach Mhile
surgery

THE SQUARE

Buth Barraigh/
Barra Bike Hire

Hebridean
Toffee
Company

PIER ROAD

A888

Our Lady Star
of the Sea

A888

MacLean grocers

Royal Bank
of Scotland

MAIN STREET

PIER ROAD

Castlebay

Castlebay

Kisimul Castle

Oban

🚶 A WALK UP HEAVAL

1.9km (1.2 miles); 1½–2¼hrs
OS Explorer 452 Barra & Vatersay
Start/finish: signposted car park between Castlebay & Breibhig (⊕ NL679986)

Barra's highest hill may be just 383m (1,256ft) high but – like many summits in the Outer Hebrides – this is a more strenuous climb than some loftier hills on the mainland. The walk starts at about 100m (320ft) above sea level, but that still leaves more than 270m (900ft) to climb at a gradient of nearly one in three. Turn right out of the car park and walk uphill for 100m and turn left through the gate. You then walk back on yourself with a fence on your right for 50m until you reach another gate. Turn right through this and simply begin climbing. There is no fixed route but, depending on your preference, you can either zig-zag your way upwards or head east along the fence for 50m or so and just head straight up, over a mixture of open ground and foot tracks shadowing the burn. Two-thirds of the way up, you encounter *Our Lady of the Sea*, a marble Madonna and Child which some postcards playfully imply has the same stature as the *Christ the Redeemer* figure that overlooks Rio de Janeiro in Brazil (it doesn't). This is nevertheless a fantastic vantage point and, if you've had enough of the steep ascent, is a good place to call a halt. The summit is another 10–15 minutes above you, and various paths coil around the rocky cone-shaped summit, where there is a trig point and superb views in all directions. Expect to take 45–90 minutes to climb up and 30–45 minutes to descend. Every July, the Heaval race tests the lungs of the fittest fell runners, who start and finish in Castlebay Square. If you wish, you can extend the walk by descending the north side of Heaval and walking through Borve on to the A888, where you can arrange for the bus to pick you up. This is a distance of 1½ miles and will take most people around 40–60 minutes at an easy pace. The descent is straightforward: there is no single continuous path, but you can follow a combination of path, burns and sheep tracks to drop you down at the top of road's end in Borve.

Just below Dualchas is the **herring trail**, a small waymarked walk along the shoreline that takes you past a series of herring barrels where you can read about the importance of the industry to Barra. At its peak in the late 19th century, 600 Castlebay boats fished for herring; it's said that you could walk across to Vatersay without getting your feet wet by hopping from boat to boat.

Around the island

Almost all Barra's points of interest are found along the coast. The route here is described in a clockwise direction from Castlebay, but either way is just as good. Some beaches along the west coast can be fiddly to access – fences seem to be in place everywhere to keep Barra's beef and dairy cattle in check – so be prepared to have to walk up and down the coastal ring road until you find a gate or stile. If you're travelling by bus, drivers will know where to drop you for any beach or coastal walk.

West coast bays Heading west out of Castlebay along the A888, you quickly come upon a clutch of fine beaches. The first is Halaman Bay, also known as Tangasdale, whose sands command a dramatic sweep of coast. Just north of here, the township of Borve runs inland through a valley. Just across the road from Borve, the walk out to the headland at Gob Buirgh makes for a gentle excursion. To get there, follow the sandy track out past Borve cemetery to the crumbled remains of a broch dating to the Iron Age. Immediately north are two more fine beaches: **Tràigh Tuath** (also known as Craigston beach) and the adjoining **Tràigh Hamara**. Be aware of the quicksand warning here.

The beach further north at the township of **Alladale (Allathasdal)**, known as **Seal Bay**, is some distance and hidden from the road but particularly picturesque.

FROM TANGASDALE TO DÙN BAN

5km (3 miles) return; 2–3hrs
OS Explorer 452 Barra & Vatersay
Start/finish: telephone box to the south of the Isle of Barra Beach Hotel (⊕ NF649002)

Superbly elemental but straightforward when it comes to navigation, this walk combines beach, machair and moorland as it winds its way along the coast to the dizzyingly located Iron Age hill fort of Dùn Ban. Be prepared to get your feet wet.

The bus will drop you off by the start; there is also space for bicycles and a handful of cars here. Go through the gate and follow the path ahead into the dunes and on to the beach. Bear left to cross the burn (if not wearing boots, you will have to take your trainers off) and pick up the path that runs along the coast with a fence on your left. Go through a gate and follow the path as it weaves through grass, with Loch na Doirlinn on your left. Almost imperceptibly, the soft machair is displaced by sparse moorland, interspersed with granite. Barra always appears picturesque in tourist brochures; here it is rocky, wild and desolate – what might be described as a 'greyscape' dominates the field of vision. This monochrome edge to the island makes the green of the interior look richer.

Waymarker posts show the route, although some of these have been flattened by the wind. Self-evident as it may seem, so long as you keep the sea to your right, you are on course. Aim for the conspicuous cairns on the brow ahead (the landmarks were not originally put in place for walkers, but for fishermen).

From these cairns you can finally pick out the *dùn*, which is perched on the far, westernmost headland. Several paths lead towards the *dùn* but try and keep the waymarkers in sight. The views offshore are tremendous, with Atlantic rollers pummelling the craggy shoreline, while even at low tide the sea seems to fill a succession of coves to the brim. The path drops down to a fence with a stile. Cross this (at the time of writing, the stile was very high, and will be awkward for some walkers) and turn seawards to approach the *dùn*.

The location is tremendous, with enough of the *dùn* remaining, intact – much has been pilfered for local houses and stone walls – and standing hard above the sea, to excite the imagination. Be mindful of the drop on the far side. The *dùn* dates back around 2,000 years and features irregular blocks that run across the headland, while the promontory site is defended by an outer wall, now much infilled with peat, and there are also traces of an entrance and of a subcircular building. Return the same way.

As the name suggests, harbour seals sometimes haul out on the rocks here. To reach it, pass through the gate that leads to another cemetery and cross the machair and dunes. Please note: if you are driving, there is parking above Tangsadale beach and Tràigh Tuath; do not park in the passing places. Bus drivers will drop you off here.

A pleasant beach and hill walk can be compiled from Alladale. If you walk the whole distance described here, you'll cover no more than 5km (3 miles) in total, but this will take an easy 3 hours to complete with stops. If driving, park by the junction of the A888 with the small lane signposted for Allathasdal a Deas/South Alladale. Go through the gate opposite and across the dunes to the beach (this is Seal Bay). If you bear right following the curve of the beach you can work your way easily enough up on to the rocks and the machair behind. The further you walk out towards the headland of **Ceann Àird Ghrèin**, the more dramatic the views. The walking here is easy: just walk as far as you wish towards the headland. Among the rocks above the shoreline on the west of the headland are what geologists consider to be the most impressive examples in the UK of pseudotachylite rocks. These were formed by the movement of the Outer Hebrides Fault (page 6), which generated temperatures so fierce and intense that the rock melted and cooled quickly, forming a network of glassy veins. (That said, the pseudotachylite rocks are hard for the lay eye to pick out; you may decide it is comforting simply to know they are there.)

While you have the option to return the same way, a steady but undemanding climb will bring you to the top of the hill on the headland, **Cnoc an Fhithich** (91m/299ft), topped by a communications mast. From here you can see not only Tràigh Mhòr (of beach landing fame) but also the beautiful dunes of its west-facing counterpart, Tràigh Eais, as well as the hills of South Uist. Immediately below you to the east is the island golf course (you can hire clubs from Bùth Bharraigh). If no-one is playing, drop down the hill to pick up the narrow road that winds further downhill to the A888. If players are present, as a courtesy, follow the same track, but join it from the top of the hill by the mast so as not to disturb them. Once on the A888, turn right to return to the Alladale turning.

Cleit and North Bay A mile or so further on in the township of Cuidhir, turn left signposted for **Cleit** and keep ahead, ignoring the golf club road. At the road end, park in the small stony lay-by. Just to the east is a truly gorgeous north-facing, crescent-shaped beach that backs on to dunes beneath the glowering crags of Beinn Cleit. To the left of the parking area, a short walk through a gate leads to a small geo that is a good spot for birdwatching. From May to July, fulmars nest on the cliffs up to the left; they will let you know if you get too close by flying low and squirting a liquid deposit in your direction.

Back on the circular A888, you pass a dammed Loch an Dùin and then, just above Bàgh Thiarbhagh, a small but pleasant **stretch of woodland** (✤ NL697033). There is parking for two cars here, and a short, signposted stroll runs for some 400m through the woods along boardwalks and paths. This is a rare sylvan experience and a reminder that you are that little bit further south than the elemental wilds of Ness. The path comes to an abrupt dead end, so you must retrace your steps.

The junction of the A888 with the airport road is a pretty spot, centred upon a large islet and caressed by Bàgh Thiarbhagh's peaty waters, which in turn flow out into North Bay. This looks like it should be good walking territory, but fences – with no gates in sight – seem to thwart you at every turn. The Scottish Outdoor Access Code (see box, page 58) prohibits you from damaging fences and, in the absence of any rocks that might provide the elevation to step over the fence, you'll have to make do with a bench conveniently positioned on the north shore.

Tràigh Mhòr and Eoligarry Turning up the airport road, after 450m a road to the right leads to the factory of **Barratlantic**, the island's fishing and processing business. Ten trawlers are contracted to fish the surrounding waters and bring back shellfish and white fish. The company has a £7 million turnover and, with around 30 staff, is the largest employer on the island, making Barra's economy hugely reliant on its success. There is a small **shop** ✳ (📞01871 890341; **w** barratlantic.co.uk;

🚶 AROUND CILLE-BHARRA CHAPEL AND DUN SCURRIVAL

Map, page 284

9km (5½ miles); 2–3hrs
OS Explorer 452 Barra & Vatersay
Start/finish: jetty at Eoligarry (✦ NF713076)

This walk explores the crofting township of Eoligarry and takes in two marvellous beaches, a culturally important cemetery and wonderful hilltop views. It's probably best to park at the jetty at Eoligarry. From the jetty, walk up the road and go straight ahead at the junction to reach the Cille-bharra chapel. From here, continue along the road heading northwest until it bends sharply right in front of the beach of Bàgh nan Clach. Go through the gate on the left and make your way up the slope of the hill ahead; it's awkward walking at times with a need to hop from one large tussock of cattle-cleaved turf to another. The pay-off is a delectable view from the top: you get your first impression of the tombolo and the remains of the Iron Age hill fort, Dun Scurrival (Dùn Sgurabhal).

Perhaps a slightly more daunting view ahead is that of Beinn Eolaigearraidh Mhòr. This higher hill is deceptive but in fact barely scrapes above 105m (300ft) in height, so you should reach it more quickly than you might think. To do so, follow the fence line, then the stony track around its northwestern foothills and finally make for the waymarker post that becomes visible just below the summit cairn. There can be few better views in the whole of the Outer Hebrides, with the back-to-back beaches and a panorama of the mountains of South Uist. In spring, the southern flanks of the hill are smothered in clusters of miniature primroses. Drop down the hill towards the west-facing beach and look for a stile to the right of the track ahead; cross over and make your way through the dunes to the beach. Walk for as long as you wish along the beach and then take one of the narrow breaks in the dunes to the left; there are some tracks here, but if you walk over open ground you will still quickly reach the machair and see gates ahead that lead to the airport road.

If the tide is in, you'll have to follow the road back to Eoligarry. If it's out, then you have the opportunity of a magnificent beach walk across the sands of Tràigh Mhòr. The beach is different in nature from its windward counterpart on the west of the tombolo; the shoreline is higher, the white shell-sand even more striking and laced with seaweeds of all shapes and sizes. Walk around the headland with the island of Orosay (Orasaigh) to your right and keep going across the beach of Tràigh Cille-bharra to the jetty at Eoligarry. If the tide is rising, you will see a wide grassy track that leads up from this beach between houses; follow this track as it winds its way on dry land more or less in parallel with the road to the jetty.

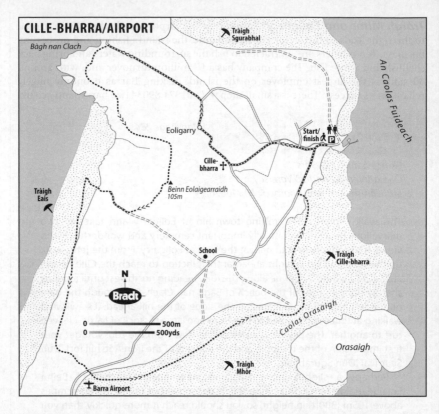

CILLE-BHARRA/AIRPORT

Bàgh nan Clach

An Caolas Fuideach

Tràigh Sgurabhal

Eoligarry

Start/finish

Cille-bharra

Tràigh Eais

Beinn Eolaigearraidh 105m

Tràigh Cille-bharra

School

N

Brodt

0 — 500m
0 — 500yds

Caolas Orasaigh

Orasaigh

Tràigh Mhòr

Barra Airport

⏱ 08.30–17.00 Mon–Fri, 08.30–noon Sat) here that sells fresh and frozen fish, whole sides of smoked salmon (around £25), prawns, fresh monkfish and battered haddock. They will vacuum and freezer-pack goods so that you can get them back home in fresh condition.

Returning to the airport road, the vast sands of **Tràigh Mhòr** soon come into view. A single-track lane winds around its edge for almost 2 miles, passing the small airport terminal along the way. Beyond the airport, take the upper road at the fork through **Eoligarry** (Eolaigearraidh) to reach the remains of the 12th-century church of **Cille-bharra,** or St Barr. At first glance, it is easy to assume the conspicuous but minuscule roofed building is the church; in fact this is the north chapel. The graveyard now contains remains of the original medieval church and a small chapel. This is the ancestral burial ground of the Macneils, and inside the north chapel you'll find atmospheric 16th-century grave slabs thought to have once covered the remains of various Macneils. The chapel was also where the Norse stone was housed. This stone was dated by a runic inscription that proclaimed: 'After Thorgeth, Steiner's daughter, this cross was raised.' The stone was whisked off – much to local indignation – to the National Museum of Scotland in Edinburgh in 1880. Outside, wander around and you'll find the grave of Sir Compton Mackenzie, author of *Whisky Galore*.

East coast: Loch Ob and Bolnabodach
Returning to the A888, **Loch Ob** is another picturesque stretch of water, squeezing eastwards out to sea in a fashion that is easy on the eye. On the southern shore of the loch are the ruins of the

abandoned village of **Bolnabodach**. Reaching them involves a 10-minute walk from the road. Park with care between the red telephone box and the transmitter mast, being careful not to block the passing places. On the loch side of the road, look for a faint track immediately to the south and east of the bungalow (⊕ NF714016). The track cuts down towards the lake, is a little boggy and veers to the right below a hillock to bring you upon the ruins. With a burn trundling into the loch and hill views all around, this is an idyllic spot where you could easily enjoy a picnic. While Iron Age structures have been identified, the major interest is the collection of collapsed blackhouses, some of which have stood the passage of time better than others. The houses date to 1810–40 so may well have been barely occupied before the inhabitants were evicted during the clearances. Among the artefacts uncovered by archaeologists were 19th-century necklace beads and a thimble, in their way as historically resonant as Iron Age tools.

Just before you come full circle back to Castlebay, you pass the turn-off for the township of **Breibhig**. The shoreline here, unusually for Barra, is both rocky and accessible, so is a good place for exploring rockpools.

VATERSAY (BHATARSAIGH)

For decades, Vatersay has held the title of the most southerly inhabited island of the Outer Hebrides, and it can sometimes feel that those who have stayed have hung on only by the skin of their teeth. Following clearances in the 19th century, the island population plummeted to 13 by 1901, yet only ten years later immigration from Barra and Mingulay had seen this soar to 288. By 1971, the population was down again, to 77. Today, the small community is huddled around the south

---

🚶 FROM BARRA TO VATERSAY

9km (5½ miles) one-way; 2½–3hrs
OS Explorer 452 Barra & Vatersay
Start: The Square, Castlebay, at the junction with Main St
Finish: Vatersay Bay

This is a lovely walk and, although it mostly follows the paved road that links the two islands, traffic is minimal and not intrusive and the views are hugely rewarding. You'll need either to retrace your steps to return or co-ordinate your walk with the bus service. Simply head west out of Castlebay along the A888, turn left on to the Vatersay road and keep going. This is a steep hike, with two ascents; the first as you leave Barra and climb through Nasg and the second as you clamber back up from sea level around Heisabhal Beag on Vatersay. The payback for the latter climb is a simply breathtaking panorama of Vatersay's twin beaches and the southernmost and uninhabited islands, Sandray (Sanndraigh), Mingulay, Pabbay (Pabhaigh), and, finally, just sneaking out behind Pabbay and southern end of the Outer Hebrides, another Berneray (not to be confused with its namesake close to North Uist). Once over the Heisabhal Beag pass and on the downhill road to Vatersay, look out for the wreck of the *Catalina* on the shoreline side of the hill. This flying boat crashed here in 1944, killing three of the nine crew. The aircraft was on an operational flying exercise but failed to gain enough lift after taking off from Mull.

of the island, where the single-storey wooden houses have a distinctly Nordic tint. The population is mainly bilingual in Gaelic and English, and Roman Catholic in religion. Work started on the £3.7 million causeway linking Vatersay and Barra in 1989. The 250m gap – with a depth of 37m – presented a formidable engineering challenge because it linked the Atlantic Ocean on one side with the Sea of the Hebrides on the other. That the location is 75 miles out from the mainland made for ferocious tidal currents. A total of 220,000 tonnes of rock was required and, perhaps in recognition of the exhausting engineering demands, the causeway was never formally declared open. The link made life a good deal easier for farmers who until then had to swim their cattle across the Sound of Vatersay to Barra.

GETTING AROUND The island has barely 5 miles of road, all of which are single track. The W33 bus runs to Vatersay, but services are infrequent. Your feet or two wheels will be the main means by which you explore the island.

WHERE TO STAY AND EAT, AND OTHER PRACTICALITIES A seasonal **café** [map, page 268] (🅵 Vatersay Hall Café; ⏁ usually May–early Sep 11.00–16.00 Mon–Sat) operates from the village hall at the northern end of Vatersay Bay, serving toasties, home bakes and hot drinks. There is also a wheelchair-accessible toilet here. You'll find a tiny **post office** behind the southern end of the beaches (⏁ 09.00–14.00 Mon–Tue & Thu–Fri, 09.00–13.00 Wed, 09.00–12.30 Sat) but there are no shops on the island. Nor is there any hosted accommodation. You can, of course, camp as long as you adhere to the outdoor access code (see box, page 58). For motorhomes, the nearest chemical disposal point is the campsite at Eoligarry (page 274).

WHAT TO SEE AND DO Shaped rather like an anvil, with a narrow 'waist' in the middle, Vatersay repays exploration. There are really just two things to do: enjoy the back-to-back beaches and walk. In summer, the machair can be breathtaking, smothered with red and white clover, kidney vetch and field gentian, while swallows swoop back and forward and meadow pipits scurry.

The east-facing **beach** ✴ overlooking **Vatersay Bay (Bàgh Bhatarsaigh)** is as beautiful as anything you will find up or down the Outer Hebrides. Generally

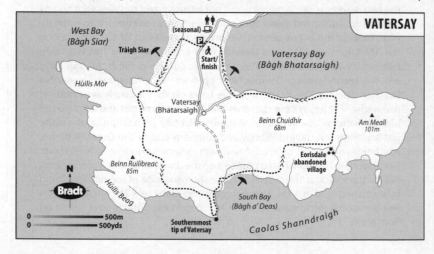

6½km (4 miles); 2–3hrs
OS Explorer 452 Barra & Vatersay
Start/finish: car park behind dunes of Vatersay Bay (⊕ NL633952)

This hike is one of the most exquisitely beautiful walks in the Outer Hebrides but is also tougher than it looks, boggy in wet weather and demands negotiation of open moorland. Don't attempt it in fog or low cloud as you'll struggle to locate the waymarkers and – of course – miss out on the views that are the reason for undertaking this walk.

From the car park behind the east beach, make for the *Annie Jane* monument overlooking West Beach (Tràigh Siar). Walk south along West beach to the far end. Go left through the gate by the blue waymarker and then turn right uphill, walking just to the right of the *dùn* to the next waymarker. The posts can be erratic and hard to spot; moreover, some have succumbed to the elements. If in doubt, make your way over the next brow to the south then follow the narrow valley, keeping the hill of Beinn Ruilibreac on your right, heading southeast and then south. Where a waymarker gives two options, turn left and keep to the higher ground to avoid the boggier sections. Head east over open ground until you come to a tiny beach (⊕ NL634936). If you wish, you can reach the most southerly point of the inhabited Outer Hebrides by turning south here for 200m across a small geo to a rocky foreshore known as Heillanish. The southerly islands Sandray, Pabbay, Mingulay and Berneray pull away into the ocean like giant stepping stones. This can be an evocative part of the world: when the sea is calm, a wave will suddenly erupt over a submerged reef, and then the ocean returns to its steady state.

Make your way north with the sea on your right to Bàgh a Deas, but be wary of the hidden geo just before the first fenceline. On the east side of the beach, pick up the waymarker posts that first head north then east. It's worth leaving the trail and making for the ruins of Eorisdale. This village was built shortly after the land raids of 1909 and was inhabited as recently as the 1970s. The standalone gables and roofless house make for a striking skyline. From here, head north over sometimes boggy open ground. Keep Beinn Chiudhir well to your left and pick up the waymarker posts once again. The path then becomes much easier and turns left (west) to follow the shoreline above Vatersay Bay.

sheltered from any wind, the fine shell-sand runs for 600m and slips below shallow waters that on sunny days turn a transluscent aquamarine. Show the folks back home a picture of this beach and ask them to name which Caribbean island you are visiting. The west-facing beach, **Tràigh Siar**, has more pebbles but is also graceful.

There is a concrete plinth overlooking Tràigh Siar in memory of emigrant ship *Annie Jane,* which foundered on rocks off Vatersay in 1853, with the loss of more than 350 lives. Given the forced clearances that bedevilled these islands, it's a dreadful irony that most of those on board were skilled craftsmen and their families, willingly bound for Canada to build that nation's railway system. Their bodies were interred in the ground nearby.

Hidden to the south of Vatersay is the beautiful **South Bay (Bàgh a Deas)**, a golden beach that looks out towards Sandray. Getting there can be surprisingly fiddly, as the beach is separated from the two back-to-back beaches by Vatersay township, gates, fences and 600m of machair. The easiest route is to step over the stile at the southern end of the east beach and walk along the wide grassy tracks between the dunes and find a gate on to the beach. The fences can be frustrating for walkers, but they keep the cattle from straying on to the beach.

SANDRAY, PABBAY, MINGULAY AND BERNERAY

South of Vatersay, the Outer Hebrides archipelago continues to include a few stragglers that can be visited by boat.

Just across the water from Vatersay is the mountainous rock of Sandray, and beyond lie Pabbay, Mingulay and Berneray, the full stop at the bottom of the Outer Hebrides. The last three of these are owned by the National Trust for Scotland, who purchased them from the Barra Head Sheep Stock Company in 2000. Together with Vatersay, the islands are collectively known as the Bishop's Isles, though this appears to be a relatively recent moniker, applied in the 20th century by geologist Daphne Pochin Mould. The title suggests that the Macneils paid rent to the Iona bishopric; in reality, it seems unlikely that the Macneils would let any wealth from these islands go anywhere but to Kisimul.

The undisturbed and pristine environment of these islands briefly came under threat in 2005, when a Freedom of Information request revealed that Sandray had been shortlisted as a suitable site for the long-term geological storage of the UK's nuclear waste. The list, prepared by nuclear disposal company NIREX, also identified the island of Fuday, which is clearly visible in the sound between Barra and Eriskay and which is used for rough grazing. An outcry saw NIREX backtrack and the hunt for a suitable location move elsewhere. While using the islands as a nuclear waste disposal site is now highly unlikely, locals keep a wary watch on the issue.

MINGULAY Mingulay requires some effort to visit, but those who do so often compare it favourably with the more epic journey out to St Kilda. The history and, to some extent, the geology of Mingulay, shadows that of its better-known counterpart out in the North Atlantic. Lying 12 miles south of Barra and clearly visible from any high vantage point there or on Vatersay, the island was abandoned by its residents in 1912. This decision brought to an end at least 2,000 years of human occupation. (It is thought humans occupied or used the island as early as 5000BC.) The island rapidly rises from a sandy bay to Macphee's Hill in the north and Carnan to the west. Beyond these hills are striking sea cliffs of Lewisian gneiss and those near Carnan, at 250m (820ft), are the third highest in the UK. Iron Age sites and the ruins of a more recent abandoned village have been documented on the island, and people on Barra still like to regale visitors with tales of ghosts rising from Macphee's Hill to wander around the village.

Perhaps the most striking memory you take away from a visit is of the remaining houses, whose roofs were deliberately stripped upon evacuation to ensure no change of heart could take place among islanders.

The only way to experience the island is to take a boat trip from Barra. This can be a stomach-churning affair in even modest swells, but the close-up views of the sheer western cliffs are unforgettable, particularly from May to July, when they are smothered in nesting seabirds such as kittiwake, fulmar, guillemot and razorbill.

Guillemots appear to be doing well, with a population of around 19,000 but the National Trust for Scotland has expressed 'serious concern' over the fortunes of the island's colony of Leach's storm petrel. In autumn, grey seals congregate and pup in their hundreds on the beach at Mingulay Bay in a spectacle that would not be out of place in a David Attenborough documentary.

A visit to the island is a special experience and can be arranged from April until September with Francis Gillies of **Mingulay Boat Trips** (\ 01871 810679; m 07970 854147; w barrafishingcharters.com; e mingulayboattrips@outlook.com). The tours, requiring a minimum of five adults, depart from Castlebay at 10.00 and last around 6 hours, which includes 3 hours on Mingulay. The National Trust for Scotland (w nts.org.uk) manages the island and can also provide information. By arrangement, tours can also include visits to **Pabbay** and **Berneray**. Known as the Hermit's Isle, Pabbay has sand dunes, heathland and sheer cliffs. A handful of families lived here, but a hammer blow to the community came when a disaster at sea in 1897 claimed the lives of five men; by 1911 the island was abandoned. **Berneray** – you may also see the island referred to as Barra Head – is a peat-free island so instead has cultivated grasslands and a few remaining blackhouses. A lighthouse stands proud high on the cliffs of **Sloc n Bèiste** on Barra Head, providing a suitably dramatic sign-off to the southern end of the Outer Hebrides chain – and mimicking the stature of the lighthouse at the Butt of Lewis, 130 miles to the north.

OUTER HEBRIDES ONLINE

For additional online content, articles, photos and more on the Outer Hebrides, why not visit w bradtguides.com/outerhebrides?

Appendix 1

LANGUAGE

You will have no problem using English in any situation in the Outer Hebrides; it is understood as it is anywhere in the UK. However, it can be both enjoyable and rewarding to learn a few phrases of Gàidhlig, as the Gaelic language spoken in the Outer Hebrides is called. There is an intense pride in Gàidhlig, so any effort on the part of visitors to speak a few phrases by way of introduction or as an ice-breaker – even if this is not necessary on a practical level – will be warmly welcomed. Some words are also decidedly useful to avoid social faux pas: men's toilets are often marked with an 'f' (*fir*) while women's toilets can be marked with a 'm' (*mnathan*).

GUIDE TO PRONUNCIATION With thanks to Dr Simon Taylor (Lecturer in Celtic and Gaelic, School of Humanities, University of Glasgow) and the Ordnance Survey

Gaelic spelling is more regular than English spelling, which means that it reflects more accurately the actual sounds of the language. Gaelic uses an alphabet of 18 letters, namely: a, b, c, d, e, f, g, h, i, l, m, n, o, p, r, s, t, and u. A major feature of the Gaelic spelling system is the concept of broad and slender vowels, which are also referred to as back and front vowels. The broad or back vowels are a, o, u; the slender or front vowels are e, i. All vowels can be long or short, with length being indicated by a grave accent (`` ` ``). In Gaelic, an adjective usually follows its noun.

Vowels
Single vowels
- a: like a in 'hat', often like u in 'but'; before nn it is like ow in 'cow'
- à: like a in 'half'
- e: short closed e like a in 'rate' and short open e like e in 'fetch'
- è: long closed e like ay in 'bay' and long open e like e in 'cortege'
- i: like ee as in 'keep'
- ì: like ee in 'keep' but longer
- o: short closed o like oa in 'boat', and short open o like o in 'lot'
- ò: long closed o like 'owe', and long open o like 'awe'
- u: like oo in 'book'
- ù: like oo in 'book', but longer

Vowel groups Most groups of two or three vowels are pronounced much as would be expected, ie: as separate sounds rapidly following one another. However, one of the vowels is often there simply to indicate whether a consonant is broad or slender, for example, in *fearann* the a following the e indicates that the r is broad, so that ea is pronounced simply as e (as in 'get'). However, note the following:

- ao: a long sound with no equivalent in English. Try saying Gaelic ù (like oo in 'book', but longer) without rounding your lips.
- eu: like ia in 'Maria' or like ay in 'bay'.

Consonants Consonants or groups of consonants that are most unfamiliar to someone used to the English spelling system are given below, with their approximate English value:
- bh: like v at the beginning of words, otherwise like w, or silent (ie: not heard at all); for example *dubh* is pronounced approximately as 'doo'.
- c: like c in 'cat' or c in 'cue'; when it occurs between two vowels or as the last letter of a word it is preceded by the sound ch in 'loch'.
- ch: like ch in 'loch'.
- cn: like cr.
- d slender (ie: in contact with one of the slender vowels e, i): like j in 'jam'.
- dh broad (ie: in contact with one of the broad vowels a, o, u): the same sound as Gaelic broad gh, almost like French r in 'rire'. When it is not at the beginning of a word, it is often pronounced only very lightly or not at all.
- dh slender (ie: in contact with one of the slender vowels e, i): the same sound as Gaelic slender gh, like y in 'yet'. When it is not at the beginning of a word, it is often pronounced only very lightly or not at all.
- fh: silent, ie: not pronounced at all.
- gh broad (ie: in contact with one of the broad vowels a, o, u): the same sound as Gaelic broad dh, almost like French r in 'rire'. When it is not at the beginning of a word, it is often pronounced only very lightly or not at all.
- gh slender (ie: in contact with one of the slender vowels e, i): the same sound as Gaelic slender dh, like y in 'yet'. When it is not at the beginning of a word, it is often pronounced only very lightly or not at all.
- l broad (ie: in contact with one of the broad vowels a, o, u): like a hollow or dark l, as in 'full', with the blade (as opposed to the tip) of the tongue touching the teeth.
- l slender (ie: in contact with one of the slender vowels e, i): like lli in 'million' when it is at the beginning of a word; otherwise like ll in 'silly'.
- mh: like v at the beginning of words, otherwise like w, or silent (ie: not heard at all). It also makes the vowel before it sound very nasal.
- ph: like f.
- r slender (ie: in contact with one of the slender vowels e, i): can be pronounced like r in Scottish English 'tree', but in several dialects it is pronounced like th in 'the'.
- rd and rt: in many Gaelic dialects this is pronounced with a light sh as in 'she' between the two consonants.
- s slender (ie: in contact with one of the slender vowels e, i): like sh in 'she'.
- t slender (ie: in contact with one of the slender vowels e, i): like ch in 'church'.
- th: like h in 'he' at the beginning of words, otherwise silent.

Lenition You will sometimes notice that the spelling of a place name is slightly different from a nearby feature that shares the same name, eg: the township of Geocrab on Harris overlooks Loch Gheocrab, while Dail Beag on Lewis overlooks a bay called Bàigh Dhail Beag. This is an example of lenition, literally 'softening', whereby consonants at the beginning of words can change according to gender, number and case. It is usually signalled by putting the letter h after the lenited or softened consonant.

BASIC WORDS AND PHRASES With thanks to Eilidh MacMillan and Liam Alastair Crouse at Ceòlas, and Magaidh (Maggie) Smith
Gaelic has no direct equivalent of the words 'yes' and 'no'. Instead, they are

conveyed by repeating the verb in the question put to you. For example, were you to be asked 'Do you understand?', you would reply in Gaelic 'Tha mi 'tuigsinn' ('I understand') or 'Chan eil mi 'tuigsinn' ('I don't understand').

Good morning	*Madainn mhath*	*(mat-in va)*
Good afternoon	*Feasgar math*	*(fes-gar ma)*
Good evening	*Feasgar math*	*(fes-gar ma)*
Good night	*Oidhche mhath*	*(oi-che va)*
Hello/Welcome	*Fàilte*	*(fahl-tche)*
Goodbye	*Beannachd leat*	*(benn-ichk let)*
How are you?	*Ciamar a tha thu?*	*(ki-marr a ha oo?)*
What is your name?	*Dè an t-ainm a th'ort?*	*(je an t-n-am a ha-ort?)*
My name is...	*Is mise...*	*(is mis-eh...)*

I am...

English	*Tha mi à Sasann*	*(ha me a Sass-ing)*
Welsh	*Tha mi às a' Chuimrigh*	*(ha mi as a Chum-ri)*
Irish	*'s e Èirinneach a th' annum*	*(shay Air-un-nach a ha anum)*
American	*'s e Aimeireaganach a th' annum*	*(shay America-nach a ha anum)*
Australian	*'s e Astràilianach a th' annum*	*(shay Australia-nach a ha anum)*
Canadian	*'s e Canadach a th' annum*	*(shay Canadach a ha anum)*

How do you say...	*Ciamar a chanas tu...*	*(ki-mar a chan-as tu...*
in Scottish Gaelic?	*ann an Gàidhlig?*	*ann an Gah-lic?)*

Please	*Ma's e do thoil e*	*(mass eh doh holl eh)*
Thank you	*Tapadh leat*	*(ta-pa let)*
Sorry!	*Tha mi duilich!*	*(ha me due-liech!)*
Cheers!	*Slàinte!*	*(slann-tch!)*

Numbers

0	*neoni*	*(neon-i)*
1	*a h-aon*	*(a h-oon)*
2	*a dhà*	*(a dha)*
3	*a trì*	*(a tree)*
4	*a ceithir*	*(a kay-ar)*
5	*a còig*	*(a co-ig)*
6	*a sia*	*(a shea)*
7	*a seachd*	*(a sh-achk)*
8	*a h-ochd*	*(a h ochk)*
9	*a naoi*	*(a nu-ai)*
10	*a deich*	*(a je-ch)*
11	*a h-aon deug*	*(a h-oon jee-ag)*
12	*dà dheug*	*(da yee-ag)*
13	*trì deug*	*(tree jee-ag)*
14	*ceithir deug*	*(kay-ar jee-ag)*
15	*còig deug*	*(co-ig jee-ag)*
16	*sia deug*	*(shea jee-ag)*
17	*seachd deug*	*(sh-achk jee-ag)*
18	*ochd deug*	*(ochk jee-ag)*
19	*naoi deug*	*(nu-ai jee-ag)*

20	fichead	(fee-ch-at)
21	a h-aon air fhichead	(a h-oon ar ee-ch-at)
22	dà air fhichead	(da ar ee-ch-at)
30	deich air fhichead	(je-ch ar ee-ch-at)
40	dà fhichead	(da ee-ch-at)
50	dà fhichead is a deich	(da ee-ch-at is a je-ch)
60	trì fichead	(tree fee-ch-at)
70	trì fichead is a deich	(tree fee-ch-at is a je-ch)
80	ceithir fichead	(kay-ar fee-ch-at)
90	ceithir fichead is a deich	(kay-ar is a je-ch)
100	ceud	(key-ad)
200	dà ceud	(da chey-ad)
1,000	mile	(me-lu)

Time

What time is it?	Dè 'n uair a tha e?	(jey en ooh-ar a ha eh?)
noon	meadhan-latha	(me-yann la)
one o'clock	tha e uair	(ha eh ooh-ar)
two o'clock	tha e dà uair	(ha eh da ooh-ar)
early/late	tràth/anmoch	(t-rah/an-a-moch)

Days

Monday	Diluain	(je-lu-ing)
Tuesday	Dimàirt	(je-mar-tch)
Wednesday	Diciadaoin	(je-key-at-ing)
Thursday	Diardaoin	(jers-do-ing)
Friday	Dihaoine	(je-who-in-ye)
Saturday	Disathairne	(je-sah-her-n-ye)
Sunday	Didòmhnaich	(je-doh-n-ich)

Months

January	am Faoilleach	(um foo-luch)
February	an Gearran	(an ger-an)
March	am Màrt	(um mar-tch)
April	an Giblean	(an ge-bling)
May	an Cèitean	(an kay-ching)
June	an t-Ògmhios	(an t-og-ve-as)
July	an t-Iuchar	(an t-uch-ar)
August	an Lùnastal	(an lu-nas-tal)
September	an t-Sultain	(an t-ult-ing)
October	an Dàmhair	(an da-vur)
November	an t-Samhain	(an t-ow-ing)
December	an Dùbhlachd	(an do-lach-k)

Getting around

port	pòrt	(porst)
plane	itealan	(eecha-lan)
ferry	aiseag	(ash-ig)
Bon voyage!	Turas math dhut!	(too-ras ma ghoot!)
bus station	stèisean bus	(station bus)
airport	pòrt-adhair	(port ah-ar)

toilet	*goireasan*	*(gor-es-an)*
Men	*Fir*	*(fear)*
Women	*Mnathan*	*(mna-han)*

Shopping

How much is it?	*Dè a' phrìs tha seo?*	*(jay a frish a ha sho?)*
expensive/cheap	*daor/saor*	*(d-ur/s-ur)*
beautiful/ugly	*àlainn/grànnda*	*(ah-ling/gran-da)*
old/new	*seann/ùr*	*(shen/ur)*
good/bad	*math/dona*	*(ma/donna)*

Descriptions

difficult/easy	*doirbh/furasta*	*(dor-ive/fu-ras-tah)*
It's boring/	*Tha seo a' cur fadalachd orm/*	*(ha sho a kur fa-da-lachk urum/*
interesting	*inntinneach*	*ha sho innchinn-ach)*

Weather

hot/cold	*teth/fuar*	*(che/fu-are)*
It's raining/sunny	*Tha i sileadh/grianach*	*(ha e she-luch/gre-an ach)*
It's warm/cold	*Tha i blàth/tha i fuar*	*(ha e blah/ha e fu-are)*

If you want to learn more about Gaelic and even prepare some phrases, then *Everyday Gaelic* by Morag MacNeill (Birlinn) is a good introductory guide. If you're in need of a shortcut, it has to be said that Google Translate is often quite good for Gàidhlig; or you can look up individual words through w faclair.com, and you can further cross-reference for reassurance with w focloir.ie

Appendix 2

FURTHER READING

A great deal of fact and fiction, historical accounts and travelogues have been written about the Outer Hebrides. The following select bibliography is far from exhaustive but is intended to suggest books that the author has personally read and that, in sometimes very different ways, shine a light on the islands. It's also well worth exploring the lists of works produced by the specialist publishers Birlinn and the Islands Book Trust who cover many aspects of island life.

HISTORY

Beveridge, Erskine *North Uist* Birlinn, 2008. Originally published in 1911, this detailed account of the island's prehistory from pagan times to Christianity is written by an antiquary who lived on the tidal island of Vallay.

Boddington, David *A Record of the Early Re-occupation of St Kilda* Islands Book Trust, 2010. A diary kept by the island's medical officer, recounting tales of treating injured seabirds and military personnel along with off-duty hikes around the island.

Burnett, Ray *Benbecula* Mingulay Press, 1986. A definitive and politically forthright history of the island that has worn well since its first publication in the 1940s.

Hunter, James *From the Low Tide of the Sea to the Highest Mountain Tops* Islands Book Trust, 2012. An account of the development of community ownership in the Highlands and Islands by the authoritative Emeritus Professor of History at the University of the Highlands and Islands.

Hunter, James *The Making of the Crofting Community* Birlinn, 2010. Described by the *Scottish Historical Review* as 'one of the most significant books of its generation', the book has been in print for more than 35 years.

Lawson, Bill *Lewis in History and Legend – the East Coast* Birlinn, 2011. The definitive and most authoritative account of the social history of Stornoway and the east of Lewis. Several other equally informed historical books by Lawson can be found at the Seallam! Visitor Centre on Harris.

MacDonald, Malcolm and Macleod, Donald John *The Darkest Dawn* Acair Books, 2018. Comprehensive record of the *Iolaire* disaster with details and life stories of those on board.

Rae, Frederick *A School in South Uist* Birlinn, 2007. An account of Rae's life as a school master between 1896 and 1913, a time when the island was reeling from the changes of the 19th century.

Randall, John *The Historic Shielings of the Pairc* Islands Book Trust, 2017. Authoritative book that tells the stories of the time when the Pairc, now empty, was home to crofters.

Steel, Tom *The Life and Death of St Kilda* Harper Press, 2011. A stirring and sometimes viscerally angry account of the culture and struggles involved in living on St Kilda, the evacuation and subsequent varied fates of the islanders. First published in 1965.

ARCHAEOLOGY The following are outstanding guides to the archaeology of the islands. Written in accessible language they include good practical sections of sites to visit, as well as illuminating accounts of their history, from first settlers to the clearances.

Branigan, Keith *Ancient Barra* Comhairle nan Eilean Siar, 2007
Burgess, Christopher *Ancient Lewis & Harris* Comhairle nan Eilean Siar, 2008
McKirdy, Alan *The Outer Hebrides: Landscapes in Stone* Birlinn, 2018. Everything you ever want to know about gneiss (and other rocks). Geology in readable form.
Parker Pearson, Mike, Sharples, Niall, Symonds, James, Robbins, Heidi and Badcock, Anna *Ancient Uists* Comhairle nan Eilean Siar, 2013

CULTURE

Kjellberg, Sven and Hasslöf, Olof *A Swedish Field Trip to the Outer Hebrides* National Museums Scotland Enterprises, 2012. A curious account of a 1934 journey by bicycle through the islands by two Swedish ethnologists in search of connections between fishing communities there and in Scandinavia.
MacLellan Angus *Stories from South Uist* Birlinn, 2005. Compendium of storytelling and oral history that remains a feature of the island (see box, page 256).
Meades, Jonathan, Hicks, Dan and Boyd, Alex *Isle of Rust* Luath Press, 2019. Book form of Meades's stirring documentary of Harris and Lewis, illustrated and accompanied by Boyd's photographs and thoughts, all complemented by the insights of archaeologist Hicks.
Shaw, Margaret Fay *Eilean* Birlinn, 2018. Stirring and elegiac images of St Kilda, South Uist, Barra and Mingulay – among other Hebridean islands – taken by this 20th-century American photographer and folklorist.
Shaw, Margaret Fay *Folksongs and Folklore of South Uist* Birlinn, 2014. Fascinating and hugely authoritative account of Shaw's often scholarly insights into South Uist land and culture. The book is said to have never been out of print since it was first published in 1955.
Shaw, Margaret Fay *From the Alleghenies to the Hebrides* Birlinn, 2008. Shaw's autobiography serves as a useful counterpoint to her other major work.

NATURAL HISTORY

Cunningham, Peter *Birds of the Outer Hebrides* Melven Press, 1983. Possibly the original – if now a little dated – compendium of the avian residents and visitors to the islands, accompanied by striking sketches.
Holden, Peter and Housden, Stuart *RSPB Handbook of Scottish Birds* Bloomsbury Natural History, 2016. Beautifully illustrated, comprehensive and extremely practical guide. Keep it in your daypack.

LANGUAGE

Maciver, Donald John *Gaelic Is Fun!* Acair, 2014. A light-hearted, breezy and sometimes risqué cartoon-based introduction to the basics of Gaelic.
MacNeill, Morag *Everyday Gaelic* Birlinn, 2006. A good introductory guide that includes words and phrases for meeting people, travelling, weather, and food and drink.

GENERAL

Boyd, Alex *The Silent Islands* Luath Press, 2018. Outstanding photographic record of St Kilda by the former curator of the An Lanntair arts centre in Stornoway.
Fraser Darling, Frank *Island Years, Island Farm* Little Toller, 2011. There are shades of *Mosquito Coast* in this account of an academic and conservationist who takes his young family off to the Summer Isles and North Rona, a small rock north of Lewis (see box, page 111).

Johnson, Alison *A House by the Shore* London Victor Gollancz, 1987. A jolly yet incisive and searing account of two university graduates who seek out the 'good life' on Harris in the 1970s. Based on their time establishing Scarista House (page 157). Possibly now out of print but worth seeking out from secondhand bookshops.

Mackenzie, Compton *Whisky Galore* Vintage Classics, 2004. Highly entertaining – if slightly embellished – account of the sinking of the SS *Politician* and the tale of low-level law-breaking that ensued (see box, page 266).

Mackenzie, Greta *Return to Patagonia* Islands Book Trust, 2010. One of the best accounts of what happened to Hebridean people who migrated to the New World.

Nicolson, Adam *Sea Room: An Island Life* HarperCollins, 2001. Wonderfully written and thoughtful account of one man's inheritance of the Shiant Isles.

Strand, Paul *Tir A'Mhurain – Land of the Bent Grass* Aperture, 2002. A truly superb photographic study of South Uist in the 1960s by an American photographer. The book has rightly achieved iconic status.

TRAVELOGUE AND TRAVEL BOOKS

Bunting, Madeleine *Love of Country: A Hebridean Journey* Granta, 2016. Lewis is one of seven islands visited by the author on an insightful journey through culture and history.

Campbell, Angus Peter and Maclean, Cailean *Suas Gu Deas* Islands Book Trust, 2009. Not a walkers' handbook as such but a wonderful tale of two Hebrideans walking the entire chain of the Outer Hebrides.

Cawthorne, Mike *Wild Voices, Journeys Through Time in the Scottish Highlands* Birlinn, 2014. An excellent account of how the author reinterpreting the landscape of the highlands through its history. Includes an atmospheric account of deftly canoeing across the lochs and moors of southwest Lewis.

Hedderwick, Mairi *An Eye on the Hebrides* Birlinn, 2009. A beautifully illustrated account of a tour of the Western Isles undertaken by the author, who displays an acerbic and arch quill that is not apparent in her *Katie Morag* stories.

MacFarlane, Robert *The Old Ways: A Journey on Foot* Penguin, 2013. High prose as the author explores tracks from pre-history that cut across the moors of Lewis and Harris and sails to Sula Sgeir (see box, page 111).

Margulies, Martin *Mhòr and More, Hill Walks in South Uist* Islands Book Trust, 2011. Not a particularly practical guide but rather a series of enjoyable vignettes by the former author of an engaging column for the local newspaper *Am Paipear*.

Martin, Martin *A Description of the Western Islands of Scotland* Birlinn, 1999. First published 1716. Tales of cows with second sight, islands almost paralysed with superstition but eking out an existence against ferocious odds. Essential reading.

Murray, Donald S *The Guga Hunters* Birlinn, 2008. A gripping, often raw yet fluent account of the astonishing annual journey by the men of Ness to the island of Sula Sgeir to hunt young gannets, or guga.

Riddoch, Lesley *Riddoch on the Outer Hebrides* Luath Press, 2007. Bouncy account of broadcaster Riddoch's cycling tour from bottom to top of the islands. She ruffles a few feathers along the way but her often sweeping generalisations are more hit than miss, saved by her sharp journalistic eye, and always entertaining.

Other Scotland guides For a full list of Bradt's Scotland and other British Isles guides, see w bradtguides.com/shop.

Featherstone, Katie *Inner Hebrides* Bradt Travel Guides, 2020

Greig, Donald and Flint, Darren *Dumfries & Galloway* (Slow Travel) Bradt Travel Guides, 2020

Rowe, Mark *Orkney* Bradt Travel Guides, 2019

Smith, Phoebe *Britain's Best Small Hills* Bradt Travel Guides, 2017

Smith, Phoebe *Wilderness Weekends: Wild Adventures in Britain's Rugged Corners* Bradt Travel Guides, 2015

WALKING BOOKS AND SMALL POCKET GUIDES

Townsend, Mike *Walking on Uist and Barra* Cicerone, 2015. Extremely good on the technical routes of the South Uist hill walks that have a strong mountaineering element to them.

Webster, Paul and Helen *The Outer Hebrides: 40 Coast & Country Walks* Pocket Mountains, 2013

Welsh, Mary *Walking the Western Isles* Clan Books, 2006. Excellent selection of walks throughout the Outer Hebrides, beautifully annotated with drawings by Christine Isherwood.

Williams, Luke *Western Isles: 34 walks from 1–12.5 miles (1.5–20kms)* Hallewell, 2009

FICTION Given their extraordinary social history and spectacular landscapes, the Outer Hebrides have been the subject of surprisingly little fiction.

May, Peter *Coffin Road* Quercus, 2016. A 4th – but unelated – Hebridean book, based on Harris and documenting the shadowy links between a drug company and colony collapse disorder in bees.

May, Peter *The Lewis Trilogy* Quercus, 2016. Comprises *The Blackhouse* (2011), *The Lewis Man* (2012) and *The Chessmen* (2013). Dark deeds among the moors and scattered townships of the isles. Phenomenal bestseller: the trilogy has already sold more than 1 million copies in the UK.

Pollen, Bella *The Summer of the Bear* Pan, 2011. Novel loosely related to the extraordinary tale of Hercules, the bear who escaped on Benbecula and North Uist in 1980 (see box, page 211).

Ransome, Arthur *Great Northern?* Jonathan Cape, 1982. The last of Ransome's *Swallows and Amazons* series was researched and based on Lewis. The title refers to the bird – great northern diver – at the centre of the children's adventures.

OUTER HEBRIDES ONLINE

For additional online content, articles, photos and more on the Outer Hebrides, why not visit w bradtguides.com/outerhebrides?

Index

Page numbers in **bold** indicate main entries; those in *italics* indicate maps

INDEX OF ADVERTISERS